Errors and Intelligence in Computer-Assisted Language Learning

Routledge Studies in Computer-Assisted Language Learning

EDITED BY CAROL CHAPPELLE

1. Changing Language Education Through CALL
Edited by Randall P. Donaldson and Margaret A. Haggstrom

2. Errors and Intelligence in Computer-Assisted Language Learning
Parsers and Pedagogues
Trude Heift and Mathias Schulze

Errors and Intelligence in Computer-Assisted Language Learning

Parsers and Pedagogues

Trude Heift and Mathias Schulze

Routledge
Taylor & Francis Group
New York London

Routledge
Taylor & Francis Group
270 Madison Avenue
New York, NY 10016

Routledge
Taylor & Francis Group
2 Park Square
Milton Park, Abingdon
Oxon OX14 4RN

Routledge is an imprint of Taylor & Francis Group, an Informa business

Printed in the United States of America on acid-free paper
10 9 8 7 6 5 4 3 2 1

International Standard Book Number-10: 0-415-36191-5 (Hardcover)
International Standard Book Number-13: 978-0-415-36191-0 (Hardcover)

Library of Congress Cataloging-in-Publication Data

Heift, Trude.
Errors and intelligence in computer-assisted language learning : parsers and pedagogues / Trude Heift and Mathias Schulze.
p. cm. -- (Routledge studies in computer assisted language learning ; 2)
Includes bibliographical references and index.
ISBN-13: 978-0-415-36191-0 (hardback : alk. paper)
1. Language and languages--Computer-assisted instruction. 2. Language and languages--Study and teaching--Error analysis. 3. Parsing (Computer grammar) I. Schulze, Mathias, 1962- II. Title.

P53.28.H455 2007
418.028'5--dc22 2006033133

Visit the Taylor & Francis Web site at
http://www.taylorandfrancis.com

and the Routledge Web site at
http://www.routledge-ny.com

To Gabi and Chris

Contents

There is an educational theory prevalent that might be called Hydraulic Theory. It is a practical rather than a formal theory in that its disciples do not advocate the theory in any formal way: they merely act as though they believe in it. Nevertheless, the Hydraulic Theory is respectable, its practitioners many, its tradition long, and its influence dominant. According to the Hydraulic Theory, knowledge is a kind of liquid which resides copiously in teachers and books, as in great vessels, and hardly at all anywhere else. Particularly is it scarce in the small vessels known as students. The purpose of education, then, is to transfer this liquid from the larger to the smaller vessels. Fortunately, this liquid has certain peculiar and mysterious properties that facilitate the process of transfer. For one thing, effluence from the larger container in no way diminishes the supply. (In some cases, it actually appears to have the opposite effect, as witness the increasing authority with which lecturers repeat the same material in consecutive terms.) Another remarkable property is that the effluence can be shared among a number of recipient vessels with no apparent reduction in the amount received by each. There are cases on record in which as many as 600 containers have been simultaneously filled from one great vessel in this way. The most recent advance in Hydraulic Theory, and certainly the most exciting, is the use of the computer and the multimedia console, with its graphic display and audio channel, is able to inundate the student with a flood of visual and auditory stimuli, literally filling every channel, inlet, passage, and canal leading to the student's brain.

Davies, P. M. (1969) "The Hydraulic Theory of Education" quoted in O'Shea & Self, 1983, p. 67.

Preface

Most of the ideas articulated in this book were formed over the past ten to fifteen years and, many of them, were strengthened and expanded in discussions with other people: first as PhD students with our respective supervisors, Paul McFetridge and Allan Ramsay, and later as faculty with colleagues in our respective departments and at conferences and workshops. They challenged our thoughts, concepts and understanding of natural language processing in computer-assisted language learning, second language acquisition, and linguistics in general. Equally important, other scholars offered encouragement and fresh ideas: Paul Bennett, Chris Bowerman, Tom Carey, Robert Fischer, Piklu Gupta, Marie-Josée Hamel, Marie Hayet, Sake Jager, Peter Liddell, Mike Levy, John Nerbonne, Devlan Nicholson, Maeve Olohan, Janine Toole, Cornelia Tschichold, and Christoph Zähner. Our students in language or linguistics classes have also helped us shape our ideas over the years. In particular, we are very grateful to Anne Rimrott, who prepared parts of the bibliography of this book and proofread earlier drafts. Mohammad Haji-Abdolhosseini and Barbara Schmenk also provided valuable feedback on an earlier version of the manuscript. Last but not least, we would like to acknowledge the support and encouragements from the two series editors, Carol Chapelle and Graham Davies. Many thanks to all of you!

List of Figures

List of Tables

Abbreviations

AI	Artificial Intelligence
ALE	Attribute Logic Engine
ASL	American Sign Language
ATN	Augmented Transition Network
CA	Contrastive Analysis
CAL	Computer-Aided Learning
CALL	Computer-Assisted Language Learning
CATN	Cascaded Augment Transition Network
CBM	Constraint-Based Modeling
CF-PSG	Context-Free Phrase Structure Grammar
CL	Computational Linguistics
CMC	Computer-Mediated Communication
CSCL	Computer-Supported Collaborative Learning
DCG	Definite Clause Grammar
EA	Error Analysis
FPSG	Functional Phrase Structure Grammar
FSA	Finite State Automata
GB	Government Binding
GPSG	Generalized Phrase Structure Grammar
HLT	Human Language Technology
HPSG	Head-Driven Phrase Structure Grammar
HTML	Hypertext Mark-up Language
ICALI	Intelligent Computer-Assisted Language Instruction
ICALL	Intelligent Computer-Assisted Language Learning
IL	Interlanguage
ILE	Interactive Learning Environment
ILTS	Intelligent Language Tutoring System
IPG	Incremental Procedural Grammar
ITS	Intelligent Tutoring System
LFG	Lexical Functional Grammar
LMS	Learning Management System
MT	Machine Translation

NLP	Natural Language Processing
PL	Programmed Learning
POS	Part of Speech
PPT	Principles and Parameters Theory
RTN	Recursive Transition Network
SG	Systemic Grammar
SLA	Second Language Acquisition
SM	Student Modeling
SQL	Standard Query Language
TAG	Tree Adjoining Grammar
TN	Transition Network
ZPD	Zone of Proximal Development

1. Introduction

> I would like to offer a test for the seriousness of the claim that a computer has a conscience. I will only accept this claim from someone who is willing to give a present to a computer. If he answers: "But that's impossible!" I will reply: "Indeed! The computer does not have a world but only pieces of information that it processes by means of pre-programmed procedures, which it can do much better than us. In comparison, we can be quite appalled upon realizing that we act like a computer program, without sense or reason, and without any consideration of the world in which we live." (Schröder, 1998)[1]

1.1 INTELLIGENCE AND PARSERS

The concept of intelligence as applied to Computer-Assisted Language Learning (CALL[2]) have been a source of contention since the early 1980s. The actual and potential contributions of Artificial Intelligence research and techniques to CALL has been exaggerated (O'Brien, 1993), misunderstood (Last, 1989), and doubted (Salaberry, 1996). At the same time, areas of Artificial Intelligence which are relevant to CALL, such as Natural Language Processing (NLP), Student Modeling (SM), and Intelligent Language Tutoring Systems (ILTSs) have played a significant role in the development of our thinking about CALL, its design and implementation. For instance, Nerbonne (2003), in his chapter on NLP in CALL in the *Oxford Handbook of Computational Linguistics*, argues that recent advances in NLP have much to contribute to CALL. Borin et al. (2003) put forward a similar argument in their proposal to the European Union to establish a Network of Excellence (Supporting Second Language Acquisition with Human Language Technology (SLAinTe)). They ascertain that there is a need for research in this area because recent research in language technology has had little impact on approaches in CALL.

Marshall (1988) identifies the significant interactive qualities of CALL as one advantage of using the computer in the language classroom. True interaction, however, requires intelligent behavior on the part of the computer. Without intelligence, the system is merely another method of presenting information, one not necessarily preferable to a static medium like print. Instead of multiple choice questions, relatively uninformative answer keys and gross mainstreaming of students characteristic of workbooks, NLP-based CALL is aiming at interactive computer systems possessing a high degree of artificial intelligence and capable of processing natural language input (Holland, Maisano, Alderks, & Martin, 1993). The strength of NLP is that it allows for a sophisticated error analysis where student tasks can go beyond multiple-choice questions and/or fill-in-the-blanks. Many simple drills, on the other hand, are usually based on string matching algorithms, that is, the student response is compared letter for letter against an answer key. However, one obviously cannot store the infinitely many sentences required for meaningful practice for purposes of comparison. NLP provides the analytical complexity underpinning an ILTS.

Matthews (1993) identifies Linguistic Theory and Second Language Acquisition (SLA) Theory as the two main disciplines which inform and have been informed by Intelligent Computer-Assisted Language Learning (ICALL). He adds that "the obvious AI research areas from which ICALL should be able to draw the most insights are Natural Language Processing (NLP) and Intelligent Tutoring Systems (ITSs)" (1993, p. 5). Matthews also shows that it is possible to "conceive of an ICALL system in terms of the classical ITS architecture" (Matthews, 1993, p. 6). An ITS generally consists of three modules: an expert, a student, and a teacher module.[3] The expert module houses the language knowledge and, ideally, it is this part that can process any piece of text produced by a language learner. This is usually achieved by a parser. A parser produces a formal linguistic representation of natural language input by identifying the grammatical functions of the parts of a sentence[4]:

> The use of parsers in CALL is commonly referred to as intelligent CALL or 'ICALL', it might be more accurately described as parser-based CALL, because its 'intelligence' lies in the use of parsing — a technique that enables the computer to encode complex grammatical knowledge such as humans use to assemble sentences, recognize errors, and make corrections. (Holland et al., 1993, p. 28)

This notion of parser-based CALL not only captures the nature of the field much better than the somewhat misleading term *Intelligent CALL* (Is all other CALL *un-intelligent*?), but it also identifies the use of human language technology as one possible approach in CALL alongside others, such as multimedia-based CALL and web-based CALL. In some cases, the (technology-defined) borders between these sub-fields of CALL are not even clearly identifiable, as illustrated in some of the projects described later. For this reason, the terms *parser-based systems*, *ICALL systems*, and

Intelligent Language Tutoring Systems (ILTSs) are used interchangeably throughout this book although, for the reasons outlined above, the terms *parser-based systems* or *parser-based CALL* are preferred.

The following quote illustrates that the notion of intelligence is perceived in a number of different ways in CALL. Rüschoff (1987) contrasted two of these notions and concluded his discussion of *intelligence* in CALL as follows:

> Returning, however, to the question of how "intelligent" computer assisted language learning materials have to be in order to make them suitable for effective self-study use, the solution to this problem does not necessarily lie in the development of true expert systems or any other form of artificial intelligence. Such systems are still very much a thing of the future and we shall have to investigate their possible points of application for computer assisted language learning materials when they become available. However, I do hope we do not have to wait until then to develop useful CALL materials for self-study. Such programs would not need an "intelligence" of their own, but their quality would rather depend on the intelligence with which they have been programmed. (pp. 81–82)

This is certainly true, but at the same time, it does not suggest that a parser-driven CALL application will not prove useful in language learning. Examples throughout this book illustrate that parsing technology can provide CALL with significant advantages over traditional workbook instruction. For instance, studies addressing the question of what kind of feedback a computer program should give have shown that not only do students appreciate the more sophisticated, error-specific feedback made possible by NLP, but also perform better on the language skills being taught (e.g., van der Linden, 1993; Nagata, 1996, 1998a, 1998b; Heift, 2001, 2002, 2003, 2004). The fact that students learn better provides the rationale for employing parsers in CALL. Ideally, the advantages of a grammar-checking component in CALL software are complemented by intelligent communicative tasks that facilitate effective language learning.

Higgins (1987), in his article entitled "Artificial Unintelligence: Computer Uses in Language Learning," puts forward an interesting notion of the term *intelligence* in CALL:

> Yet there is intelligence present during the interaction [students using software programs produced by Higgins] — the learner's intelligence in assessing, responding to, criticizing, or enjoying what the machine sets up — and it seems that the learner's recognition of the machine's stupidity is a factor in releasing their own intelligence and zest for experiment. (p. 162)

Most misgivings identified in the CALL community with the term *Intelligent CALL* can be put down to two reasons:

1. The term *intelligence* has been transferred from the area of Artificial Intelligence (AI) without making its background in this discipline transparent in CALL. For instance, for many language teachers, *intelligence* by its very definition is an inherently human category. In contrast, the notion of intelligence in computing has been defined with computers in mind (e.g., a test proposed by Alan Turing, in which a (conversation) machine is said to have intelligence if a human interrogator cannot distinguish it from a human (Brookshear, 1997, p. 359)).
2. The use of *intelligent* for programs that can be said to approximate the passing of the Turing test appears to be common practice which probably led to the coining of the term Intelligent CALL. A closer linguistic analysis of the terminology reveals another problem, that of scope ambiguity of the modifier *intelligent*. The modifier is adjacent to the noun *computer* which is part of the compound *computer-assisted*. If *intelligent* were to refer to *computer* then its use would be justified because of the artificial intelligence nature of the programs to which the whole term refers. The problem is that *intelligent* is much more likely to be interpreted as the modifier of the head noun *learning* and thus it stipulates that only CALL that relies on parsers is intelligent. Undoubtedly, this notion cannot have been intended by the proponents of the use of artificial intelligence techniques in CALL.

The notion is certainly not intended by us in this book in which we will discuss different aspects of artificial intelligence in CALL in some detail.

1.2 THE STRUCTURE OF THE BOOK

The use of NLP techniques and tools in CALL has indeed become one of the major areas of research and development in the field of new technologies and language learning. An increasing proportion of articles in journals dedicated to CALL (e.g., CALL, ReCALL, CALICO) are devoted to the discussion of NLP techniques relevant to the field. However, there is no book that gives a comprehensive overview of the research issues involved and that offers a solid introduction for students and researchers working in CALL, Applied Linguistics and/or Computational Linguistics. Unlike recent publications (e.g., Swartz & Yazdani, 1992; Holland, Kaplan, & Sams, 1995; Jager, Nerbonne, & van Essen, 1998; Schulze, Hamel, & Thompson, 1999; Heift & Schulze, 2003a) which are compilations of papers usually derived from a conference, this book provides an overview of theoretical issues, historical developments and current trends and gives due attention to all of these areas in a balanced way. It assumes a basic familiarity with Second Language Acquisition (SLA) theory and teaching, CALL and linguistics. The book is written for upper undergraduate and/or graduate students who study CALL, SLA, Language Pedagogy, Computational Linguistics, or Artificial Intelligence as well as researchers with a background in any of these fields.

The book consists of four main parts. Starting off with a short review of (artificial) intelligence in CALL and describing the role it has played and how it has been discussed, the authors offer an overview of research and development at the intersection of NLP and CALL. This overview introduces key concepts in the area of parser-based CALL systems by discussing individual projects. Moreover, the reader gains an understanding of grammar formalisms and parsing algorithms and their relevance to language learning software. Relevant literature from neighboring disciplines that have provided insights into error diagnosis and feedback are reviewed and contextualized within the area of parser-based CALL. Error diagnosis and feedback are two processes in language learning that are of importance to the research, development, and implementation of ICALL systems. Both concepts are investigated in considerable detail to discuss current trends in research and development and related work that has been carried out in SLA theory. The final part provides an overview of language learning systems that make use of student modeling techniques to achieve a more individualized language learning environment. Student modeling techniques that have been applied to both NLP-based systems and other CALL programs will be presented. A concluding chapter considers future directions including empirical research.

The following sections provide a more detailed description of each part of the book.

1.1.1 Part 2: NLP in CALL

Part 2 introduces the reader to important concepts in natural language understanding and processing and aims at familiarizing the reader with different approaches of NLP techniques in CALL, its success stories and failures. The notion of a computational grammar will be discussed and different parsing techniques will be introduced. For instance, parsers designed for language instruction typically contain components that anticipate or search for errors in the event that a grammatical rule is not successful, buggy rules being a common instance. Lately, researchers have also analyzed L2 corpora to determine certain buggy rules that are needed for a language parsing system. In addition, statistical methods have also been applied to error detection and diagnosis.

Selected research and development projects of the past 25 years will be presented in chronological order to introduce key concepts, such as different parsing techniques and programming, and natural languages, and to show the development of the field.

1.1.2. Part 3: Error Analysis and Description

Part 3 begins with an overview of the inherent challenges of designing spell and/or grammar checkers. It then continues with a discussion of Error Analysis (EA), a branch of Applied Linguistics that influenced our understanding of Second Language Acquisition (SLA) in the late 1960s and early 1970s. The advent of electronic learner corpora and the need for elaborate error data has sparked a recent renewed interest in the methodologies employed by Error Analysis. We will show how findings in EA can be successfully employed in parser-based and other CALL systems. In the final part, corpus studies will be discussed in some detail. Their role in our understanding of language learning in general, and CALL in particular, will be presented.

1.1.3. Part 4: Feedback

Part 4 discusses the notion of feedback in language learning and CALL under five different aspects: human-computer interaction (HCI), learning theories, SLA, formal grammar and, of course, CALL.

Human-computer interaction (HCI), as a research area, generally deals with questions of interface and dialogue design. The discussion here focuses on interface design. Findings of HCI research that are applicable to corrective feedback generated by parser-based software for foreign language learners will be presented. The concept of reinforcement is frequently employed in behaviorist learning psychology and is related to the concept of feedback. The assumption is that feedback of a certain kind can act as a reinforcer. Sociocultural concepts in psychology form the basis for our discussion and relevant phenomena and findings of behaviorist and cognitive psychology will be outlined. SLA research that is relevant to feedback and the design of parser-based CALL systems will also be reviewed at this stage. Formal Linguistics provides the tools to describe learner language in a systematic and mathematical way with the goal for it to be *understood* by a computer. We will discuss the representation and connection of well-formed and ill-formed sentences. This part will then conclude with an overview of related topics, for example, design issues and research on feedback in CALL.

1.1.3. Part 5: Student Modeling

Part 5 discusses the theoretical issues surrounding individualized instruction and provides examples of parser-based and other CALL systems that have implemented different kinds of student models and modeling techniques. Individualized language instruction has long been recognized as a significant advantage of CALL over workbook tasks. A *one size fits all* approach is not appropriate for a learning environment. Students learn at their own pace and often work for their own purposes. Learners also vary with respect to prior language experience, aptitude, cognitive needs, beliefs, attitudes and/or learning styles and strategies.

Student models are challenging in a number of ways. Self (1979), for example, in opposition to a number of other researchers who list the advantages of student models, discusses the difficulties of how to capture, maintain and implement certain kinds of information about the learner. Such difficulties have since been the subject of some discussion and we will provide glimpses of these debates and report steps towards solving these problems.

1.1.4. Part 6: The Past and the Future

Part 6 provides concluding remarks that consider the past 25 years and future directions of NLP in CALL. We look at different ways of identifying current trends and future developments and apply these to the field of NLP in CALL. We will pay particular attention to the need for future empirical studies.

2. NLP in CALL

2.1 CALL: LEARNING AND TECHNOLOGY

Computer-Assisted Language Learning (CALL) is the result of the convergence of several fields of research, development and pedagogic innovation that address the use of computers in language learning. According to Levy (1997),

> the study of CALL as a body of work has been complicated because it has had to contend with the rate of technological change and from the uneven introduction of technology into language teaching and learning. (p. 227)

CALL stands for a wide and varied set of methods and approaches in foreign language learning and teaching which all have in common that they employ a computer. These methods and approaches are applied by language teachers and trainers in many countries around the globe. They are not limited to a few selected languages or to any educational and/or language proficiency level. In addition to this rather practical aspect of CALL, commonly labeled as *practice* or *pedagogic innovation*, CALL can be described as a field of investigation that combines *research* and *development*. Research aims to lay the theoretical foundations for (efficient) development and (effective) application of CALL resources whereas development is mainly concerned with the design, implementation and evaluation of learning and teaching resources for CALL. Pedagogic innovation, research and development are defined in a policy document which has been adopted by Eurocall, the European organization for CALL (Eurocall, Calico, & IALLT, 1999) and also by CALICO, the North American organization for CALL professionals (Calico, Eurocall, & IALLT, 1999). All three areas are eclectic in that they draw on useful information, approaches, findings, experience and knowledge from a wide range of disciplines, often without attempting to adopt the entire body of research of the other disciplines. Levy (1997) describes CALL as follows:

> Computer-Assisted Language Learning (CALL) may be defined as 'the search for and the study of applications of the computer in language teaching and learning'. The name is a fairly recent one: the existence of CALL in the academic literature has been recognizable for about the last thirty years. The subject is interdisciplinary in nature and it has evolved out of early efforts to find ways of using the computer for teaching or for instructional purposes across a wide variety of subject areas, with the weight of knowledge and breadth of application in language learning ultimately resulting in a more specialized field of study. (p. 1)

Throughout its short history, which will be outlined in brief in this chapter, CALL has always been treated and described as a multi-disciplinary area. For example, when discussing two CALL projects, Holland (1994) states that "CALL design in particular demands communication among experts in diverse disciplines – linguistics, psychology, language pedagogy and computer science" (p. 227) (see also Matthews, 1993). Levy (1997), who discusses CALL in more general terms than Holland (1994), provides the list of disciplines that informed recent CALL projects (see Table 2.1).

CALL can be described as a particular approach to language learning. As such it has been influenced by different learning theories that were dominant at certain times. Warschauer (1996) outlines three phases of CALL:

1. behaviorist CALL, which is based on behaviorist learning theories;
2. communicative CALL, which is based on the communicative approach in language teaching; and
3. integrative CALL, which Warschauer (1996) considers to be based on two technological developments: multimedia and the Internet.

Table 2.1 Disciplines with relevance to CALL

Applied linguistics	*Artificial intelligence*
Cognitive psychology/science	Computational linguistics
Curriculum development	Educational psychology
Educational technology	Expert systems
Human-computer interaction	Information processing
Instructional design	Instructional technology
Language data processing	Language teaching methodology
Linguistics	Machine translation
Materials design	Natural language processing
Parsing theory	Programmed instruction/learning
Psycholinguistics	Second language acquisition
Sociolinguistics	Systems theory

Levy, 1997, p. 49.

Warschauer (1996) argues that in integrative CALL, a computer can be a tutor which offers language drills and exercises, as intended by the behaviorist framework. In addition, it also provides stimuli for discussion and interaction, which then refers to the computer-as-tool metaphor and has been used widely in communicative CALL. These types of programs do not necessarily provide any language material, but rather empower the learner to use or understand language.

Künzel (1995), when considering *Learning Theory and CALL*, compares the development of computer technology throughout the thirty-year history of CALL with the dominant psychological theories that have had an impact on language learning in general, and CALL in particular. He identifies the three approaches of behavioral, developmental, and cognitive psychology, which we discuss in the following sections.

2.1.1 Influence of behavioral psychology

Behavioral psychology "was employed in a wide variety of disciplines in the 1950s and 1960s, supported by the work of B. F. Skinner, who in turn based his research on the ideas of Edward L. Thorndike" (Künzel, 1995, p. 108). Learning was designed in a linear fashion, that is, the learner's task was broken down in a sequence of smaller tasks through which the learner was guided, in this case, by the computer program. This so-called Programmed Instruction (PI) had particular appeal to a number of early developers in CALL. For instance, in the late sixties, CALL systems were primarily developed on large-scale, mainframe systems in universities where computer sessions were intended to replace classroom instruction. PI proposed the view that the best way of learning a task is to split it into small units, where the successful completion of one building-block leads to the next. The generally sound pedagogical principle of dividing a large learning task into conceptually smaller units was, however, distorted by an overemphasis on rote memorization manifested in repetitive drills and uninformative feedback. For example, in a typical drill exercise, the student was asked to type in the answer, which was checked as each character was entered. If an error resulted, the computer assumed control and typed out the word "wrong" (Barker & Yeates, 1985). CALL questioned the effectiveness of such systems. A program with a simple letter to letter match is incapable of differentiating types of errors: not only is it, therefore, incapable of providing any valuable, evaluative feedback, but, in ignoring the source of the error when selecting another language problem, it relies upon an inflexible, program-centered, rather than student-centered, definition of difficulty. While, in considering the early systems, one should make allowances for the limitations of the technology available at the time, the fact remains that, although PI had been refined over the years, it never achieved a high degree of popularity (Price, 1991). The original linear programs with fixed sequences of instruction were replaced by more sophisticated branching programs; most, however, remained based on multiple choice answers.

> 'Branching', in which the material presented to the student depends upon the last response of the student, was introduced by the mathematician Norman A. Crowder and expanded its (programmed instruction) repertoire. Branching meant that the material presented to the learner was constantly and directly 'steered' by the learner's achievements in problem solving. (Künzel, 1995, p. 109)

This approach is still widely used in CALL, resulting in programs that involve a substantial drill element, emphasizing reinforcement (see part 4). However, there are claims that this rigid approach does not make use of the potential of the computer (Künzel, 1995, p. 109). Inasmuch as the new is often an offshoot of the old, CALL is historically related to PI, adopting however a concern for individualized learning, self-pacing and immediate feedback.

The metaphor of *magister and pedagogue*, introduced by Higgins (1983), was also often employed in the discussion of the role of the computer in CALL (e.g., Späth, 1994):

> For years people have been trying to turn the computer into a magister. They do this by making it carry the learning system known as Programmed Learning (PL). Underlying PL is the belief that a body of knowledge can be reduced to a set of very small strips, each of which is easily learnable. Each step is turned into a frame which contains a line or two of exposition and a comprehension question. PL in fact does not need a computer or any other machinery; it can be used just as effectively in paper form and computers which are used exclusively for PL are sometimes known disparagingly as page-turners. The real magister is the person who wrote the materials and imagined the kind of conversation he might have with an imaginary student. Suppose, instead, that we try to make the machine into a pedagogue. Now we cannot write out the lessons in advance, because we do not know exactly how they will go, what the young master will demand. All we can do is supply the machine with a template to create certain kinds of activities, so that, when these are asked for, they are available. The computer becomes a task setter, an opponent in a game, an environment, a conversational partner, a stooge or a tool. (Higgins, 1983, p. 4)

The concept of *pedagogue* is already much closer to a cognitive understanding of learning psychology, which we address in the following section.

2.1.2 Influence of developmental psychology

Developmental psychology deals with "the analysis of the phases the human being traverses when processing from childhood to adulthood" (Künzel, 1995, p. 109). This notion of development and learning is often linked to a constructivist framework: the learner is meant to explore and manipulate the learning material in order to discover underlying rules and principles and to construct knowledge, either individually (e.g., Piaget) or in a social interaction (e.g., Vygotsky). Künzel (1995) suggests that "the limitations set on this method by the computer could very well be considerably lessened by CALL programs being written in 'hyper'-mode" (p. 110).

Many CALL programs published in the 1990s attempt to offer this kind of flexibility to the student by using the concept of hypertext. Visual and object-oriented programming languages (e.g., Visual Basic, Delphi) enable the CALL developer to implement hypertext features in their CALL applications. The worldwide use of the Internet and the inception of hypertext, the World Wide Web (WWW), have opened up a new field for CALL in the second half of the 1990s (see e.g., Felix, 1998, 2001, 2003). The relative simplicity of HTML (Hypertext Mark-up Language) and the fact that HTML editors and browsers are widely available and relatively inexpensive, offers language teachers the opportunity to present their learning material in a hypertext. So far, this approach has mainly been used to display text (on-line/off-line). It has given the learner the opportunity to explore learning material by browsing through a hypertext environment. The latter consists of multimedia documents that link on-screen information with exercises that are still mainly constructed using the drill-and-practice approach.

It has been argued that the Web has given new life to such exercise types as fill-in-the-blank or multiple-choice. However, both presentation and processing of answers were more sophisticated in packages on stand-alone computers of either dedicated hypertext software (e.g., *Guide*) or exercise authoring software (e.g., *Question Mark, CALIS*). It is probably fair to say that exercise creation packages for Web browsers have still not reached a level of sophistication comparable to that of earlier stand-alone versions. However, the exploitation of hypertextual capacities of the Web and dedicated software has often been connected with a particular school of developmental psychology: constructivism. In opposition to behaviorist methods, here learners construct knowledge with the help of facilitators and resources made available to them.

2.1.3 Influence of cognitive psychology

According to Künzel (1995), cognitive psychology believes that "it is necessary to understand inner mental states (i.e., storage and organization of knowledge, generation of new knowledge and so forth) in order to explain human cognitive capacities and learning patterns" (p. 110). He further notes that "cognitive psychology is also closely linked [to] research in the field of Artificial Intelligence (AI). Questions of representation, acquisition, recall and application of knowledge by humans are essential to the creation of 'intelligent' computer programs" (p. 111). In more general terms, the metaphor of computers has been frequently used in cognitive psychology. Some cognitive psychologists view learning as a process of construction. This understanding of process refers to information that has to be *processed* and *integrated* by the learner and not just *received* (see part 5). However, models of information processing (in terms of information storage and retrieval, for example) also exist and, with respect to their computational metaphors, they are closely related to ideas in AI.

Learning, according to one branch of cognitive psychology, takes place within a social context of interaction and not in isolation. Eminent scholars in this field of psychology, in particular in the context of learning and language acquisition, are Aleksei Leontier and Lev Vygotsky. Both scholars are proponents of Activity Theory, a theory that views knowledge construction in the context of social interaction (see Vygotsky, 1978).

Within language learning in general, and CALL in particular, questions of retention of linguistic knowledge (e.g., of vocabulary) in relation to learning activities and resources, of noticing of cultural and linguistic aspects in language input, of learner autonomy and learner centeredness have played a pivotal role. These questions have influenced the design of language learning software, the process of development and implementation as well as evaluation and research.

2.1.4 Learning psychology and CALL

Learning theories in CALL and their implications for program design have been discussed by several scholars. In addition to Künzel (1995), Levy (1998), for instance, compares the influence of two conceptions of learning on CALL and states:

> The first orientation is represented by the work of Piaget, whose conception of learning is individualistic, whereas Vygotsky is the prime example of a theoretician who has focused on social factors. The two perspectives imply widely differing classroom practices, research agendas and techniques. (p. 86)

The widely acknowledged importance of learning theories in CALL informs all three facets: pedagogic innovation, development, and research. They often serve as a starting point for individual researchers and developers and determine important variables in many CALL projects. We will revisit these theories in the context of our discussion of error correction (part 3) and feedback (part 4).

CALL has not only been influenced by teaching theories and psychology, but also by developments in the field of computing. Many innovations in CALL were preceded by the introduction of new computer hardware and/ or software. Of particular interest here are the developments in Human Language Technology (HLT). These are technologies that rely on our understanding of (computational) linguistics and computer science.

2.2 HUMAN LANGUAGE TECHNOLOGY

The influence of Computational Linguistics (CL) and Machine Translation (MT) on CALL may be indirect but modern CALL systems draw heavily upon the findings of these two areas. The processing of natural language by the computer contributes greatly to the fluency of interaction between the human user and the machine.

> ...there is no doubt that the development of tools (technology) depends on language — it is difficult to imagine how any tool — from a chisel to a CAT scanner — could be built without communication, without language. What is less obvious is that the development and the evolution of language — its effectiveness in communicating faster, with more people and with greater clarity — depends more and more on sophisticated tools. (European Commission, 1996, p. 1)

Language and Technology. From the Tower of Babel to the Global Village (European Commission, 1996), by using an admittedly broad understanding of the term, provides the following examples of language technology: typewriter, ballpoint pen, spell checker, word processor, grammar checker, thesaurus, terminology database, printing, photocopier, laser printer, fax machine, desktop publishing, scanner, modem, electronic mail, machine translation, translator's workbench, tape recorder, database search engines, and telephone. Many of these are already used in language learning and teaching. Today most of the research and development that aims to enable humans to communicate more effectively with each other (e.g., e-mail and Web-conferencing) and with machines (e.g., machine translation and natural language interfaces for search engines) is done in Human Language Technology.

> The field of human language technology covers a broad range of activities with the eventual goal of enabling people to communicate with machines using natural communication skills. Research and development activities include the coding, recognition, interpretation, translation and generation of language. (Cole, 1996, n.p.)

Human Language Technology, Natural Language Processing (NLP) and sometimes also Language Engineering are used as synonyms in the literature. However, the former two are used far more frequently and will be used synonymously in this book.

The following section explores some of the aspects and challenges in HLT that are of relevance to CALL. Starting with a brief outline of some of the early attempts in HLT, namely in machine translation, it will become apparent that experiences and results in this area had a direct bearing on some of the developments in CALL. CALL soon became a multi-disciplinary field of research, development and practice. Some researchers began to develop CALL applications that made use of human language technology. A number of such applications will be discussed in this book.

2.2.1 Computers and language: a brief look back

Facilitating and supporting all aspects of human communication through machines has interested researchers for a number of centuries. The use of mechanical devices to overcome language barriers was proposed first in the seventeenth century. Then, suggestions for numerical codes to mediate between languages were made by Leibnitz, Descartes, and others (Hutchins, 1986, p. 21). The beginning of what we describe today as HLT is, of course, closely connected to the advent of computers:

> The electronic digital computer was a creation of the Second World War: The ENIAC machine at the Moore School of Electrical Engineering in the University of Pennsylvania was built to calculate ballistic firing tables; the Colossus machine at Bletchley Park in England was built to decipher German military communications. (Hutchins, 1986, p. 24)

In a report written in 1948, Alan Turing, one of the fathers of AI, who was heavily involved in the cryptanalysis using the so-called Colossus machine at Bletchley Park, mentions a number of different ways in which these new computers could demonstrate their *intelligence*:

> (i) Various games, for example, chess, noughts and crosses[1], bridge, poker; (ii) *The learning of languages*; (iii) Translation of languages; (iv) Cryptography; (v) Mathematics. (Turing, 1948 quoted in Hutchins, 1986, pp. 26–27)

The term *machine translation* (MT) was coined shortly after the first computers and computer programs had been produced in March 1947 by Booth and Weaver. MT enjoyed a period of popularity with researchers and funding bodies in the United States and the Soviet Union:

> From 1956 onwards, the dollars (and roubles) really started to flow. Between 1956 and 1959, no less than twelve research groups became established at various US universities and private corporations and research centres.... The kind of optimism and enthusiasm with which researchers tackled the task of MT may be illustrated best by some prophecies of Reifler, whose views may be taken as representative of those of most MT workers at that time: '...it will not be very long before the remaining linguistic problems in machine translation will be solved for a number of important languages' (Reifler 1958, 518) and, 'in about two years (from August 1957), we shall have a device which will at a glance read a whole page and feed what it has read into a tape recorder and thus remove all human co-operation on the input side of the translation machines' (Reifler 1958, 516). (Buchmann, 1987, p. 14)

Linguists, language teachers, and computer users today may find these predictions a vast exaggeration. However, the enthusiasm and the work during this time provided the basis for many developments in HLT today.

> By 1964, however, the promise of operational MT systems still seemed distant and the sponsors set up a committee, which recommended in 1966 that funding for MT should be reduced. It brought to an end a decade of intensive MT research activity. (Hutchins, 1986, p. 39)

It is then perhaps not surprising that the mid-sixties saw the emergence of another discipline: Computer-Assisted Language Learning.

> In order to explain how CALL originated and the form its development took, it is necessary first briefly to consider the history of the application of the computer to language and literature in general. And in the context of cryptographical investigations in the Second World War, language applications were involved in the very earliest developments of the electronic digital computer. (Last, 1992, p. 227)

The PLATO Project is widely regarded as the beginning of CALL: "CALL may be said to have begun with the PLATO (Programmed Logic for Automatic Teaching Operations) Project which was initiated at the University of Illinois in 1960" (Levy, 1997, p. 15). *PLATO IV*, implemented on mainframe computers, was probably the version of this project that had the biggest impact on the development of CALL.

> Over the years, we explored many CALL design problems such as the use of hierarchical menus, the organization of student controlled help systems, the proper use of automatic review features and the

> possibilities of matching-driven grammar error diagnosis, feedback and error markup. We experimented extensively with multilingual writing systems, touch driven selection activities, combination of graphics and audio with text material and performance history and data basing. The solutions to these problems eventually provided a rich design vocabulary for PLATO CALL. Indeed, before the appearance of true multimedia courseware, I never saw a micro based CALL design we hadn't already approximated on PLATO. (Hart, 1995, p. 25)

At the time, PLATO was developed at the University of Illinois. Another American university, Brigham Young University, received government funding for a CALL project called TICCIT (Time-Shared, Interactive, Computer Controlled Information Television) (Levy, 1997, p. 18). Sanders (1995), in her introduction to the "Thirty Years of Computer Assisted Language Instruction," Special Issue of the *CALICO Journal*, recalls the beginnings of CALL with the "Stony Brook Project", PLATO, and TICCIT, in the United States. Other still well-known and widely used programs were developed soon after: CALIS (Computer Aided Language Instruction System) at Duke University (Borchardt, 1995) and TUCO[2] at Ohio State University. In Britain in the 1980s, Higgins developed *Storyboard*, a text-reconstruction program for the microcomputer. Davies (1996) notes that the original idea of text-reconstruction programs for language learning probably emanates from Tim Johns. "Other programs such as Fun with Texts [Camsoft] extended the total text reconstruction idea considerably by adding further activities" (Levy, 1997, p. 25).

In recent years, the development of CALL has been greatly influenced by the technology itself as well as by our knowledge of the technology and our expertise with it. For this reason, both the design and classification of CALL software have generally been technology-driven. Wolff (1993, p. 21), for example, provides a classification which takes into account the most recent developments in Information Technology and European standards. He distinguishes five groups of applications:

1. Traditional computer-assisted language learning applications
2. Multimedia applications
3. Utility applications (tools and help systems)
4. Artificial intelligence applications
5. Communication applications

It is important to note that most CALL packages combine features that make it possible to assign them to more than one group. However, traditional computer-assisted language learning applications, the first group mentioned by Wolff (1993), are pieces of software that emulate the approach of the programs that were produced in the early CALL projects. They usually incorporate a *lecturing* element that introduces the learning concepts and provides some help with the task at hand. This *lecturing* section is then followed by a set of exercises. The interface of these packages has improved significantly due to the incorporation of multimedia (text, sound, picture, animation, and video). However, most of the programs offer a limited choice of exercise types such as gap filling, text reconstruction, multiple choice and/or ranking. Feedback is achieved by pattern matching of various levels of specificity.[3] These packages can be created using dedicated authoring tools (e.g., *WinCALIS*, *Question Mark Designer, Hot Potatoes*), authoring programs (e.g., *Guide*, *Toolbook*, *Authorware*) or high-level programming languages (e.g., C++, *Delphi*, *Visual Basic*). Authoring tools are specifically designed for the creation of computer-assisted (language) learning programs. Authoring programs, on the other hand, are more flexible than authoring tools. However, they also require the developer to learn a scripting language and become familiar with a visual interface for designing software. Programming languages are even more flexible, but provide less built-in functionality dedicated to the design of learning activities.

In contrast to traditional language learning software, multimedia applications generally refer to programs that implement (fairly) recent technology. In addition to text, they commonly contain a visual component or combine text, sound, graphics and video. The mid-1980s and the early 1990s saw a significant increase in using multimedia technology for language learning. This can be illustrated with a list of desiderata of CALL programs published at the time:

The courseware should utilize many items, methods, and options:

- Extended silent listening (pre-production phase)
- Natural Approach Techniques (Terrell)
- Spoken and illustrated dialogs (VCR)
- TPR with spoken, written and graphic commands (Asher)
- Vocabulary-building segments with graphics
- Pictionary (extensive photo inventory of actions, places, things, etc.)
- Digitized voice questions and answers
- Constant Interaction (Student instigated movement of the program)
- Simulation sequences (Student with teacher/with another student/ with policeman, etc.)
- Multiple-choice tests (text, voice, graphics)
- Branching frames (according to degree and nature of error in test frames)
- Intrinsic programming (nonlinear sequencing)
- Cloze exercises (graduated from every 6th, 5th, 4th, 3rd word blanked)
- Traditional grammar approaches (where learning style patterns indicate potential)
- Dictation exercises (with immediate correction feedback)
- Writing practice (with immediate correction feedback)
- Visual Phonetics (Displaying native to students' formant wave patterns) (Barrutia, 1985, p. 38)

Barrutia's (1985) wish list contains a majority of items that clearly depend on advances in multimedia technology. Only one item, writing practice, depends on progress in natural language processing and other artificial intelligence technologies. This widespread interest in multimedia applications shifted the interest of language teachers away from applications that focused on the manipulation and/or creation of written texts. Statements like Underwood's (1989) plea for a combination of "hypermedia, simulation and artificial intelligence" (p. 80) were rare.

Utility applications, the third group in Wolff's (1993) classification system, include software that has not been written specifically for the language learner, such as monolingual, bilingual and multilingual dictionaries, spell checkers, word processors, databases and occasionally even spreadsheets.

Artificial Intelligence (AI) applications, the fourth group of applications mentioned by Wolff (1993), are programs that contain knowledge of the subject matter and/or the user. An example is a CALL system in which the program has grammatical knowledge of the target language. If the program has an adaptive component, it will also contain some information about the user. For instance, the program might store mistakes the user makes or entail knowledge of the language learner's first language and then select exercises accordingly. These applications will be discussed in much more detail in part 5. It has to be noted at this point, however, that many CALL applications that make use of AI techniques also rely on learning activities that are remarkably similar to those in traditional CALL applications. Wolff (1993), however, is highly critical of them:

> Complex computational grammars, lexicons and parsers underlie these systems, which as far as I can see do not yet work efficiently. This has not prevented AI researchers from designing, at least in theory, more and more complex systems for modelling discourse, learner behaviour and learning environment. Although I believe that these ambitious endeavours will help us to understand more fully the relationship between these factors in the learning process, I doubt that intelligent tutoring systems will ever be of much use in practical language learning. As far as I am concerned, I think that such systems, at least in their present state of development, go against most of the language learning assumptions discussed above. (p. 22)

Wolff does not, however, provide a list of projects and publications on which he bases his skepticism. The application of AI techniques to language learning undoubtedly faced serious problems at the time and had a number of significant shortcomings. For instance, many projects resulted only in a proof-of-theory prototype and were not scalable. Several systems were also based on outdated beliefs about language learning processes and language learning pedagogy. Examples of these will be given later in this part when individual projects are discussed (see section 2.5).

Some of the challenges mentioned by Wolff still exist today, but it is interesting to note that one of the *language learning assumptions* he is referring to in his quote is that of individual learner differences. This is exactly the area in which AI-based error diagnosis and feedback has made significant progress (Heift & Nicholson, 2000a; Heift, 2001, 2003 2004, 2005, 2006; Heift & Schulze, 2003b). Admittedly, many systems that make use of parser technology are still very form-focused in their teaching and learning approaches which Wolff argues in his second assumption (1993, p. 18). However, an increasing number of research in parser-based CALL has made innovative contributions to new learning approaches and scenarios (e.g., DeSmedt, 1995; Sanders & Sanders, 1995). Several researchers in the area of Natural Language Processing in CALL have also frequently argued that NLP is a necessary prerequisite for further advancement in CALL (e.g., Handke, 1989b, p. 30).

Communication applications, the final group of applications discussed by Wolff (1993), have become more popular over recent years because an increasing number of users have gained access to the Internet. Electronic mail, bulletin boards, mailing lists, news groups, chat groups, computer conferencing, Web-conferencing and video-conferencing are examples of communication applications that provide abundant possibilities in language learning and teaching. These learning activities are most commonly subsumed under the term *computer-mediated communication* (CMC). Chapelle in her keynote address at Eurocall 2000 ascertained that about one third of recent CALL publications deals with the subject of CMC for language learning. For an overview of CMC in CALL, see, for example, Paramskas (1999).

Especially the second half of the 1990s saw an increased interest by language teachers in the use of the Internet (see e.g., Felix, 1998, 2001, 2003). In the language learning classroom, Web-based technology is increasingly used not only as a means of disseminating information for language learners, but also to provide easy access to exercises that mainly consist of multiple choice, gap filling, and the like. Authoring tools for these types of exercises are readily available (e.g., *Question Mark Perception, Hot Potatoes, MaxAuthor*[4]) and an ever increasing number of educational institutions, in particular in higher education, offer online courses for distance education and/or make their learning resources available online. Course management systems, such as *WebCT, Blackboard, Angel,* and *Moodle*[5] are widely used. By now, many students have fairly easy access to fast Internet connections and are sufficiently computer-literate to learn online. At the same time, storing large data files such as audio and video files has become much more feasible with the availability of enormous storage devices. Download and connection speeds permit access to good quality audio and video resources. Naturally, these technological developments have also led to a much more widespread usage of such multimedia resources in language learning. Interesting possibilities for CALL lie ahead in the not too distant future, especially because of e-learning in all kinds of academic disciplines and at a variety of educational levels, from primary schools and children's edutainment to specialized courses in higher education and on-the-job training in large companies and organizations.

The previous sections are, by no means, intended as an in-depth overview of CALL; these can be found elsewhere (e.g., in Langenscheidt Redaktion, 1985; Davies, 1988; Levy, 1997; Fotos & Browne, 2004). Instead, they are meant as a brief introduction to the following section on Natural Language Processing with the main focus on parser-based CALL.

2.2.2 NLP and CALL

Natural Language Processing is one of the branches of Artificial Intelligence (AI) and also one of its main research problems. AI, however, does not exclusively deal with natural language. In general, AI attempts to replicate aspects of human intelligence in machines. Therefore, AI researchers deal with knowledge representation, reasoning and searching and they apply such algorithms and techniques to game playing, machine learning, computer vision, robotics, expert systems and intelligent agents (Sharples, 1989; see e.g., Finlay & Dix, 1996). NLP with its two parts, Natural Language Understanding[6] (see Allen, J., 1995, for an introduction) and Natural Language Generation, is not just an important branch of AI, but also closely linked to Computational and Formal Linguistics and Cognitive Science. According to Jurafsky (2000),

> by speech and [natural] language processing, we have in mind those computational techniques that process spoken and written human language, *as language*.... What distinguishes these language processing applications from other data processing systems is their use of *knowledge of language*. (p. 2)

Computational Linguistics (CL) is the branch of linguistics that aims to develop computational models for written and spoken language. Traditionally, this branch of linguistics informed the development of HLT. More recently, ten Hacken (2003) argued that a revolution in Computational Linguistics has now taken place in that CL no longer concentrates on Natural Language Understanding exclusively (often in the context of MT) in its sentence-based approach and linguistics-driven research. In general, he detected a move away from highly structural research:

> CL has turned to the detailed analysis of practical problems. CALL provides an interesting set of such practical problems. A revolution does not mean that all earlier knowledge is lost. In fact, researchers try to save as much of it as possible by reinterpreting it in the new frame-

> work. Parsing techniques and theories of grammar are still used, but in a more interesting way than before. CALL is likely to be among the typical fields of application of CL in the future. In ten Hacken (2001a) it is argued that the revolution in MT took place between 1988 and 1998. The post-revolutionary future with its bright prospect of the collaboration of CALL and CL has already begun. (p. 36)

With respect to CALL, the strength of NLP is that it allows for a sophisticated error analysis where student tasks can go beyond multiple-choice questions and/or fill-in-the-blanks.[7] Many simple drills, on the other hand, are usually based on string matching algorithms, that is, the student response is compared letter for letter against an answer key. However, one obviously cannot store the infinite number of sentences required for meaningful practice for purposes of comparison. NLP provides the analytical complexity underpinning intelligent CALL (ICALL) or parser-based CALL.

Handke (1989b, p. 22), when discussing the link between CALL and AI, criticizes the CALL software available at the time and identifies three areas of deficiencies:

1. Didactic deficiencies (many programs lack features for error diagnosis and therefore concentrate on exercise types that have been proven to be ineffective).
2. Software engineering deficiencies (problems occur in the user interface, documentation, robustness and help facilities. All of these have an influence on motivation and learning).
3. Deficiencies in the linguistic material (these occur because the programs rely on a finite number of words, phrases, or sentences which the learner has to match in order to receive (positive or corrective) feedback).

More than fifteen years later, many of these problems have been widely recognized and overcome, sometimes in software which relies on artificial intelligence technology, but more often through the employment of modern communication methods and multimedia in (computer-assisted) language learning. The following section looks at developments and general concepts in parser-based CALL.

2.3 PARSERS IN CALL

The lack of linguistic modeling and the insufficient deployment of natural language processing techniques have been cited as reasons for the lack of progress in some areas of CALL (Levy, 1997, p. 3). Levy quotes Kohn (1994):

> Learning a language for the purpose of real-life communication is a demanding task and any attempt to develop congenial computer-based learning-support tools is soon confronted with major limitations. Certainly, there is a particular challenge in the fact that the natural 'intelligence' of a computer, fast algorithm-based processing, is hardly the kind of intelligence required for the strategic processing of discourse in natural communication. There have been attempts in CALL development to bypass such restrictions, in particular, by putting some of the burden of the human-machine interaction on learners and tutors. But in the long run, the need for 'intelligent' CALL will increase, that is, applications will be needed which simulate relevant aspects of the typically human competence underlying the comprehension and production of meaningful discourse. (p. 32)

Kohn (1994) also lists "the insufficient deployment of Natural Language Processing technologies" (p. 32) as one of the reasons why CALL falls short of expectations. Admittedly, there are very few CALL applications that incorporate NLP. This is probably due to the fact that parsing techniques and our knowledge about linguistics have only fairly recently reached a level that permits the development of fully functional parsers (see Matthews, 1993, for an overview of grammatical frameworks applied in ICALL). Moreover, the development of a parser with a computational grammar and its integration in a CALL package is still a very complex, onerous and extremely time-consuming and thus expensive endeavor.

A variety of examples in this book demonstrate that it is possible to apply certain linguistic theories (e.g., for phonology and morphology) to human language technology and implement this technology in CALL software. Opponents of a parser-based approach in CALL, however, claim that

> AI architecture is still a long way from being able to create anything close to mirror the complex system of communication instantiated in any human language and is, hence, unable to introduce any qualitative leap in the design of CALL programs (Salaberry, 1996, p. 11).

Salaberry backs up this claim by adding that "the most important reason for this failure [of ICALL] is that NLP programs — which underlie the development of ICALL — cannot account for the full complexity of natural human languages" (p. 11). This is certainly true. However, at the same time, it does not mean that interesting fragments or aspects of a given language cannot be captured by a formal linguistic theory and hence implemented in a CALL application. In defense of HLT and CALL, this point has been successfully argued by Nerbonne, Jager, and van Essen (1998).

Salaberry (2000), in his review of the conference proceedings (Jager et al., 1998) for which Nerbonne et al. (1998) provided the introduction, concludes that many of the contributions in this volume are a long way from our current knowledge about second language acquisition and language didactics. In his contribution to the *Oxford Handbook of Computational Linguistics*, Nerbonne (2003) continues his advocating of the employment of NLP technology in CALL by listing a number of techniques, such as alignment, lemmatization and parsing, which can be used to facilitate language learning tasks. He discusses the fact that misconceptions in CALL about NLP (e.g., inflated expectations) as well as misconceptions in Computational Linguistics about CALL (e.g., solving problems of the formal representation of a language fragment is a sufficient solution for CALL software development) have to be addressed in order to facilitate successful collaboration between the two fields.

Natural language parsers take written language as their input and produce a formal representation of the syntactic and sometimes semantic structure of this input. A number of earlier papers on ICALL contain a discussion of general parsing algorithms. Cook and Fass (1986), for example, discuss syntactic parsing in the introduction to their article. Loritz and his colleagues provide overviews of parsing which are situated in the context of CALL (Loritz, 1987; Loritz, Parhizgar, & Zambrano, 1990). The following sections provide a more detailed overview of parsing for error diagnosis in the context of different grammatical formalisms.

2.3.1 What are parsers good for?

Parsers designed for language instruction typically contain components that anticipate or search for errors in the event that the grammatical rules are not successful. For example, buggy rules, which enable the parser to process a sentence that contains one or more errors and to identify these errors, are a common instance. Lately, researchers have also analyzed learner (L2) corpora to determine the buggy rules needed for a language parsing system. In addition, statistical methods have been applied to error detection and diagnosis (see the section on learner corpora in part 3).

The role parsers play in CALL has been under scrutiny in the last decade (e.g., Matthews, 1992b, 1992c; Holland, Maisano, Alderks, & Martin, 1993; Nagata, 1996). Holland et al. (1993) discussed the "possibilities and limitations of parser-based language tutors" (p. 28). When comparing parser-based CALL to *conventional* CALL, as they label it, they conclude that

> in parser-based CALL the student has relatively free reign and can write a potentially huge variety of sentences. ICALL thus permits practice of production skills, which require recalling and constructing, not just recognizing [as in conventional CALL], words and structures. (p. 31)

However, at the same time, parsing imposes certain limitations. Parsers tend to concentrate on the syntax of the textual input, thus "ICALL may actually subvert a principal goal of language pedagogy, that of communicating meanings rather than producing the right forms" (Holland et al., 1993, p. 32). On the other hand, implementing newer approaches to grammar teaching and thus focusing *on form* within relevant, authentic communicative tasks might address these shortcomings.

Others (e.g., Loritz, 1992) saw the role of parsers in CALL in a generally more positive light by also emphasizing the additional help such tools can provide for learners:

> Instructional parsers can contribute significantly to more efficient humanistic language study. To do so they must yield in-depth parses despite the additional ambiguities inherent in learners' error-prone language. (p. 19)

Cook and Fass (1986) discuss a number of different uses of NLP in CALL:

- *Structure drills*, which they argue can achieve more variation with the help of NLP. The evaluation and feedback of student responses can also be made more contextualized.
- *Grammatical explanation* is very similar to structure drills. Here, grammatical rules are first presented with or without the help of the parser (e.g., a syntactic tree). The rules are then practiced and the parser facilitates error-specific feedback.
- *Word guessing* is an activity that is related to traditional cloze exercises, but with a parser, the student can be given grammatical clues about the missing word.
- *Query-answering systems* "enable users to retrieve information from and add information to a database, by asking natural language questions" (Cook & Fass, 1986, p. 166). These include text comprehension (as done in Weischedel, Voge, & James, 1978) and communicative teaching exercises. Moreover, they contain information gap exercises in which the student has to query the system to close this information gap, as well as dialogue systems such as ELIZA-type[8] exercises.

The efficacy of syntactic parsers in language learning has also been tested empirically. Juozulynas (1994), for example, evaluated the potential usefulness of syntactic parsers in error diagnosis. He analyzed errors in an approximately 400-page corpus of German essays written by American college students in second-year language courses. His study shows that

> syntax is the most problematic area, followed by morphology. These two categories make up 53% of errors … The study, a contribution to the error analysis element of a syntactic parser of German, indi-

> cates that most student errors (80%) are not of semantic origin and therefore, are potentially recognizable by a syntactic parser. (p. 5)

Juozulynas adapted an error taxonomy that was initially developed by Hendrickson (1979) and that consists of four categories: syntax, morphology, orthography and lexicon. Juozulynas argues for splitting orthography into spelling and punctuation. This choice is easily justified in the context of syntactic parsing. Parts of punctuation can be described with syntactic bracketing rules and punctuation errors can consequently be dealt with by a syntactic parser. According to Juozulynas, lexical and spelling errors form a rather small part of the overall number of learner errors. Some of these errors will be identified during a dictionary look-up.[9] Yet, if words that are in the dictionary are used in the wrong context (e.g., as in the sentence **Their are many programs*), the parser will not recognize them unless specific error rules have been included in the system (e.g., for homophones). However, a parser is commonly employed in conjunction with a spell checker and, in this case, most of the orthographic errors will be eliminated before the parser starts its analysis. Moreover, learners generally know what they intend to say and thus errors of a semantic nature can be largely avoided. Consequently, a parser-based CALL application can play a useful role in detecting many of the morpho-syntactic errors that constitute a high percentage of learner errors in freely produced texts.

However, there are also some limitations of parser-based CALL: "A... limitation of ICALL is that parsers are not foolproof. Because no parser today can accurately analyze all the syntax of a language, false acceptance and false alarms are inevitable" (Holland et al., 1993, p. 33). This is a constraint not only developers of parser-based CALL have to be aware of but also language learners using such software. Accordingly, this limitation has to be taken into consideration during the design, implementation and integration of parser-based CALL software. Higgins (1987) argues similarly but appears to be much more optimistic about students' perception of parser-based CALL. However, it is important to note that Higgins discusses the use of parsers in 1987 and in the context of developing parsing algorithms for CALL software to be run in BASIC on small microcomputers of the time:

> One gets a little closer to the domain of artificial intelligence if one designs programs in which the communication is more genuinely two-way, programs in which the learner has to get messages across to the machine as well as receive messages from it. This means equipping the machine with a parser. The parser, however, does not need to be perfect, provided that we have not endowed the machine with an aura of omniscience. Users will be perfectly ready to modify their language

> and try other formulations to find ones which work as long as they see the machine as basically stupid. (p. 32)

The fact remains that the development of ICALL software has to take into consideration the potential perception by learners: Will they be aware of certain limitations and will the perception of such limitations facilitate or hinder their learning?

Holland et al. (1993) list one final limitation of ICALL:

> A final limitation of ICALL is the cost of developing NLP systems. By comparison with simple CALL, NLP development depends on computational linguists and advanced programmers as well as on extensive resources for building and testing grammars. Beyond this, instructional shells and lessons must be built around NLP, incurring the same expense as developing shells and lessons for CALL. (p. 33)

This is probably the main reason for a lack of commercially available (and commercially viable) parser-based CALL applications that make good use of human language technology. However, it is to be hoped that this hurdle can be overcome in the not too distant future. Certainly, sufficient expertise in the area of HLT has accumulated over recent years and an increasing number of computer programs exploit this technology.

Holland et al. (1993) answer their title question *What are parsers good for?* based on their own experience with BRIDGE, a parser-based CALL program for American military personnel learning German, and based on some initial testing with a small group of experienced learners of German. They present the following points:

- **ICALL appears to be good for form-focused instruction** offering learners the chance to work on their linguistic errors by themselves, not only to improve their performance in the foreign language but also to improve their language awareness.
- **ICALL appears to be good for selected kinds of students.** They list the following characteristics which might influence the degree of usefulness of ICALL for certain students:
  - intermediate proficiency,
  - analytical orientation,
  - tolerance of ambiguity,
  - confidence as learners.
- **ICALL is good for research** because the parser automatically tracks whole sentence responses and detects, classifies and records errors. This might facilitate the assessment of student grammatical competency and thus help to discover patterns of acquisition.

- **ICALL can play a role in communicative practice.** They argue for the embedding of parser-based CALL in *graphical microworlds* which help to capture some basic semantics.

These conclusions have been confirmed by tests of other parser-based CALL applications. For example, Nagata (1996), in reviewing documented comparisons between CALL and non-CALL instruction, complains that many attempts have actually failed to demonstrate the higher efficiency of CALL methodology.[10] She concludes that only CALL programs that make good use of the full potential of the computer, mainly by providing immediate and appropriate feedback, which a workbook will not do, will produce higher learning results. In her study, she uses *Nihongo-CALI*, a CALL program that employs NLP to provide more sophisticated error feedback. Nagata (1996) concludes the following:

> The results of the study show that given the same grammar notes and exercises, ongoing intelligent computer feedback is more effective than simple workbook answer sheets for developing learners' grammatical skill in producing Japanese particles and sentences. A significant difference between Nihongo-CALI and the workbook instruction was observed in the production tests but not in the comprehension tests. This is consistent with Flynn's[11] hypothesis that grammatical competence is less critical in comprehension than in production. As suggested by Pederson [1987] and Dunkel [1991], the present study also confirms that the use of a medium (i.e., the computer) alone does not bring better effects; rather the quality of the messages produced by the medium affects the result. This is based on the fact that the intelligent version of Nihongo-CALI is significantly more effective than the workbook instruction but the traditional version of Nihongo-CALI does not show a significant difference. (p. 67)

In many parser-based CALL projects, developers and researchers allow for so-called *free input* by severely constraining the input domain. Claydon, Hietala, and Nissilä (1992) argue that

> conventional CALL methods and authoring systems appear to cope reasonably well with short range agreement and specific areas where lexical choice becomes narrowed down, due to a predetermined context, to a very small number of alternatives. (p. 15)

They conclude that, what they label a knowledge-based approach should be able to cope with a wider domain and a wider range of exercises than software using conventional methods. In section 2.5, we discuss projects in parser-based CALL. Some of these provide solid evidence of the benefits of artificial intelligence techniques in CALL.

2.3.2 Formal grammar

The knowledge of a parser-based system is not only to be found in its parsing algorithms, but, more importantly, in its representation of linguistic phenomena, that is, in the representation of the spelling, grammar, meaning and textual structure of the language. Here we are concentrating on the most common aspect of linguistic representation in parser-based CALL: the representation of grammar (i.e., morphology and syntax). The main types of grammar formalisms used in ICALL systems are Head-Driven Phrase Structure Grammar (HPSG) (Pollard & Sag, 1987, 1994; Sag, Wasow, & Bender, 2003), Lexical Functional Grammar (LFG) (Bresnan, 1982), Government and Binding (GB) (Chomsky, 1981), Principles and Parameters Theory (PPT) (Chomsky, 1986), Logic Grammars (e.g., the Metamorphosis Grammar by Colmerauer, 1978) and Definite Clause Grammar (DCG) (Pereira & Warren, 1980). The grammar formalisms fall into two main categories: feature and rule-based grammar formalisms.

In feature-based grammars (e.g., HPSG), linguistic information is formally represented as feature structures. Feature structures specify values for various attributes as partial descriptions of a linguistic sign. Feature-based grammars adopt a lexicalist approach in which syntactic information is described within each lexical entry and, for this reason, they require only a few generalized syntactic rules to specify how words and phrases combine into larger units. In contrast, in rule-based grammar formalisms (e.g., DCG), the bulk of syntactic information is contained in the syntactic rules thus leading to a vast number of syntactic rules while leaving the lexical entries minimally specified.

Two related questions arise at this point:

1. How can we implement a natural language grammar in a computer program?
2. How does this grammar have to be adapted if it has to capture an entire variety space of learner grammars as well as the target grammar?

The answer to the first question is connected to the mathematical nature of computers. It is the fact that computers were invented to perform calculations as opposed to something almost *organic* like a natural language. In order to make language palatable for a computer, certain aspects, features and characteristics have to be captured in a mathematical way. With respect to grammar, we will refer to such a grammar as a *formal* grammar and it can be defined as follows:

$$G(V_N, V_T, R, S)$$

Equation 1: Formal grammar

The domain of this function, that is, the set of all input values, contains words of the language in question. The co-domain of this function, that is, the set of possible output values, refers to the trees which represent the sentences from this language. The grammar **G** is here defined as a function with four arguments which are all sets: $\mathbf{V}_N$ is the set of non-terminal symbols of a language such as noun phrase (NP) and verb phrase (VP); $\mathbf{V}_T$ is a set of terminal symbols, that is, words of that language; **R** stands for the rules which describe the formation of non-terminal symbols out of terminal and/or non-terminal symbols; and **S** is a start symbol. Each set has a finite number of members. The biggest set is the set of lexemes[12] of a given language and although this is a finite set at any given point in time, it would be difficult to enumerate all its members. On the other hand, it is certainly possible to list the vocabulary items that need to be acquired by a learner to reach a certain level of language proficiency.

Various formalisms have been developed to describe natural language in a formal grammar. Matthews (1993, p. 9), for example, lists eight major grammar formalisms that have been used in CALL:

1. Various Augmented Phrase Structure frameworks (including Definite Clause Grammars)[13] as used, for example, by Chen and Kurtz[14] (1989a), Schwind (1990a), Labrie and Singh (1991) and Sanders (1991). Also included are systems embedded under PATR-II-like environments as in Levin, Evans, and Gates (1991) and Chanierr, Pengelly, Twidale, and Self (1992).
2. Augmented Transition Networks (ATNs) used by Weischedel et al. (1978). Handke (1992) uses a Cascaded ATN variant.
3. Lexical Functional Grammar (LFG) used by Feuerman, Marshall, Newman, and Rypa (1987).
4. Systemic Grammar used by Fum, Pani, & Tasso (1992).
5. Tree Adjoining Grammar (TAG) used by Abeillé (1992).
6. Incremental Procedural Grammar (IPG) used by Pijls, Daelemans, and Kempen (1987).
7. Word Grammar used by Zähner (1991).
8. Preference Semantics used by Wilks and Farwell (1992).

After his discussion of existing grammatical formalisms in CALL, Matthews (1993) adds that "the…list does not include some of the frameworks…for instance, Categorial Grammar (CG), Generalized Phrase Structure Grammar (GPSG) and Head-Driven Phrase Structure Grammar (HPSG)" (p. 9). He argues for the use of PPT (Principles and Parameters Theory, Chomsky, 1986) as a grammar framework for CALL applications, basing his judgment on three criteria: computational effectiveness, linguistic perspicuity and acquisitional perspicuity.[15] In later parts of his paper, Matthews compares rule-based with principle-based frameworks, using DCG (Definite Clause Grammar) as an example of the former. He concludes that principle-based frameworks (and consequently principle-based parsing) are the most suitable grammar frameworks for ICALL. In an earlier article, however, Matthews (1992c) mentions the potential of "grammars where lexical information plays a crucial organizational role" (p. 25), listing HPSG, among others. He also highlights their great potential in relation to Second Language Acquisition (SLA). Hagen (1995), for instance, describes "an object-oriented, unification-based parser called HANOI" (p. 13) which uses formalisms developed in HPSG. He quotes Zajac (1992, p. 160):

> Combining object oriented approaches to linguistic description with unification-based grammar formalisms...is very attractive. On one hand, we gain the advantages of the object oriented approach: abstraction and generalization through the use of inheritance. On the other hand, we gain a fully declarative framework, with all the advantages of logical formalisms. (p. 10)

Before discussing some of the grammatical frameworks and their role in ICALL more specifically, we need to address the problem of parsing ill-formed input in a more general way.

2.3.3 Parsing ill-formed input in CALL

Given a language L that has a grammar G and a vocabulary V consisting of a set of word forms, we can state, although somewhat simplistically, that a sentence S is a list of selected word forms which are all members of V. Grammar G contains rules that specify selecting and ordering criteria which need to be applied to members of the vocabulary V in order to form a grammatical sentence in language L. In other words, grammar G *forbids* certain combinations of members of V by declaring them ungrammatical. These morpho-syntactic rules will be referred to as constraints. An example of such a constraint in English is the rule that requires a verb to agree with its subject in number (e.g., *she goes*).

The set of possible strings that can be constructed using V is called the closure of V or V*.[16] The number of possible strings would be infinite without any restrictions on how to construct strings because each vocabulary item of V can be repeated infinitely in order to construct a string. However, any language L adheres to a finite set of (grammar) rules. Accordingly, L contains only those strings in the closure V* that satisfy the grammar rules of L (see Figure 2.1). All members of V* which cannot be described with the rules of grammar G, that is, they contain one or more errors, are then to be found in the set V*-L. All three sets — V*, L, V*-L — have an infinite number of members. We know that the number of sentences in any language is infinite, which is our set L. If we then assume that each sentence

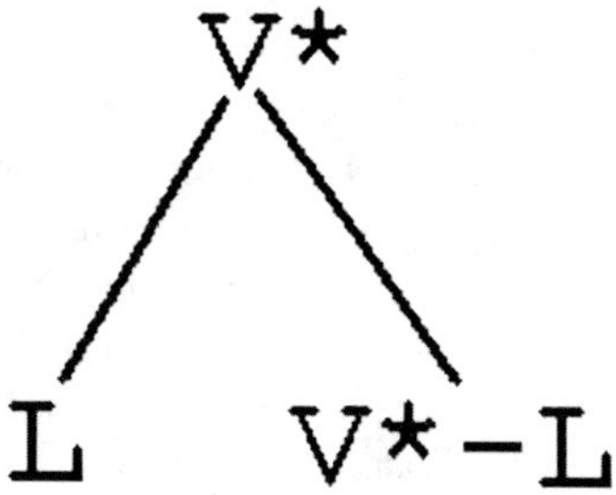

Figure 2.1 Closure of V and L

can potentially be an incorrect sentence by containing a single error, we realize that the number of incorrect sentences (V*-L) is also infinite.

Although parsing ill-formed input has been a challenge for all NLP applications, ICALL systems differ fundamentally from other NLP applications in how and why they handle ill-formed input. In most NLP applications, the goal is to successfully parse and analyze a sentence, despite any errors. In ICALL systems, however, the focus lies on tracing the student's language knowledge rather than on the linguistic analysis of well-formed input. Such systems are inherently prescriptive and, to provide error-specific feedback, they need to analyze where the student deviated from the expert knowledge. In this respect, ICALL systems have a more difficult task (see section 4.5 for a discussion of grammatical formalisms and feedback). Fortunately, however, they usually do not deal with the relatively large input domain found in other NLP applications. Along those lines, DeSmedt (1995) states:

> There is . . . a presumption of grammaticality built into production-rule parsers at a fundamental level. This presumption can make dealing with the productions of someone just learning a language . . . a non-trivial exercise for standard NLP systems. Their parsers can certainly detect ill-formed input (by the simple device of running out of applicable rules without finding a match), but error diagnosis and recovery can be serious issues. (p. 158)

In ICALL, errors occur, not because the student's knowledge is a strict subset of the expert knowledge, but because the learner possesses knowledge potentially different from the expert in quantity and quality. For example, foreign language learners may commit errors that are influenced by their mother tongue.

In describing systems that are not specifically designed for language learners, Weischedel and Sondheimer (1983) analyze errors as either *absolute* or *relative*. Absolute errors refer to errors in the language output. Examples are gender and number mistakes or word order problems. Relative errors address grammatical structures that are correct but are beyond the scope of the grammar.

Although this definition of *absolute* errors addresses the concerns of an ICALL system, there is nonetheless a different goal behind systems that are geared at language learners: ICALL systems aim at providing the student with error-specific feedback and, for this reason, they need to analyze student errors and not simply withstand them. The error analysis performed by an ICALL system provides the source of an error and thus enables the student to learn grammatical constructions of the target language. Simply withstanding errors fails the purpose of a parser-based CALL system.

Relative errors refer to language the user possesses that is beyond the system's knowledge, which is rarely the case with parser-based CALL systems because they generally focus on a language subset as described in students' grammar books. It is a diagnostic tool for language learners to improve their second language grammar skills. The system responds to a student's work on the basis of any errors the student may have made and the model of the student that the system has constructed up to that point.

Errors are most often a symptom of an underlying rule violation. Chen and Xu (1990) provide a useful conceptualization of two different kinds of (grammatical) rules:

> We break the condition part of the grammar rules into two parts: primary and secondary. Primary conditions are compulsory. They determine the nature of the rule. Each grammar rule can be entered only when its primary conditions are satisfied. Secondary conditions are optional. They test the well-formedness of the entered input. If they are satisfied, the input is grammatical.... If they are not satisfied,... a specific error message along with the words which cause the mistake and the expected correct form are printed. (p. 67)

The following section explains the process of parsing ill-formed input in CALL.

2.3.4 Robust parsing for CALL

"Parsing is the process by which grammatical strings of words are assigned syntactic structure" (Patten, 1992, p. 29). Patten continues by stating that this syntactic analysis can then in turn form the basis for a semantic and pragmatic textual analysis.

The parser output from *Textana* given in Figure 2.2 is taken from the developer's command line interface.[17] The sentence *Ich kaufe das Auto* (I am buying the car) was successfully analyzed by the parser: *kaufe* was determined as a regular verb in first person singular, present tense. Thus it agrees with the subject *ich* which the parser identified as the best candidate for the subject position because of its theta-role, arg (von, dat, +). *Auto* agrees with its article *das* in number (singular) and gender (neuter) and the phrase was identified correctly as the direct object, marked for accusative case.

Each word of the sentence was first parsed individually to determine its morphological structure. Each morph — the root, lexical and derivational affixes and inflections — adds some information about the word, for example, its grammatical gender and number. Complete words are then combined into phrases according to grammatical rules. Each phrase is subsequently analyzed and the phrases are then combined into larger units until the sentence is fully parsed. For instance, Figure 2.3 shows the parse of the German comparative adjective, *affigere* (sillier). Figure 2.3 illustrates the number of slots used in this HPSG structure to record information about the *sign*. In the upper part (*structure*) the sign records the surface

```
| ?- go.

Input a sentence in german
|: Ich kaufe das Auto.
|: *
Found one
None like it. This one is no. 26
Parse completed - 26 edges

Time taken: ~3d seconds
Parse 26 (cost 0):
[.,
 identity
 - [kaufe,
    arg(lab(von, dat, +)) - ich,
    arg(lab(gen, -, +)) - [Auto, modifier - das]]]

DEPENDENCY TREE
***************
.
---------------
kaufe
------------
ich   Auto
      ---
      das


no
| ?-
```

Figure 2.2 Parsing results — summary in *Textana* (Schulze, 2001, p. 156)

```
sign(structure(positions(start(0),
                         end(1),
                         span(1),
                         +compact,
                         xstart(0),
                         xend(1)),
               string({{{aff,ig},er},e},affigere),
               core(???({{{aff,ig},er},e})),
               index(1),
               dtrs([]),
               misc(language(german, A), +realised, -icap, B)),
     morph(affixes([]),
           -affix,
           history(-umlauted, branch([]), C),
           frame(inflecting, [[], [105, 103], -], [])),
     syn(nonfoot(head(cat([xbar(+v, +n)]),
                      agree(third(+sing, -plural),
                            gender(-neuter, +masculine, -feminine)),
                      nform(defval(value(case(+nom, D)), -usedefault),
                            ref(+, E),
                            F),
                      G),
                 mcopy(type(H), -bracketed, I),
                 minor(mod(target("NOUN"(J)),
                           result("NOUN"(K)),
                           completion(\+(\+(---)))),
                       -conj,
                       specf(-specified,
                             def(+, -, generic(defval(-value, usedefault(L)))),
                             card(agree(third(+sing, -plural),
                                        gender(-neuter, +masculine, -feminine))),
                             M),
                       N)),
         subcat(args([]), fixed(O)),
         P),
     meaning(semantics(Q), uses(-predicative, R), S),
     remarks(constraints([]), T))
```

Figure 2.3 Morphological analysis of a German adjective (*affigere* = *sillier*)

structure of the string which has just been parsed. Grammatical information is stored in *morph* and *syn*. Very little information is recorded about the meaning of the word because the parser is used here as part of a grammar checker focusing on morphology and syntax. The slots of the *remarks* part will be used later to store the information that is needed to generate feedback if the parser locates an error.

As a result of this process, the longer the sentence and the more complex its structure, the more partial parse trees of words, phrases and phrase combinations will be generated before the parser arrives at its final result. Figure 2.4 shows only the summary of the final parsing result. However, far more detail is stored for each part and for the sentential level. Certainly, all the information including the processing effort is usually kept from the learner. The parse results are converted to learner-friendly feedback and displayed as such to the learner (compare Figure 2.2 and Figure 2.5).

Generally, a successful parse indicates a well-formed sentence and an unsuccessful parse indicates an ill-formed one, judged on the basis of the grammar and lexicon. Even if we assume that a certain parser is only intended to parse texts produced by competent native language (L1) writers, we can never be certain that a text will be error-free. For this reason,

```
Input: Die alte Friseuse gab dem netten Studenten den teuren Tisch.
(The old hairdresser gave the nice student the expensive table.)

Parser output:

Parse completed - 86 edges

Time taken: ~3d seconds
Parse 86 (cost 4.5):
[.,
 identity
 - [gab,
    arg(lab(von, dat, +))
    - [Friseuse, modifier - die, modifier - alte],
    arg(lab(gen, -, +)) - [Tisch, modifier - den, modifier - teuren],
    arg(lab(an, acc, dat))
    - [Studenten, modifier - dem, modifier - netten]]]

DEPENDENCY TREE
***************

.
---------------------------------------------------
gab
------------------------------------------------
Friseuse           Tisch              Studenten
----------         ------------       ------------
die    alte        den    teuren      dem    netten
```

Figure 2.4 Textana parsing output of a sentence

it is necessary to have parsers that can deal with ill-formed linguistic constructions. Obviously, if it is clear right from the start that the parser will be used to evaluate sentences produced by foreign language learners, then the parser must be capable of producing meaningful structural analyses of ill-formed sentences. This feature of a parser is often referred to as its robustness. Thus, parsers in a CALL environment have to achieve two conflicting goals: they have to parse all well-formed constructions of the language correctly and they have to parse sentences which are ill-formed according to the rules of the parser grammar (Dini & Malnati, 1993, p. 76). The latter set of sentences use linguistic rules of the language that have either not been implemented in the parser or do not belong to the linguistic system of that language. In CALL, the latter rules reflect the learner's interlanguage (Selinker, 1974, 1992; Corder, 1981) rather than the target language.

A number of different approaches have been developed to deal with erroneous input. For example, Mellish (1989) wrote a grammar and a parser that just dealt with simple errors: "unknown/misspelled words, omitted words, extra noise words" (p. 102). He criticizes the earliest approach in parser-based CALL by Weischedel and Sondheimer (1983)[18] who used the longest spanning edge of the parse and then applied further rules, so-called meta-rules. Mellish shows that there are problems with that approach and proposes the use of a declarative formalism, such as a Context-Free Phrase Structure Grammar (CF-PSG) or a Definite Clause Grammar (DCG), which allows to construct partial parses that do not necessarily start from the beginning of the input, thus providing left and right context for the determination of the *best* parse:

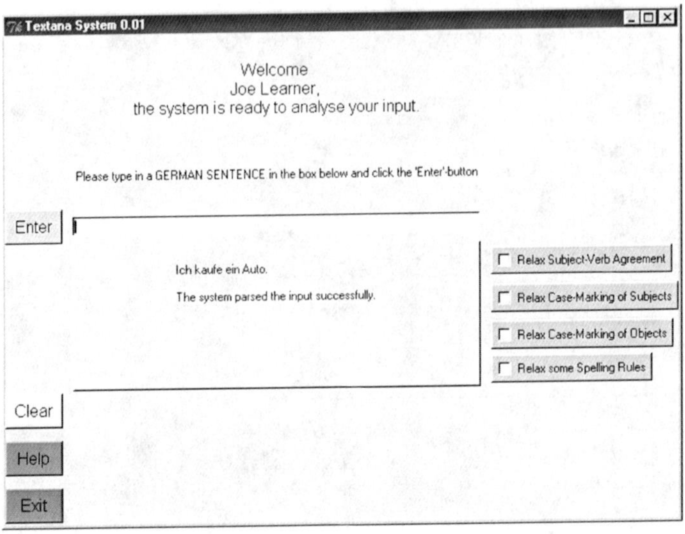

Figure 2.5 Textana user interface for a successful parse

> Our basic strategy is to run a bottom-up parser over the input and then, if this fails to find a complete parse, to run a modified top-down parser over the resulting chart to hypothesise possible complete parses. (Mellish, 1989, p. 103)[19]

Other approaches have been adopted in parser-based CALL. Many of them use an error grammar, that is, they capture individual and/or typical errors of language learners of a certain language in a separate rule system. The advantage of this error grammar approach is that feedback can be very specific. Moreover, the error analysis is generally fairly reliable because each error can be attached to a very specific rule. The big drawback, however, is that individual learner errors have to be anticipated in the sense that each error needs to be covered by an adequate rule.

Klein and Dittmar (1979) proposed to describe the interlanguage of learners computationally by starting off with a description of the standard grammar of the target language. The rules and phenomena peculiar to the learner language are captured by adding new rules and symbols that also carry a probability value. This probability value indicates the likelihood of the application of a different rule for each stage in the learner's development. The difficulty of this error anticipation becomes apparent when considering the huge variety space with its infinite number of possible deviations from the standard grammar. These variations are contained in the different learner varieties that exist over time and for different learners.

However, we do not only find erroneous structures in texts that have been produced by language learners: machine translation faces similar problems. In addition to a structure actually deviating from the standard variety, it is also possible that the parser grammar lacks a rule for parsing a fragment of well-formed text. Both phenomena result in the same fact in that the parser will fail to provide an output of a complete parse. Dini and Malnati (1993) review approaches "concerning the design and the implementation of grammars able to deal with 'real input'" (p. 75), that is, natural language input that does contain errors and/or constructions which are not covered by the computational grammar. They list the following four approaches to treating ill-formed input:[20]

1. the rule-based approach,
2. the metarule-based approach,
3. the preference-based approach, and
4. the constraint-based approach.

The rule-based approach relies on two sets of rules: one for grammatical input and one for ungrammatical input. The latter rules are also referred to as buggy rules. Dini and Malnati (1993) point out quite rightly that, in general, well-formedness conditions should be sufficient and the second set of rules, the buggy rules, result in linguistic redundancy. This approach also requires that the program designer anticipates the errors language learners are most likely to make. This presents a number of problems in addition to the disadvantage with respect to the coverage of learner varieties described in section 2.3.3.

First, due to the vast error scope and unpredictability of some errors, ill-formed input can only be partially anticipated (Yazdani & Uren, 1988). Sentences containing errors that have not been anticipated by the designer cannot be processed by the system. Inevitably, this results in generic rather than error-specific feedback and thus it fails to achieve one of the primary goals of a parser-based CALL system.

Second, anticipating errors lacks generality. Most systems base the search for errors on the native language (L1) of the student. Any system which anticipates errors requires that the same error in the target language is presented in each different source language. The fewer source languages considered the more user-limited the system. For example, a system which anticipates errors made by English learners of German, will tend not to handle errors specifically made by French learners of German.

The metarule-based approach uses a set of well-formedness rules and, if none of them can be applied, the system calls an algorithm that relaxes some constraints by applying so-called meta-rules and recording the particular violation.[21] Dini and Malnati (1993) note that the procedurality of the algorithm causes problems when confronted with multiple errors, something very likely in any text produced by a language learner. Courtin et al. (1991), for example, present a system which only checks for agreement errors in French. Whenever an error is encountered, the system generates "the corresponding correct form" (p. 163) and proposes it to the user.

If the user confirms it, this choice is added to the syntactic dependency tree and the system continues to build the tree without reparsing the phrase or the sentence. However, it is often difficult to determine a *correct* equivalent of an erroneous structure, particularly when dealing with agreement errors: if two constituents do not agree, which one contains the error? It is also difficult to handle multiple errors with this very localized approach to correction.

The preference-based approach comprises an overgenerating grammar and a set of preference rules.

> ...each time a formal condition is removed from a b-rule[22] to make its applicability context wider, a preference rule must be added to the grammar. Such a p-rule must be able to state, in the present context of the b-rule, the condition that has been previously removed (Dini & Malnati, 1993, p. 77).

This is again a source of linguistic redundancy that might result in inconsistencies in the grammar. Dini and Malnati (1993) claim that due to the overgeneration of possible interpretations, "the system would be completely unusable in an applied context" (p. 79).

The constraint-based approach is based on the following assumptions:

- each (sub)tree is marked by an index of error (initially set to 0);
- the violation of a constraint in a rule does not block the application, but increases the error index of the generated (sub)tree;
- at the end of parsing, the object marked by the smallest index is chosen. (Dini & Malnati, 1993, p. 80)

Consequently, the "most plausible interpretation of a...sentence is the one which satisfies the largest number of constraints" (p. 80). The authors then claim that some constraints are better left *strong* if their weak counterpart causes a loop. The example provided is a mother node with one obligatory daughter. In this case the "mother node is always interpreted as the daughter node with some violated constraint" (p. 80). For example, in a rule VP -> V the intransitive verb (V) will always be interpreted as a V verb phrase and the rule will be triggered over and over again.

After sketching the DIMAcheck framework, Dini and Malnati (1993) conclude that "weak constraint-based parsing has proven to be useful in increasing the robustness of an NLP system" (p. 88). basing their conclusion on the following advantageous features of the approach: non-redundancy, built-in preference mechanism, globality, efficiency and linguistic flexibility. Non-redundancy refers to the fact that similar rules will not have to be recorded twice. Only one rule is recorded and the constraints of this rule can then be violated because they are encoded in their weak form.

This approach also means that preference will always be given to the parse result for which no weak constraints had to be violated (built-in preference mechanism). Globality refers to the advantage that the interpretation of violated constraints is left until the end of parsing so that the interactions of violated constraints can be taken into consideration. This makes the approach advocated by Dini and Malnati very efficient and relatively flexible.

With respect to parsing erroneous texts for CALL, Menzel views parsing as constraint satisfaction (Menzel, 1990; Heinecke, Kunze, Menzel, & Schröder, 1998). He argues that due to the general ambiguity of natural languages and the ambiguity of erroneous utterances in particular, it is necessary to reduce the search space, that is, the number of generated parses. Menzel (1990) proposes the following heuristics:

- exclusion of compatibility constraints which are unlikely to be violated (e.g., two prepositions in one prepositional phrase);
- exclusion of "useless permutations during category attachment to the grammar tree by maximising the locality measure." (p. 424)
- reuse of phrases already parsed in the analysis (chart parsing).

Later Menzel and his colleagues investigate the use of graded constraints. Graded constraints start off with the assumption that the use of additional constraints will reduce the ambiguity in the analysis, but also exclude the successful parsing of other constructions (Heinecke et al., 1998).

> Obviously, there is a trade-off between the coverage of the grammar and the ability to perform the disambiguation efficiently. To overcome this problem one wishes to specify exactly which constraints can be relaxed in case a solution can not be established otherwise. Therefore, different types of constraints are needed in order to express the different strength of strict conditions, default values and preferences. (not paginated)

The authors then introduce the annotation of constraints c with weights w(c). They distinguish hard constraints with a score of $w(c)=0$, which should never be violated (e.g., a sentence must have one and only one subject); well-formedness conditions with a score near $w(c)>0$, which can be violated (e.g., agreement); and weak constraints with a score near $w(c)<1$, which are mere preferences (e.g., attachment preferences). The best parse is found by multiplying all constraint violation scores (II w(c)) and determining the parse with the highest product. Any constraint can be violated more than once by a given structure, "the constraint grade w(c) is raised by the power of n(c,s), which denotes the number of violations of constraint c by the structure s" (Heinecke et al., 1998, not paginated).

$$s' = \arg\max_{s} \prod_{c} w(c)^{n(c,s)}$$

Figure 2.6 Formula for a partial constraint satisfaction (Heinecke et al., 1998)

The formula given in Figure 2.6 determines that structures that contain a violation of a hard constraint (multiplication with score 0) are not considered at all.

Menzel and Schröder (1998b, 1999) continue the discussion of graded constraints and present a system in which morpho-syntactic and semantic constraints are taken into consideration. The semantic relations are determined on the basis of a graphically represented market-place scenario. Menzel (2004) "tries to adopt intentions as an additional dynamic source of knowledge, which can be used to bias feedback generation components of a tutoring system for foreign language learning" (not paginated). Intention is introduced as a category that facilitates the reduction of possible parse solutions. It is, of course, most effective to use the constraint with the greatest reductive power which, very often, also corresponds to the learner's intention. What did the writer really intend to say?

This question is notoriously difficult to answer on the basis of a textual analysis by a computer. Menzel investigates two different options. First, learners can be queried, in case of an error and asked to elaborate on their intentions. For example, in the case of non-agreement of subject and verb, they are asked to state whether they mean one entity or multiple entities of the subject (Menzel, 2004).

Example 2.1

* the children plays in the yard

a) intended : the child plays

b) intended : the children play

If the learner states the intention given in Example 2.1a, the system will provide feedback on the noun error to help correct the unintended plural. If the learner states Example 2.1b, as the intention, the system will flag an agreement error and propose to change the verb ending.

For the second option, the system will ask students to demonstrate what they intended to say. Thus, in a microworld students are asked to drag and drop an object to a position after querying the system on its location with a possibly erroneous, verbal command. Menzel (2004) remarks:

> Such a non-linguistic approach even becomes the only feasible option whenever the direct communication in the language to be learnt breaks down due to the insufficient proficiency of the learner. Given the sophistication of the contemporary graphical user interface, fairly complex propositions can be communicated that way. (not paginated)

In a later paper, Menzel and his colleagues show that parsing with weighted constraints is not just a suitable approach within CALL, but it is a valid approach to parsing texts which often contain unexpected input (Foth, Menzel, & Schröder, 2005). These discussions support the view put forward by Dini and Malnati (1993) that weak constraint relaxation is the most efficient algorithm for error detection. However, a number of problems still remain. This is evident in several projects that attempted implementations of this approach. For example, Vandeventer (2001) reports on a feasibility study using relaxed constraints. She concludes that although recall is fairly good when three constraints (gender, number, person) are relaxed, precision (i.e., false positives) is unacceptably low.[23]

The methods available to detect errors, that is, violations of grammatical rules, however, are determined by the programming language and the grammar formalism. ICALL systems have been implemented in both procedural and declarative programming languages. Procedural programming languages such as BASIC specify the steps the computer needs to apply chronologically. Early programs even had line numbers and the computer moved to line one, carried out the command listed, moved to line two and performed this command and so forth. In contrast, declarative programming languages such as *Prolog* contain rules that do not describe a procedure by specifying steps that have to be followed in a chronological order. Instead, the computer employs a rule when it can match its head.

```
job(susan, department_chair).
job(janet, department_secretary).
   who_is(Name, X) :-
   job(Name, X).
```

If the small program above is set the task of determining *who_is(janet, X)*, then it matches the *who_is* predicate first, instantiates the variable *Name* with the value *janet* and successfully matches the clause which tells us that *janet* is the *departmental secretary*.

Programming language, to some extent, determines the choice of grammar formalism which in turn determines what detection methods can be applied and how errors are perceived by the system (Sanders & Sanders, 1989; Matthews, 1993, 1994).

In the following sections the two major formalisms, procedural and declarative formalisms, are presented in some detail.

2.4 FORMALISMS AND PARSING FOR ERRORS

A thorough introduction to procedural and declarative formalisms cannot be provided in this book. Instead, we are focusing on the role the formalisms have played in parser-based CALL.[24] Before these two formalisms are introduced, however, a necessary distinction between deterministic and non-deterministic parsing algorithms has to be made. These differ in the way they handle the instances where a parser fails:

> ... when a non-deterministic parser fails at a certain point, it does not necessarily mean the sentence is wrong at this point, maybe the parser has chosen the wrong path [it will now backtrack]. But when a deterministic parser faces several paths, it looks ahead and also looks back if necessary to see which path is the correct one. As soon as it decides on a path which is considered to be the only correct path, it never backtracks. (Chen & Xu, 1990, p. 65)

Deterministic as opposed to non-deterministic parsing has an impact on the system when deciding whether or not it is actually dealing with an error. This is an important question that leads us to a discussion of the processing of erroneous language by using distinct formalisms.

2.4.1 Procedural formalisms: augmented transition networks

The late 1980s saw the beginning of what is known as *Intelligent CALL* (ICALL) — a "mix of AI techniques and CALL" (Matthews, 1992a, p. i). Very little earlier work is documented. Courtin, Dujardin, Kowarski, Genthial, and De Lima (1991) list Courtin's *Thèse d'état* from 1977 with the title *Algorithms pour le traitement des langues naturelles*. Bowerman (1993, p. 31) notes that "Weischedel et al. (1978) produced the first ICALL system which dealt with comprehension exercises. It used syntactic and semantic knowledge to check students' answers to comprehension questions."[25] The system is a prototype German tutor implemented as an Augmented Transition Network (ATN) with a semantic and syntactic component.

Transition Networks (TNs) consist of a set of states. Movement between states is controlled by rules according to the next element in the input. States are referred to as *nodes*; transitions between states are referred to as *arcs*. TNs are inherently procedural.

Augmented Transition Networks (ATNs) additionally employ *registers* which hold grammatical information, for example, information on agreement. ATNs also allow actions to be associated with each arc, for instance, the setting of a register, or the calling of another network.

The ATN given in Figure 2.7 parses sentences such as *Mary sleeps* by going through the steps listed in the figure. The ATN follows the arcs and accepts, from the input string, constituents that are on the arc labels. The ATN can either accept a word, a proper noun for instance, or it can call another entire subnetwork (VP in the present example). Parsing proceeds until a node is reached in which parsing can stop, indicated by the double circle. In addition, the arcs set and test register *NUM* to control number agreement between the subject and the verb.

Start in state 1 of S network.
Accept NP (Mary, NUM = singular).
Set register NUM of NP = singular.
Set register NUM of S = singular.
Proceed to state 2 of S network.
Call VP network.
Start in state 1 of VP network.
Accept V (sleeps, NUM = singular).
Set register NUM of VP = singular.
set NUM of S test NUM of S = NUM of NP = NUM of VP
Proceed to state 2 of VP network and exit.
Test that NUM of S = NUM of VP
(the test succeeds since both have the value singular).
Proceed to state 3 of S network and exit.

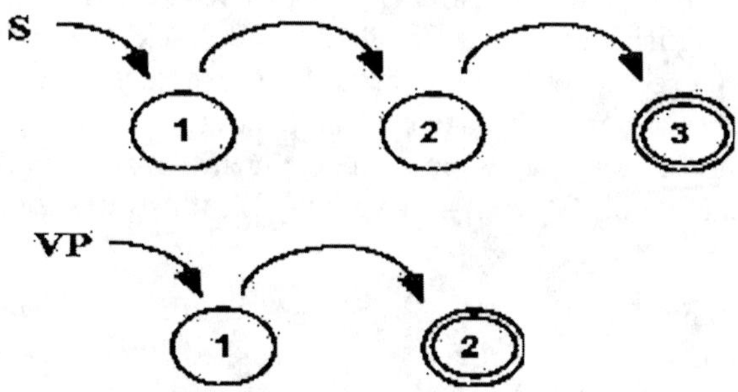

Figure 2.7 An Augmented Transition Network (Covington, 1994)

The ATN can successfully parse *Mary sleeps* but the sentence *Mary sleep* will fail since the register on number agreement is violated. Violations of this kind, however, are common among second language learners. An ICALL system needs to parse such sentences and analyze the errors to provide error-contingent feedback.[26]

Meta- and buggy rules are the most common procedures employed for handling students' errors in parser-based systems.[27] In ATN systems, agreement constraints are commonly relaxed with meta-rules, while buggy-rules are used for errors in word order. Buggy rules might also make up a complete second grammar, the student's native language. In this case, meta-rules are used for analyzing overgeneralization errors. Overgeneralization errors are the effects of particular interlanguage strategies on items within the target language, that is, overgeneralization of target language rules. For example, for the verb *sleep*, a student might choose the regular past tense suffix *-ed *sleeped* as opposed to the correct irregular form *slept*.[28]

ATNs are limited in their application to parser-based systems. In procedural programs, the data and its implementation are interwoven. This makes a system less general and makes it more difficult to provide a large coverage of errors, because errors need to be anticipated and encoded similar to a pattern-matching mechanism. Johnson's (1983) evaluation of general ATN systems can be applied to parser-based systems:

> Like any procedural model, an ATN gives extensive possibilities for optimization and tight control over details of parsing strategy. The price to be paid in return is a danger that as the system increases in size, its logic becomes obscure, modification progressively more risky and debugging more and more problematic. (p. 72)

Furthermore, the ATN systems developed for CALL are commonly tied to a specific native language of the student, in Weischedel's system (1978), for example, English. However, Weischedel and Black (1980) conclude that it is efficient to relax predicates which the parser designer designates as "failable". For students with different native languages, the systems would require even more buggy rules since the error anticipation is derived from the native language of the student. Example 2.2 illustrates the problem:

Example 2.2

a) German:	Ich habe es gesehen.	*I have it seen*
b) French:	Je l'ai vu.	*I it have seen.*
c) English:	I have seen it.	

In German, the direct object appears in between the auxiliary and the past participle, the auxiliary always being in second and the past participle in final position in main clauses. A French learner of German is likely to commit errors concerning the position of the auxiliary, while the English learner of German will have problems with the position of the past participle. For an ATN to deal with the error caused by either native language, buggy rules of each error would have to be implemented.

A further shortcoming of procedural systems is that they are not modular. Such systems cannot be easily altered and applied to another language. The whole system has to be rewritten, when preferably one could replace only the language-dependent grammar within a language-independent shell.

2.4.2 Declarative formalisms

The bulk of parser-based systems are implemented as declarative representations. The main types of grammar formalisms used are Definite Clause Grammar (Pereira & Warren, 1980), phrase structure grammars, such as

Head-Driven Phrase Structure Grammar (Pollard & Sag, 1987, 1994; Sag et al., 2003), Generalized Phrase Structure Grammar (Gazdar, Klein, Pullum, & Sag, 1985; Bennett, 1995), as well as Government and Binding (Chomsky, 1986; Cook & Newson, 1996).

In distinction to Augmented Transition Networks, in declarative implementations, the grammar makes heavy use of the operation on sets of features called unification. Unification-based grammars place an important restriction on unification, namely that two categories A and B fail to unify if they contain mutually inconsistent information (Gazdar et al., 1985; Knight, 1989). However, this inconsistent information constitutes exactly the errors made by second language learners. For example, if the two categories A and B do not agree in gender a parse will fail. A system designed to accommodate the errors of second language learners requires either a modification of the unification algorithm itself or feature specifications capable of overcoming the gender restriction.

There are three common methods of analyzing ill-formed input in declarative-based ICALL systems. In the first approach, in addition to the target grammar, the student's native language is explicitly encoded to cover errors due to native language interference. Depending on the error scope of the system, meta-rules may be added for overgeneralization errors. The second approach does not rely on the native language of the student but on meta-rules to relax the constraints of the target language. In the third approach, the unification algorithm is altered in such a way that the system, despite clashing features, performs a parse and keeps track of the conflicting features. The following sections will discuss the three distinct approaches and provide examples of each.

2.4.3 Use of the native language

An example of the first approach which encodes the native language grammar is Schuster's (1986) *VP2* system for Spanish learners of English. The system focuses on the acquisition of English verb-particle and verb-prepositional phrase constructions. The program contains two grammars, Spanish and English. A shortcoming of the system is that it mainly deals with native language interference errors. Overgeneralization errors, another significant source of students' errors cannot be recognized by the system.

Catt and Hirst (Catt, 1988; Catt & Hirst, 1990) overcome the shortcoming of Schuster's system by implementing meta-rules for overgeneralization errors. Their system *Scripsi* consists of three grammars: English as the target language, and French and Chinese as the native languages of the learners. Whenever the input cannot be recognized by English rules alone, the system applies the rules of French or Chinese. Although the system represents an extension of Schuster's system, nonetheless, an important error class passes unrecognized: errors in word order can only be detected if they are due to native language transfer. A further limitation of this approach lies in its lack of generality. First, the same error in the target language has to be encoded in each source grammar, French and Chinese. Second, identical grammatical structures are encoded in all three grammars leading to redundancies.

Wang and Garigliano (1992, 1995) designed a *Chinese Tutor* for English native speakers. In their design, they attempted to avoid the kind of redundancies found in Catt and Hirst's system. The *Chinese Tutor* models only the fragments of the grammatical rules in the native language which are different from the corresponding rules in the target language. Additionally, the authors address only those transfer errors justified by empirical data they collected. They found that 78% of the errors made by English learners of Chinese are due to transfer. The remaining 22% are ignored in their system.

The deficiencies of the systems employing native grammars are either lack of generality and/or poor coverage of errors, as in the case of neglecting errors due to other variables than native language interference (e.g., influence of other learnt languages, overgeneralization or simplification of target language rules, cognitive misconceptions about target language rules). The systems also overtly rely on a particular native language of the user and are thus limited in their scope. This limitation becomes more problematic due to the increase in online distance education. Any overt presumption of the native language of the student is severely restrictive.

2.4.4 Using meta-rules with declarative formalisms

A variation of error handling is found in other declarative systems. For example, Kurtz, Chen and Huang (1990) developed a DCG system called XTRATE for Chinese learners of English that does not rely on the native language of the student. Instead the authors only use correct grammar rules with meta-rules that relax grammatical constraints at multiple levels. Level 1 contains all grammatical constraints, Level 2 relaxes syntax, Level 3 semantics and Level 4 both syntax and semantics. In addition, for translation exercises the system performs a literal word-by-word translation. The authors' system is more general in the sense that they do not anticipate errors on the basis of the native language of the student. However, the system cannot handle errors in word order. The only constraints which can be relaxed in their system are agreement errors, both syntactic and semantic.

A similar pitfall can be found in a system for learning English developed by Covington and Weinrich (1991). The program is written in Gulp, an extended form of Prolog which includes a notation for feature structures (Covington, 1994). The system focuses on agreement, insertion and omission errors. Insertion and omission errors are due to a violation of the subcategorization list of the verb. For example, a student might use an inherently transitive verb without an object. The authors relax constraints by implementing a lenient rule for each rule which parses well-formed input, that is, they combine the feature-checking approach with buggy rules, not constraint relaxation (see below). Consequently, errors in word order pass unrecognized.

Meta-rules, by definition, cannot address errors in word order. They can only relax constraint violations of grammatical features. All systems which handle word order errors anticipate these by implementing buggy rules. However, in all cases the result is very user-specific since the systems rely on a particular native language of the student. The ones which implement more than one native language lack generality. The same error in the target language is presented in each source language. However, others have argued that buggy rules function adequately (Bender, Flickinger, Oepen, Walsh, & Baldwin, 2004) because a system which can detect some errors and provide accurate diagnosis and feedback for them is, nonetheless, valuable.

2.4.5 Adapting the feature grammar formalism

The third approach in error detection within declarative systems makes use of the feature grammar formalism itself. For example, Hagen (1995) developed a parser-based system, *GrammarMaster*, for French as a second language. The program is driven by an object-oriented, unification-based parser written in HyperTalk. The system addresses three particular grammatical constructions: conjunctions, reflexive binding and dislocated, missing and superfluous constituents.

The goal of the system is to show an implementation of some "thorny problems of complex grammatical constructions" (1995, p. 5). Hagen's system borrows analyses from a number of grammar formalisms: Head-Driven Phrase Structure Grammar (HPSG), Generalized Phrase Structure Grammar (GPSG) and Government Binding (GB). Missing constituents are handled with the SUBCAT feature of HPSG, reflexive binding makes use of the foot feature principle (GPSG) and superfluous constituents are controlled by thematic assignment (GB).

Hagen (1995) relaxes the unification algorithm to block parsing failure such that if the parser

> detects contradictory features like [genM] and [genF] [genM and genF indicate masculine and feminine gender, respectively], it preserves the features on the major part of speech (in the case of noun phrases, the noun) and inserts the contradictory feature on a minor part of speech like an article into an error stack along with a corrective message. (p. 16)

Hagen's implementation of the principles from GPSG, HPSG and GB allow for a general treatment of the errors considered. The errors do not need to be anticipated. If any of the grammar principles do not hold, the constituent is flagged and an error message is attached. However, the system seems linguistically rather than pedagogically motivated because grammatical constructions which are linguistically and computationally complex do not necessarily present difficulties for the language learner. For example, the errors second language learners make with conjunctions are generally limited to subject/verb number agreement and case assignment of the subject or verb complement. While conjunctions present a challenge from a computational point of view since it is of utmost importance for the linguist that the parser displays the correct analysis, for the language learner it is the feedback that outweighs the linguistic and computational analysis (Farghaly, 1989). In addition, altering unification implies inserting procedural techniques in an inherently declarative algorithm. Thus the analysis becomes closely tied to its implementation, that is, the grammar only works if unification is changed in a certain way.

Schwind (1990a, 1995) developed a system for German based on Metamorphosis Grammar (Colmerauer, 1978).[29] Her system covers a broad range of errors: agreement, syntactic and semantic errors. Her method of analyzing agreement errors is based solely on the feature grammar formalism. The class of agreement errors covers errors in gender, number, person and case of noun phrases. The system does not anticipate these errors. Instead, each lexeme is specified for every possible grammatical occurrence (see also McFetridge & Heift, 1995). In addition, the unification-based algorithm builds up two sets of feature structures:

> ... unify (a,b,r,e) holds whenever r is the result of the unification and e is the set consisting of all the pairs of values for which a and b could not be unified, together with all the symbols contained in the symmetrical difference between a and b. (Schwind, 1995, p. 305)

Thus Schwind's definition of unification differs from the usual one (Karttunen, 1984) in the sense that the parse does not fail but instead records the elements which do not unify.

Schwind's analysis also allows for discriminating among errors that are phonetically identical, but differ in their source. These errors occur within noun phrases. The problem with noun phrases, for example in German, derives from the fact that there are three features (gender, number and case)[30] any of which can be wrong. Consider Examples 2.3–2.5 as they appear in Schwind (1995, p. 312):

Example 2.3

a) *Der Kind spielt.
b) Das Kind spielt.
   nominative
   The child is playing.

Example 2.4

a) *Er gibt der Kind Milch.
b) Er gibt dem Kind Milch.
dative
He is giving the child milk.

Example 2.5

a) *Sie kennt der Kind.
b) Sie kennt das Kind.
accusative
She knows the child.

In Examples 2.3–2.5, the error occurs with *der Kind*. According to Schwind, the desired feedback in Example 2.3a and Example 2.4a is *The determiner is incorrectly inflected for gender*, while in Example 2.5a it is *The determiner is incorrectly inflected for case*. In the three examples, although the surface error *der* is identical, the sources of the errors are distinct. This is due to the distinct case requirements of the three examples and the ambiguity of the determiner *der*. In Example 2.3a, the source of the error is gender since *der* is a possible article in the nominative (*der, die, das*). However, since *der* is not a possible accusative article (*den, die, das*) as required in example (2.5), the source of the error lies in case. Schwind (1995) applies case filtering to achieve the desired feedback. Her system first checks whether the article is a possible determiner for the required case. If it is, the system responds with a gender error; if not, the source of the error is case. The shortcoming of her analysis is that the system assumes that students in general are more likely to know grammatical case than gender. This is apparent in Example 2.4a, which Schwind analyzes as an error in gender as opposed to in case. The error is ambiguous due to the grammatical ambiguity of *der*. If the student incorrectly assumes that *Kind* is feminine, the error is due to wrong gender. However, if the student knows the correct gender (neuter) but does not assign the correct case, the error source is wrong case.

Schwind uses the same analysis for semantic errors. The system recognizes the violation of semantic restrictions on verbs and their complements. For this, she provides a semantic network where semantic constraints are expressed as features.[31] For example, while computer is [inanimate], woman is marked as [animate, human]. The analysis is again very general, that is, the errors do not have to be anticipated.

One significant deficiency of Schwind's system is its handling of high-level syntax errors. In syntax, Schwind makes a distinction between low-level and high-level, a classification of syntax errors that reflects the way in which the errors are treated in her system. Low-level syntax errors are errors of insertion or omission while high-level errors refer to errors in word order. Schwind uses one buggy rule for each constituent of insertion and omission. High-level syntax errors, however, must be anticipated and, according to Schwind (1995), their treatment is not general.

Feature grammars are more promising than ATNs for ICALL systems. The data and implementation are kept separate which allows for easier expansion. Feature grammars also accommodate more methods of error detection. In addition to meta- and buggy-rules, they allow for alteration of the unification algorithm itself. Altering the unification algorithm has its pitfalls as mentioned; however, a more general treatment of errors than with meta- and buggy rules alone can be achieved (for a detailed discussion on feature grammars, see Black, 1986).

2.5 PROJECTS IN NLP AND CALL

After an overview of the historical development of parsers in CALL and a review of relevant theoretical concepts and approaches to parsing, this section provides an overview of research and development projects that have employed NLP techniques or resources for CALL. The aim is to show general tendencies, common patterns and typical approaches and practices. Accordingly, individual projects will only be discussed in passing, often used as a mere illustration of a certain phenomenon. Aspects of a given project that warrant a detailed discussion can be found in relevant sections of this book. For example, if the parsing algorithm used in a project or its student model is of particular interest to the discussion at hand then the project will be discussed under the heading of parsing or student modeling, respectively.

2.5.1 Documentation and literature overview

The literature on NLP in CALL projects is scattered. Overviews are often given as part of Master's theses (e.g., Catt, 1988) or unpublished doctoral dissertations (e.g., Nagata, 1992; Bowerman, 1993; Heift, 1998b; Schulze, 2001). Krüger-Thielmann (1992, pp. 52–61), for example, lists and summarizes the following early projects in ICALL: ALICE (Cerri, 1989), ATHENA (Kramsch, Morgenstern, & Murray, 1985; Morgenstern, 1986; Murray, 1991), BOUWSTEEN & COGO (Pijls et al., 1987), EPISTLE (Heidorn, Jensen, Miller, Byrd, & Chodorow, 1982; Jensen, Heidorn, Miller, & Ravin, 1984), ET (Fum, Giangrandi, & Tasso, 1988, 1989), LINGER (Barchan, 1986; Barchan, Woodmansee, & Yazdani, 1986; Yazdani & Uren, 1988), Menzel (1988, 1990), VP2 (Schuster, 1986), XTRA-TE (Chen & Kurtz, 1989a, 1989b; Kurtz et al., 1990), Zock (Zock, Sabah, & Alviset, 1986; Zock, 1988).

Notable exceptions among published works, in that they do not just review a few selected projects, are the chapter by Nerbonne (2003) in the *Oxford Handbook of Computational Linguistics* as well as papers by Matthews (1993) and Gamper and Knapp (2002). To our knowledge, there have been only two dedicated bibliographies on ICALL (Matthews, 1992a; Bailin, 1995). A number of books contain collections of articles on different projects in parser-based CALL. Some of them discuss almost exclusively several related projects (Yazdani, 1984, 1993), others provide a useful snapshot of important research and development at the time (Swartz & Yazdani, 1992; Holland et al., 1995). Proceedings of workshops and smaller conferences were also made available in a number of dedicated publications (Thompson & Zähner, 1992; Jager et al., 1998; Olsen, 1999) as well as special issues of academic journals (e.g., Bailin & Levin, 1989; Bailin, 1991; Chanier, 1994; Schulze et al., 1999; Tokuda, Heift, & Chen, 2002; Heift & Schulze, 2003a). We are only aware of three monographs, that are not published dissertations (Last, 1989; Menzel, 1992a; Dodigovic, 2005). The book by Menzel (1992a) is written in German and contains a detailed discussion of constraint-based parsing of errors. Last (1989), on the other hand, pays little attention to the research in ICALL that had been done up to the publication of his book (almost 20 projects were documented by 1987). His book also lacks a convincing account of the role of artificial intelligence in CALL. Last's book, which was the only one at the time, was widely reviewed (Hubbard, 1990; Schwind, 1990b; Sinyor, 1990; Wolff, 1991). It possibly did a lot of damage to the field of NLP in CALL because it created a distorted and incomplete impression of AI-related research in the CALL community. The book was confusing, especially to people neither familiar with Artificial Intelligence nor NLP (see Wolff, 1991). The most recent of the three books, Dodigovic (2005), discusses an ESL tutor in a wide theoretical context. Chapters 1 to 5 provide a detailed discussion of the pedagogic and linguistic considerations as well as the design decisions for a program for advanced learners of English for Academic Purposes (EAP). The system contains an error detection module that relies on NLP. In her discussion of her ICALL project, Dodigovic provides reasons for her design decisions which are based, among others, on second-language acquisition theories, error analysis and second language writing. These are the strongest sections of the book due to their interesting and well-articulated insights. In contrast, the implementation of the NLP components of her system are described in much less detail. Dodigovic concedes in her conclusion that the "project was notably far from completed" (p. 264).

Many introductory or overview books on CALL, monographs as well as collections of articles, do not contain a thorough discussion of AI techniques in CALL. However, there are some notable exceptions. Smith (1987) contains a chapter by Underwood entitled *Artificial Intelligence and CALL* in which he reviews many smaller projects of the time. He also introduces the challenges faced by AI-based research in CALL. Kenning and Kenning (1990) include a thorough discussion of basic concepts of NLP, AI and CALL in their section 1.2 (pp. 18–24). They sketch the then current state of affairs in AI research and link it to the work in computer-aided learning in general. The relevance of AI research to CALL, the challenges faced and the opportunities provided by it are discussed thoroughly and presented to the CALL researcher and developer. However, they provide very few references. Similarly, the chapter by Hamburger, Schoelles, and Reeder (1999) in Cameron's (1999) collection of papers on different aspects of CALL provides an overview of the work in ICALL.

Quite commonly, academic papers include very little detail about the design, development and implementation of a particular system. The information included is generally limited to the theoretical research question at hand. For that reason, the insights gained from such papers and, to a much smaller extent, from theses and dissertations are often not as complete as one would hope. For instance, some articles provide detailed information on the underlying grammatical formalism (e.g., Loritz, 1992), others discuss the specifics of the student model (e.g., Bull, 1994a, 1994b) and again others discuss the linguistic coverage (e.g., Fum et al., 1988) and the learners and/or researchers who used the software (Molla, Sanders, & Sanders, 1988) and/or evaluated it (Reuer, 2003).

For the present book, more than one hundred projects were reviewed. To our knowledge, this is the largest number ever examined inthe field. None of the overview publications listed above relied on a literature survey of a similar size. Only some of the projects reviewed for this book are quoted in the CALL literature, many appeared outside the mainstream journals of CALL. This might explain why there is a perception among CALL researchers and developers that the field of NLP in CALL is relatively small. Jung (2002) may serve as an example here: among the 558 publications indexed, eleven are listed under the keyword *Artificial Intelligence*, seven under *Parser* and only two under *ICALL* because very few articles from the field of Computational Linguistics are actually listed in the various installments of his bibliography. However, there are many more publications on different aspects in CALL than on NLP in CALL. Dedicated journals on CALL, particularly the *CALICO* Journal, *ReCALL* and *CALL*, contain a comparatively high number of articles on ICALL. The number of NLP in CALL papers compared with the total number of publications in the ACL Anthology — a digital archive of research papers in computational linguistics (http://acl.ldc.upenn.edu/), nevertheless, pales in comparison. CALL projects have not received the kind of attention within Computational Linguistics which they probably deserve. Zock (1996) states:

> Surprising as it may be, one of the biggest markets for products of computational linguistics (CL) has been largely overlooked: the classroom.

> ... CALL ... has hardly ever received the attention it deserves. Actually there seems to be a communication problem and a mutual lack of interest concerning the work done in the neighbouring disciplines. (not paginated)

2.5.2 Chronology and coverage

One reason for the limited number of publications in the field might be that ICALL is relatively young even within a young discipline such as CALL. The project by Weischedel, Voge, and James (1978) was the first and only one in the 1970s.

The first half of the 1980s saw the beginning of projects such as EPISTLE (Heidorn et al., 1982; Jensen et al., 1984), which was intended to help with the correction of business letters in English. It was not specifically designed as a language learning system (see also Krüger-Thielmann, 1992, p. 55, for a discussion). CRITIQUE was an extension of EPISTLE for which three application areas were identified: office environments, publication organizations and educational institutions.

Use by educational institutions has proven to be the most challenging of the areas. There is a wide range of ill-formed text to deal with, originating from classes in composition, business writing, technical writing and ESL (English as a Second Language). The professors in these varied areas also sometimes have differing opinions on grammar and style (Richardson & Braden-Harder, 1988, p. 196).

A number of much smaller projects by Yazdani and his colleagues were created at this time (e.g., Imlah & du Boulay, 1985), The big ATHENA Language Project at MIT (Kramsch et al., 1985; Felshin, 1995) started in the mid-1980s. The number of projects that received attention in the academic environment increased in the second half of that decade: between 1985 and 1994 about seventy projects were reported, that is, about half of all projects started, were carried out or completed in these ten years. Some of them are unpublished PhD theses (e.g., Johnston, 1988; Bowerman, 1993), many were published in the dedicated collections mentioned above, others appeared in proceedings of CL conferences.

The second half of the 1990s as well as the first five years of the current decade saw each about twenty new projects (McCoy, Pennington, & Suri, 1996a, 1996b; Dokter & Nerbonne, 1998; Dokter, Nerbonne, Schürcks-Grozeva, & Smit, 1998; Nerbonne, Dokter, & Smit, 1998; Vandeventer, 2001; L'Haire & Vandeventer Faltin, 2003). The numbers are increasing again, mainly due to a renewed interest in Computational Linguistics, although, maybe not so much in CALL. Figure 2.8 provides an overview of the number of NLP in CALL projects from 1980 to now. Altogether, we identified 119 projects.

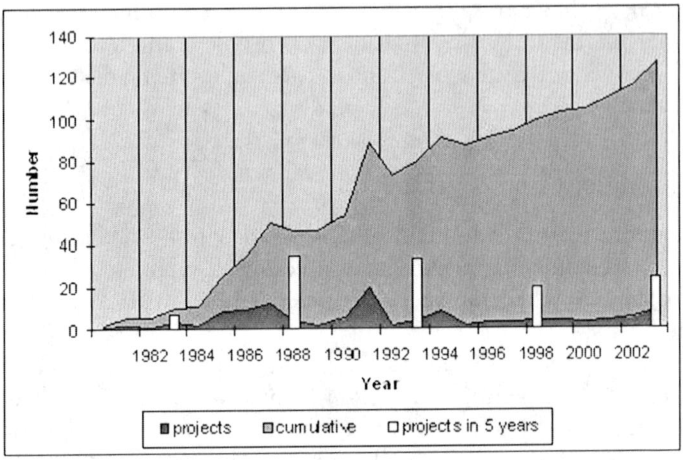

Figure 2.8 Number of NLP in CALL projects over time

The projects are surprisingly diverse in nature in almost every aspect. The following section considers the target languages for which parser-based CALL systems have been written.

2.5.2.1 *Target languages*

Our review of NLP in CALL projects revealed a wide range of languages that have been covered both in terms of the target languages as well as the range of native languages of intended users. Moreover, we found that the majority of systems are written for ESL learners (see Table 2.2). There are three probable reasons for this phenomenon. First, resources for learning English as a second language (ESL) are in high demand. Second, English has received much attention in formal linguistics, which is a prerequisite for a successful implementation of a computational grammar. Third, the literature reviewed for this book is mainly written in English. Only selected publications in other languages, mainly German, were considered.

In addition to the systems that concentrate on a single language, a number of systems were written for more than one language. For example, GPARS (Loritz, 1995) was developed, although to a different extent, for English, Russian, Chinese, Japanese and Uzbek. Similarly, the ATHENA Language Project (Kramsch et al., 1985; Morgenstern, 1986; Murray, 1991; Felshin, 1995; Murray, 1995) covers, again to a different extent, German, French, Spanish, Russian, English, Japanese and Greek. Yazdani and his graduate students asserted that they developed a language-independent system (LINGER: Language Independent Grammar Error Reporting) (Yazdani, 1991; Bolt & Yazdani, 1998).

Generally, formal descriptions of a natural language only ever cover a certain fragment of a language. The fragments described in language learn-

Table 2.2 NLP in CALL projects by language

Language	*Example(s)*
Arabic	(Weinberg, Garman, Martin, & Merlo, 1995)[32]
Basque	(Diaz de Ilarranza, Maritxalar, & Oronoz, 1998; Diaz de Ilarranza, Maritxalar, Maritxalar, & Oronoz, 1999)
Chinese	(Loritz, 1992)
Czech	(Smrž, 2004)
Dutch	(Pijls et al., 1987)
English	(Heidorn et al., 1982; Jensen et al., 1984)
French	(Zock et al., 1986; Emirkanian & Bouchard, 1988b; Zock, 1988; Vandeventer, 2000; L'Haire & Vandeventer Faltin, 2003; Vandeventer Faltin, 2003)
German	(Sanders & Sanders, 1982; Molla et al., 1988; Schwind, 1988,1990a; Heift, 1998b; Schulze, 1998; Sanders & Sanders, 1999; Schulze, 1999,2001; Heift, 2002,2003)
(Classical) Greek	(Murray, 1995)
Hebrew	(Anderson, 1995)
Italian	(Cerri & Merger, 1983; Cerri, 1989; Cerri, Cheli, & McIntyre, 1992; Delmonte, 2002,2003)
Japanese	(Nagata, 1992,1993,1995,1996,1998b,1998a; Yamura-Takei, Fujiwara, Yoshie, & Aizawa, 2002)
Latin	(Culley, Mulford, & Milbury-Steen, 1986; Mulford, 1989)
Portuguese	(Bull, 1993; Bull, Pain, & Brna, 1993; Bull, 1994b,1994a)
Russian	(Kramsch et al., 1985)
Spanish	(Feuerman et al., 1987; Rypa & Feuerman, 1995)
Thai	(Dansuwan, Nishina, Akahori, & Shimizu, 2001)
Turkish	(Güvenir, 1992)
Uzbek	(Loritz et al., 1990)

ing systems differ significantly in size as well as nature. Borissova (1988), for instance, planned a system for Russian and claimed that a dictionary with about 150–200 words would be sufficient for beginners. This claim can be easily refuted by any instructor who has ever taught an elementary language course. Learners progress very quickly beyond a 200-word limit. Liou (1991), however, reports a dictionary size of 1,400 words (English), others (Chen & Xu, 1990) worked with a 60,000 word dictionary for English. The largest dictionary, with 130,000 entries, was reported for the EPISTLE project (Heidorn et al., 1982; Richardson & Braden-Harder, 1988). This is a system written with a particular genre in mind, in this case business English. There is also a grammar checker for Dutch intended for native speakers, not necessarily language learners. It contains 275,000 word forms which are built from 90,000 lemmas as opposed to inflected forms (Vosse, 1992).

Yet there are instances where a small dictionary consisting of 20 nouns and 20 verbs appears quite adequate for the purpose of the grammar. GENERATE (Hackenberg, 1984), for example, aims to introduce students to some of the rules of Transformational Grammar as opposed to teaching a language. This implies that it is not only the dictionary that determines the linguistic coverage of a given language. In more general terms, the underlying goals of the system decide on the size of the vocabulary and grammar rules needed.

The following section discusses the range of grammatical phenomena that are covered in different systems.

2.5.2.2 Grammatical phenomena

Many projects focus on more specialized grammatical phenomena. Johnston (1988), for instance, reports that his system, GIBBER, deals with adjectival endings, determiner gender, subject-verb agreement and verb and object positions in German. His system was neither used nor evaluated for a learning context. Yet, he maintains that it could be used with a CALL host, a program with language learning exercises that can make use of GIBBER's grammar checking capabilities. Klenner and Visser (2003), who also work with German, focus on agreement, word order and dominance rules by relying on restricted exercise vocabulary. Zock (Zock et al., 1986; Zock, 1988) concentrated on the use of French clitics. Yamura-Takei et al. (Fujiwara & Yamura-Takei, 2002; Yamura-Takei et al., 2002) focus on zero pronouns in Japanese in their exercises and the TDTDT project (Pijls et al., 1987) checks the conjugation of Dutch verbs for morphotactic errors. Pijls et al. also worked on two other, related projects for Dutch. One of these (Cogo) teaches sentence analysis (construction of sentence trees), the other (Bouwsteen) emphasizes sentence construction with drag and drop exercises. Many projects, probably in part due to the nature of our knowledge of syntactic parsing, focus on the processing of isolated sentences. Teutsch (1996), for example, discusses his system MARPLE, which processes sentences of a translation exercise.[33]

The research reports indicate that the systems with smaller coverage and less ambitious goals are the ones that commonly went beyond a research prototype and were used by language learners. Larger, more ambitious projects yielded interesting results from a research point of view, but they tended not to be used in the language classroom. For example, the *Textana* system for German explored the use of relaxed constraints for feedback generation (Schulze & Hamel, 1998; Schulze, 1998, 1999, 2001, 2003) and attempted a larger coverage of the grammar by accepting all the inherent problems and difficulties. It discovered a number of interesting points on feedback and German from a computational grammar point of view, but it was never used by students. On the other hand, there are systems which set out to diagnose errors in a limited domain (e.g., the ALICE system, which concentrates on the analysis of temporal conjunctions in Italian, French and English (Cerri, 1989). Such systems were widely used, at least for a limited time and usually at the university where they were developed. The problem with these projects is that the results do not scale or transfer easily.

2.5.2.3 Evaluation

A number of projects also started with a learner corpus to construct a grammar although the size of the corpus varies vastly. For example, only 48 Japanese sentences were analyzed for a system by Kang & Maciejewski (2000). The system was intended to aid the reading of technical Japanese although the exercises consisted merely of sentence translation. When run on its test-bed essay, LICE parsed 30 out of 35 sentences successfully (Bowerman, 1993, p. 198). For a benchmark test of EPISTLE (Heidorn et al., 1982; Jensen et al., 1984), 2,254 sentences from 411 business letters were parsed; 64% of them parsed successfully (Heidorn et al., 1982, p. 318). These numbers can be deceptive because, if the prototype represents a large variety of distinct items and even user groups then scaling up the computational dictionary and/or grammar is a well-defined task; only more of the same need to be added. However, if the prototype works only in the context of the data analyzed thus far then enlarging the scope of the program usually means re-writing the system.

Vosse (1992) reports on his evaluation: a text of about 6000 words contained 30 spelling errors of which the system only missed 2 and produced 18 false alarms; 14 other errors were corrected appropriately. Another text of 7,443 words in 468 sentences was parsed for morpho-syntactic errors, finding 11 errors and correcting 4 of them adequately and producing 12 false alarms. The evaluation was conducted for a system intended for technical writers in publishing houses or departments rather than for language learners. Thus the proposed use explains the comparatively low number of errors. Probably, the system did not have to deal with multiple errors in a sentence.

The meticulous measuring of CPU (Central Processing Unit) time for various analyses[34] is also interesting in Vosse's article because processing times were too long for interactive use. For example, the 468 sentences they tested were processed in 30 minutes CPU time in 1992 (see also a benchmark test by Heift & Nicholson, 2001). Given the increased processing speed of computers in general, measuring time become almost irrelevant nowadays. However, it is not only the actual processing time that needs to be kept in mind. In some projects, students spent on average 20% of the time off task (Mostow et al., 2002) with activities such as logging in, waiting for a system response, and so forth.

When evaluating and measuring success of a project, the quality of coverage, including error detection and diagnosis, has become more important than ever. Surprisingly, few projects carried out thus far have been evaluated adequately and, if so, the evaluations were often performed by the developers and/or researchers themselves. However, more independent evaluations conducted either with learner data in form of a learner corpus or with real learners in an authentic teaching context are needed.

2.5.3 Grammar and parsers

2.5.3.1 Different formalisms

A number of projects do not identify a grammatical framework at all or rely on different algorithms such as finite state automata (FSA) for the buggy rules of the system (Chen & Tokuda, 2003). The more successful projects, however, generally employ a well-established, comprehensive and widely used grammatical framework such as HPSG, LFG, or GB. Yet, at the same time, it is surprising how little of the proven approaches in (formal) linguistics have been incorporated into the systems. Often projects failed because they ignored or underestimated the necessity of a formal and theoretically sound description of the grammar, which provides a strong basis for the parser. Accordingly, the robustness and scalability of a computational grammar depends, to a large extent, on the choice of linguistic formalism.

As discussed in more general terms in section 2.4.1, many early projects made use of augmented transition networks (ATNs) (e.g., Weischedel et al., 1978; Weischedel & Black, 1980; Weischedel & Sondheimer, 1983). Different versions of these were implemented: Cascaded Augment Transition Networks (CATNs) (Handke, 1992), ATNs complemented by Case Grammar (Hellwig, 1987) and a generalized transition network (Loritz, 1992, 1995). Such transition networks were sometimes used with actual words instead of phrasal and part of speech categories at the nodes. An example of such a system is ACQUIRE (see Brand, 1987). The system was intended to acquire English by inserting correct and erroneous sentences into two different networks and learn on the basis of this positive and negative evidence. Brand (1987) concludes "I am very hesitant to claim that Acquire has any real practical value for language teaching..." (p. 30) because the system began to reject all sentences after a short while.

Another syntactic framework in earlier ICALL projects (as well as other work in NLP at the time) is Definite Clause Grammar (DCG), a context-free grammar which relies on a number of syntactic re-write rules. In fact, recursive transition networks (RTNs) are expressively equivalent to context-free grammars, that is, an RTN can be converted to a context-free grammar and vice versa (J. Allen, 1995, p. 70).

Table 2.3 lists several ICALL projects that use DCGs.

Other authors also describe their approach as a context-free grammar (Emirkanian & Bouchard, 1988a, 1988b; Labrie & Singh, 1991; Kang & Maciejewski, 2000). DCG-based frameworks are nowadays rarely used in NLP because, by now, their limitations are well known and have been widely documented.

Other researchers have used Generalised Phrase Structure Grammar (GPSG) (Menzel, 1988, 1990, 1992a, 1992b; Heinecke et al., 1998; Menzel & Schröder, 1998a, 1998b, 1998c, 1999); Head-Driven Phrase Structure

Table 2.3 ICALL projects using DCG

Project	*References*
VP2	(Schuster, 1986)
SYNCHECK	(Sanders & Sanders, 1987; Sanders, 1991; Sanders & Sanders, 1995, 1999)
XTRA-TE	(Chen & Kurtz, 1989a, 1989b; Kurtz et al., 1990)
no-name prototype	(Claydon et al., 1992)
published PhD project	(Krüger-Thielmann, 1992)

Grammar (Brocklebank, 1998; Heift, 1998b, 2001, 2002, 2003; Schulze, 1999, 2001; Heift & Nicholson, 2000b; Heift & Schulze, 2003b); Incremental Procedural Grammar (Pijls et al., 1987); Lexical Functional Grammar (Feuerman et al., 1987; Levin et al., 1991; Levin & Evans, 1995; Rypa & Feuerman, 1995; Delmonte, 2002, 2003; Reuer, 2003); Link Grammar (Brehony & Ryan, 1994); PATR II (Kiss et al., 1997); and Tree Adjoining Grammar (TAG) (Abeillé, 1992; Kagegawa, Kanda, Fujioka, Itami, & Itoh, 2000). Bowerman (1991, 1993) relies on Functional Phrase Structure Grammar (FPSG), which he describes "as a declarative, three-tiered description of German sentences drawing on GPSG (Gazdar et al., 1985), LFG (Sells, 1985) and Montague grammars (Dowty et al., 1981)" (Bowerman, 1993, p. 84, and see also Bowerman, 1991). Hagen (1995) also used a unification-based grammatical formalism.

Matthews (1993), when reviewing grammatical frameworks in ICALL, argued for the use of a principles and parameters based approach. There are indeed a number of projects that relied on a Chomskyan understanding (Transformational Grammar, Government and Binding, Principles and Parameters) of grammar (Weinberg et al., 1995; Hamel, 1996; Schulze & Hamel, 1998; Vandeventer, 2000, 2001; Vandeventer & Hamel, 2000; L'Haire & Vandeventer Faltin, 2003; Vandeventer Faltin, 2003). Schwind (1988, 1990c, 1990a, 1995) took the Logical Metagrammar by Colmerauer (1978) as the basis for her system and Wilks and Farwell (1992) used Preference Semantics (Fass & Wilks, 1983) for their project.

The surprising multitude of grammatical formalisms used in the different projects provides evidence that successful projects usually relied on a well-established and reasonably tested grammatical formalism. Such formalisms (Head-Driven Phrase Structure Grammar, Lexical Functional Grammar, Principles and Parameters Theory) have not only been employed and tested when applying NLP to CALL, but also in many other projects which relied on computational linguistics in general.

2.5.3.2 Borrowing tools for language learning

A number of projects used parsers and grammars that had been developed for other purposes and with different goals in mind (e.g., machine translation). Vandeventer and Hamel (2000), for example, explicitly discuss issues connected to re-usability. Parsers and grammars are adapted in such a way that they can process erroneous language input. Nagata (1992) as well as Levin and colleagues (Levin et al., 1991; Levin & Evans, 1995), for instance, used the Tomita parser and a morphological analyzer developed by Hausser. The Tomita parser was also employed by Emirkanian and Bouchard (1988b, 1988a). The *Freetext* Project which incorporated the Fips parser by Wehrli and Laenzlinger (Vandeventer, Faltin, 2003)[35] and FipsVox, a speech synthesizer for French, was integrated in SAFRAN (Système d'Apprentissage du Français) (Vandeventer, 2000). All of these tools were initially written for native speakers.

In other projects, the grammar of an existing parser was adapted to another language or to a different application domain altogether. For example, Schulze (1999, 2001) modified a parser with a grammar for English (developed by Ramsay) and designed a grammar for German. The same parser was used for the analysis of sentences produced by Japanese learners of English (Brocklebank, 1998). Later, Ramsay's parser was also used for basic French (Lusuardi, 2005). Along the same lines, Hamburger and his team expanded the parser that was created for the ATHENA Language Project (Felshin, 1995; Murray, 1995) in his FLUENT project (Hamburger & Hashim, 1992; Hamburger, Tufis, & Hashim, 1993; Hamburger, 1995). The XTRA-TE system (Chen & Kurtz, 1989a, 1989b; Kurtz et al., 1990) relied on a parser which was originally developed for machine translation by Huang. Anderson (1995) evaluates a machine translation system, Targumatik, for its usefulness for teaching Hebrew and concludes "that MT with a properly constructed and applied learning algorithm can definitely be used to enhance language learning" (p. 90). Another machine translation system, METAL, was proposed for a CALL program which would check grammar and style. However, the author concludes that "this example shows that much fine tuning is necessary to make a checking device a really useful tool and improve its value to users" (Thurmair, 1990, p. 370).

Given the huge development times and the considerable expertise needed, the re-use of suitable parsing technology gave these projects a significant advantage. Our literature review identified only one project (Lawler, 1990, 1993) in which the system was ported across platforms (and countries) and then evaluated and extended. Lawler ported LINGER (Yazdani & Uren, 1988; Yazdani, 1991) to the Macintosh. It was originally written for the PC with about 74 context-free grammar re-write rules and a dictionary of about 50 to 70 words per language. Even after extending the dictionary by a factor of 20 he maintains that "the LINGER system ... is not usable in the classroom today" (Lawler, 1990, p. 49). As stated earlier, employing a computational grammar with a fixed goal in mind has certainly its merits.

It is not necessarily the technology per se which is going to be re-used in a new project. For example, evaluation technology from machine translation was used to measure English language proficiency of Japanese learners of English. These tested algorithms are sometimes implemented as a computer program that can perform the algorithm (Yasuda et al., 2004).

2.5.3.3 *Authoring tools*

Re-usability has also been discussed with respect to authoring tools. ICALL systems generally demand significant computational expertise as well as subject-domain expertise to design appropriate learning content for the student. In addition, since authors are dealing with a complex learning system, the task of providing frequently updated, authentic and relevant practice exercises can be very time-consuming. For this reason, there is a noticeable trend toward developing authoring environments for Intelligent Tutoring Systems (ITSs) that can be used by instructors within a reasonable time frame (Murray, 1999).

The goal of these authoring tools is to reduce the cost in time and expertise that is required to produce a usable intelligent learning environment. For instance, Toole and Heift (2002) developed the *Task Generator*, a prototype for a component of an authoring tool for an ILTS. The *Task Generator* allows teachers to automatically create learning material by merely specifying the learning objective and providing samples of text that are likely to contain examples of the learning objective. The primary advantage of the *Task Generator* is that the authoring tool is more usable since the tasks and expertise required of the user are reduced. The prototype of the *Task Generator* is implemented for English.

The *Task Generator* is part of their main authoring tool, the *Tutor Assistant,* which allows instructors to create on-line vocabulary and grammar exercises for a beginner and intermediate language skill level. In addition, instructors can author teaching strategies and the student model.

When adding or editing an exercise, the instructor has two main tasks:

1. create the student task
2. list all the possible answers

The student task is a set of words and prompts that the student must use to complete the task. In the case of the Build-a-Sentence example (Figure 2.9) the student task lists the words that the students must use in their answer. The user of the authoring system can also add additional prompts like present conditinuous to further restrict the student's task, as illustrated in Figure 2.9.

A previous study by Toole and Heift (2002) showed that ESL teachers who are inexperienced with both the authoring system and the ILTS, can develop one hour worth of learning material in about two to three hours. While this is a significant improvement over development times for authoring tools in other domains, the participants indicated they found some

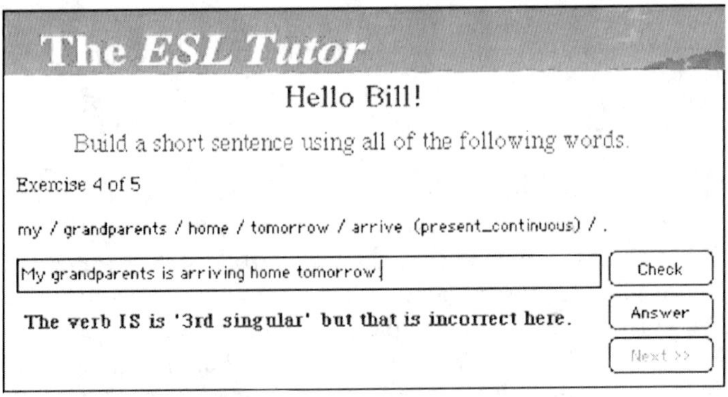

Figure 2.9 The *ESL Tutor*

sections of the process difficult. In particular, they found it challenging to create student tasks that were varied, interesting and relevant. Significant time was spent thinking of relevant examples.

In order to alleviate this problem and to decrease the overall development time for authoring learning material, they decided to automate the process of creating the learning task by designing the *Task Generator.*

The goal of the *Task Generator* is to extract learning material from unedited texts. Unlike similar work by Kunichika et al. (1998), the *Task Generator* creates examples from texts which already contain the target learning objective. Kunichika et al. on the other hand, generate questions for reading comprehension from assertions existing in the text. The disadvantage of the Kunichika approach for the current task is that significant syntactic, semantic, as well as discourse information must be supplied — either automatically, or by the author.

According to Toole and Heift (2002), this level of analysis is infeasible given the goals of their system. First, their goal is to reduce the skill level and time required from the human authors. Second, from a computational perspective, one of the design goals for the *Task Generator* system is portability between languages. This is motivated by the fact that the system needs to be used by ILTSs from more than one language. Hence, in order to develop a system that is both usable and portable, all of the task generation must be done by the system and minimal linguistic resources should be used.

The *Task Generator* meets these goals. The user is required only to specify a particular learning objective, such as past tense, passive, or plural nouns and to provide a range of texts that contain examples of the learning objective in use. Furthermore, the linguistic resources are restricted to a sentence boundary detector, a part of speech (POS) tagger and a lexicon containing syntactic information. These resources are generally available for the more widely studied languages and are what is minimally required to disambiguate the input text.

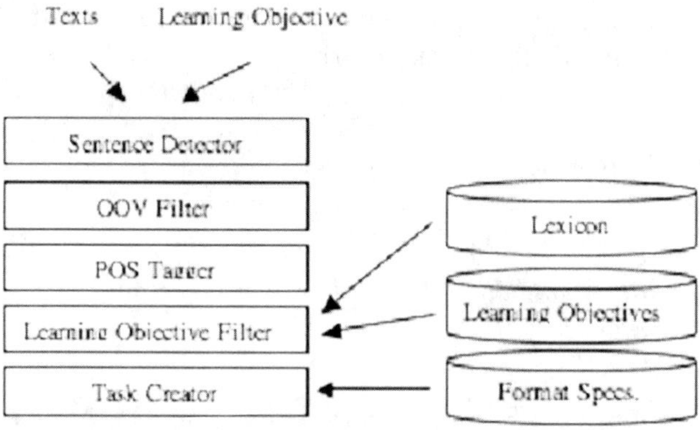

Figure 2.10 System architecture of the *Task Generator.*

The overall architecture of the system is given in Figure 2.10. The first module of the system detects sentence boundaries and separates the text into its constituent sentences. The *Task Generator* uses the MXTerminator system (Reynar & Ratnaparkhi, 1997). The next stage is the out-of-vocabulary (OOV) words filter. The ILTSs for which the learning material is being created perform significant linguistic analyses on the student input. Hence, all words in the task must be known to the ILTSs. The purpose of the OOV Filter is to remove sentences which contain out-of-vocabulary words.

The part of speech tagger assigns one of 14 tags to each word token. The POS tagger is a Hidden Markov Model based on Church (1988). The tagger disambiguates the input so that the correct lexical information can be retrieved from the lexicon. The lexicon is derived from the XTAG lexicon (Egedi & Martin, 1994).[36]

The Learning Objective Filter removes all sentences that do not contain an instance of the specified learning objective. For each possible learning objective a Learning Objective Filter has been developed which specifies positive and negative constraints on the lexical entries that occur in a given sentence. For example, the filter for the Present Continuous learning objective specifies that the sentence must contain an auxiliary with a base form of be and an additional verb in present participle form. It is also possible to specify a window within which the lexical items that match the constraints must co-occur.

The sentences remaining after the learning objective filter each contain at least one example of the learning objective. These sentences form the input to the Task Creator.

The Task Creator converts the sentence into one or more of the grammar-practicing exercise types used in the ILTSs: Build-a-Sentence, Fill-in-the-Blank and Drag-and-Drop. The Format Specification file contains information about how the words in the sentence should be converted for each exercise type. In the case of converting a present continuous sentence into a Fill-in-the-Blank, the main verb is converted to base form, the auxiliary is removed and the remaining words remain in their original form. This is illustrated in Example 2.6. In the case of converting the same sentence to Build-a-Sentence, a similar process is followed except that all words are converted to their base form, as illustrated in Example 2.7.

Example 2.6
But more than half also said they [save (present continuous)] for a dream vacation.

Example 2.7
but more than half also say they save (present continuous) for a dream vacation.

This following section describes an evaluation of the *Task Generator* conducted by Toole and Heift (2002). The main aim in their study was to evaluate the accuracy of the system in producing learning tasks for the ESL Tutor. To this end, the accuracy of each individual component, as well as the overall accuracy of the system was evaluated. Since the OOV Filter achieves 100% accuracy (it is not a difficult task), this filter was excluded from the system for the purpose of the evaluation. This provided a wider range of input to the later parts of the system.

The input to the *Task Generator* was 7,600 words from 13 texts that were selected by an independent analyst. The texts covered a range of subject areas from personal descriptions to family finances to net access for business travelers. Ten learning objectives were selected from the forty that are currently implemented. These were selected to include objectives for a variety of parts of speech, with an emphasis on the inflecting classes. The selected learning objectives are listed in Table 2.4. The input text was submitted to the system, once for each of the selected learning objectives.

The performance of each system component (the sentence boundary identifier, the tagger, the learning objective filter and the lexicon itself) is given in Table 2.5. The accuracy of a component for a specific learning objective was determined by considering just those sentences that contained the learning objective. For example, the accuracy of the sentence boundary detector for the Passive learning objective was determined by evaluating all of the sentences that were identified as containing a passive construction. The percentages specify the percentage of sentences that were analyzed correctly by each component. The Correct column specifies the percentage of the created examples that are correct. The Total Produced column specifies the number of examples that were created for each learning objective — there is an upper limit of 150. Finally, the Total row provides the total calculated by averaging the original scalar values of each column (for reason of brevity original values are not provided in the table. They can be calcu-

Table 2.4 Learning objectives used in Toole and Heift (2002)

Any / Some / No words
Comparative and superlative - Adjectives
Count / Mass nouns
Indefinite articles
Prepositions
Passive
Present continuous
Reflexives
Singular pronouns (masc., fem., neuter, accus., nomin.)
Verb agreement

lated from the information provided in the table). For example, in 99.5% of the tasks created, the Learning Objective Filter performed correctly.

The results show that 90.8% of the examples produced were correct. In 8.2% of the cases, there was some error that was caused by one of the preceding modules.

By far the largest source of errors was the sentence boundary identifier. In 7.4% of the created examples there was an incorrect sentence boundary. This comprised 80% of the errors. A review of the data found that the

Table 2.5 Results of Toole and Heift (2002)

	Sentence Boundary	*Tagger*	*LO Filter*	*Lexicon Problem*	*Correct*	*Total Produced*
Any/Some/ No Words	95.0%	100.0%	100.0%	100.0%	95.0%	40
Comparative & Superlative Adjectives	78.1%	100.0%	100.0%	84.4%	62.5%	32
Count/Mass Nouns	100.0%	100.0%	100.0%	100.0%	100.0%	6
Indefinite Articles	95.3%	100.0%	100.0%	100.0%	95.3%	150
Prepositions	92.0%	100.0%	100.0%	100.0%	92.0%	150
Passive	94.7%	100.0%	100.0%	100.0%	94.7%	38
Present Continuous	90.9%	100.0%	100.0%	100.0%	90.9%	11
Reflexives	85.7%	100.0%	100.0%	100.0%	85.7%	7
Singular Pronouns	94.0%	100.0%	98.0%	100.0%	92.0%	150
Verb Agreement	84.0%	76.0%	100.0%	100.0%	72.0%	25
Total	92.6%	99.0%	99.5%	99.2%	90.8%	609

detector used appears to rely heavily on periods and capitalization as an end of sentence identifier. In cases where periods do not frequently occur, such as at the end of headings, a sentence boundary was omitted, leading to problems as illustrated in Example 2.8. In addition, there were cases with a period and appropriate capitalization that were not identified as sentences. Hence, in order to increase the overall accuracy, an improved sentence boundary identifier is required.

Example 2.8

Effective vs. Ineffective One way to distinguish effective from ineffective employees is in how they act and react to the demands of their positions.

The remaining modules each achieved very high accuracy. The tagger performed extremely well, except in the case of the verb agreement category. In this case, the tagger occasionally incorrectly tagged a noun as a verb. One example is the input given in Example 2.9.[37] In this case the noun Hikes was tagged as a verb. This is not surprising since the input is not a complete English sentence. This type of error accounted for three of the six tagging errors. In order to reduce this type of error it will be necessary to include filter mechanisms that exclude input items which are not complete sentences. The existence of an increased proportion of punctuation and capitals may provide sufficient indication of this.

Example 2.9

CALIFORNIA Great Day Hikes In & Around Napa Valley (Ken Stanton, Bored Feet Publications, Mendocino, CA, 1995, 707/964-6629; $12).

The Learning Objective Filter also performed very well: the only source of error was with the singular pronoun filter. In three instances this filter incorrectly identified cases like the one provided in Example 2.10 as containing an example of the singular pronoun *it*. In each case the actual word was an acronym. A solution to this problem is to consider capitalization as a factor in the learning objective filters. At present, the filters only place constraints on information that is present in the lexical entry for this word.

Example 2.10

The most significant case is that of Lois Franxhi, an IT manager who was sacked for using the Internet during her lunch break to track down a bargain holiday.

The final source of error in the system is the lexicon itself. First, the lexicon incorrectly identifies *modest* as a superlative adjective (Example 2.11). Second, the lexicon incorrectly lists the base form of *lower* as *lower* instead of *low* (Example 2.12). These two types of errors accounted for all of the five lexicon problems.

Example 2.11

They tend to defer to others, are less likely to take risks, are [modest (superlative adjective)] and cautious and try to avoid conflict.

Example 2.12

People with [lower (comparative adjective)] dominance are congenial and cooperative.

With the exception of the examples influenced by the sentence boundary detector, the *Task Generator* appears to be quite accurate. In particular, the shallow approach to analyzing the sentence has proved sufficient for the purposes of producing learning tasks for a specific learning objective.

According to Toole and Heift (2002), however, the analysis of the data indicated several areas for improvement. First, the sentence boundary detector needs to be significantly improved. The detector needs to be able to deal with text in context, that is, text that includes components such as headers. Second, an additional module is required that can identify incomplete sentences which generally contain an unduly high proportion of capitals and punctuation. This should reduce the number of tagging problems as illustrated previously in Example 2.8. Third, the language for stating learning objectives needs to be updated so that word capitalization can be used as a constraint.

The system designed by Toole and Heift (2002) is the only prototype of an authoring system we know of. Yet, such a system has many advantages and great potential for the language learning classroom. The system automatically creates learning content from existing texts and is designed to require minimal linguistic resources. The current version of the system requires a sentence boundary detector, a POS tagger and a lexicon with syntactic information. The results suggest these resources are sufficient to automatically produce learning content for a range of learning objectives.

2.5.3.4 Different programming languages

When tools were developed from scratch, a surprisingly large number of programming languages have been used to create different language learning systems as illustrated in Table 2.6

Procedural programming languages such as BASIC, Pascal and C were used in quite a number of projects. This is not surprising because programming languages like BASIC were very popular among CALL developers for some time. This popularity has never been shared by (I)CALL developers and researchers in Computer Science and Computational Linguistics. For example, Handke (1989b, p. 23), a computer scientist, expresses disbelief about Skehan's very positive review of BASIC as a tool which has exceptional qualities for the manipulation of text. Note that Skehan is an applied linguist.

Table 2.6 Projects by programming language

Programming / Scripting Language	*Project*	*References*
BASIC (QuickBasic)	BASIC Parser for CALL	(Cook, 1988)
C	Miniprof, GIBBER	(Johnston, 1988; Labrie & Singh, 1991; Tschichold et al., 1994)
C++	Francophone Stylistic Grammar Checking	(Brehony & Ryan, 1994)
Hypertalk	FrenchWriter	(Hagen, 1995)
LISP	Nobile, ALICE, GPARS, CALLE, SWIM	(Weischedel et al., 1978; Weischedel & Black, 1980; Cerri & Merger, 1983; Weischedel & Sondheimer, 1983; Feuerman et al., 1987; Jehle, 1987; Loritz, 1987; Cerri, 1989; Loritz et al., 1990; Cerri et al., 1992; Loritz, 1992, 1995; Rypa & Feuerman, 1995)
LISP and C	WIZDOM	(Handke, 1989a, 1989b, 1990; Zock, 1992)
Logo	Die Sprachmaschine	(Harroff, 1986)
Pascal	DRIP, AL	(Hellwig, 1987; Güvenir, 1992)
Prolog	VP2, ET, German Tutor,[38] Grammar Debugger, Textana	(Schuster, 1986; Fum et al., 1988, 1989; Chen & Xu, 1990; Fum, Pani, & Tasso, 1991; Fum et al., 1992; Krüger-Thielmann, 1992; Tasso, Fum, & Giangrandi, 1992; Heift, 1998b; Schulze, 2001)

Sometimes the limitations of a certain programming language in its NLP application in CALL are documented: *Die Sprachmaschine* (Harroff, 1986), for instance, a system written in Logo, recognizes 65 nouns, 18 verbs, 2 adverbs,[39] and 9 prepositions which the student can use to build sentences by following certain pre-programmed patterns. Harroff, the system designer, describes *Die Sprachmaschine* as a "narrowly focused microworld for language learning" (p. 34) and concludes that an expanded version would exceed the capabilities of the Logo interpreter. Most suitable for the writing of a computational grammar are languages such as Prolog and LISP. These languages are declarative in that they do not require the programmer to stipulate procedures the machine has to follow. Instead there are rules that are being applied.

Last (1989), for instance, argues against the use of Prolog and similar programming languages, such as LISP. He finds both Prolog and LISP too specialized and too recursive. Johnston also disagrees with the use of these two programming languages (Johnston, 1988, p. 161). He instead uses regular expressions[40] to describe morphological structures of German (p. 163).[41] He also includes linguistic features for association and evaluates words bitwise for unification (p. 162). While this approach may be appropriate and efficient for the limited domain Johnston worked in, the code will be difficult to maintain and even more difficult to port to other linguistic phenomena and/or languages. A better founded and much more convincing argument for the use of Prolog or LISP in NLP in CALL projects is provided by Handke (1989b). Most work in NLP these days, including the work in CALL, uses versions of Prolog[42] or LISP, often supplemented with dedicated grammar-writing tools (e.g., the Prolog-based Attribute Logic Engine (ALE) (see Heift, 1998b)).

The importance of linguistic coverage and a suitable parsing algorithm can be illustrated with projects that lacked one or the other or both. The *Passive Voice Tutor* (Virvou, Maras, & Tsirigia, 2000) relies on restricted natural language processing. It counts the words, generates the correct passive form of the English verb and searches for it in the sentence (see also Virvou & Maras, 1999; Virvou & Moundridou, 2001). Such an approach might work if the system concentrates solely on passive constructions, but may not be scalable. Bailin (1990) in his VERBCON project seems to concentrate only on analyzing verbs that students have to insert into blanks. Again the question arises whether such an approach can be scaled up to include other morpho-syntactic phenomena.

Last (1986), who argues against approaches used in Artificial Intelligence, discusses an AI-like CALL program which contains simple search algorithms programmed in BASIC. These algorithms are neither informed by linguistic theory nor grounded in Second Language Acquisition (SLA) theory and could therefore not be developed further. However, employing relatively simple techniques does not always and necessarily lead to a limited program. Soria (1997), for instance, discusses the merits of what he terms *Expert CALL*, an approach which he places in between intelligent and traditional CALL. His morphological analysis of Spanish makes use of simple NLP techniques such as recording features of verbs. He argues convincingly that this augmentation of existing string information enables the program to generate more meaningful feedback for students. Along the same lines, Emanuelli (1986) developed a small system in BASIC for the Commodore 64 computer which relies on a database that is used to store entities and facts about them (such as *has wings*, *has horns*, *flies*). The simple expert system engages the learner in a dialogue, generated through canned text, by asking yes-no questions. The learner's task is to identify an entity from the system or to describe certain features of a new entity, for which the system presents a choice of six statement patterns. Emanuelli (1986) concludes that such simple AI-related systems "provide interesting learning environments for students of foreign languages" (p. 53).

2.5.3.5 Diverse parsing algorithms and applications

Many papers in ICALL are dedicated to the discussion of parsing algorithms, in particular, the notion of robust parsing of second language input (see section 2.3.4). Other studies investigated the effectiveness of NLP technologies in CALL. For example, Nagata (1992, 1996, 1998a, 1998b) provides empirical and statistical evidence that parser-based technology is capable of providing superior learning support. Sanders and Sanders (Sanders, 1985, 1991; Sanders & Sanders, 1987, 1989, 1999) worked on a grammar checker for German and tested parsing technology in this context. They provide a very useful overview of parsing techniques available at the time and their use in parser-based CALL (Sanders & Sanders, 1989).

In contrast, some of the publications only suggest certain applications for CALL, but present work which is grounded in computational or formal linguistics (Hellwig, 1987; Abeillé, 1992). Zock, for example, explored the utilization of natural language generation in CALL (Zock et al., 1986; Zock, 1988). In his SWIM (See What I Mean) project (Zock, 1992), students choose certain concepts and ideas and answer questions posed by the system. Depending on the answers, the system then generates the French sentence. Bailin (1988), in his PARSER project, used sentence generation to ask students to identify parts of a sentence, for example, a noun phrase. Language generation also played a role in LingWorlds (Douglas, 1995; Tomlin, 1995). Lessard, Maher, Tome, and Levison (1994) modeled what they termed language creativity and they were able to generate examples of erroneous sentences. More recently, Mansilla (2004) proposes to use the KPML language generation tool (http://purl.org/net/kpml) to detect errors in fill-in-the-blank exercises and provide feedback on them. He argues that an initial small-scale experiment shows that KPML is capable of handling simple, single morphological and lexical errors.

Natural language understanding and natural language generation have also been combined in an interesting way. For example, in the Arboretum project (Bender et al., 2004) the parser grammar, that is, the English Resource Grammar by Flickinger, is complemented by mal-rules which map ill-formed strings to well-formed semantic representations. This allows the system to generate a possible correct(ed) response on the basis of the semantic representation. To resolve sentence ambiguity, possibly playing a role in both error analysis and generation of the corrected version of the string, Bender et al. (2004)

> developed a strategy for best-first generation which [they] call 'aligned generation'. In aligned generation, the goal is to generate the sentence which most closely matches some reference sentence in structure and lexical yield. (not paginated)

In addition to natural language parsers, speech technology has also been employed (Hamburger & Hashim, 1992; Hamburger et al., 1993, 1999; Hamburger, 1994, 1995; Delmonte, 2002, 2003). Even back in 1984, the GENERATE program, which ran on a Commodore 64 computer, made use of this machine's "Software Activated Mouth" to have individual words pronounced in a still rather artificial way (Hackenberg, 1984). GENERATE was intended to teach students of linguistics the basics of Transformational Grammar by showing them how sentences are generated by a computer. Others (Güvenir, 1992) use NLP technology to support drill-and-practice exercises, a language learning activity which contributes little to successful language acquisition and language proficiency.

There are also a few projects that focus on the intersection of syntax and orthography. Bouwer (1998), for example, describes a prototype of a system for teaching Dutch spelling to university students. Students are presented with a small text (2–8 lines) that contains some punctuation. The chunks are predetermined and the student is asked to provide a corrected punctuation sequence including the relevant punctuation mark for each chunk, for example, *1,2.3;4!5*. The system can provide feedback on punctuation errors because the chunks have been tagged with syntactic and some rhetorical information.

2.5.4 Implementation, research, integration

2.5.4.1 Virtual contexts

A number of projects embed the language learning software with its tasks and technology in a virtual context. Some of the earlier systems are based on simpler NLP technology. Underwood (1982, 1984, chapter 7), for instance, reports on FAMILIA, a project which heavily borrowed from the ELIZA program by Weizenbaum. In FAMILIA, the system recognizes certain keywords, mainly family terms, and searches for verb complement combinations that are erroneous in Spanish. The entire lexicon, as well as the sophisticated pattern matching technique, are geared towards this scenario. Unfortunately, the technique does not seem to be scalable or easily transferable to other contexts although it is probably effective and liked by students. *Spion* (Sanders & Sanders, 1982; Molla et al., 1988; Sanders, 1995), which was based on a program without NLP (Sanders, 1984), was a spy game for students of German. Its main character, Robotky, is placed in Berlin and students have to give him advice on a variety of situations. If students respond in a complete and well-formed sentence, the recommended action will be performed. However, the circumvention of the problem of a limited parser dictionary is quite interesting. If the system does not recognize a word, it stays in character but tells the student that such a word should not be used in the spy milieu or genre. Another project,

Herr Kommissar (DeSmedt, 1995), also relies on a crime story scenario to engage students of German in a written exchange and uses NLP. Menzel and Schröder (1999) have their students communicate about a market place scenario that is represented graphically. They are able to check input utterances for their semantic truth value by comparing what the student said to what is actually displayed in the graphic representation of the market scene. FLUENT-1 (Hamburger & Hashim, 1992) asks students to move objects in a bathroom per request.

Hamburger and his team also developed an interface for teachers to create exercises that utilize the natural language processing tools of FLUENT-2, both written and spoken. The teacher can use the tutorial schema tool to design interactive exercises, the language tool to influence the language generated by FLUENT-2 and the drawing tool to manipulate the graphical microworlds (Schoelles & Hamburger, 1996). A very different scenario has been used in a series of related projects: American soldiers learning a foreign language are provided with a military scenario in Bridge and MILT (Kaplan & Holland, 1995; Sams, 1995; Kaplan, Sabol, Wisher, & Seidel, 1998).

The *L2tutor* (Price, McCalla, & Bunt, 1999) uses natural language understanding technology in an interesting way. The proof-of-theory system immerses the student in an English language dialogue, a restaurant scenario. The system analyses the student input for keywords in context in order to generate a suitable response. The system plays the role of the waiter. The parser analyzes the written dialogue text for errors and feeds the information to a student model once the dialogue sequence has been completed.

More recently, projects have emerged in which both NLP tools and techniques from virtual realities are used in a language learning system. For example, Segond & Parmentier (2004) report that their system uses bilingual dictionaries, a morphological analyzer, a syntactic tagger, a language identifier and a phonetic spell checker. These NLP tools are used in a virtual reality environment (work situation at a printing company) to facilitate the comprehension of texts and student writing in chat rooms or discussion boards. It is interesting to note that language learners are, for example, asked to use the syntactic tagger to find errors in their own writing. The authors do not report on the effectiveness of this approach, but the question arises whether students with no formal background in linguistics are indeed able to use a syntactic tagger effectively.

In our opinion, the most ambitious goal was put forward by Culley, Mulford, and Milbury-Steen (Culley et al., 1986; Mulford, 1989). They proposed a foreign language adventure game for both Latin and French. However, they only ever documented that they implemented some morphological rules for Latin and some semantic relations of words in their database. Yet, they had scripted their adventure game on paper and had tested it with a group of French teachers who had been invited along with one student for a workshop. During this workshop, teachers were asked to respond like a computer would. They were shown pre-scripted cue-cards (similar to a text-based adventure computer game) in response to input that was provided by the student on their cards. This helped them to thoroughly test their scripts and identify some traits of learner behavior in such games.

However, this is not the only example of a project that reports such an experiment at the conceptual stage. Michel and Lehuen (2002), for instance, reported a project that relies on a human-computer dialogue which has only been tested in a wizard-of-oz experiment. Such experiments support the conceptualization of the design, but all too often, they raise false hopes as to what can be achieved once the computer program takes on the role of humans.

2.5.4.2 Semantics and pragmatics

For systems to be able to recognize linguistic structures and provide feedback on the accuracy and adequacy of the utterance, they need to be able to consider at least some level of semantics and pragmatics. In many projects, researchers concentrated on the morphological and/or syntactic analysis of the textual (and very often only sentential) input. However, projects such as the ones mentioned above were successful for two reasons: first, they restricted the possibilities of semantic input by providing a scenario that was known to the developers. Often they also explicitly excluded world knowledge outside of these scenarios. Second, they implemented semantic and/or pragmatic aspects of such scenarios. In spite of the fact that these solutions might not be very satisfactory in terms of scientific elegance, they certainly were effective. On the other hand, projects that relied on a much wider approach in semantic processing indicate the necessity and usefulness of such an approach. They, however, also illustrate the immense effort required to implement semantic relations even in small(er) linguistic domains such as in aspects of finance (Segond & Parmentier, 2004).

Lelouche (1994), for example, claims that when he began his project in 1985, pragmatics was very rarely considered for a CALL program. He compares his approach to Cerri's (1989) and notes that Cerri, in spite of employing the term pragmatics in his description of the ALICE project, uses it only in its every-day, popular sense. This differs from its academic, linguistic definition of pragmatics that considers any knowledge which lies outside of textual surface structures. This is not implemented in the ALICE project. Lelouche demonstrates with two greeting scenarios the kind of pragmatic inferences that have to be evoked. He designed two prototypes in Prolog which, for their input, both require pragmatic information and their relations. PILÉFACE-Generation "generates utterances that are semantically acceptable and pragmatically plausible" (Lelouche, 1994, p. 527) and PILÉFACE-Analysis "takes an analysis and a summarized context as input and produces a diagnosis to determine whether this utterance is adequate" (p. 527). His experiment and subsequent discussion clearly show the immense difficulty of implementing pragmatic knowledge in a computational system. The main reason for this challenge is the combinatorial explosion of semantic rules. However, Lelouche also demonstrates convincingly that pragmatic knowledge ought to be considered in a system that is intended for communicative language teaching.

The communicative approach played an important role in a very large project, the ATHENA Language Learning Project. This project was heavily influenced, at least initially, by Kramsch and her ideas about the role of discourse in communicative language learning (Murray, 1991). As a result, aspects such as dialogue and narrative structures were considered. Murray (1991) reports on the problems encountered at MIT when not considering the pragmatic level:

> Language teachers are concerned about complex communicative functions such as exchanging greetings, speaking topically, conducting an argument, asking for clarification. Computational linguists, on the other hand, although interested in these larger forms, have done their most concrete work on a tighter level of semantic analysis, such as questions of underspecified referents. Of course these reference ambiguities are basic technical problems that are going to have to be solved if the computer is to become a potent medium for conversational exchanges. But pronoun reference alone does not take us very far toward mimicking human conversation. (p. 7)

Another project which incorporated some selected discourse features is *Simone Says* (Lehman, 1999a, 1999b) in which processing at all linguistic levels appears to have remained at a rather basic level, but a level suited to the task at hand. A combination of grammatical, semantic and discourse analysis is also employed by Delmonte (2004) in his GETARUNS project. He proposes to use his text summary software to evaluate student text summaries and to achieve an evaluation of both the student's work and the system.

Sometimes, however, there are claims of future possible uses of a system for CALL that are only vaguely or not at all linked to the linguistic and computational capabilities of the current implementation of the system. A few papers outline ambitious project plans, however, there are no follow-up publications that discuss any outcomes of these projects. For example, Borissova (1988) proposed a system with a dictionary of a total of 200 words. The program relied on a few, quite simple grammatical rules to diagnose errors in texts produced by learners of Russian. Along the same lines, Yazdani (1990) anticipated that his system could be used as a grammar checker for a wide variety of texts and as part of e-mail clients or word processors. However, we are not aware of subsequent publication of an implementation. In other cases, very ambitious, well-planned goals were laid out (Lian, 1992), but again, it was impossible to determine whether or not the project was completed. These, quite often, exaggerated prospects contributed to inflated expectations among the wider CALL community as well as in language teaching in general. These expectations were not met and CALL practitioners and developers who had heard about the ambitious plans were disappointed. This all too often led to a wholesale rejection of the work done in ICALL. For example, while Loritz (1987) was still optimistic about parsers in CALL stating that "it now appears instructional parsers will enter widespread use within a decade" (p. 52), his optimism waned just five years later: "In education, sophisticated interactive grammar-checkers built on instructional parsing systems might eventually be used for direct student interaction, but we do not expect such use will soon be widespread" (Loritz, 1992, p. 17). The latter judgment was based on a small experiment with an English parser to which only one third of the students reacted positively.

2.5.4.3 *Different target groups*

Often it was the specific requirements of the intended target group of a project that inspired the development and led to interesting research questions. For example, relatively simple NLP techniques, SHRDLU by Winograd, were used to support small language games for profoundly deaf teenagers (Ward, 1986; Ward, Foot, & Rostron, 1999). Loritz (Loritz et al., 1990; Loritz, 1992, 1995) also tested his early English version of the parser with deaf students and reported that only one third of the students reacted positively (Loritz, 1992). McCoy and colleagues were more successful with their ICICLE project (McCoy et al., 1996a, 1996b; Schneider & McCoy, 1998; Michaud & McCoy, 1999, 2000). Students who acquired American Sign Language (ASL) as their first language are supported in learning written English as a second language. The ICICLE system uses both a model of English and ASL.

2.5.4.4 *Systems in use*

It is only recently that we have seen reasonably sized systems that have been tested with a large group of language learners or are in constant use. For example, the GLOSSER system at the University of Groningen in the Netherlands (Dokter & Nerbonne, 1998; Dokter et al., 1998; Nerbonne, Dokter et al., 1998; Nerbonne & Dokter, 1999; Nerbonne, Kleiweg, Smit, Kuipers, & Dokter, 2001) provides students with access to a morphological analyzer and an online dictionary. Students can extract linguistic information on any word from a reading text chosen by the learner or the instructor. GLOSSER is a COPERNICUS project that demonstrates the use of language processing tools (Locolex, a morphological analyzer and part of speech disambiguation package from Rank Xerox Research Centre, relevant electronic dictionaries (e.g., Hedendaag Frans) and access to bilingual corpora).

> The project vision foresees two main areas where GLOSSER applications can be used. First, in language learning and second, as a tool for users that have a bit of knowledge of a foreign language, but cannot read it easily or reliably." (Dokter & Nerbonne, 1998, p. 88).

Roosma and Prószéku (1998) draw attention to the fact that GLOSSER works with the following language combinations: English-Estonian-Hungarian, English-Bulgarian and French-Dutch. They also describe a demonstrator version running under Windows. The French-Dutch demonstrator which runs on UNIX

- uses morphological analysis to provide additional grammatical information on individual words and to simplify dictionary look-up;
- relies on automatic word selection;
- offers the opportunity to insert glosses (taken from the dictionary look-up) into the text;
- relies on string-based word sense disambiguation ("Whenever a lexical context is found in the text that is also provided in the dictionary, the example in the dictionary is highlighted." (Dokter & Nerbonne, 1998, p. 93)

Dokter et al. (1998) conclude in their user study "that Glosser-RuG improves the ease with which language students can approach a foreign language text." (p. 175).

Knapp (2004) describes ELDIT — Elektronisches Lernwörterbuch Deutsch-Italienisch[43] — for which she and her team employed NLP tools to generate information-rich content. The dictionary has 4000 word entries in each language and is linked to 800 texts in Italian and German which prepare students for the bilingual examinations in Tyrol. The texts are augmented with linguistic information and are encoded in XML. The linguistic information is partially generated by a part-of-speech tagger, lemmatizer, WordManager[44] and word nets. Some tasks, for example, semantic disambiguation of words, are carried out manually when the texts are augmented. The system is still available at http://www.eurac.edu/eldit (accessed January 15, 2007) and the user can clearly detect the focus on vocabulary acquisition.

Other systems in use concentrate more on help on morpho-syntactic errors made by learners. The *E-Tutor* at Simon Fraser University in Canada (Heift, 1998b 2001, 2002, 2003, 2004; Heift & Nicholson, 2000a, 2000b) is an ICALL system that accepts input from a variety of beginner to advanced vocabulary and grammar exercises for German and provides error diagnosis and feedback. The Web-based system (http://www.e-tutor.

org) has been employed for several SLA research projects and is used by hundreds of students every semester at various North American universities. The system consists of 15 chapters with a variety of learner tasks. It covers the main grammar concepts of German and provides learning content for the first few semesters of university German. In addition to the grammar and vocabulary tasks, a number of language learning resources, including grammar notes and explanations, context-sensitive grammar help, a dictionary, authentic pictures, audio and cultural information, are contained in the Web-based learning environment.

Finally, there is one commercial Web-based system for Japanese, *Robo-Sensei* developed by Nagata (2002). The system was presented earlier under the name of BANZAI. It is written in Java and combines parsing technology with a multimedia interface. The system provides 24 lessons on Japanese grammar and culture with authentic photographs and audio recordings. Learners can input Japanese characters. BANZAI's lexicon covers the vocabulary of a three-year Japanese language learning program. Verbs and adjectives are stored in their base form and inflected forms are generated by a morphological generator (Nagata, 2002, p. 3). In a first step, the parser separates lexical items from each other because, in Japanese, words are not divided by spaces. Compound nouns and inflected forms are then morphologically analyzed. "The BANZAI syntactic parser's job is to determine whether the input string is a grammatical (well-formed) or ungrammatical (ill-formed) sentence." (Nagata, 2002, p. 4). The system relies on context-free grammar rules. They are used in conjunction with the analysis of the data provided on the correct answer. Correct answers are supplied by the exercise designer. Each word is listed with its "grammatical category" (p. 6) and alternatives and optional items can also be stored. Feedback on missing words, unexpected words, particle errors, predicate errors and word order errors can then be generated.

2.5.4.5 Teaching different skills with different teaching approaches

Not all applications focus on learning grammar through explicit teaching and/or error correction. Burstein and colleagues (Burstein, Kaplan, Wolff, & Lu, 1996; Burstein & Chodorow, 1999; Shermis & Burstein, 2003) describe the *E-rater*, a system for automatic scoring of essays written by both native and non-native speakers of English. Payette and Hirst (1992) present a sentence-based style checker for English. The system only accepts a sentence for statistical analysis if it is error-free because it does not comprise a grammar or spell checking component. The question remains whether this kind of software is useful in a second-language learning context. The system relies on a small dictionary with 800 words and was never tested with language learners.

There are also tools that focus on communicative language instruction. Jehle (1987), for instance, designed a tool for Spanish (SPANLAB) which resembles the ELIZA program by Weizenbaum. It also attempts to engage the learner in a written dialogue without correcting any linguistic errors. Lehman (1999a, 1999b) proposes a language learning system, *Simone Says*, for children with pervasive developmental disorders. It provides processes for conversational turn-taking and conversational repair using a very small set of core vocabulary (about 200 words) and only basic syntax.

An interesting pedagogic approach, the Silent Way, is utilized in CALEB (Cunningham, Iberall, & Woolf, 1987). The project's name is derived from Caleb Gattegno, the developer of the Silent Way. This instructional approach requires the teacher to provide minimal input and, through trial and error, students invent new rules and receive feedback on errors.

Sometimes outdated and less successful approaches to SLA formed the basis for a project. For instance, Schuster (1986) parsed an English text with Spanish grammar rules in order to get a better understanding of transfer errors when an error was found. However, this project relies exclusively on a contrastive understanding of second language acquisition and thus fails to recognize errors which are due to other interlanguage processes. Rypa and Feuerman (1995), in quoting Schuster, also mention Contrastive Analysis as their main approach. They use it, however, to establish grammatical phenomena which their system explains to students. Yet, Pulman (1984) is rather direct in his rejection of modern communicative and/or cognitive approaches to language learning:

> Second language learning, especially during the early stages, is one [activity], where quite a lot of the time what is important is practice and training in correct usage of basic grammatical forms, not the conveying of facts about the world. (p. 84).

Oxford (1993) summarizes the situation in the mid-1990s as follows:

> It was somewhat surprising to me to discover that most of the papers presented at the ARI Workshop contained only outdated language learning and teaching references ... ICALL must devote as much attention to its language learning / teaching principles as it does to its exciting technology. (p. 174)

She then continues with nine key desiderata:

1. Communicative competence must be the cornerstone of ICALL.
2. ICALL must provide appropriate language assistance tailored to meet student needs.
3. ICALL must offer rich, authentic language input.
4. The ICALL student model must be based in part on a variety of learning styles.

5. ICALL material is most easily learned through associations which are facilitated by interesting and relevant themes and meaningful language tasks.
6. ICALL tasks must involve interactions of many kinds and these interactions need not be just student-tutor interactions.
7. ICALL must provide useful, appropriate error correction suited to the student's changing needs.
8. ICALL must involve all relevant language skills and must use each skill to support all other skills.
9. ICALL must teach students to become increasingly self-directed and self-confident language learners through explicit training in the use of learning strategies. (p. 174)

More recently, the number of CALL-oriented projects in the field of Computational Linguistics has increased. Unfortunately, the focus is still too often on parsing algorithms and grammatical formalisms. While this is important, the understanding of language learning often remains rudimentary and this leads researchers to develop software prototypes which do not sit well with our current understanding of SLA. Fortmann and Forst (2004), for instance, present a prototype of an LFG-based grammar checker for German as a foreign language and describe L2 learning as a process of conscious rule learning. This understanding has been shown to be inadequate by research in SLA over at least the last quarter of a century although Krashen's (1982) hypothesis that the learning of rules has no bearing on second language acquisition has been refuted in its strong version (Long, 1991). Instead, a foreign language has to be acquired in meaningful communication (Swain, 1985; Swain & Lapkin, 1995) and knowledge of grammatical rules only facilitates focus on form (Long, 1991). This lack of SLA understanding partially leads Fortmann and Forst (2004) to treat word order errors with a number of mal-rules. They hereby ignore the fact that any interlanguage will have a potentially infinite number of possible word orders, in addition to a fair amount of different interlanguages.

2.5.5 Developmental stages

The foregoing discussion mainly illustrates two developmental stages in parser-based CALL systems that primarily focus on form rather than on content. The early programs, as the one by Weischedel et al. (1978), concentrated solely on tackling the computational problems of parsing ill-formed input as opposed to embedding pedagogic considerations into such systems. For example, while Weischedel's system considers ambiguous readings, they are addressed from a computational rather than a pedagogic point of view. This is evident in the algorithm used to handle such errors. Selecting the parse with the fewest errors is a computationally effective method but it does not address the likely cause of error. A pedagogic system would consider the performance level of the learner and/or the language learning task in order to address ambiguous readings. The second phase of parser-based CALL, while still extending the parsing capabilities of ill-formed input, also attempts to emphasize pedagogic considerations. For example, Schwind (1995) and Holland (1994) seek a wider error coverage in a computationally more general way and also address language learning pedagogy in considering ambiguous errors.

The previous discussion of existing systems shows that neither phase has been completed. From a computational point of view, some errors such as errors in word order still need to be anticipated and thus are not addressed in a general way. In addition, semantics and pragmatics have not received their due attention in ICALL systems. From a pedagogical perspective, ambiguous, contingent and multiple errors, for example, are important for the development and evaluation of CALL programs. In addition, current research in SLA needs to be considered carefully in order to determine in what ways language learning software that relies on artificial intelligence techniques in general, or natural language processing in particular, can best contribute to successful learning.

3. Error analysis and description

3.1 INTRODUCTION

Part 3 starts with a brief overview of the two best known, commercially available computational tools which deal with errors in written texts: spell checkers and grammar checkers. A discussion of these tools leads to a review of the foundations of Error Analysis (EA), a branch of Applied Linguistics that began to influence our understanding of second language acquisition in the late 1960s and early 1970s.

In parser-based CALL, the treatment of grammatical errors has received the most attention (Nerbonne, 2003). Identifying and describing errors has played an essential role in research and development albeit often in a purely computational framework by designing parsers that can process erroneous language input. This focus meant that some ICALL researchers (e.g., Schuster, 1986), in their practical pursuit of error diagnosis, relied on a theoretical framework, such as that of Contrastive Analysis (CA) (Lado, 1957). Contrastive Analysis was already outdated at the time and had been heavily criticized within Seond Language Acquisition (SLA) research (see, for instance, Oxford, 1995 who discusses these problems that often derive from the lack of an appropriate theoretical foundation in some of the ICALL research and development). Others confirm our view that the processing of texts produced by language learners is a non-trivial problem: "Computational error analysis (as opposed to competency analysis) is also a significant and immediate challenge for diagnostic parsing. We think this problem is more subtle and difficult than some recent researchers realize (e.g., Weischedel & Sondheimer, 1983; Mellish, 1989)" (Loritz, 1992, p. 20). To be fair to researchers and developers in NLP and CALL, one has to take into consideration that the knowledge base in SLA has been developed in the same time frame in which work in ICALL progressed. The interest of linguists and language teachers in errors, their diagnosis and correction, however, is much older than the foundations of EA and CA (e.g., Leather, 1932). The advent of electronic learner corpora and the need for elaborate error data in parser-based CALL research has recently sparked renewed interest in the methodologies employed by Error Analysis (EA). In this section, we will show examples of successful implementations of research findings in CALL in general, and in parser-based CALL in particular. This part concludes with an overview of current trends in corpus research as it pertains to parser-based CALL. We discuss the uses of corpora both in CALL in general, and as a resource for NLP and CALL.

3.2 SPELL CHECKERS

The use of word processors has become an integral part of the language learning classroom and spell checkers, in particular, have turned into a highly desirable tool for both native and non-native writers.[1] With little controversy, spell checkers are praised for their effectiveness in treating spelling mistakes. However, generic spell checkers are based on the assumption that their users are competent speakers of the language who primarily make accidental typographical mistakes. For this reason, they are best at correcting single typographical errors of letter addition, omission, substitution, and transposition (e.g., as in the misspelling **lannguage* for *language*). A number of studies, however, have indicated that spell checkers are less successful in dealing with errors made by writers with spelling deficits or non-native speakers. Non-native writers, for example, are just as likely to make accidental typographical mistakes as native writers are, but they also make errors that are due to their insufficient command of the foreign language. These errors tend to deviate from the correct spellings in more substantial but also somewhat predictable ways. For instance, a language learner might provide the word *goed* for *went* which deviates more from the correct spelling than an accidental typographical mistake such as *wwent* for *went*. However, this error is also predictable because the learner incorrectly overgeneralized the regular English past tense marker — ed.

The detection and correction algorithms of commercially available spell checkers are largely based on two empirical research findings. First, the vast majority of misspellings (80–95%) contain only a *single* error of omission, addition, substitution, or transposition (Damerau, 1964; Pollock & Zamora, 1984). Second, the *first* letter of a misspelled word is usually correct (Yannakoudakis & Fawthrop, 1983; Pollock & Zamora, 1984). The algorithms assume that most spelling errors are performance-based, that is, a result of accidental mistypings rather than conscious, or systematic misspellings (Pollock & Zamora, 1984; Pedler, 2001). Mitton (1996) discusses a variety of methods for detecting and correcting spelling errors and confirms that apart from problems with proper nouns, homophones, rare words and grossly deviating misspellings, generic spell checkers can treat the majority of spelling mistakes made by typical native speakers effectively (for spell checking techniques, see also Peterson, 1980; Berghel, 1987; Kukich, 1992). Kukich (1992), for example, notes that "most researchers report accuracy levels above 90% when the first three guesses [in a spell checker's list of suggested spelling corrections] are considered" (p. 142).

However, when it comes to non-native writers, there are several shortcomings concerning the usefulness of spell checkers. Allerton, Tschichold, and Wieser (2005), for example, state that

> as learners' errors often do not correspond to typical typing mistakes, the algorithms used by spell checkers are of relatively little help in this situation. What is needed to detect this type of variation and generate appropriate feedback is an algorithm (coupled with a database) designed to deal specifically with learner language. (p. 147)

Very few studies have investigated the effectiveness of spell checkers in treating misspellings made by second language learners. A study by Holmes and de Moras (1997), however, examines the spelling correction component of a generic grammar checker. The French Grammar Analyzer *Le Correcteur 101* was tested on eight French essays written by native English university students. Overall, 76.5% of the orthographical errors were detected. However, of those misspellings that were not related to the incorrect inclusion or omission of accents, *Le Correcteur 101* detected only 44%. The researchers conclude that "the software's usefulness would be extended if it were taught to anticipate some typical Anglophone errors" (Holmes & de Moras, 1997, p. 104). Similarly, Burston (1998) discusses the effectiveness of the French grammar and spell checker *Antidote 98* when tested against 40 second-year advanced student essays. In contrast to *Le Correcteur 101*, *Antidote 98* frequently alerts writers of possible misuse of Anglicisms. While the program handles most misspellings effectively, Burston notes that *Antidote 98* misidentifies "some fairly obvious spelling errors" (p. 209) and fails to recognize sentence initial misspellings.

In an attempt to address the shortcomings of generic spell checkers in the language learning context, a few researchers have designed programs that assist non-native writers with their spelling problems. Fallman (2002), for example, presents a descriptive spell checker that uses the Internet as a database to retrieve the number of hits of a given string. The number of hits for different possible spellings of a word can be compared to determine the correct spelling (i.e., the alternative with the most hits is most likely the correct spelling). Bos and van de Plassche (1994) describe a tutoring system for the conjugation and spelling of Dutch verbs as a spelling aid for children and non-native writers. If a student misspells a word, the system tries to determine the cause of the misspelling (e.g., overgeneralization of a spelling rule) and guides the student to the correct answer. De Haan and Oppenhuizen (1994) introduce us to SPELLER, an intelligent tutoring system to support the learning of L2 English spelling. The system aims to diagnose and remedy spelling errors in cooperation with the users. Apart from treating common typographical errors, it is mainly concerned with spelling errors caused by misrepresentations of English phonemes (i.e., phonologically-motivated spelling errors). Ndiaye and Vandeventer-Faltin (2003) have developed a spell checker for learners of French. Similar to de Haan and Oppenhuizen's program, the spell checker is geared towards the correction of both typographical and phonologically-motivated spelling errors. It also includes an ad hoc method for treating a specific type of morphological spelling error (the incorrect plural formation of words ending in *–al* and *–ail*). Some additional spelling and grammar checking tools are available for non-native writers of French. For example, *Le Correcteur didactique* is a version of *Le Correcteur* targeted at non-native writers and the educational version of *Sans-Faute* is a grammar and spell checker directed at beginning and intermediate learners of French. In addition, recent versions of *Antidote* incorporate non-native error lists. Murphy-Judy (2003) evaluated the performance of *Sans-Faute* and compared it to the performance of *Le Correcteur didactique* and *Antidote* among others. She concludes that overall *Sans-Faute* is "currently the most powerful" (p. 219) tool for non-native writers of French.

The programs described above are all geared towards non-native misspellings, however, they are generally not based on an extensive empirical analysis of L2 spelling errors. Many researchers however, recognize the need to consider authentic learner errors in the design of useful language learning programs (see e.g., Juozulynas, 1994; Mitton, 1996; Cowan, Choi, & Kim, 2003; Ndiaye & Vandeventer Faltin, 2003; Allerton et al., 2005). For example, Cowan et. al. (2003) state that "basing the selection of errors to be targeted for correction research on empirical data ... provides us with many examples of error types that can be built into the CALL program" (p. 455).

Rimrott and Heift (2005) conducted a study on non-native German spelling errors and evaluated the performance of the generic spell checker in the *Microsoft® Word® 2003* word processing software, which is not specifically designed for second language learners. One of the study goals was to determine the kinds and frequencies of errors it can successfully correct. Thirty-four students enrolled in one of the first three introductory classes of university German participated in the study and the authors analyzed 374 spelling errors that were collected from an English-to-German translation exercise.

In classifying the spelling errors, they made a primary distinction between competence and performance errors. Within the category of competence errors, they further distinguished errors according to language influence (interlingual vs. intralingual)[2] and linguistic subsystem (lexical, morphological, phonological and orthographic).[3] Performance errors were subdivided into single letter violations (additions, omissions, substitutions, and transpositions), multiple letter violations and word boundary violations.

Frequency counts indicated that 80% of the errors were competence-based, while 20% were performance-related, that is, they were accidental typographical mistakes. In the competence category, intralingual errors were much more frequent than interlingual misspellings. In addition, phonological and lexical errors were more prevalent than morphological or orthographic errors. Performance errors were largely comprised of single letter violations. Multiple letter violations and word boundary errors constituted the minority.

In assessing to which extent the *Microsoft® Word® 2003* spell checker can successfully correct the misspellings, the authors found that, contrary to claims with respect to L1 misspellings, only 52% of the non-native misspellings were corrected. However, the spell checker was much more successful in treating performance errors than competence-based misspellings. Competence errors tend to deviate more substantially from the target words than performance errors. This difference in degree of deviation makes it harder for a spell checker to suggest the target words. Furthermore, within the competence category, lexical misspellings were most frequently not corrected, followed by morphological and finally phonological misspellings. Again, greater target deviation was the principal explanation: on average, lexical misspellings have a greater target deviation than morphological misspellings, which in turn deviate more from the target words than phonological misspellings. The results confirm that the spell checker is effectively serving its primary purpose: correcting performance-based single letter violations. However, the error data also demonstrate quite clearly that the spell checker's task is different in foreign language writing where most misspellings are competence-based and thus, most commonly, involve greater target deviations. Along the lines of Tschichold's (1999a, 1999b) strategies for improving foreign language grammar checking, Rimrott and Heift (2005) propose two main strategies to overcome the shortcomings of generic spell checkers in the CALL classroom:

1. increasing the spell checker's effectiveness in treating non-native misspellings and/or
2. decreasing the language learners' dependence on the spell checker.

3.3 GRAMMAR CHECKERS

There is a genuine need for grammar checkers in language learning. Learners certainly perceive the correctness of second language utterances to be important in written and oral communication. Language learning often has phases of form-focused activities (Long, 1991) in which students shift away from the negotiation of meaning in a communicative setting to concentrate on the surface form of their utterances. The thorough proof-reading for errors of a text is such an activity. For these form-focused activities grammar checkers can be very useful tools, if they function adequately. However, the shortcomings of commercially available grammar checkers used by language learners have been discussed widely (Granger & Meunier, 1994; Wei & Davies, 1997; Tschichold, 1999a, 1999b). Evaluations of these grammar checkers usually indicate that, for grammar checkers to be useful, they need to be geared toward language learners. More linguistic rules are also needed to avoid simplistic pattern and keyword matching. Bolt (1992) published a detailed comparison of six commercially available grammar checkers for English with LINGER (Yazdani & Uren, 1988; Yazdani, 1991, 1992; Bolt & Yazdani, 1998), a small NLP-based prototype and concludes that

> there is a major division between the commercial programs and LINGER. This is not to say that LINGER is in any general or sustainable sense superior. As with all small programs it has the virtue of dealing with a small part of data [which was selected by one of the developers] reasonably well but the vice of not being easily scaled up so as to continue to perform as well with larger data sets. (p. 90)[4]

But how should grammar checkers work within the context of SLA and what kinds of foreign language learning activities should grammar checkers be part of?

Word-processing and e-mail have been mentioned as potential host applications for grammar checkers for students of foreign languages (Yazdani, 1990). However, we are not aware of any such non-commercial tool that is available to learners of a foreign language.[5] According to the projects described at the end of this chapter, an error diagnosis performed by a parser-based CALL system is also much more likely to occur within the well-defined context of a sentence-based language learning activity. However, for all these activities it is necessary to consider the underlying SLA processes, the ways to describe learner language and the kinds of errors that constitute the nature of the problems a grammar checker claims to address.

3.4 FOUNDATIONS OF ERROR ANALYSIS

When learning a second language, the learner can rely on an existing cognitive system, that is, the native language (L1). The learner might also have learnt or acquired other languages in addition to the declarative and procedural knowledge about (language) learning, cultures, societies, people and the world in general. How do these systems or other cognitive devices contribute to language learning? How do they interact?

In an attempt to answer these questions by analyzing learner language (L2), it is useful to remember the distinction between text as a process and text as a product (e.g., Antos, 1982). The former refers to an understanding of text production processes during which communicative goals are modified, specified and finally met by searching for, selecting, connecting and uttering appropriate linguistic signs such as words, phrases and sentences. If verbalized, some of these processes can be observed in spontaneous spoken speech. It is much more difficult to detect traces of the preceding processes in the written result, that is, the text as product. If an utterance in such a text adheres to all orthographic, grammatical, stylistic and pragmatic norms of the L2 as judged by a native speaker, then it is very difficult to determine whether language learners have internalized the linguistic constraints of the L2 or whether they applied normative knowledge from outside the L2 system and coincidentally produced a well-formed utterance. Errors, on the other hand, provide an excellent window into text production processes because they deviate from the L2 norms. Most often, the errors made by language learners reflect hypotheses of linguistic norms that learners form about the L2. Insights into the process of second language acquisition and the de-emphasizing of the notion of errors as failures are clearly benefits of the application of error analysis in language learning software (Chanier et al., 1992).

3.4.1 The beginnings of error analysis

The school of *Contrastive Analysis* (CA) (Lado, 1957) tried to explain all errors through reference to the native language of the learner. This process was either described as transfer or interference. The chapter headings in Lado's book (*How to Compare Two Sound Systems; How to Compare Two Grammatical Structures; How to Compare Two Vocabulary Systems; How to Compare Two Writing Systems; How to Compare Two Cultures*) indicate the parts of the language system that should be compared. Some proponents of CA claimed that the learner language could be *constructed* by contrasting the system of L1 with that of L2. If related linguistic phenomena differ vastly between L1 and L2 (e.g., adjectives are inflected in one language, but not in the other), then they are very difficult to learn and are frequently a source of errors. If, on the other hand, such linguistic phenomena are very similar (e.g., a certain letter represents the same sound in both languages), then they are very easy to acquire and rarely cause errors. Lado (1957) summarized this in his CA hypothesis:

> ... the student who comes into contact with a foreign language will find some features of it quite easy and others extremely difficult. Those elements that are similar to his native language will be simple for him and those elements that are different will be difficult. (p. 2)

For both predictions, analyses of learner language provide counter-evidence. The main reason is that many researchers in CA did not examine utterances or texts produced by language learners. Instead, they often compared two abstract constructs, the two language systems, with their inventory of rules and lexical items in order to predict the occurrence of errors. However, in spite of these limitations, CA has made significant contributions to our understanding of SLA processes in general, and, perhaps even more importantly, CA has informed the design of language teaching materials for a long time.

Some of the problems of CA were overcome in later works and through studies in *Error Analysis* (EA) (Corder, 1974; Dulay & Burt, 1974). In opposition to the stronger view of the CA hypothesis, that is, errors can be fully predicted on the basis of a comparison, EA incorporated a weaker view of the CA hypothesis. It began with an analysis of the errors and returned, if necessary, to a comparison of native and target language (Gass & Selinker, 2001, p. 73). The main difference, which is already emphasized in the respective names of the two theoretical approaches, is that EA shifts the focus onto the learner language. It is no longer sufficient nor necessary to analyze typological differences between L1 and L2 to arrive at a better understanding of SLA processes. Errors in texts produced by language learners are seen as evidence for language learning processes. In a first approximation, an error, in this sense, can be described as a deviation from a norm (Ellis, 1994, p. 51).

> A learner's sentences may be deviant, ill-formed, incorrect or erroneous only in the sense that they are not fully describable in the terms of his mother tongue or the target language. They are, however, presumably 'well-formed' in terms of the grammar of his own transitional idiolect at that point in time. I shall, however, hereafter use the term erroneous to mean either superficially deviant or inappropriate in terms of the target language grammar as is the usual practice. (Corder, 1974, p. 122)

The three steps taken in traditional error analysis (Corder, 1974), effective recognition, description and explanation of errors,[6] have to make use of language technology if they are to be performed by a computer program. For a high-quality error analysis of morpho-syntactic errors in written texts, NLP techniques are necessary (Menzel & Schröder, 1999). Errors are detected because they deviate from the norm.

In parser-based CALL, this norm is constituted by morpho-syntactic rules contained in the grammar and, far less often, by semantic and/or pragmatic rules. Moreover, most often only a fragment of the grammar rules of a language have been implemented. This fragment is based on linguistic knowledge available at the time of writing the parser grammar. It is not only limited by the linguistic knowledge of its designer but also by choices that have been made to describe certain phenomena.[7] The designer's grammar is the grammar that constitutes the norm in a parser-based CALL program. Textual input that cannot be described and thus analyzed by the parser is a deviation from the grammar's norm; but is it an error?

Corder (1974, p. 122) distinguishes between errors versus mistakes, or lapses. Only errors are the result of a lack of competence on the part of the second language learner. Mistakes are performance-based. Their number increases under certain adverse conditions like stress or fatigue. As far as computer-aided text production is concerned, typographical mistakes should also be subsumed in the performance-based categories of mistakes and lapses.

Mistakes and errors are both deviations from the norm and as such, they will be detected by the parser. The difference lies in the feedback for the learner: an error that is due to a lack of language competence calls for some kind of support to build up competence in this area. A mistake, on the other hand, can easily be corrected by the learner and without a lengthy explanation in the feedback.[8]

A number of error analysts have indicated that the notion of error is highly subjective (Shaughnessy, 1979; Lennon, 1991). There might always be a native speaker who finds an utterance acceptable, however difficult it might be for others to understand. From his corpus of spoken learner English, Lennon (1991), for instance, shows in some detail the heterogeneity found among native speaker judgments when it comes to errors. Accordingly, he applies a very cautious definition of an error:

> a linguistic form or combination of forms which, in the same context and under similar conditions of production, would, in all likelihood, not be produced by the speakers' native speaker counterparts. (p. 182)

The subjectivity of a parser is certainly an indirect one. It goes hand in hand with the notion of the parser grammar, that is, the grammar of an informed idiolect on which the judgment of well-formedness is based. This problem is compounded by the fact that the parser will only consider grammatical errors. Errors of other classes (e.g., semantic or pragmatic errors) are thus often overlooked.[9] Corder (1974, pp. 123–124), for example, separates errors of well-formedness from errors of appropriateness. For the latter he distinguishes four major error classes:

1. referential errors (calling a hat a cap),
2. register errors (referring to a ship as a boat in a naval context),
3. social error (addressing a teacher as "old man"),
4. textual errors (not selecting the structurally correct form to express the intended relation, e.g., providing a personal narrative when a project report is required).

superficially well-formed	*and*	appropriate	**erroneous or correct**
superficially well-formed	*but*	inappropriate	**erroneous**
superficially deviant	*but as far as can be judged*	appropriate	**erroneous**
superficially deviant	*but as far as can be judged*	inappropriate	**erroneous**

Corder's distinction of *superficially ill-formed sentences* and *errors of appropriateness* is a useful one in understanding the limitations of a morpho-syntactic parser that can only detect the former errors. The four possible combinations of error classes are shown above (Corder, 1974, p. 124).

Only the latter two combinations will be detected by a parser, whereas the first two will go unchallenged. Corder states that even the first combination can be erroneous because an underlying error can be presumed if the learner achieves a correct answer by chance. Corder's four combinations assume that all deviations from the norm are detected correctly and adequately. This cannot be said about a parser. There is a likely scenario in which the parser judges a sentence as erroneous although it is both well-formed and appropriate. This is possible because the parser is unable to provide a complete analysis of the sentence due to a missing or over-restrictive rule. This is commonly referred to as overflagging. Accordingly, feedback provided for certain deviations from the parser grammar has to be formulated very cautiously because it might be difficult to determine whether or not the parser detected a genuine error.[10]

Corder (1974, p. 126) also makes a distinction between spontaneous and controlled text production, free composition versus translation, précis, paraphrases, and retelling of stories. He argues that the spontaneous text production is error-avoiding while controlled text production is error-provoking (see also Schachter, 1974). The rationale behind this claim is that students in free composition, that is, spontaneous text production, are more likely to avoid grammatical structures with which they are less familiar and by which may trigger unwanted errors. In contrast, in controlled text production, the task can be specified in such a way that the learner must use certain grammatical constructions and possible errors are unavoidable. This explains why errors that have been detected by the parser can be used to provide help and support for the learner because they indicate the grammar areas in which the learner has difficulties. However, the errors alone cannot be used to form an adequate picture of the learner's linguistic competence. An extreme example of this is a learner who produces an error-free text. The text, however, contains endless repetitions of the same simple structures and recurring lexical patterns: although the text is error-free, the language learner is certainly not a proficient writer. This problem can be addressed if the parser does not only output an error analysis and feedback but also stores parsing results in a learner model.[11] Consequently, the model can maintain a record of lexical and syntactic constructions used by the learner. Given *standard* frequency of certain constructions in a given text type (i.e., genre) or language learning task, the student model can then flag overuse or (partial) avoidance of some constructions. However, if the input the student submitted contains an error, what can the parser actually do in terms of error analysis?

The three stages of error analysis are effective recognition, description and explanation (Corder, 1974). The first two stages can be carried out by a parser that is coupled with a feedback module. The third stage, however, is difficult for any analyzer but particularly difficult, if not impossible, for a parser that relies on morpho-syntactic knowledge only. As described in section 2.3, a morpho-syntactic parser does not have sufficient information about other linguistic levels, the situational context and the world in general. Yet, this kind of information is often necessary in determining a plausible well-formed utterance on the basis of a corresponding ill-formed one. The parser can relate the ill-formed sentence to a well-formed counterpart on the basis of the violated constraint. The violated constraint is thus seen as the underlying cause of the error. This approach to reasoning about the underlying cause of an error relies exclusively on linguistic features and fails to consider non-linguistic reasons such as learning strategies or misconceptions about language and the world. An even higher level of error anticipation is necessary when buggy rules are used. Such rules describe the morpho-syntactic structure of erroneous utterances and the error diagnosis and feedback generation is often embedded in the rules. The complete set of these rules in a parser grammar essentially represents an error classification with all its advantages and limits.

Error analysis has been criticized for two main reasons: its weakness in methodological procedures (one of them is the ad hoc error classifications which were sometimes employed) and its limitations in scope (its concentration on *negative* learner language phenomena) (Ellis, 1994, p. 67). Error classifications which appear to employ rather heterogeneous classification criteria as opposed to structured, systematic ones can also be found in the CALL literature (see e.g., Dalgish, 1991, p. 41). Such ad hoc classifications should best be avoided. They often unduly skew the results of the error diagnosis and, consequently, influence the quality of the feedback in a negative way.

In this sense, parser-based analyses inherit some of the limitations of the error analysis approach. Usually, learners receive information about the errors they make and parsers create a student profile on the basis of the errors found. However, learners do not commonly receive any feedback on the correct structures they use. As a result, *negative* features are over-emphasized. Moreover, the problem of ascribing a cause to an error is another difficulty parser-based approaches share with EA approaches (Gass & Selinker, 2001, pp. 83–84).

Despite justified criticism leveled against Error Analysis, this (methodological) approach has seen some renewed interest recently, particularly from the field of corpus-based studies of learner language (see section 3.6). The merits of EA with its concentration on observable surface phenomena and its close analysis of texts produced by learners are still important. "EA, in fact, continues to be practiced, although now it is more likely to serve as a means for investigating a specific research question rather than for providing a comprehensive account of learners' idiosyncratic forms" (Ellis, 1994, p. 70). It can function and is used as a tool to develop our understanding of interlanguage, which we discuss in the next section.

3.4.2 Interlanguage

The term *interlanguage* was coined by Selinker in 1969 and discussed in an article in 1972 (Corder, 1981, p. 87). The article was reprinted in Richards (1974a) as Selinker (1974). Selinker (1992) explicitly contextualizes his understanding of interlanguage in a historical framework of Contrastive Analysis and Error Analysis. Granger (2003) points out that the study of errors in interlanguage texts is an important prerequisite for their successful automatic detection and processing in CALL.

Interlanguage generally refers to a specific learner variety of the target language at a given point in time and/or the learner's progress over time (Ellis, 1994, p. 350). It captures the fact that the language used by a learner lies somewhere in between the native language and the target language. Selinker (1974) originally proposed

> five psycholinguistic processes which establish the knowledge which underlies IL [interlanguage] behaviour. I would like to suggest that there are five central processes (and perhaps some additional minor ones) and that they exist in the latent psychological structure referred to above. I consider the following to be processes central to second language learning; first, language transfer; second, transfer of training; third, strategies of second language learning; fourth, strategies of second language communication; and fifth, overgeneralisation of TL [target language] linguistic material. (p. 35)

In later works, Selinker describes three processes of interlanguage construction: language transfer, simplification and overgeneralization (Ellis, 1994, p. 351). He emphasizes the importance of language transfer among the three (Selinker, 1992, pp. 171–214). Simplification and overgeneralization both work on the basis of target variety rules, whereas language transfer introduces rules from another language into the interlanguage.

Simplification refers to the writer ignoring certain rules in order to save processing time (in a psycholinguistic or cognitive sense). For example, this might apply to a rule which requires using one and the same verb form consistently with the subject (e.g., the infinitive). A similar algorithm can be observed in overgeneralization. This process extends the scope of a rule of the target variety beyond its standard boundaries, for example, an irregular verb is conjugated as a regular verb.Although it can be safely assumed that all three processes play some role in constituting an interlanguage, it is not always clear which of the processes can be used to describe the cause of a learner's deviation from the standard variety. This is not only true for the distinction between overgeneralization and simplification processes but also between either of the two and transfer processes. The decision as to what process caused an error is complicated by the fact that transfer does not only occur between the native and target languages but also between other previously learnt languages and the language currently being learnt. Again, it appears to be impossible to establish the language from which the transfer originated given similarity or even identity of rules covering a linguistic phenomenon in different languages. However, this needs to be determined in order to establish the exact cause of a deviation in the learner variety. The problem of establishing error classes on the basis of such processes, which is probably an impossible task, has been discussed in more detail in Ellis (1994, p. 61).

Simplification and overgeneralization attempt to provide a psycholinguistic account of interlanguage phenomena. Hence they are also meant to identify causes of deviations in the interlanguage grammar from the grammar of the target variety. The claim that interlanguage is as systematic as any other language is frequently made. Only systematicity makes it possible to consider a computational implementation because in its absence, there are no rules to be captured. Moreover, systematicity is based on the three interlanguage processes (i.e., language transfer, simplification, and overgeneralization).

Using this concept of interlanguage in relation to a formal grammar is problematic because the parser almost exclusively relies on the surface of the text, or in this particular context, on the surface of the grammar deviations. It is very difficult, if at all possible, to establish a one-to-one relationship between an error class and the interlanguage process, independent of the granularity of the classification. In some cases, it is impossible to identify the single interlanguage process underlying an error while, in other instances, it is equally realistic to identify two possible interlanguage processes for the same error. In the worst case scenario, it is feasible that identical surface errors made by different learners are caused by different interlanguage processes.

Interlanguage processes are certainly intuitive and they seem to provide a good explanation of the linguistic varieties in the learner language. They also provide evidence that interlanguage is systematic. However, they do not appear to fully explain individual deviations from the target variety within a certain learner variety. Nevertheless, the knowledge of the interlanguage processes proves very valuable for identifying linguistic phenomena of the target variety that learners are more likely to misconstruct, that is, to which they apply interlanguage processes.

3.4.3 Error classification

An important prerequisite for the adequate description of errors and the generation of helpful feedback in CALL is an appropriate error classification. The use of an error classification has the following advantages for a grammar checker:

- Error description and feedback can be based on both the individual error and the error class. This will result not only in computational efficiency but also in consistent description and feedback. The latter is identical for all errors belonging to the same error class.
- Errors that belong to the same error class can be treated in the same way. Their description and feedback can be provided on the basis of the frequency of the learner's errors of the same error class.
- Error classification enables parser-based systems not only to record the occurrence of individual errors but also to tally the errors that belong to the same error class. This results in more precise feedback because the feedback can be based on a more informative and comprehensive student model (see Heift & Schulze, 2003b).

Error classifications in CALL vary considerably in granularity. Yang and Akahori (1995), for example, who were first and foremost interested in the discussion of errors in Japanese passive constructions, provide a list of nine different types of errors. Others rely on a much smaller set of types. For instance, Krüger and Hamilton (1997) use an error classification for the RECALL system (Kiss et al., 1997) that relies on compound descriptors which consist of class name, subclass and subtype, for example, syntactic_agreement_person_verb_noun.

For illustrative purposes, this book proposes an error classification that is based on Taylor (1998) and Lee (2003). Both proposals were developed for the computer-aided analysis of written texts. Here, they will merely serve as a concrete example of the challenges associated with classifying learner errors. By classification we refer to entities that are assigned to a class on the basis of whether or not they contain a certain feature. The features we use for the classification are organized along different axes. Taylor proposed three axes: interlanguage processes, systematicity and surface.

Taylor's first axis relies on the classification of errors by interlanguage processes (i.e., simplification, overgeneralization and language transfer)

(Selinker, 1992). The main difficulty with this classification is that the class-determining features are based on psycholinguistic explanations as part of the error analysis. However, it is impossible to determine a one-to-one relationship between these processes and the surface phenomena observed. These processes can only be used for a classification performed by a human observer and would be very subjective at best. A parser can only pick up the surface phenomena.

Taylor's second axis (systematicity) is based on a distinction made by Corder (1974, p. 131). Corder uses *pre-systematic* for errors that occur in an unsystematic way because the learner is unaware of a particular rule in the target language. In the language learning classroom this generally applies to instances where the rule has not yet been introduced in the course of the curriculum. The *systematic* stage is characterized by the learner relying systematically on an interlanguage rule that is not part of the target language rule system. At the *post-systematic* stage, a deviation can be described as a lapse, that is, the learner usually applies the target language rule consistently, but has failed to do so in a particular case. This might be due to external factors that, for example, result in a lack of concentration. Within a parser-based CALL system, such a distinction can be made by the instructor who, from time to time, sets configurational switches that indicate whether learners of a particular group have been exposed to, learned, or acquired a certain linguistic phenomenon. This can be applied to certain linguistic rules such as subject-verb agreement, different tenses and case marking. Alternatively, these categories can be assigned as part of statistical calculations of the student model. Figures such as frequency of an error type and ratio of correct versus incorrect usage of grammatical structures will need to be taken into consideration. However, we are not aware of any validated statistics for such a computation.

The third axis provided by Taylor relies on a classification of errors by part of speech as well as error heurisms (omission, insertion, and invention). For the latter, she also assumes a category of inappropriateness (Taylor, 1998, p. 48). Accordingly, she distinguishes invented forms, that is, forms, which are not part of the target language system from inappropriate forms, which exist in the language system, but should not have been used in this particular context. This distinction is an important one for a parser because invented word forms will not be found in the lexicon nor be parsed at the morphological level. Errors of inappropriateness, on the other hand, would have to be detected by the parser because they are violating a syntactic, semantic, or pragmatic constraint.

Lee (2003), in continuation of Taylor's work, applied her classification to an analysis of German texts produced by English-speaking learners. She used two approaches previously suggested by Dulay, Burt, and Krashen (1982, p. 146): surface strategy and linguistic category. For surface strategy, Lee distinguishes among omission, addition, misselection, misordering, and malformation. All five strategies are observed at the word level, that is, it is a word (rather than a single character or a phrase) that is omitted or added. The unit of analysis has to be determined for any error analysis as evident in the following example:

Example 3.1
a) *developped
b) *Peter is read a book.

Lee describes the error in Example 3.1a as a malformed word and not an addition of a character. In contrast, the word *read* in Example 3.1b is classified as a misselected word because the verb form exists but is not appropriate in the present tense. Example 3.1b illustrates the difference between misselection and malformation. Lee uses the former to describe an error where a chosen linguistic form is part of the language system, but cannot be used in the given sentence. Accordingly, Example 3.1b is not a malformed word because malformation refers to a word form that does not exist at all in the language system. This difference is important in two ways: First, from a computational point of view it is a different task detecting a word form that does not exist as opposed to spotting a word form that exists but has not been used in the correct context. Second, and even more importantly, Lee argues that the two error classes are viewed rather differently by learners. With malformation, the learner most likely does not know how to construct the target language form while, with misselection, the learner has some familiarity with the word form. In contrast, misordering refers to an existing word form that is used correctly in a given context but its positioning violates a word order constraint. This category is particularly useful because, instead of marking two errors, in one place of omission and in another of addition, there is one misordering error. In cases where entire phrases occur in an inappropriate position in the sentence, Lee, nonetheless, labels the error(s) at the word level for reasons of consistency. For example, *the <u>of my father</u> house is very near* consists of three misordering errors at positions 2, 3, and 4.

Lee's analysis is word-based and, for this reason, she splits linguistic category, her second classification axis, into two steps of analysis: part-of-speech (i.e., lexical category) and syntactic category. Part of speech takes the word as the main unit of analysis.[12] Figure 3.1 illustrates a classification of lexical categories for German which, however, can be easily adapted to other, at least Indo-European, languages.

The lexical category of a word can be augmented by the grammatical constraint that has been violated (case marking, agreement, etc.). This will assist in determining the exact nature of a malformation or misselection more precisely. Information on the nature of the error can also be included. For example, it can indicate whether the error is predominantly orthographical or perhaps lexical. This allows for the treatment of errors

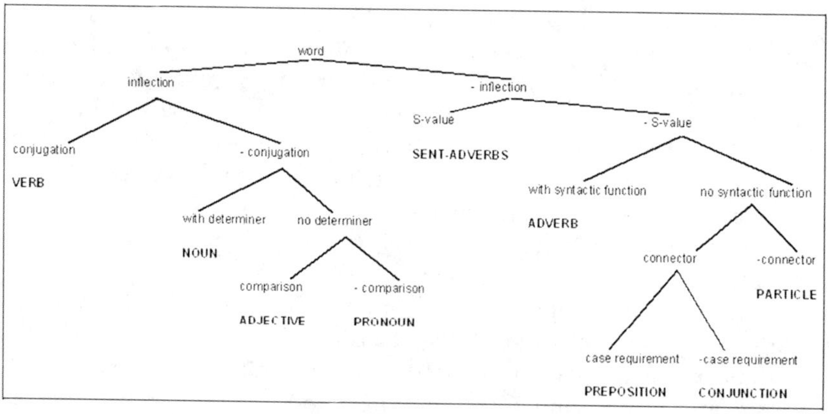

Figure 3.1 POS — binary decision tree (adapted from Flämig, 1991, p. 358)

of similar nature in the same way. For instance, errors due to case marking of determiners, adjectives and nouns can all entail similar help features. However, it is often difficult to decide on the precise cause and/or nature of an error because errors themselves can be ambiguous. For example, in German an error with a determiner can be due to either incorrect gender or case. It is also sometimes hard to distinguish between orthographical and morphological errors or orthographical and lexical errors (e.g., *external* vs. *eternal; vocation* vs. *vacation*).

3.4.3.1 *An example of an error classification*

To further illustrate the inherent difficulties of any error analysis, the following example provides an analysis of German texts produced by language learners. Following Lee (2003), we use words[13] as the unit of analysis and description. Our classification uses two axes:

Surface strategy (addition, malformation, misordering, misselection, omission)

Part of speech (POS) (adjective, determiner, noun, preposition, verb)

The *surface strategy* axis refers to errors that are characterized by different constraint violations. In contrast, the *POS* axis corresponds to what Dulay et al. (1982) subsumed under linguistic strategy. The following parts of speech are important in the error classification: noun, verb, adjective, preposition and determiner. None of these can be omitted, with the exception of adjectives, which are optional in any sentential environment.[14]

Nouns[15] are marked for morphological ill-formedness (*Messers* [*knives*, correct form *Messer*: incorrect plural suffix]), case-marking errors (*des Lehrer_* [*of the teacher*, correct form *Lehrers*: missing genitive marker]) and agreement errors (*Dort ist der Tisch. Es ist rund.* [*There is the table. It is round.*, correct form *Er*: non-agreement of pronoun and antecedent]).

Verbs are marked for morphological ill-formedness (*gehte* [*went*, correct form *ging*: incorrect past tense formation]) and agreement errors (*ich gehen* [*I walk*, correct form *gehe*: use of infinitive for first person singular]). For agreement errors, it is the verb that does not agree with the subject and not vice versa. This is based on the belief that learners know whether one or more actors perform a certain action. However, they might not know the grammatical agreement with the verb.

Adjectives can fail to agree with the noun phrase (*das schönes Haus* [*the beautiful house*, correct form *schöne*: adjective does not agree with NP]) and can be morphologically ill-formed (*gutester* [*best*, correct form *bester*: incorrect superlative form]). Case-marking prepositions can violate a case-marking constraint (*er interessiert sich in Musik* [*he is interested in music*, correct form *für*: incorrect prepositional case marker]).

Determiners can signal agreement and case-marking errors (*die Haus* [*the house*, correct form *das*: agreement error]; *mit das Haus* [*with the house*, correct form *dem*: case-marking error]). Again, the learner probably knows the noun and it is the determiner that lacks agreement or case concord. In some cases, both errors occur simultaneously (*er sieht der Haus* [*he sees the house*, correct form *das*: non-accusative and non-neuter determiner]).

The POS axis provided for the error classification at hand excludes a number of lexical categories (e.g., adverbs, particles, and numerals) for the following reasons:

First, from a computational point of view, it is more efficient to subsume lexical categories such as adverbs under the broader heading of adjectives. In this respect, they are treated as adjectives that do not inflect. This approach emphasizes commonalities between the two classes and thus facilitates the construction of clearer type hierarchies, in this instance, of lexical types.

Second, these word classes are generally less prone to errors because they do not inflect. For this reason, there is less need to include them in the error classification. Table 3.1 provides a number of examples to illustrate the scope and limitations of such a classification. For brevity, errors of misordering (violations of linear precedence) and orthography have been omitted for the different word classes.

In addition to annotating the parts of speech with the morpho-syntactic category that underlies the error (e.g., agreement, case-marking, or orthography), we also propose to include the syntactic function of the erroneous word. This allows us to preserve some additional information about the error. Here again we follow Lee (2003, p. 43) and use the following syntactic functions that were loosely based on Durrell and Hammer (2002): subject, accusative object, dative object, genitive object, prepositional object, place complement, direction complement, subject complement, object complement, temporal adjunct, local adjunct, and adverbial adjunct.

Table 3.1 POS and surface strategy for error classification

Part of speech	*Surface strategy*	*Example*	*Gloss*
noun	omission	*er beeilt _ (er beeilt sich)	he is in a hurry
noun	addition	*er antwortet die Frage (er antwortet)	he answers the question
noun, morph	misselection	*die Computers (die Computer)	the computers
noun, agree	misselection	*dort ist der Tisch, es ist rund (..., er ist rund)	there is the table, it is round
noun, case	misselection	*das Haus des Lehrer_ (das Haus des Lehrers)	the house of the teacher
adjective	addition	*er schreibt einen Brief gutes (er schreibt einen Brief)	he writes a letter good
adjective	misselection	*das schönes Haus (das schöne Haus)	the beautiful house
verb	omission	*er __ einen Brief geschrieben (er hat einen Brief geschrieben)	he a letter written
verb	addition	*er ist schreibt einen Brief (er schreibt einen Brief)	he is writes a letter
verb, morph	malformation	*er gehte (er ging)	he goed
verb, agree	misselection	*er gehen (er ging)	he walk
prep	omission	*ich interessiere mich __ Musik (ich interessiere mich für Musik)	I am interested music
prep	addition	*in 1999 werde ich ... (1999 werde ich ...)	in 1999, I will ...
prep	misselection	*ich interessiere mich in Musik (ich interessiere mich für Musik)	I am interested in music

Continued

Table 3.1 Continued

Part of speech	*Surface strategy*	*Example*	*Gloss*
det	omission	*ich habe __ Brief geschrieben (ich habe einen Brief geschrieben)	I have written letter
det	addition	*ich bin nach die Berlin gefahren (ich bin nach Berlin gefahren)	I have gone to the Berlin
det, agree	misselection, agree	*die Haus (das Haus)	the house
det, case	misselection, case	*mit das Haus (mit dem Haus)	with the house

3.4.3.2 *Some problems with error classifications*

Classifications do not exist in a vacuum. They are intrinsically linked to the objects that are being classified and to the (research) goal of the overall project. The strict focus on the project at hand appears to be one possible solution to a practical problem. However, error classifications are generally fraught with the following problems:

Coverage: In an ideal world, all possible errors should be classifiable and not only those that are found in a particular text. However, as indicated earlier, errors can be difficult to anticipate.

Homogeneity: In a homogeneous, more stringent classification, the characteristics that are used for a classification are all of the same generic type (e.g., a classification that is only based on part of speech). This, however, makes it impossible to achieve sufficient coverage of errors and a meaningful description of them, for example, preposition errors can not be classified as agreement errors.

Classification characteristics: Most part of speech classifications are not only language-dependent but clear distinctions of classes such as adverb versus adjective, particle versus adverb or preposition versus conjunction are problematic in many languages.

For the reasons stated above, a more general, theoretical solution to error classification in CALL seems unlikely. Instead, researchers and developers of CALL will need to work with classifications that prove to be workable, robust and effective for their project.

In the realm of NLP in CALL, however, error classifications frequently make use of surface features of the (written) language. They also emphasize morpho-syntactic and lexical phenomena and, most importantly, they are language-specific. Frequently, they are also a reflection of the grammar formalism and thus the ways in which grammatical information is encoded within an NLP system. For instance, the *German Tutor* (Heift & Nicholson, 2001) uses Head-Driven Phrase Structure Grammar (HPSG) (see Pollard & Sag, 1994; Sag et al., 2003) and the error classification is based on the concept of phrase descriptors, which we discuss in the following section.

3.4.4 Phrase descriptors

In the *German Tutor* (Heift & Nicholson, 2001), a phrase descriptor is implemented as a frame structure that models a grammatical phenomenon. Each member of the frame consists of a name followed by a value. For example, subject-verb agreement in number is modeled by the frame [number, *value*] where *value* represents an as yet uninstantiated value for number. If the grammatical phenomenon is present in the student's input, the value is either *correct* or *error* depending on whether the grammatical constraint has been met or not, respectively. If the grammatical constraint is missing, the feature value is *absent*. Consider Example 3.2:

Example 3.2
a) *Er gehen.
b) Er geht.
He is leaving.

The phrase descriptor for subject-verb agreement in number in Example 3.2a is [number, *error*], while that for the sentence in Example 3.2b is [number, *correct*]. For either sentence, the information may be used in a student model that records correct and incorrect usages of grammatical phenomena. A system presented with **Er gehen*, however, will also instruct the learner on the nature of subject-verb agreement in number.

In addition to the grammatical features defined, the grammar uses a type *descriptor* representing the description of the phrase that the parser builds up. This type is set-valued and is initially underspecified in each lexical entry. During parsing, the values of the features of *descriptor* are specified. Ultimately, *descriptor* records whether the sentence is grammatical and what errors were made.

The *German Tutor* takes all incoming phrase descriptors as input and returns learner model updates and potential error feedback at different levels of granularity for each phrase descriptor. Such levels of granularity have been previously applied to an Intelligent Tutoring System for LISP programming (Greer & McCalla, 1989; McCalla & Greer, 1994). In their system SCENT, Greer and McCalla (1989) implemented granularity to "recognize the strategies novice students employ when they solve simple recursive LISP programming problems" (p. 478). In the *German Tutor*, however, granularity is used in establishing the error classification for ultimately framing responses to learners' errors: inexperienced students obtain detailed instruction while experienced students receive higher level reminders and explanations. For instance, consider the ungrammatical sentence in Example 3.3a:

Example 3.3
a) *Der Mann dankt dem Frau.
b) Der Mann dankt der Frau.
The man thanks the woman.

In Example 3.3a, the student has provided the wrong determiner for the indirect object. For the error *dem Frau*, the system generates feedback of increasing abstraction that the instruction system can use when interacting with the student. The level of the learner, either expert, intermediate, or novice according to the current state of the Student Model, determines the particular feedback displayed. The responses, given in Example 3.4a–c correspond to the three learner levels for the error in Example 3.3a, respectively:

Example 3.4
a) There is a mistake with the indirect object.
b) There is a mistake in gender with the indirect object.
c) This is not the correct article for the indirect object. The noun is feminine.

For the expert, the feedback is most general, providing a hint to where in the sentence the error occurred (indirect object). For the intermediate learner, the feedback is more detailed, providing additional information on the type of error (gender). For the beginner, the feedback is the most precise. It not only pinpoints the location and type of the error but also refers to the exact source of the error (feminine noun).

Figure 3.2 displays the partial Granularity Hierarchy for constraints in feature matching. The Granularity Hierarchy is a representation of the instructions given to the student correlated with the grammatical constraints monitored by a phrase descriptor. Each term in a phrase descriptor corresponds to a level in the Granularity Hierarchy. For example, for the indirect object of the sentence **Der Mann dankt dem Frau*, given in Example 3.3a, the grammar and the parser will generate the phrase descriptor [main_clause [vp_indirobj [fem error]]]. The top node of the Hierarchy specifies in which kind of clause the error occurred. The phrase descriptor indicates that a mistake was made in a main-clause. The next level in the Granularity Hierarchy lists possible errors in each clause type. As indicated by the phrase descriptor, the mistake refers to the indirect object. An even finer-grained constraint specification is found in the next lower level of the Granularity Hierarchy. For instance, an indirect object can be incorrectly

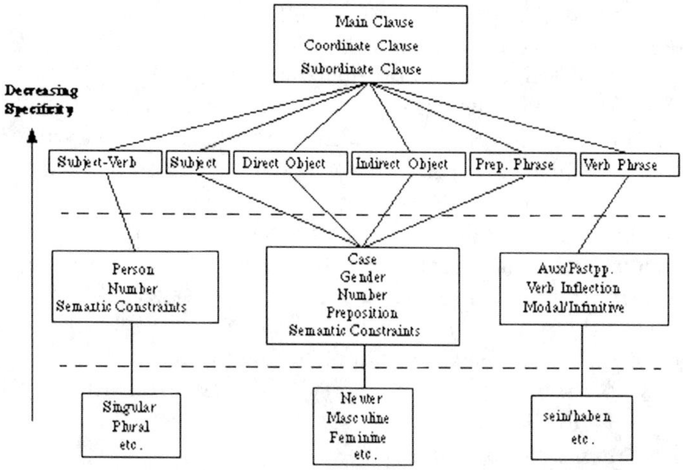

Figure 3.2 Granularity Hierarchy for constraints in German (Heift, 1998b)

inflected for either case, number, or gender. The phrase descriptor specifies that an error in gender occurred, specifically with a feminine noun, which corresponds to the lowest level in the Granularity Hierarchy.

The Granularity Hierarchy is implemented in DATR (Evans, 1992), a language that is designed for pattern-matching and incorporates multiple inheritance. Nodes in DATR are represented by the name of the node followed by paths and their values. For example, the node given in Figure 3.3 corresponds to the phrase descriptor that records the position of a finite verb in a subordinate clause.

The paths in a node definition represent descriptions of grammatical constraints monitored by phrase descriptors. The matching algorithm of DATR selects the longest path that matches left to right. Each path in a node is associated with atoms on the right of '=='. For example, if there has been an error in word order in a subordinate clause, the parse will contain the phrase descriptor [sub_clause [position_subclause [finite error]]]. This will match the path <sub_clause position_subclause finite error> which specifies four atoms for each of three groups (see Figure 3.3). Each group

```
<subclause position_subclause finite error> ==
('possubclfin' '3' 'true'
        'The verb in the subordinate clause is not in the correct position.'
'possubclfin' '2' 'true'
        'The finite verb in the subordinate clause is not in the correct position.'
'possubclfin' '1' 'true'
        'The finite verb in the subordinate clause is not in the correct position.
         It has to be the last element of the sentence.')

<subclause position_subclause finite correct>  == ('possubclfin' '1' 'false'
                                                   'possubclfin' '1' 'false'
                                                   'possubclfin' '1' 'false')

<subclause position_subclause finite absent>  == ('').
```

Figure 3.3 DATR code for a finite verb in a subordinate clause (Heift, 1998b)

represents a learning level. The three learning levels considered are: expert, intermediate and novice.

The first atom in each group specifies the grammar constraint as described by the incoming phrase descriptor. For example, the grammar constraint *possubclfin* represents finite verb position in a subordinate clause. The second atom specifies a value that is decremented or incremented depending on whether a grammatical constraint has been met or not, respectively. The Boolean values, as the third atom, indicate whether it is an increment or decrement: true for increment, false for decrement. Finally, the fourth atom specifies a feedback message. For example, for the path <sub_clause position_subclause finite error> provided earlier, the specificity of each response corresponds to the grammar constraints in the Granularity Hierarchy which frames responses to constraints on verb position, given in Figure 3.4.

The three instructional responses associated with each node correspond to the three learner levels. The feedback for the beginner student reflects the lowest node in the Granularity Hierarchy, while for the intermediate and expert student the message will refer to nodes higher in the hierarchy. In a typical student-teacher interaction, as the student becomes more proficient in the use of a grammatical construction, error feedback becomes less specific.

If there has been no error in the student's input, the phrase descriptor is [sub_clause [position_subclause [finite correct]]] and no message is associated with the name of the grammar constraint. However, the first three atoms, that is, the grammar constraint, the decrement, and the Boolean

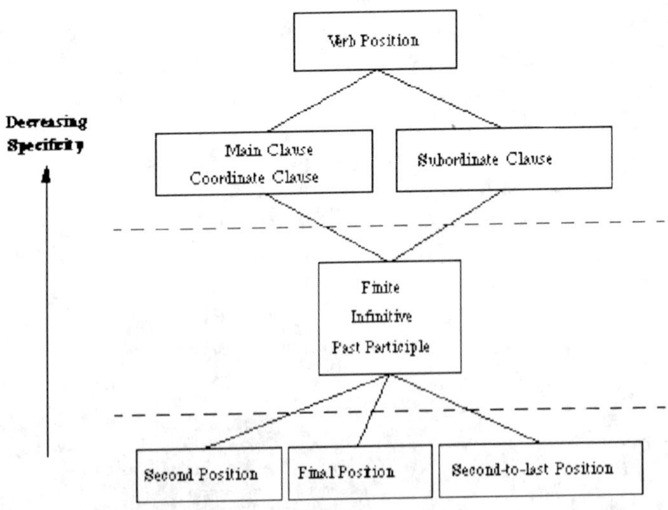

Figure 3.4 Granularity hierarchy for constraints in linear precedence (Heift, 1998b)

value are still specified, as shown in Figure 3.3. They contribute to a Student Model update to record the success.

Finally, if the phrase descriptor is [sub_clause [position_subclause [finite absent]]], then the grammatical phenomenon was not present in the student input. As a result, the phrase descriptor is ignored by the system, indicated by an empty list in Figure 3.3.

The final output is a list of possible instructional responses from a coarse to fine grain size for each incoming phrase descriptor. The more expert the student with a particular grammatical construction, the more general the feedback.

3.5 EMPIRICAL STUDIES

The error classifications described in the previous sections all aim at errors that can be detected by a morpho-syntactic parser. Errors of a semantic or pragmatic nature are not considered. Is it then at all useful to employ this technology in a language learning context?

In addition to the study by Juozulynas (1994) described in section 2.3.1,[16] Sanders (1991), using the same corpus of student essays, discusses their computational error analysis and reports a number of challenging cases generally found with definite-clause grammar parsers. She concludes that parsers are useful in error analysis but more empirical work on texts written by language learners is required to determine how exactly parsers for such grammar checkers need to function. Furthermore, Rogers (1982) reports on an error analysis that concentrated on the positioning of the finite verb in German in main and sub-clauses. Her analysis included errors by beginner and advanced learners. She concludes:

> The mother tongue [English] has been rejected as a major influence in the production of these errors. The errors [made by both beginners and advanced learners alike] appear to stem largely from attempts to operate within the rule system of German. The failure to operate the rule system correctly in all cases cannot be trivialized as carelessness, but can be traced not only to complexity and in some cases the variability of rules (verb-second with dual status adverb/conjunctions), but also to a too powerful use of grammatical rules in the face of perceptual constraints (verb-final "artichoke" errors). (p. 77)

A study by von Wittich (1967) is typical for many other studies in Error Analysis. She analyzed errors made by students in the Pimsleur German Writing Proficiency Test. After her mainly quantitative analysis of surface structures, von Wittich (1967) concludes that "the degree of error may be indicative of the learner's stage on the interlanguage ... continuum" (p.

316). However, from the previous discussion we can conclude that it is often difficult to distinguish errors from non-errors (Shaughnessy, 1979; Lennon, 1991). How much more difficult is it then to even differentiate degrees of errors? Such distinctions are often highly subjective and depend on the circumstances of an individual study.

Many studies show that a high number of errors by language learners are of a morpho-syntactic nature and can be analyzed by a parser. On the other hand, a number of errors will not be found and, therefore, no feedback can be provided. However, Ellis (1994) shows that even in regular classroom situations not all errors are dealt with:

> The main conclusions are that certain types of errors are much more likely to be treated than others: discourse, content and lexical errors receive more attention than phonological or grammatical errors; that many errors are not treated at all; that the more often a particular type of error is made, the less likely the teacher is to treat it; and that there is considerable variation among teachers regarding how frequently error treatment takes place. Edmondson (1985) has also pointed out that teachers sometimes correct 'errors' that have not in fact been made. (p. 585)

Assuming that language learning in the classroom is, nevertheless, effective, we can hypothesize that it will be useful and sufficient to treat selected errors that occur in learner output (e.g., selected morpho-syntactic errors). It is important, however, to inform learners about possible limitations of a parser-based system. Learners should not assume that a document that has been analyzed by a parser will be 100% error-free. However, the same applies to any computer-aided tool used in the classroom such as, for example, a spell checker.

A number of parser-based CALL projects have included a significant element of error analysis. For example, Liou (1991) designed a grammar checker for Chinese learners of English by compiling a small corpus of 1,000 compositions with 200 words each from engineering students. Liou identified 1,659 errors which he grouped under 93 subtypes. The study informs the design of an ATN-parser (see section 2.4.1). Other projects started with a collection of learner data for constructing a grammar, for example, test papers written by Japanese learners of English (Brocklebank, 1998) (see also Heidorn et al., 1982; Jensen et al., 1984).

It is, however, still rare that parsers that are part of a CALL program are subjected to a thorough evaluation of learner data. Moreover, it is just as atypical that the design of a parser-based CALL system is built on a large-scale, theoretically founded error analysis or, even better, on an interlanguage analysis. This investigation, however, can determine the nature of learner errors, provide a test bed for an error classification and inform the design of the parser technology of the language learning environment. But what exactly is the link of corpus linguistics, language learning, and parser-based CALL?

3.6 LEARNER CORPUS STUDIES AND CALL

3.6.1 Corpus Linguistics

Corpus Linguistics has become a large and varied field of scientific investigation. Charles C. Fries is usually credited as the first modern corpus linguist. His 1952 article and many other seminal papers in Corpus Linguistics have been republished (Sampson & McCarthy, 2004). The volume by Sampson and McCarthy (2004) contains 43 chapters and provides a good overview of the scope of the discipline[17] as well as its development over time. Chapters on the use of corpora in the evaluation and development of NLP resources can also be found in this book. In the following, we can only provide a short, sketchy introduction that focuses on the intersection of corpus linguistics, NLP, and CALL.

Electronic corpora are large principled collections of text which are often annotated for specific purposes. The annotations provide additional information such as author and text type, but also part of speech tags as well as syntactic bracketing and analysis. Some corpora are also annotated for semantic or discourse phenomena. Additionally, a distinction between corpus-based linguistics and corpus-driven linguistics is frequently drawn. Sinclair (2004a), for instance, argues that the annotation of corpora by linguists is based on a pre-corpus understanding of language and subject to human error. This is what he labels corpus-based research. Sinclair's corpus-driven approach attempts to avoid preconceived theoretical notions and yields very detailed study results. They are, however, difficult to generalize and to apply to NLP-oriented research and development unless there is some guarantee that presuppositions about a phenomenon currently under investigation are excluded from the corpus analysis.

Electronic corpora have become a widely used research tool not just in Corpus Linguistics, but also in many other linguistic disciplines. For example, researchers in descriptive and formal linguistics (e.g., Biber, Conrad, & Reppen, 1998; Nerbonne, 1998), lexicography (e.g., Baker, Francis, Sinclair, & Tognini-Bonelli, 1993) and translation studies (e.g., Olohan, 2003) use large corpora to study examples of language use. Large electronic corpora have become more widely available in recent years. Meyer, Grabowski, Han, Mantzouranis, and Moses (2003) even see the World Wide Web as a corpus and therefore a research tool for linguists.

3.6.2 Corpus studies and language learning

In SLA research, large annotated collections of texts produced by learners of various backgrounds, proficiency levels and native languages are employed to study selected phenomena of interlanguage. Leech (1997) maintains that it was not until 1992 "that there was an item in the ICAME conference program referring to the use of corpora in language teaching" (p. 1). He further concludes that corpora had played a role in data-driven language learning (Johns, 1991a, 1991b, 1994, 1997) and were a good example of discovery learning. Corpora in language learning have existed at least since the mid-seventies, but there was no substantial link to research in language learning at that time. Sinclair (2004b, p. 1), in his introductory chapter, laments the gap between linguistics and language teaching and argues that corpora can bridge this gap if they play an important role in language learning.

> The convergence mentioned in ...[the] title *[Teaching and Language Corpora: A Convergence]* is a natural coming together of teaching with research from various points of view. This is natural whether we consider it from the 'trickle down' point of view, where the resources and techniques used in research progressively become available for teaching, or from the John's 'trickle up' point of view, where the development of language teaching techniques naturally appropriates to itself the resources available for research and becomes a topic for research in its own right. (Leech, 1997, p. 4)

Leech (1997) distinguishes three distinct areas of corpus use related to teaching:

1. Direct use of corpora in teaching:

- Teaching about corpora, that is, the teaching of corpus linguistics as a branch of linguistics or a method of analysis;
- Teaching to exploit, that is, teaching students how to use corpora for their own language learning;
- Exploiting to teach, that is, the use of corpora in otherwise non-computational language or linguistics classes;

2. Use of corpora indirectly applied to teaching:

- Reference publishing, for example, corpora as the 'data mine' for a new dictionary;
- Language learning materials development, that is, making use of available information from corpus-based research such as already existing frequency lists;[19]

- Language testing, that is, using the corpus for the preparation of testing items;

3. Further teaching-oriented corpus development:

- LSP [language for specific purposes] corpora, that is, the use of corpora to document a particular genre, for example, that of law or medicine and the subsequent use of such materials as teaching aids;
- L1 and L2 developmental corpora, that is, the principled collection of texts produced by language learners for research purposes;
- Bilingual / multilingual corpora[20], that is, the exploitation of parallel (and aligned) and comparable corpora with texts from different languages in language teaching. (p. 16)

In addition to the uses of electronic corpora that are more or less directly linked to the teaching and learning of a foreign language, some studies of learner corpora contain texts produced by second language learners. They are situated within SLA research (e.g., Belz, 2004) and are generally not intended for the development of teaching materials.

3.6.3 Corpora in CALL

The CALL literature reflects discussions and experiments with corpora in language learning (e.g., Johns, King, & University of Birmingham. Centre for English Language Studies, 1991). Corpora are employed for language teaching in many different ways:

- to gain a better understanding of grammar in general, and of a learner in particular (Biber et al., 1998);
- to prepare learner dictionaries (Gillard & Gadsby, 1998);
- to compile textbook materials (Kaszubski, 1998);
- to develop a computer-based learning environment (Milton, 1998); and
- to enhance foreign-language classroom instruction (Granger & Tribble, 1998).

More recently, researchers have begun to question the straightforward applicability of any (foreign-language) corpus in language learning and teaching. For instance, Braun (2005) states that "the successful use of corpora for learning and teaching hinges to a great extent on a successful 'pedagogic mediation' between the corpus materials and the corpus users" (p. 61). According to Braun, learner support and reconstruction of discourses from which the corpus texts are taken are reasons for mediation. Moreover, coherent, relevant content, restricted size, multimedia format and pedagogic annotation are the necessary methods of mediation. After their study, Gaskell and Cobb (2004) conclude that "learners are willing to use concordances to work on grammar, that they are able to make corrections based on concordances" (p. 317). All of these approaches require further processing of corpus texts before they are genuinely useful in a communicative language learning context. Some of this processing can potentially be supported by NLP tools.

It is not just in the realm of language learning that corpora are being used by students. For instance, Borin and Dahllöf (1999) describe work in progress on a corpus-based tutoring system which teaches grammar and grammatical analysis for students of linguistics.

3.6.4 Corpora and NLP in CALL

Generally, there are three different ways of employing corpora in NLP and CALL:

First, the use of corpora to evaluate NLP tools in CALL is relatively common. However, the amount of linguistic data used often does not approximate the size of modern electronic corpora. They usually consist of small collections of sentences or samples of student essays. Examples of parser-based projects that have utilized electronic collections of sentences or texts produced by learners are given in section 2.5.2.3.

Second, corpora are employed in the design of NLP tools. To some extent, this has been implemented by Granger and her team, who examined authentic errors from second language texts. The annotated FRIDA (French Interlanguage Database) corpus was analyzed to extract detailed error statistics and to carry out concordance-based analyses of specific error types (Granger, 2003). The results were then used to improve the error diagnosis system integrated in the *Freetext* CALL program (L'Haire & Vandeventer Faltin, 2003). However, according to Dagneaux, Denness and Granger (1998) they also performed an analysis of learner errors to advance research in computer-aided error analysis (CEA). The authors hope that CEA

> will give new impetus to Error Analysis research and re-establish it as an important area of study. The data used to demonstrate the technique consist of a 150,000-word corpus of English written by French-speaking learners of intermediate and advanced level. After the initial native speaker correction, the corpus is annotated for errors using a comprehensive error classification. This stage is a computer-aided process supported by an 'error editor'. The error-tagged corpus can then be analyzed using standard text retrieval software tools and lists of all the different types of errors and error counts can be obtained in a matter of seconds. (p. 163)

While other projects have used similar information on learner errors, they are usually extracted from significantly smaller samples of learner text.

There are also applications in machine translation that employ parsing and other text analysis techniques that are solely based on the analysis of large (parallel) corpora. However, we are not aware of any NLP software in CALL that uses such an approach although Briscoe and Carroll (2004 [1995]) have shown that the analysis of a parallel corpus can be applied to more general NLP projects. In their introduction to the reprint of this article, Sampson and McCarthy (2004) write:

> When computational linguists began to exploit theoretical linguistics for natural language processing purposes by building formal generative grammars into automatic parsing systems, they tested these on artificial invented example sentences. For some years, in conformity with the generative tradition, these researchers showed little interest in exposing their systems to real-life data. This was perhaps sensible as an early research strategy. New technologies need to be allowed an easy ride initially, if they are to have a chance of developing into robust contenders rather than falling at the first hurdle. That is not a strategy that would have been acceptable indefinitely, though and in due course a more realistic approach emerged. (p. 267)

Probably, this statement still holds true for NLP-based research in CALL. The general lack of intelligent employment of large (learner) corpora in parser-based CALL indicates that researchers in ICALL can still benefit significantly from current advances in corpus studies. This, however, assumes that such new evidence and new approaches to natural language will provide a significant impetus for further developments in NLP in CALL.

The third and last approach to using corpora in ICALL is probably the most straightforward. A number of projects have successfully combined NLP tools and corpora and applied them to CALL environments. The Glosser project (Dokter & Nerbonne, 1998; Dokter et al., 1998; Nerbonne, Dokter et al., 1998; Roosmaa & Prószéky, 1998; Nerbonne et al., 2001) as well as the Irakazi project (Aldabe & Maritxalar, 2005), for instance, combine tools for morphological analysis (lemmatizer, morphological analyzer) with the opportunity for the language learner and/or teacher to consult a relevant corpus. This combination enables the user to select an inflected form to look up instances of different inflected forms of the same word as they appear in the corpus and potentially even other words of the same word family.

4. Feedback

4.1 INTRODUCTION

Once errors have been detected and classified, the ground is prepared for learner feedback. Issues regarding the role and contribution of corrective feedback for language learning have been central to CALL and SLA theory and pedagogy. Feedback is often understood as a technical term:

> **feedback** — a principle used in self-regulating control systems. Information about what is happening in a system (such as level of temperature, engine speed or size of a workpiece) is fed back to a controlling device, which compares it with what should be happening. If the two are different, the device takes suitable action (such as switching on a heater, allowing more steam to the engine, or resetting the tools). (Upshall, 1993, p. 337)

This understanding of feedback is usually associated with the notion of a servo system:

> **servo system** — an automatic control system used in aircraft, motor cars and other complex machines. A specific input, such as moving a lever or joystick, causes a specific output, such as feeding current to an electric motor that moves, for example, the rudder of the aircraft. At the same time the position of the rudder is detected and fed back to the central control, so that small adjustments can continually be made to maintain the desired course. (Upshall, 1993, p. 829)

The term feedback, however, is also commonly used in psychology and pedagogy in a surprisingly similar way. Annett (1969, p. 26), in his book *Feedback and Human Behaviour*, claims that the concept of feedback can be used to analyze behavior and usually occurs in the form of *knowledge of results*. He further distinguishes between intrinsic and extrinsic feedback. Intrinsic feedback is inherent to the task while for extrinsic feedback, an additional feedback loop is added. For example, this might include additional information on the standard of performance or information on results that is available after a task has been completed (Annett, 1969, p. 27). The efficiency of such feedback, even in written form, has been confirmed in a number of studies (for an overview see Kulhavy, 1977).

The complex nature of feedback in language learning necessitates a multifacetted approach to its description, design and implementation. Given that we are interested in the provision of feedback in a language learning situation and, more specifically, in the learning of a foreign language grammar within a parser-based CALL application, this part discusses the concept of feedback from five general points of view: human-computer interaction, learning theories, second language acquisition theories, formal grammar and CALL.

Before we begin with the discussion of the concept of feedback, however, a first attempt is made to sketch a feedback loop for computer-assisted grammar acquisition and learning (Figure 4.1). Grammar is used here in a wider sense, going beyond morphology and syntax. However, as in our previous discussion of error analysis and description in part 3, the feedback discussion presented here concentrates on form aspects of student input, simply because this is what parser-based CALL systems generally do.

As illustrated in Figure 4.1, the learner submits textual input to the computer. The input is constructed on the basis of the grammatical structures available to the learner. The parser compares the structures provided by the user with the structures defined in the system's computational grammar and generates feedback that is based on the results of this comparison. Learners then have the option to confirm their structures or revise the submitted input according to the feedback given. It is at this point that the feedback loop for a (human) learner differs from a similar feedback loop

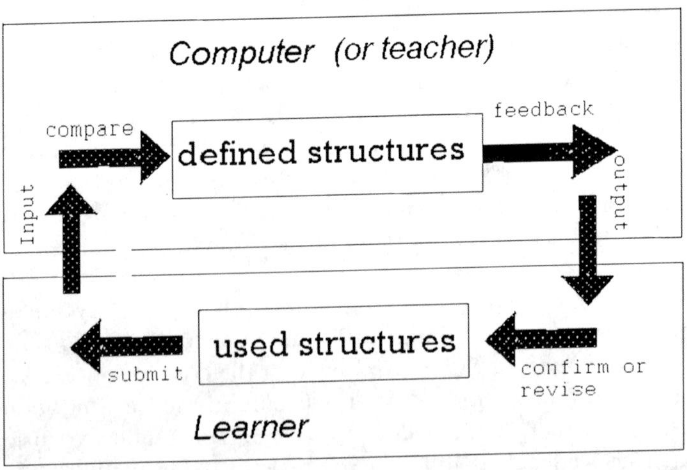

Figure 4.1 Feedback loop on text well-formedness

for a technical device: a machine has no choice but to revise the subsequent input based on the feedback information.

The following section considers feedback from the point of view of Human-Computer Interaction.

4.2 FEEDBACK IN HUMAN-COMPUTER INTERACTION

Human-Computer Interaction (HCI) as an area of research deals with questions of interface and dialogue design. It is solely the latter that will concern us here. The two main questions for this section are:

1. What are the characteristics of human-*computer* interaction by comparison to human-*human* interaction?
2. Which findings of HCI research are applicable to the provision of feedback by parser-based software for foreign-language learners?

Let us begin with the first question.

If learners are given full control over their linguistic input by relying on parsing technology, what are the terms that define the communicative interaction between the computer (program) and the learner? Naturally, the differences between humans and machines must be taken into consideration in order to understand the interaction of learners with CALL programs. The list below is based on Schmitz (1992, p. 209):

- Machines are compiled out of individual parts for a very specific purpose whereas humans are holistic entities whose parts can not be differentiated.
- Humans process all sorts of experiences and, repeatedly and interactively, create their own environment, something machines cannot do. Machines *calculate* a problem on the basis of pre-wired rules.
- The main feature of human thoughts is their inherent contradictions and the ability to cope with them, something that is not computable due to its complexity, variety and degree of detail.

Schmitz (1992) bases this distinction on a philosophical argument:

> Our world of thoughts is split into two realms: here the abstract example, there the deficient reality, here the perfect plan, there the resistance against its realization, here the universal rules, there the numerous exceptions, here the manageable model, there the real chaos, here the 'pure' ideal, there the 'dirty' reality. ... And here the technically masterable and there the rebellious everyday life. This approach was thoroughly rejected by Ludwig Wittgenstein. He radically threw the thinking in ideas, abstractions and identities over board ... and showed

> in the same line of argument that rules do not exist independently of their application and that we change them by using them. Outside of their application we do not have any control over them. ... Because they [the computers] are instruments, language can only be used in an instrumental way with them. Tools incarnate abstract technical knowledge; language-enabled computers are abstract incarnations of human knowledge about rules. The computer is awaiting its application without being able to significantly change within this application. (p. 62)[1]

Schmitz, by no means, attempts to diminish the capabilities of computers. He claims that computers can theoretically carry out all operations but never actions because they do not recognize aims, purpose and position of the action. Obermeier (1985) provides a counter-argument and distinguishes "proponents of *weak* AI (i.e., people who consider the program as a useful tool only) and *strong* AI (i.e., people who believe that a program is a mind)" (p. 154). He argues for *strong* AI whereas most projects in NLP in CALL were probably aimed at *weak* AI.

For our purposes, the theoretical description of human-computer interaction, the differences between humans and machines can be legitimately reduced to the distinction between actions and operations, as is done in Activity Theory.

Activity Theory is an approach to psychology that originated in the former Soviet Union and later influenced thinking about human behavior in many Western countries. This theory was originally an attempt to overcome some of the perceived weaknesses of behaviorist psychological theory without having to revert back to introspection.

> When we do speak of activity, we do not intend it as a synonym of 'behavior' as, for instance, the behaviorists understand it. For the behaviorist, man is, in effect, an automaton, albeit a very complex one. Like any automaton, he 'switches on' when external forces somehow exert an influence on him, by pressing a button, inserting a coin, or intercepting a ray leading to a photoelectric cell. As soon as such influence is exerted, man starts to 'behave', to act in some way and to react. (Leontiev, 1981, p. 12)

The proponents of Activity Theory, for example, Leontiev and Vygotsky, view humans as social beings whose psyche is developed in activity, that is, mainly in social interaction and in actions within an environment. The main categories used are *activity*, *action*, and *operation*. They argue that an activity has a motive, an action is linked to an aim and an operation is triggered by a condition (Leontiev, 1981, pp. 17–18).

Accordingly, communicative activities can be divided into actions and actions can be sub-divided into operations. Operations are usually learnt as actions. The concepts are best illustrated with an example: switching gears when driving a car. Gear-switching is learnt as an action. The learner-driver is asked by the driving instructor to change gear and this becomes the goal of the learner. However, once the learner-driver has performed this action a sufficient number of times, this action becomes increasingly automated. A proficient driver might have the goal to accelerate the car which will necessitate switching into higher gear, but this is now triggered by a condition (the difference between engine speed and speed of the car).

It can thus be argued that humans learn to perform complex actions by learning to perform certain operations in a certain order. Machines, on the other hand, are only made to perform certain (sometimes rather complex) operations. Sequences of such operations can be performed by sophisticated machines like computers in rapid succession or with powerful computers even in parallel, but each and every one of them is initialized by a condition (e.g., a mouse-click, keyboard input). They are also not subordinated to an intention and, as a result, they cannot be described as actions (Schmitz, 1992, p. 169).

Activity Theory has some bearing on our understanding of the human-computer interaction that takes place when a learner uses language learning software. For instance, word-processing software that contains a spell checker does not have the intention to proof-read the learner's document. Instead, the computer simply responds to a selection of the spell checker menu and performs an operation, that is, comparing the strings in the document against the entries in a machine dictionary. The result of the comparison triggers the next operation: if an identical string has been found in the dictionary, the next string from the document is being compared; if an identical string could not be found in the dictionary, similar strings are then selected from the dictionary according to an established algorithm. The list of spelling suggestions will then be displayed to the user. For the computer user, in our case the language learner, it might look like the computer is proof-reading the document as long as the computer does not flag a correctly spelled word as incorrect and/or provide absurd spelling alternatives for a simple spelling error.

Let us compare this interaction with an interaction between two people. Person X interacts with Person Y in that s/he observes Person Y's action, reasons about the likely intention for that action and reacts according to this assumed intention. Learners tend to transfer this approach to the interaction with a computer in a language learning situation, that is, they interpret the sequence of operations performed by the computer as an action, reason about the 'intention' of the computer and react accordingly. For this reason, learners get just as frustrated with a computer as with a human tutor when the system rejects an answer they believe to be right.

The ideal CALL system will avoid such pitfalls and not reject a correct response or overlook an incorrect one. However, any existing system can only approximate this ideal. Hence, researchers and developers in parser-based CALL aim to build systems that can perform complexly structured sequences of (linguistic) operations. This allows learners to interact with the computer in a meaningful and successful manner.

This conclusion takes us to the second question posed above: Which findings of HCI research are applicable to the provision of feedback, for example, by a grammar checker for foreign-language learners?

To reiterate, the main focus here is on the dialogue aspect of HCI. Accordingly, O'Shea and Self (1983) emphasize the importance of implementing a *dialogue system* in any Intelligent Tutoring System (ITS). Similarly, Sutcliffe (1995, pp. 165–166) discusses principles of dialogue design from the perspective of HCI. As the first criterion of dialogue design he uses the term *feedback* by which he refers to the information continuously provided to the computer user according to the criteria shown in Table 4.1.

These principles enable the user to exercise control over the program and not be controlled by the machine, in the sense of being restricted in performing all possible actions at any given point in time (e.g., the ability to close the program at any time, to call up help at any time, etc.).

In addition to determining the kind of information that needs to be provided, the question remains how this information should be shared with the user. With regard to error messages in general, Shneiderman (1992, p. 305) outlines the following principles:

- specificity
- constructive guidance and positive tone
- user-centered phrasing
- appropriate physical format

With respect to user-centered phrasing, Shneiderman (1992, pp. 312–313) argues against the use of anthropomorphic instructions because the pretence that the computer is a human cannot be sustained for a long

Table 4.1 Feedback criteria in HCI (Sutcliffe, 1995, pp. 165–166)

Status	Tell the users what part of the system they are in.
Escape	Allow them to terminate an operation at any time, permit them to leave this part of the program or the program altogether.
Minimal work	A minimal number of dialogue steps should be needed to communicate user decisions to the program.
Default	Predictable answers should be displayed prominently and 'reached' easily.
Help	Provide on-line contextualized help on how to operate the program and/or particular tools within it.
Undo	Always allow the user to recover a previous state.
Consistency	Allow the user to perform identical actions in an identical way through consistent commands, object labels and procedures.

period of time. Generally, this approach is also not appreciated, at least by adult computer users. Moreover, the principles and guidelines that have been established for a more general human-computer interaction certainly also apply to a foreign language learning situation. Sutcliffe (1995, p. 256), when discussing features of intelligent help systems, outlines the following components: dialogue manager, user model, diagnostic module (lexical, syntactic, semantic) and a remediation-repair planner. Note, that this catalogue of desiderata is very similar to that for an intelligent tutoring system. For instance, in an ideal system, users will be able to pose questions in everyday prose and the machine will engage in a natural language dialogue with them (dialogue manager). The system will be familiar with user preferences, background knowledge, etc. (user model). The program will also know about the source and nature of an error or user problem (diagnostic system) as well as the algorithms to remedy errors and to address user problems (remediation-repair planner).

HCI research also provides some guidance concerning the timing of feedback: only one problem at a time should be presented to the user. "Novices to tasks ... prefer to work at slower speeds than knowledgeable frequent users" (Shneiderman, 1992, p. 283). Short response times are quick and enjoyable, longer response times motivate the users to exercise more care and make fewer errors. Shneiderman (1992) reports from an experiment:

> Overall, subjects working at the shorter response time completed their lessons more quickly and had a favorable attitude toward the system. There were clear indications that subjects tried to work more carefully and made fewer errors with the longer response time. (p. 290)

Kulik and Kulik (1988) conclude from their investigation of several studies that delayed feedback only seems to be effective in a few experimental settings and that error feedback needs to be immediate to be effective.

Our view of feedback so far has focused on our understanding of how the use of computers impacts on the process. In the next section, we will focus specifically on feedback in a learning context.

4.3 FEEDBACK AND LEARNING

4.3.1 Reinforcement and feedback

Behaviorist psychology provides the starting point of this excursion into learning psychology for two reasons: First, behaviorist psychologists imposed strict rules on their experiments. They concentrated on observable stimuli and responses and avoided any speculation about unobservable processes. These observations were very often recorded using quantitative measures. Second, the concept of *reinforcement* is frequently used in behaviorist learning psychology and appears to be related to the concept of feedback under investigation here. The assumption is that feedback of a certain kind can act as a reinforcer.

Much of the research in learning psychology has been based on experiments with animals. Is reinforcement indeed a factor that has to be taken into consideration when discussing human behavior? Lieberman (1990) argues in that context that "when reinforcement is used in accordance with all these principles, it can be substantially more powerful than our everyday experience might suggest" (p. 208). The principles he refers to are as follows:

First, the kind of reinforcer used is important. The Premack principle states that the strength of a reinforcer can be determined by observing the amount of time subjects dedicate to the reinforcer if it is freely available. Under these conditions, secondary reinforcers, that is, reinforcers that satisfy no immediate basic need (e.g., money, grades), can be as powerful as primary ones (e.g., social recognition, group status) if they are paired with a primary reinforcer.

Second, reinforcement should not be used after each response, but only intermittently and, in a fashion, that is not transparent to the learner:

> To generate a high rate of responding, which will persist even if reinforcement is not available for some period, partial reinforcement schedules are preferable to continuous reinforcement — especially variable ration and interval schedules, in which the reinforced response cannot easily be predicted. (Lieberman, 1990, p. 207)

Third, the quality of responding to a reinforcer depends on the motivation which in turn depends on the incentive value of the reinforcer.

> The Yerkes-Dodson law says that the optimum level of motivation for learning depends on the difficulty of the task. For simple tasks, high motivation is helpful; on more difficult tasks, strong motivation can narrow attention in a way that interferes with learning. (Lieberman, 1990, p. 207)

Fourth, in order to achieve a response in a wide variety of situational settings, it has to be reinforced in a variety of settings. "When a response is difficult to learn, it may be possible to shape it by first reinforcing a simpler response and only gradually requiring closer approximations to the target behavior" (Lieberman, 1990, p. 208).

In the following, a brief, historical excursion into learning theory and relevant aspects of reinforcement will be pursued in order to answer questions about the practicalities of corrective learner feedback. The link between feedback and reinforcement will be clarified in the course of this excursion.

Learning theory can be said to have originated with Thorndike (Hergenhahn & Olson, 1997, p. 72). Prior to his studies, systematic, experimental treatment of learning was simply not documented. However, an early learning theorist frequently associated with developments in CALL is Skinner.

> Skinner's position was similar to Thorndike's position after 1930 in that it emphasized the effects of a response on the response itself. Moreover, like Thorndike, Skinner concluded that the effects of reinforcement and punishment are not symmetrical; that is, reinforcement changes the probability of a response's recurring, but punishment does not. ... His work led to the development of programmed learning and teaching machines. (Hergenhahn & Olson, 1997, p. 78)

> Skinner, like Thorndike, was very interested in applying his theory of learning to the process of education. To Skinner, learning proceeds most effectively, if (1) the information to be learned is presented in small steps, (2) the learners are given rapid feedback concerning the accuracy of their learning (i.e., they are shown immediately after a learning experience whether they have learned the information correctly or incorrectly) and (3) the learners are able to learn at their own pace. (Hergenhahn & Olson, 1997, p. 105)

Skinner rejected the necessity of developing elaborated psychological theories like the one put forward by Hull (1943). Hull (1943) was the first to attempt to define reinforcement and related concepts in a precise manner. He developed his theory as a logical structure of postulates and theorems and, according to him, primary reinforcement must involve need satisfaction or drive reduction. He then defines a secondary reinforcer as "a stimulus which has been closely and consistently associated with the diminution of need" (quoted in Hergenhahn & Olson, 1997, p. 126). In keeping with Hull, Hergenhahn and Olson (1997) conclude that a reinforced stimulus-response connection strengthens the formation of a response habit. Hull (1943) developed a formula that captured the likelihood of a learned response being made. He termed this likelihood *(effective) reaction potential* (for a detailed discussion see Hergenhahn & Olson, 1997, p. 128):

$$ {}_R\overline{E}_S = {}_S H_R \times D \times K - (I_R + {}_S I_R) $$

Equation 2: Effective reaction potential (Hull, 1943)

The effective reaction potential (E) is a function of *habit strength* (H) (the strength of the association between stimulus (S) and response (R), drive (D) and the incentive motivation (K), the subjectively perceived *size* of the reinforcer. It is reduced by the influence of *reactive inhibition* (I_R), caused by fatigue which originates in responding, and by *conditioned inhibition* (${}_{S}I_{R}$), which is the learned response of not responding.

For most behaviorists, reinforcement is a necessary condition for learning (1997, p. 450). In contrast, most cognitive theorists believe that learning is independent of reinforcement. Reinforcement can at most facilitate the transformation of learnt actions into behavior. In any case, when designing a language learning tool, findings of the branch of behaviorist learning psychology cannot be ignored for practical reasons.

Shneiderman (1992), for example, showed in an experiment that certain kinds of reinforcement play a pivotal role in successful learning with the computer:

> ... positive reinforcement with value-judgment phrases (excellent ...) did not improve performance or satisfaction in an arithmetic drill and practice lesson. On the other hand, the presence of a simple numerical counter (6 correct, 2 incorrect) improved learning. (p. 134)

While we might speculate whether this predisposition towards numerical scores is peculiar to students that perform well in mathematical tasks, the experiment, nevertheless, suggests that different reinforcers are needed for different people in the context of different tasks.

The foregoing discussion, along with the many successful experiments cited in the literature on reinforcement, indicate that feedback can act as a powerful reinforcer. Verbal praise, scores and so forth not only confirm or disconfirm the correctness of grammatical structures but they also reinforce, at least potentially, certain behavioral patterns. Even if one claims that reinforcement has no influence on language learning, it is still an important factor to consider when designing a computer program or tool. Reinforcement can certainly influence the behavior towards the system and thus indirectly affect the learning experience.

On the other hand, there are inherent problems with reinforcement that need to be considered and, if possible, avoided when it comes to corrective feedback. Reinforcement should not be bribery because, in that case, the desired response will not be achieved in the absence of a reinforcer. The mildest reinforcer possible needs to be used. According to Lieberman (1990), "if reinforcement is seen as a means of control for the benefit of the controller, then it is less likely to be effective" (p. 275). This is certainly one of the differences between humans and animals when reacting to reinforcers. Humans can act adversely when praised for responding exactly the way the subject in charge of the reinforcer expected. This adverse reaction is most likely to be much stronger in a CALL situation given that the incentives and the reinforcement are controlled by a machine.

The term *bribery* does not only refer to the use of excessive material reinforcers (e.g., large sums of money), but also to the inflationary use of praise words such as *excellent* and *brilliant*. If these are given as the only feedback to all correct answers, as is the case with a number of CALL applications, then they become meaningless at first and a laughing matter and even counter-productive later.

Similar caution is necessary when attempting to weaken an unwanted response, for example, the application of an inappropriate grammatical rule. Negative reinforcement, that is, punishment, has been widely discussed in behaviorist literature. Thorndike (1913), for example, concluded in his revised 'Law of Effect' that "reinforcement increases the strength of the connection, whereas punishment does nothing to the strength of the connection" (Hergenhahn & Olson, 1997, p. 68). However, others argue that

> early research suggested that punishment had only a temporary effect on behavior, but more recently research has reversed this conclusion. When punishment is immediate, firm, accompanied by a clear (and fair) explanation and when it occurs in a variety of settings, it can be a very powerful tool for eliminating undesirable behavior." (Lieberman, 1990, p. 243)

However, the dangers are great. Punishment, already in its mildest form (e.g., negative comments), can result in harmful side effects, fear and/or anxiety, which then inhibits attention and a tendency towards increased aggression (here the punishing subject is used as a model). No computer operation should be performed that may be perceived as punishment by the learner due to the potential side effects of negative reinforcement and its relatively unpredictable and low success rate. At first, this might be self-evident. However, a number of (language) learning packages offer feedback such as *Wrong!*, *Incorrect!*, *False!*, or simply *No!*. If we accept that these short phrases can be perceived as mild social punishment, then it becomes clear that careful consideration must be given to the formulation of feedback messages on linguistic errors.

4.3.2 Cognitive perspectives

Shortly after the advent of cybernetics,[2] a branch of psychology that draws on comparisons between machines (mainly computers) and humans was founded. This branch is commonly labeled *information-processing psychology*. Feedback here is similarly defined as in servomechanisms: it forms a loop between the input and output of an action and the output serves as information on the adequacy of the input. Norman (1988), as quoted in Hergenhahn and Olsen (1997) and a representative of this approach, defined three laws of learning:

The Law of Causal Relationship: For an organism to learn the relationship between a specific action and an outcome, there must be an apparent causal relationship between them. This is the law of causal relationship.

The Law of Causal Learning: The law of causal learning has two parts: First, for desirable outcomes, the organism attempts to repeat those particular actions that have an apparent causal relationship to the desired outcome. Second, for undesirable outcomes, the organism attempts to avoid those actions that have an apparent causal relation to the undesirable outcome.

The Law of Information Feedback: In the law of information feedback, the outcome of an event serves as information about that event. (p. 368)

This information-processing approach to psychology can be subsumed under *cognitive psychology*. Cognitive psychology is a branch of psychology that considers human cognition, that is, processes such as sensory perception, memory, thinking, problem solving, and learning (Stillings et al., 1995, p. 15). Piaget, who is considered a cognitive psychologist, explained learning as given in Figure 4.2 (reproduced from Hergenhahn & Olson, 1997, p. 278).

Here, *assimilation* refers to the cognitive process of responding to the environment on the basis of one's cognitive structures; *accommodation* describes the process during which the cognitive structures are modified in accordance with the environment. The driving force of intellectual growth, caused by accommodation, is *equilibration*, that is, "the innate tendency to create a harmonious relationship between [oneself] and the environment" (Hergenhahn & Olson, 1997, p. 284). Piaget argues that learning takes place when individuals assimilate new information about the environment in their cognitive structures and then bring their modified system of cognitive structures back in line with their perception of the environment.

Tolman is another psychologist in the cognitive tradition who took his lead from the *Gestalt* theorists. Similar to Norman, Tolman (1932) argues

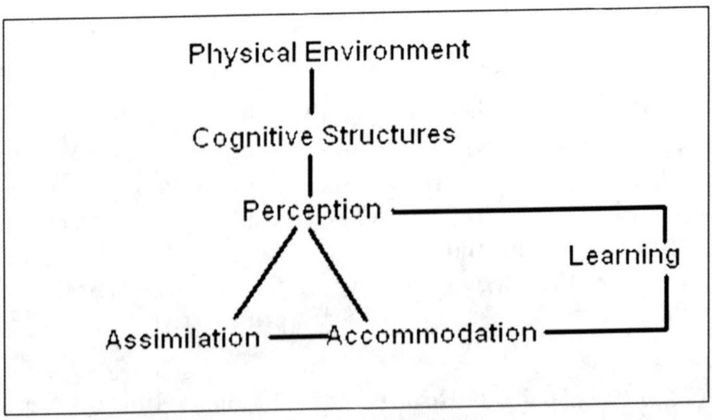

Figure 4.2 Learning (Piaget)

that learning is not the learning of stimulus-response relationships as the behaviorists believe, but the discovery of cause-effect relationships. He rejected the notion of reinforcement as unimportant,

> but there is some similarity between what Tolman called confirmation and what the other behaviorists called reinforcement. During the development of a cognitive map, expectations are utilized by the organisms. ... Early tentative expectations are called *hypotheses* and they are either confirmed by experience or not. Hypotheses that are confirmed are retained and those that are not are abandoned. (Hergenhahn & Olson, 1997, p. 302)

Hergenhahn and Olson (1997) review the use of the concept of reinforcement in cognitive psychology and provide the theoretical approach by Bandura as an example in which

> ... reinforcement has two major functions. First, it creates an expectation in observers (see observational learning) that if they act like a model who has been seen being reinforced for certain activities, they will be reinforced also. Second, it acts as an incentive for translating learning into performance. (p. 334)

These short sketches of cognitive approaches to learning in general, and feedback in particular, indicate that reinforcement remains an important concept in the attempt to explain learning processes although distinct schools of thought might define and/or label reinforcement differently.

A much stronger criticism of the concept of reinforcement as an explanatory tool for language acquisition, however, came from within linguistics.[3] The behaviorist views on feedback, in particular, were largely discredited by Chomsky (1959) in his review of Skinner's *Verbal Behavior*. This review set in motion a re-evaluation of many of the central claims for a number of reasons: First, the dangers of extrapolating from laboratory studies of animal behavior to the language behavior of humans were identified. Second, the terms *stimulus* and *response* were exposed as vacuous when applied to language behavior. Chomsky showed that language acquisition cannot be explained by the claim that learning is triggered by a stimulus and a response. Third, analogy, that is, learning by copying observed behavior as exemplified by utterances heard by other speakers, cannot account for the ability to generate novel utterances. Moreover, studies of children acquiring their L1 showed that parents rarely corrected their linguistic errors, thus casting doubt on the importance of *reinforcement* in language learning. Subsequent studies suggested that language acquisition was developmental in nature, driven as much, if not more, from the inside as from the outside.

The application of Chomsky's hypothesis of an innate universal grammar to second language acquisition is still somewhat controversial (see

Cook & Newson, 1996) because the exact influence of universal grammar (UG) on second language acquisition processes is viewed differently by different SLA researchers. UG is either seen as playing a major part, some part, or no part at all in these processes (for a detailed discussion, see Cook & Newson, 1996, p. 101ff).

However, before we focus on feedback in SLA theory in more detail in the next section, it is important to note that reinforcement is a central concept in many cognitive processes that play a role in language learning. This applies despite the fact that the concept of reinforcement does not have sufficient explanatory power to capture language acquisition processes in their entirety. As a result, researchers and developers in CALL cannot afford to ignore the concept of reinforcement altogether. This is supported by the following two examples:

If language learners are continuously forced to perform tasks which they perceive as not challenging, too challenging, or repetitive, they are likely to transfer their frustration with a particular exercise set or program onto the computer and later onto the language they are learning. In the end, they may no longer enjoy the learning of the language. Second, if learners are frequently given negative reinforcement to tasks that they have completed successfully, their behavior can change in such a way that they do no longer attempt to learn the language. So, how can learners be given feedback when they produced utterances that contain errors?

4.4 FEEDBACK IN SLA

A number of terms have been used to refer to the general area of error treatment in SLA. Most commonly, the terms *feedback*, *repair*, and *correction* have been used. Feedback serves as a general cover term for the information provided by listeners on the reception and comprehension of messages. As Vigil and Oller (1976) have pointed out, it is useful to distinguish *cognitive* and *affective* feedback; the former relates to actual understanding while the latter concerns the motivational support that interlocutors provide to each other during an interaction. In contrast, *repair* is, to some degree, a much narrower term that is used by ethnomethodologists such as Schegloff, Jefferson, and Sacks (1977). It refers to attempts to identify and remedy communication problems, including those that derive from linguistic errors. *Correction* has a narrower meaning still, referring to attempts to deal specifically with linguistic errors by providing *negative evidence* in the form of feedback that draws the learner's attention to the errors they have made (Ellis, 1994, pp. 583–584).

With reference to cognitive feedback and by considering a study by Vigil and Oller (1976), Ellis (1994) states that "positive cognitive feedback (signaling 'I understand you') results in fossilization; negative feedback (signaling 'I don't understand you') helps avoid fossilization" (p. 354). Even more precise information on the nature of effective feedback is provided by Pica, Holliday, Lewis, and Morgenthaler (1989) who found that "the crucial factor was the nature of the feedback signals that native speakers provided" (quoted in Ellis, 1994, p. 283). Learners tended to rephrase their utterances upon clarification requests, but were less likely to rephrase after confirmation or repetitions.

Communicating linguistic errors to foreign language learners, however, has been subject to recent controversies over whether the provision of *negative evidence* is necessary or helpful for L2 development. Negative evidence refers to the kind of input that informs the learner whether or not a particular form is acceptable according to the target language norms. In L2 interaction this might take the shape of a formal correction offered by a teacher, or a more informal rephrasing of a learner's L2 utterance offered by a native-speaking conversational partner. Why is there a controversy about negative evidence in L2 learning?

The problem is that correction often seems ineffective. It seems that learners often cannot benefit from correction, but instead continue to make the same mistakes independent of the amount of feedback that is offered. For some current theorists, any natural language must be learnable from *positive* evidence alone and corrective feedback is largely irrelevant. Others continue to see value in corrections and negative evidence, though it is generally accepted that these will be useful only when they relate to "hot spots" currently being restructured in the learner's emerging L2 system (see Mitchell & Myles, 1998, p. 16). Mitchell and Myles (1998) summarize the achievements of interactionist research regarding feedback by stating: "It has been shown that learners receiving certain types of explicit instruction and/or negative feedback, relating to particular target language structures, can be significantly advantaged when later tested on those structures." (p. 141).

It is proposed that environmental contributions to acquisition are mediated by selective attention and the learner's developing L2 processing capacity. These resources are also brought together most usefully, although not exclusively, during *negotiation of meaning*. Negative feedback obtained during negotiation work or elsewhere may be facilitative of L2 development, at least for vocabulary, morphology, and language specific syntax and essential for learning certain specifiable L1-L2 contrasts (Long, 1996, p. 414).

By starting off with a brief recapturing of her debate with Truscott in the *Journal of Second Language Writing*, Ferris (2004) reviews the grammar correction debate in L2 writing and provides an overview of tangible results of SLA research on error correction:

> Adult acquirers may fossilize and not continue to make progress in accuracy of linguistic forms without explicit instruction and feedback on their errors.

> Students who receive feedback on their written errors will be more likely to self-correct them during revision than those who receive no feedback — and this demonstrated uptake may be a necessary step in developing longer term linguistic competence.
>
> Students are likely to attend to and appreciate feedback on their errors and this may motivate them both to make corrections and to work harder on improving their writing. The lack of such feedback may lead to anxiety or resentment, which could decrease motivation and lower confidence in their teachers. (p. 56)

Ferris admits that these predictions are based on scarce research of error correction. She concludes that longitudinal studies are needed to provide evidence for the efficiency of error correction over time and that these studies need to look in great detail at the variables involved in error correction (error type, feedback type, supplemental grammar instruction, etc.). Russell, Valezy, and Spada (2006) also conclude in their large meta-study that too little empirical research has been done on the effectiveness of corrective feedback but that the evidence so far supports the assumption that corrective feedback does work.

In general terms, there is evidence that adult learners who combine formal instruction with exposure to the foreign language achieve the greatest gains in proficiency (Ellis, 1994, p. 612). An important factor that determines the success of formal instruction is the learner's stage of development. "Instruction may lead to more accurate use of grammatical structures in communication providing a learner is able to process them" (Ellis, 1994, p. 627). The studies reported by Ellis suggest that higher chances of successful instruction are given if instruction is linked with opportunities of natural exposure.

Another important point made by Ellis is the distinction between *focus on forms* and *focus on form* during the instruction process of second language learning (Ellis, 1994, p. 639). *Focus on forms* refers to the kind of teaching that is often described as the structural approach. Here the teacher attempts to isolate individual grammatical phenomena in order to teach and/or test them one at a time. This is the approach that is used by many of the grammar drill packages in CALL and in ICALL (e.g., *TUCO II*[4] and *Übungsgrammatik Deutsch*[5]). Ellis relies on a study by Long (1991) and argues that this approach is counter-productive if the aim is to increase communicative proficiency, "while that which allows for a focus on form results in faster learning and higher levels of proficiency" (Ellis, 1994, p. 639). By using software packages that provide exercises on selected grammatical phenomena, students are likely to learn about the grammar of that language. However, their acquisition of the language is at best facilitated in an intermediate way by, for example, providing them with knowledge for self-correction.

Focus on form is understood as the concentration on the textual phenomena of the text in production during a short phase embedded in a communicative event. Learners take time out and look back on what they have produced, assessing and, if necessary, correcting the surface level of the text. In the context of listening comprehension exercises, Levy (1999a) refers to an approach which he describes as de-coupling of the activity level and the reflection level. This is very much how the term *focus on form* is understood, that is, CALL tools that support *focus on form* rely on the fact that a phase dedicated to reflection on the activity just performed is introduced in the learning process (e.g., the introduction of a grammar checking phase in the text production process). For instance, Wiese (1983) analyzed verbalization processes of English and German native speakers. Both groups of speakers produced short narratives in both German and English based on a cartoon. Comparing the results of text production in the first and the second language, he concludes:

> Altogether, the results show that the delaying phenomena examined are an integral and necessary part of any speech production process that takes place in real time. These phenomena are necessary, more for the user of a second language than for somebody using his mother tongue, to buy time for specific planning processes, for post-process control and correction of the utterances produced, to maintain the communication during the planning pause and probably for other, yet unknown purposes. (p. 136)

Additional studies have shown the usefulness of feedback in grammar teaching in the language learning classroom. For instance, White and Trahey (White, 1991; Trahey & White, 1993; Trahey, 1996) conducted a group of studies in which they focused on the acquisition of rules of adverb placement by French children learning English. At various times, different groups of classroom learners in these studies received explicit instruction in English adverb placement (assumed to include systematic provision of negative evidence), or a so-called *flood* of positive evidence on adverb placement, or instruction in other aspects of English. In a follow-up study investigating long-term effects in children's competence of these different treatments, Trahey (1996) found that both the explicit instruction (negative evidence) group and the flood (positive evidence) group had apparently internalized the knowledge that SAV (subject-adverb-verb) is permitted in English. However, it seemed that neither group had internalized the knowledge that SVAO (subject-verb-adverb-object) is *not* permitted. Interestingly, the instructed group had seemed to demonstrate proficiency on adverb placement in assessments that took place shortly after the original period of instruction. However, in the long-term follow-up study, their ability to recognize SVAO as ungrammatical had declined significantly.

In reviewing the equivocal results, Trahey speculates along similar lines as Spada and Lightbown (1993) that perhaps some mix of both positive and negative evidence may be required to ensure effective acquisition: "An incorporation of attention to structure within the context of the flood may well have led to greater success" (Trahey, 1996, p. 136).

The list of studies above is not intended to be comprehensive, however, they are meant to illustrate the controversy that still exists around the topic of formal instruction and feedback. To some extent, the controversy might even be due to the fact that feedback can take on very different forms and many answers to questions, although intriguing, are speculative. For example, how detailed should feedback be?

Aljaafreh and Lantolf (1994) developed a *Regulatory Scale* (see Table 4.2) to illustrate how the tutor's interventions can be aligned on a continuum from implicit to explicit correction. In cases, where it could be shown over time that students require feedback that was moving closer to the *implicit* end of the scale, they were considered to be moving towards more independent and self-regulated performance. This was consequently taken as positive evidence of learning.

Table 4.2 Regulatory scale — implicit (strategic) to explicit (Aljaafreh & Lantolf, 1994, p. 471; see also Mitchell & Myles, 1998, p. 158)

0. Tutor asks the learner to read, find the errors and correct them independently, prior to the tutorial.
1. Construction of a "collaborative frame" prompted by the presence of the tutor as a potential dialogic partner.
2. Prompted or focused reading of the sentence that contains the error by the learner or the tutor.
3. Tutor indicates that something may be wrong in a segment (e.g., sentence, clause, line) — "Is there anything wrong in this sentence?"
4. Tutor rejects unsuccessful attempts at recognizing the error.
5. Tutor narrows down the location of the error (e.g., tutor repeats or points to the specific segment which contains the error).
6. Tutor indicates the nature of the error, but does not identify the error (e.g., "There is something wrong with the tense marking here").
7. Tutor identifies the error ("You can't use an auxiliary here!").
8. Tutor rejects learner's unsuccessful attempts at correcting the error.
9. Tutor provides clues to help the learner arrive at the correct form (e.g., "It is not really past but something that is still going on").
10. Tutor provides the correct form.
11. Tutor provides some explanation for use of the correct form.
12. Tutor provides examples of the correct pattern when other forms of help fail to produce an appropriate responsive action.

Similarly, Cathcart and Olsen (1976) found that ESL learners like to be corrected by their teachers and want more correction than they are usually provided with. However, it is not only a question of how much feedback to provide but also how often. Chenoweth, Day, Chun, and Luppescu (1983), for example, found that learners liked to be corrected not only during form-focused activities, but also when they were conversing with native speakers. Favoring correction, however, contrasts with the warnings of Krashen (1982) that correction is both useless for *acquisition* and dangerous in that it may lead to a negative affective response. However, Cathcart and Olsen (1976) also report that when a teacher attempted to provide the kind of correction that learners liked, as identified in their study, it led to communication which the class found undesirable (see also Ellis, 1994, p. 584).

Before turning now to issues surrounding feedback in a computer-assisted environment, we will first consider the linguistic relation of well-formed and ill-formed sentences from the point of view of formal linguistics.

4.5 FEEDBACK AND FORMAL GRAMMAR

The aspect of foreign language learning in which we are interested can be described as the production of text in the foreign language and the didactic discussion of this text. In this respect, feedback forms part of meta-communication, that is, the talking about language. The dialogue of the text produced by the individual learner relies on an accurate analysis of the *source* text and the generation of a meaningful *response* text. These two aspects of feedback in a CALL environment are informed by NLP and Text Generation, which in turn rely on an adequate description of language.

The requirement of a formal grammar for a parser-based CALL software and the necessity of robust parsing have already been discussed in section 2.3.4. However, an adequate description of the language in question has such a strong impact on the quality of an ICALL system that a lot of work is invested in the grammatical backbone of these programs. Evidently, the more linguistic information a program can retrieve and compute from a student text, the more information it can feed back to the student.

What does this formal approach to linguistic description of the target language mean in more general terms for the provision of feedback?

In its first approximation, feedback shows the relation between the produced construction in $V^* - L$ and the intended construction in L.[6] V^* is the set of all possible strings that can be generated by using a vocabulary V. L is the set of all strings that are also grammatically well-formed sentences according to a grammar G. This approach, however, will allow for an infinite number of construction possibilities and, as a result, adequate learner feedback may be difficult, if not impossible. Instead, feedback can be linked to smaller units, that is, the finite sets on which the formal grammar $G(V_N, V_T, R, S)$ relies. How can this be done?

The non-terminal symbols (V_N) like NP and VP, the words (V_T) and the set of morpho-syntactic rules (R) carry certain features that establish their behavior in a sentence and determine their relation to other signs within the sentence. For instance, in a system designed to process well-formed input, a masculine article only unifies with a masculine noun, a noun phrase in nominative case acts as the grammatical subject of a sentence, the separable preposition of a German compound main verb occupies the sentence-final position in a verb-second clause (e.g., *der Zug fährt jetzt* *ab* (the train is departing now)) etc. These features which place restrictions on what the text producer can do with a given symbol in a sentence and under what conditions a particular grammatical rule has to be applied, are commonly labeled constraints. If any of these constraints are violated in a sentence, the sentence is grammatically ill-formed. But it is precisely these ill-formed sentences a parser in a CALL system has to address to provide error-specific feedback to the learner.

There are different ways a parser can process ill-formed sentences.[7] For instance, a second grammar F can be developed. This grammar contains grammatical rules and terminal and non-terminal symbols that only exist outside of L. Another possibility to parse ill-formed sentences is to relax some of the constraints that are defined in grammar G. A relaxed constraint is not as strict on the learner input as an ordinary grammatical constraint from which it was derived. It stipulates a preference (e.g., that the grammatical subject of a sentence should be in nominative), but it would accept a noun phrase that is case-marked differently if it cannot find another nominative noun phrase. If the parser finds such a phrase, the relaxed constraint will ensure that, first, the phrase can be processed and, second, that the use of, for example, accusative instead of nominative case marking is recorded. As a result, a relaxed constraint defines one possible relation between a deviation (a rule violation and/or an inappropriate feature) and an anticipated construction in L.

This approach is necessarily based on a finite set of rules and features. In other words, because a sentence has been parsed using a particular relaxed constraint, the parser assumes that the corresponding correct sentence is one that uses the same constraint, but without its relaxation. For instance, a particular constraint specifies that if a verb requires an indirect object then it needs to be marked for dative case. The relaxed constraint stipulates that a noun marked for any grammatical case will suffice, although a phrase marked for dative case is preferred. When a sentence is parsed that contains a suitable phrase that is not marked for dative, it is assumed that the sentence will be correct once feedback is provided and the phrase receives its dative marking accordingly.

In more general terms, feedback is based on reasoning about the relation between a produced construction in V^* - L and the corresponding intended construction in L. Feedback aims to support the learner in making the transition between these two related constructions. In parser-based CALL, meta-linguistic feedback uses information from the formal representation produced by a parser and generates linguistic information about the rule violation or the use of a non-existent symbol. It uses the terminology commonly employed in a pedagogic approach to a learner grammar.

4.6 FEEDBACK IN CALL

One of the pedagogical goals of parser-based CALL is to provide informative, error-specific feedback. For example, if a student chooses an incorrect article in German the error might be due to incorrect inflection for gender, number, or case. For cognitive learning to occur, instructional feedback must address the different sources of an error (Rumelhart & Norman, 1975; Venezky & Osin, 1991) and, accordingly, the program must be capable of distinguishing between the three error types in such an instance. Nelson et al. (1976) argued many years ago that a student should be provided "with meaningful analysis of his input" (p. 32) and that a list of anticipated responses just will not suffice. The error analysis performed by the computer system forms the basis for error-specific feedback. Garrett (1987, pp. 175–176) describes four kinds of feedback for CALL:

1. The system presents only the correct answer.
2. The system pinpoints the location of an error on the basis of the computer's letter-by letter comparison of the student's input with the machine-stored correct version.
3. Based on an analysis of the anticipated wrong answers, error messages associated with possible errors are stored in the computer and are presented if the student's response matches those possible errors.
4. The system uses an intelligent, NLP approach such as the "parsing" technique in which the computer performs a linguistic analysis of the student's response.

Over the past decade, a number of studies have focused on comparisons of the different feedback types, as explained by Garrett. For example, Nagata (1993, 1995, 1996) compared the effectiveness of error-specific and traditional feedback with students learning Japanese. In all studies, Nagata found that meaningful computer feedback based on NLP which can explain the source of an error is more effective than traditional feedback (see also Yang & Akahori, 1997, 1999). There are, however, a number of computational and pedagogical issues that arise when designing a system that provides meaningful, error-specific feedback. These will be discussed in the following section with the *German Tutor* (Heift & Nicholson, 2001), an online parser-based system for German, by way of example.

4.6.1 Feedback for multiple errors: The example of the *German Tutor*

While there has been a noticeable trend towards Web-based applications in language learning, it has also been noted that very few of them follow basic instructional design principles. For example, meaningful feedback seems to be lacking in many Web-based language learning applications (Felix, 2002; Bangs, 2003).

When designing a parser-based CALL system, there are a number of pedagogical decisions to be made to achieve meaningful feedback. For instance, a standard problem in parsing is that most sentences can be assigned more than one syntactic structure. Van Noord (1997) states that the Alvey Tools Grammar with 780 rules averages about 100 readings per sentence on sentences ranging in length between 13 and 30 words. The maximum was 2,736 readings for a 29 word sentence. Although typical language exercises do not contain 29 word sentences, an unconstrained grammar generally produces more parses than systems designed for only well-formed input. As a result, NLP applications must incorporate techniques for selecting a preferred parse. Ideally, the techniques in an ICALL system are motivated by language teaching pedagogy to ensure meaningful feedback (for examples see Heift, 1998a, 1998b).

A further pedagogical challenge for ICALL systems with respect to meaningful feedback are multiple errors made by students in one sentence. While it is desirable to construct a program capable of detecting and accurately explaining all errors, it does not follow that the system should display each and every error detected. In the absence of an error filtering mechanism, the sheer amount of feedback would overwhelm the student. For example, in evaluating her own system Schwind (1990a) reports that "sometimes, however, the explanations were too long, especially when students accumulated errors" (p. 577).

A previous study by Heift (2001), for instance, showed that approximately 40% of the sentences analyzed contained more than one error. However, a language instructor typically skips irrelevant errors and discusses the remaining ones one at a time. Example 4.1a shows a sentence with multiple errors.

Example 4.1

*a) *Heute meine <u>Kindern</u> <u>haben</u> <u>gespeilt</u> mit <u>der</u> Hund.*
b) Heute haben meine Kinder mit dem Hund gespielt
Today my children were playing with the dog.

In Example 4.1, the student made the following five errors:

1. word order: the finite verb *haben* needs to be in second position
2. word order: the nonfinite verb *gespielt* needs to be in final position

3. spelling error with the past participle *gespielt*
4. wrong plural inflection for the subject *Kinder*
5. wrong case for the dative determiner *dem*

From a pedagogical and also motivational point of view, a system should not overwhelm a student with instructional feedback referring to more than one error at a time. Schwind's (1990a) solution to this problem is that multiple errors should be avoided from the outset. She suggests that sentence construction exercises should focus on specific grammatical phenomena such as prepositions or verb cases (see also Kenning & Kenning, 1990).

While Schwind's approach is probably inherent in many ICALL systems, limiting the teaching domain is only a partial solution. Even a basic sentence in German, as illustrated in Example 4.1, requires a number of rules and knowledge about the case system, prepositions, word order, etc. Holland (1994), in her system BRIDGE, applies a different approach to address the problem of multiple errors. She displays only one error at a time and permits instructors to divide errors into primary, which are automatically displayed and secondary, which are displayed only at the student's request.

In a study regarding the amount of feedback provided for different kinds of learners, van der Linden (1993) found that "feedback, in order to be consulted, has to be concise and precise. Long feedback (exceeding three lines) is not read and for that reason not useful" (p. 65). She further states that displaying more than one feedback response at a time makes the correction process too complex for the student (see also Shneiderman, 1992; Brandl, 1995). Accordingly, van der Linden's (1993) study makes three final recommendations:

1. feedback needs to be accurate in order to be of any use to the student,
2. displaying more than one error message at a time is not very useful because, at some point, the error messages probably will not be read, and
3. explanations for a particular error should also be kept short.

With regard to feedback display, van der Linden's (1993) recommendations require a system submodule to sift all incoming errors. The errors have to be reported one at a time and the error explanations should be brief. This provides the student with enough information to correct the error, but not an overwhelming amount and yet records detailed information within the student model for assessment and remediation. The question arises in which order the errors should be reported and, from a computational point of view, how this knowledge should be represented in an ICALL system.

The German Tutor (Heift & Nicholson, 2000a) implements an *Error Priority Queue* which ranks student errors so as to display a single feedback message in case of multiple constraint violations. The ranking of student errors in the Error Priority Queue is, however, flexible: the grammar constraints can be reordered to reflect the desired emphasis of a particular exercise. In addition, a language instructor might choose not to report some errors. In such an instance, some grammar constraints will display no feedback message at all, although the error will still be recorded in the student model of the system.

In the following we provide an overview of the architecture of the *German Tutor* (Heift, 2003). We discuss the Error Priority Queue that is used by the filtering module to rank student errors. Furthermore, we present data on the use of the system that show the frequency and distribution of multiple errors.

4.6.1.1 *Feedback generation*

The German Tutor consists of four major components: the domain knowledge, the analysis module, the student model, and the filtering module. Figure 4.3 illustrates how a sentence is processed by the system.

4.6.1.2 *The domain knowledge*

The domain knowledge represents the knowledge of the language. It consists of a parser with a Head-Driven Phrase Structure Grammar (HPSG).

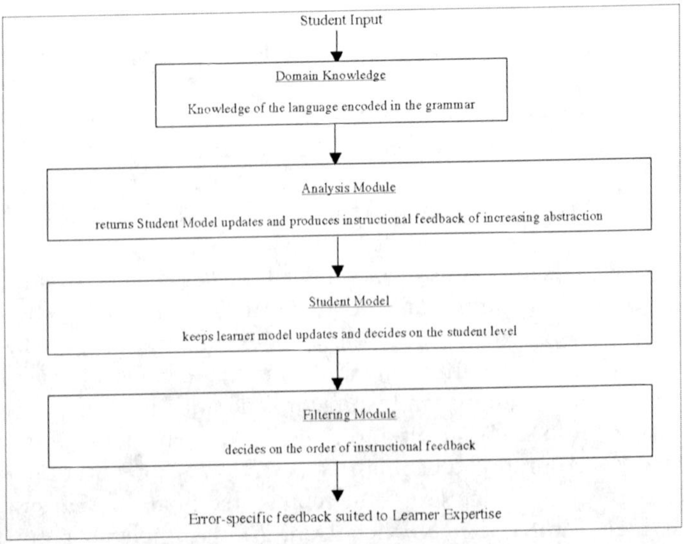

Figure 4.3 The *German Tutor* — system overview

The goal of the domain knowledge is to parse sentences and phrases to produce sets of phrase descriptors. As briefly described in part 3, a phrase descriptor describes a particular grammatical constraint (e.g., subject-verb agreement), its presence or absence in the input sentence and the student's performance on this constraint.

In HPSG (Pollard & Sag, 1987, 1994; Sag et al., 2003), linguistic information is formally represented as feature structures. Feature structures specify values for various attributes as partial descriptions of a linguistic sign. HPSG adopts a lexicalist approach in which syntactic information is described within each lexical entry. For example, the feature structure given in Figure 4.4 illustrates that the verb *gehst* subcategorizes for a subject. The subject is minimally specified as a noun and its person and number features are structure-shared with the agreement features of the verb. Structure-sharing is indicated by multiple occurrences of a coindexing box labeling the single value. Because syntactic information is expressed within each lexical entry, HPSG requires only a few generalized syntactic rules to specify how words and phrases combine into larger units.

A grammar is written as a set of constraints. To illustrate the concept, consider the simple sentence given in Example 4.2:

Example 4.2
  *a) *Er gehst.*
  b) *Du gehst.*
  You are leaving.

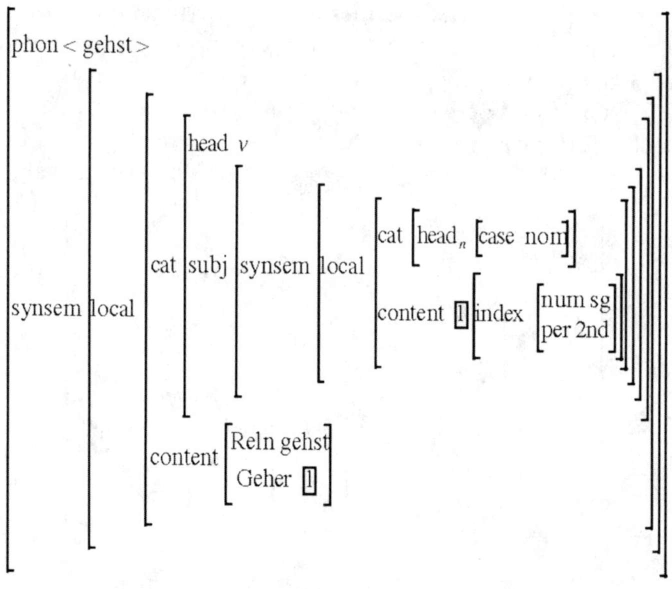

Figure 4.4 Partial feature structure (HPSG) for *gehst*

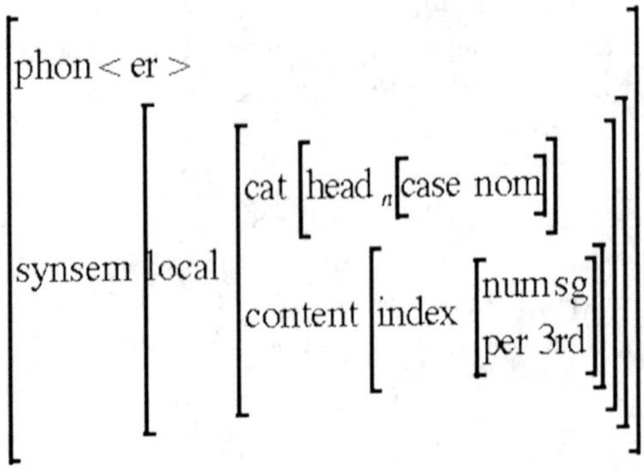

Figure 4.5 Lexical entry for *er*

In Example 4.2a, the constraints between the subject *er* and the verb *gehst* require agreement in number and person and that the subject is in nominative case. Any of the three constraints could block parsing if not successfully met. Figure 4.4 illustrates that the subject of the verb *gehst* must be a 2nd person, singular, nominative, noun. *Er*, however, given in Figure 4.5, is inflected for 3rd person, singular, nominative. Thus, **Er gehst* will fail to parse.

However, a constraint can be relaxed by changing its structure so that it records whether or not agreement is present rather than enforcing agreement between two constituents. To achieve this, the subject *er*, given in Figure 4.6, is no longer marked as (per 3rd), (num sg), (case nom). Instead the feature per, for example, specifies all possible person features, that is, 1st, 2nd, and 3rd. For *er*, the value for 1st and 2nd is error, while for 3rd it is correct. Conceptually, the feature structure states that it is incorrect to use *er* as a 1st and 2nd person pronoun, but correct for 3rd person.

The verb *gehst*, given in Figure 4.7, no longer subcategorizes for a subject marked (per 2nd). Instead, the verb *gehst* will inherit the value of 2nd

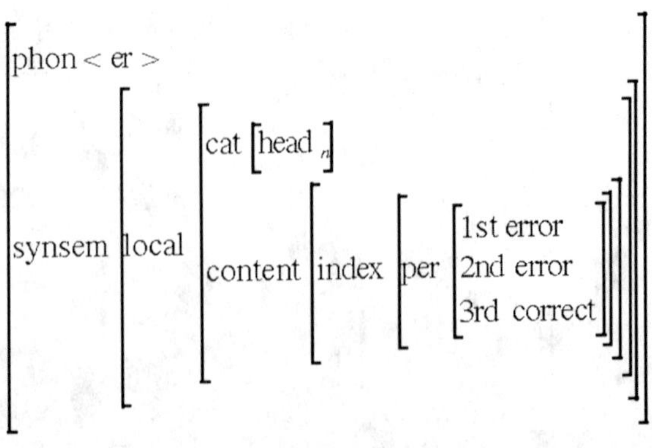

Figure 4.6 Marking person features for *er*

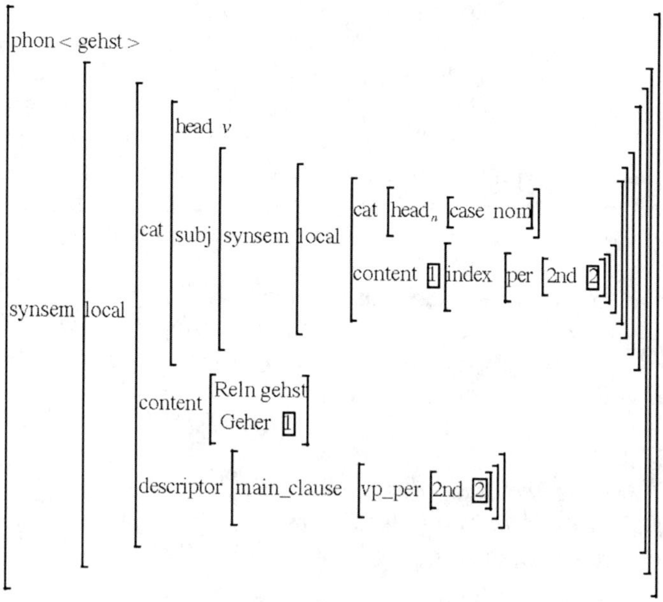

Figure 4.7 Marking person features for *gehst*

from its subject during parsing. For the subject *er*, the value for 2nd is error indicating that the constraint on person agreement has been violated, but, importantly, allowing the parse to succeed.

For the correct sentence *Du gehst*, given in Example 4.2 the value for 2nd would be correct because *du* is a second person, nominative pronoun, as illustrated in Figure 4.8. During parsing, *gehst* will inherit the value correct indicating that the constraint on person agreement has been met.

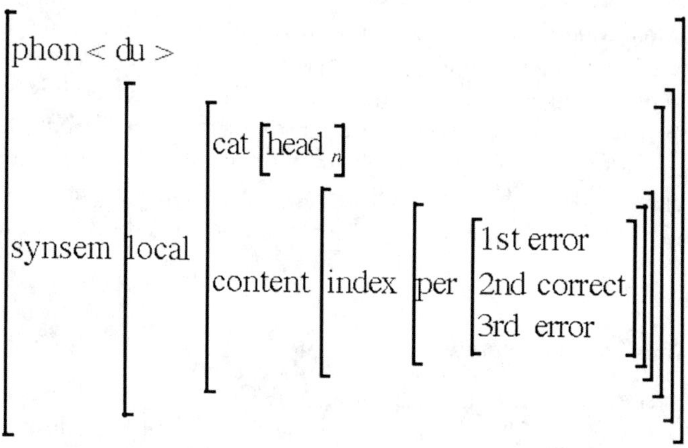

Figure 4.8 Marking person features for *du*

In addition to the HPSG features, the grammar uses a feature *descriptor* representing the description of the phrase that the parser builds up. During parsing, the values of the features of *descriptor* become specified. For example, the phrase descriptor vp_per records the constraint on person agreement. For the sentence **Er gehst*, vp_per will inherit its value from the feature 2nd, given in the lexical entry of *gehst* in Figure 4.7. The final result is the phrase descriptor (main_clause (vp_per (2nd error))), indicating that the required grammatical constraint on person agreement has not been met.

For a sentence that contains multiple errors, each phrase descriptor indicates precisely where the errors occurred. For example, the sentence given in Example 4.3 not only contains an agreement error in person but also a case error with both the direct and indirect objects.

Example 4.3

a)**Er gibst den Mann der Buch.*

b) *Du gibst dem Mann das Buch.*

You are giving the man the book.

The responsibility of the head of a phrase is to collect the phrase descriptors of its complements. To achieve this, the phrase descriptors are percolated up the syntactic tree via the Descriptor Principle which states that the descriptor features of the mother node are the descriptor features of the head daughter. As a result, the phrase descriptors for the incorrect sentence in Example 4.3 are:

(main_clause (vp_per (2nd error)))
(main_clause (indir_obj (det denerror)))[8]
(main_clause (dir_obj (det dererror)))

The advantages of the method described for analyzing constraints are: First, the technique is very general in that it can be applied to a variety of grammatical phenomena. The phrase descriptors record whether a grammatical phenomenon is present in the input and, if so, whether it is correctly or incorrectly formed. Phrase descriptors provide very detailed information indicating precisely where an error in the sentence occurred. Second, errors are not treated differently from well-formed input. Neither the parsing nor the grammar formalism needs to be altered and no additional rules are required.[9]

4.6.1.3 Generating feedback

According to Figure 4.3, student input in the German Tutor is passed onto the analysis module. The analysis module takes a phrase descriptor as input and generates sets of possible responses to the learner's input that the instruction system can use when interacting with the student. A response is a pair that contains a student model update and a message the system will use to inform the learner if a phrase descriptor indicates an error. The student model update contains the name of a grammar constraint in the student model along with an instruction to increment or decrement the corresponding cumulative total.

The analysis module generates sets of instructional feedback of increasing abstraction. As an example consider the ungrammatical sentence in Example 4.4a). An inexperienced student should be informed that *Mädchen* is a neuter noun, that the verb *danken* is a dative verb and that the determiner *das* is incorrect. A student who has mastered case assignment (as indicated by the student model) may be informed only that the case of the object is incorrect.

Example 4.4
a)**Der Mann dankt das Mädchen.*
b) *Der Mann dankt dem Mädchen.*
The man thanks the girl.

4.6.1.4 *Individualizing feedback*

The student model[10] dynamically evolves based on the student's performance. The information in the model is used for two main functions: Modulation of instructional feedback as well as assessment and remediation. The student model keeps track of an individual student's performance on a variety of grammatical phenomena (e.g., agreement, modals, verb particles) based on the information obtained from the phrase descriptors. Phrase descriptors correspond to structures in the student model and are the interface medium between the student model and the grammar of the system. The student model passes instructional feedback suited to learner expertise to the filtering module.

For each grammar constraint, the student model keeps a counter for each student with a score for each grammar skill. This score ranges from 0 - n, where we have set n to 30. The score increases when the student provides evidence of a successful use of that grammar skill and decreases when the student provides evidence of an unsuccessful use of that grammar skill. The amount by which a student's score increases or decreases can vary depending on the current value of the score. Initially, we set all scores to an intermediate level but pre-testing can determine individual differences from the offset.

For the purposes of modulating instructional feedback, we identify three categories of scores. Scores from 0–10 are assigned to the novice category, 11–20 to the intermediate category and 21–30 to the expert category. When a student makes an error on a particular grammar skill, the message they receive depends on their score for that skill. If they are ranked as novice, they will receive a more informative message than if they are ranked as expert. Since the score for each grammar skill is independent of the score for the other grammar skills, a student may be expert at subject-verb agreement, but novice at forming the passive - and receive the appropriate message.

The score information is also used for a variety of remediation and assessment tasks. By comparing the student model at the beginning and end of a session, we can provide summative feedback by listing the mistakes that a student made during that session. In our current system, these are summarized into general categories such as "Verb Tenses", "Pronouns", etc. These groups are set by means of a parameter file. Similarly, we can also identify the grammar skills where the student was correct and provide a "positive" of what the student did right. At present we show language learners a list of their errors at the end of each exercise set.

Further, one can also examine the student model overall and identify the current strengths and weaknesses of the student. We identify the strengths of a student as the five highest scoring grammar skills that have a score greater than 15 (half of the total scale). We identify the weaknesses of a student as the 5 lowest scoring grammar skills that have a score less than 15. Students can access this information.

Finally, the student model information can also be used to provide exercises to the student which focus on their areas of weakness. Instead of repeating the same exercise which the student made the mistake on, the system has the capacity to identify examples which require the same grammar skill. This avoids the problem of the student rote learning the solution to a particular example, without actually learning the general solution.

4.6.1.5 Prioritizing feedback

The filtering module determines the order of the instructional feedback displayed to the learner. The system displays one message at a time so as not to overwhelm the student with multiple error messages. The grammar constraints produced by the phrase descriptors are hierarchically organized. The student model maintains the grammar constraints and selects instructional feedback suited to learner expertise. In case of multiple errors, an error priority queue determines the order in which instructional feedback messages are displayed to the learner. It ranks instructional feedback with respect to the frequency and importance of an error within a given sentence.

The error priority queue for the grammar constraints of a main clause is partially given in Table 4.3. The names of the grammar constraints generated and maintained by the analysis module and student model, respectively, are given in parentheses.

The grammar constraints, given in the partial Error Priority Queue in Table 4.3 are grouped according to grammatical phenomena. For example, the group "Prepositional Phrases in a Main Clause" contains all constraints

Table 4.3 Error priority queue in the *German Tutor*

I. Word Order in a Main Clause

- position of a finite verb in a main-clause (posmainfin)
- position of a nonfinite verb in a main-clause (posmainnonfin)
- position of a finite verb in initial position (posmaininitial)

II. Subjects in a Main-Clause

- case of the noun of the subject (subjnounmain)
- case, number and gender of the determiner of the subject (subjmain)

III. Direct Objects in a Main Clause

- case of the noun of the direct object (dirobjnounmain)
- case, number and gender of the determiner of the direct object (dirobjmain)

IV. Prepositional Phrases in a Main Clause

- choice of preposition (prepmain)
- case of the noun of a prepositional phrase in the accusative (pp_accnounmain)
- case, number and gender of the determiner of a prepositional phrase in the accusative (pp_accmain)
- case of the noun of a prepositional phrase in the dative (pp_datnounmain)
- case, number and gender of the determiner of a prepositional phrase in the dative (pp_datmain)

relevant to prepositional phrases. Each member of a group in the error priority queue refers to a node in the student model.

The groups in the error priority queue are sorted according to the frequency and importance of an error within a sentence. The error priority queue shown reflects the default setting for the importance of an error in a given exercise. For example, grammar constraints 1 to 3 of the group "Word Order in a Main Clause" refer to errors in linear precedence. In the default setting, they are reported first since word order is one of the fundamental concepts of a language and thus likely to have high priority in most exercises.

The ordering of the groups of grammar constraints can, however, be altered to reflect the pedagogy of a particular language instructor. For example, an instructor might want to centre exercises around dative case assignment. In such an instance, the grammar constraints can be reordered so that errors of indirect objects are reported first. In addition, a language instructor might choose to suppress some errors, so as not to distract the student from the main task. These would be errors which are not relevant to a particular exercise. Suppressing certain errors, does not affect their contribution to the student model, on the rationale that behind-the-scenes information should be as detailed as possible.

4.4.1.6 *The German Tutor in use*

A study by Heift (2001) determined the frequency and types of multiple errors that occurred during system use. For data collection, a tracking system collected detailed information on the student-computer interaction (Heift & Nicholson, 2000b). Throughout the semester 33 students of two introductory university courses of German completed six chapters of the *German Tutor* with a total of 120 exercises. Each chapter contains a variety of tasks ranging from typing in words or sentences, and clicking or dragging objects, to listening to words and phrases. The grammatical structures present in the exercises were: gender and number agreement of noun phrases, subject-verb agreement, present tense of regular and irregular verbs, accusative and dative objects/prepositions, two-way prepositions, present perfect, auxiliaries, word order of finite and nonfinite verbs and modal verbs. The linguistic structures had all been practiced in communicative class activities prior to the computer sessions.

A total of 1,004 submissions with a total of 1387 errors were considered for analysis. Table 4.4 shows that approximately 30% of the 1,004 incorrect sentences analyzed contained multiple errors at initial submission. The data further indicate that, if multiple errors occurred, two errors per submission occurred most frequently with only one submission that contained five errors.

In a less constrained practice environment the percentage of multiple errors might be even higher. To some extent, the limited number of multiple errors in the current study may be due to the fact that students had practiced the grammatical structures and vocabulary in communicative activities in class before. Additionally, each chapter gradually introduced at most two new grammatical concepts.

In determining the appropriateness of the ranking of grammar constraints in the error priority queue, Heift (2001) considered the distribution of the total of errors that occurred. The error break down in Table 4.5 indicates that 409 (29.5%) out of the 1387 errors were due to spelling mistakes while the remaining 978 (70.5%) errors occurred with grammatical constructions.[11]

The data further indicate that most grammar errors occurred with direct objects (28.6%) and subject-verb agreement (18.6%). However, these were also the most frequent constructions contained in the 120 exercises of this study. For instance, only chapters 5 and 6 (40 exercises in total) focus on

Table 4.4 Error distribution (multiple errors per sentence)

Number of Submissions	*Number of Errors*	%
720	1 error	71.7%
198	2 errors	19.7%
74	3 errors	7.4%
11	4 errors	1.1%
1	5 errors	0.1%
1,004		100%

Table 4.5 Error break down

Error Type	*Number of Errors*	%
Spelling	409	29.5%
Grammar	978	70.5%
Direct objects (gender, number, case)	280	28.6%
Subject-verb agreement (person, number)	182	18.6%
Prepositional phrases: two-way (gender, number, case)	171	17.5%
Subjects (gender, number, case)	130	13.3%
Indirect objects (gender, number, case)	86	8.8%
Prepositional phrases: accusative (gender, number, case)	42	4.3%
Missing words/constituents	36	3.7%
Prepositional phrases: Dative (gender, number, case)	24	2.5%
Extra words	11	1.1%
Word order	6	0.6%
Auxiliaries	7	0.7%
Verb complements (infinitive and past participle)	3	0.3%
TOTAL	1378	100%

the present perfect and modals. These constructions are not contained in any of the previous chapters, thus there is less opportunity for errors with these grammar topics than, for example, with subject-verb agreement. However, the fact that errors with two-way prepositions rank third in the list confirms an instructor's assumption that this grammatical construction poses considerable problems to a language student of German. Only chapter 4 (20 exercises in total) focuses on two-way prepositions.

The study further examined the data with respect to multiple errors that occurred with each submission. Besides the co-occurrence of spelling and grammar mistakes, a combination of errors relating to direct objects, subject-verb agreement and prepositional phrases co-occurred most frequently. This is not surprising given the error frequency presented in Table 4.5. However, errors with subject-verb agreement were more frequent than mistakes with the subject (determiner-noun agreement) and thus the ranking of grammar constraints in our error priority queue had to be adjusted accordingly. Finally, although the data showed that errors in word order are not as frequent as initially anticipated these errors should, nonetheless, be addressed first and thus given highest priority in the error priority queue. After all, correct word order might assist the student in identifying phrasal constituents.

In summary, multiple errors pose pedagogical as well as linguistic challenges to any ICALL system. To address them effectively, computational algorithms have to be developed that take language teaching pedagogy into account. In the German Tutor, this is achieved by implementing phrase descriptors that indicate precisely the types of errors that occurred in the sentence. In addition, the filtering mechanism ranks learner errors in case of multiple errors. The filtering module uses an error priority queue that can be adjusted to instructors' and learners' needs.

4.6.2 Error-specific and traditional feedback

In their article "Parsers in Tutors: What are they Good for", Holland et al. (1993) explore the role of parser-based CALL and conclude that there are three areas in which ICALL is useful:

1. in form-focused instruction,
2. for students of at least intermediate proficiency and
3. in research.

Previous studies that focused on students' learning outcomes (results) confirm Holland et al.'s conclusion that ICALL is effective and useful, in particular, for form-focused instruction. However, it would be equally instructive to examine the learning process while students work with NLP systems that provide error-specific feedback. As Chapelle and Mizuno (1989) describe it, "when low-ability students perform poorly on a criterion measure, it remains unclear how their work with the courseware may have failed to facilitate their eventual achievement" (p. 27).

Immediate and individualized learner feedback has long been recognized as a significant advantage of CALL over more traditional language instruction, but, despite improved computing power and wider availability of authoring tools, CALL grammar exercises still often resemble traditional workbook tasks. More sophisticated error analyses are needed to provide an individualized and meaningful second language practice environment, instead of the multiple choice questions, relatively uninformative feedback and gross mainstreaming of students characteristic of workbooks.

Over the past decade, a number of NLP systems have been implemented (see section 2.5 on projects in parser-based CALL) which, to some extent, also triggered a shift in focus of CALL effectiveness research. Whereas early research in CALL emphasized comparisons of CALL and traditional face-to-face instruction, over the past decade studies have focused more on comparisons of different CALL programs (Conrad, 1996). For example, a number of studies have investigated error-specific feedback in different learning environments. Nagata and Swisher (1995) found that the computer can raise grammatical awareness by giving error-specific feedback to students. Carroll and Swain (1993), although not specifically investigating learner feedback in a CALL environment, concluded that error-specific feedback is more helpful to adult second language learners supporting earlier claims by Schachter (1984, 1986) (see also Lightbown & Spada, 1990). Brandl (1995) researched stronger and weaker students' preferences for error feedback options and responses and study results indicate that the learners' language skills influence their preference for a particular type of feedback in CALL programs. Finally, Pujolà (2001) found that delayed two-step feedback that allows students to discover the source of errors themselves before the program provides the information is perceived as ideal in his reading program ImPRESSions.

While the studies above investigated the learning outcomes and the relative effects of different types of corrective feedback, other researchers focused on learner-computer interaction during the error correction process. For instance, van der Linden (1993), in comparing learner strategies in CALL programs with different levels of feedback, found that students did not try to correct themselves when no feedback about the type of error was provided. As expected, individual differences also played a role in the students' choice strategies.

From a theoretical point of view, studying learner-computer interaction in error correction will greatly assist in the design of CALL programs (see also Hegelheimer & Chapelle, 2000). From a practical perspective, it assesses the need for a sophisticated error analysis in a CALL system, determines if and how students use error-specific feedback and which learner strategies they apply in response. In a study by Heift (2001), for example, answers to the following research questions were pursued:

Do students read and attend to error-specific feedback or overlook it?
What techniques do students apply in error correction in an ILTS?
Do learners believe the system's analysis, or, in the event of an error, perform an independent re-analysis?

She found five different modes of student reaction to system feedback:

Students corrected the error(s) explained by the system.
Students corrected an error in the sentence, however, not the one explained by the system.
Students changed a correct structure.
Students resubmitted the same sentence.
Students requested the correct answer(s).

The study further showed that for the vast majority of sentences (79.5%) students attended to system feedback. For these sentences, students corrected only the errors explained by the system while initially ignoring further errors, in the case of multiple errors. This confirms that students indeed read the feedback messages instead of independently correcting errors that incidently coincided with system feedback. Finally, as iterations increased students paid more attention to the feedback messages.

Students also corrected errors that were not explained by the system in the same feedback message (0.8%) while they disregarded the errors completely for 2.2% of all submitted sentences. Finally, for 17.5% of the erroneous sentences students requested the correct answer(s) from the system. During the three practicing sessions three out of the 33 students never requested a correct answer, resubmitting sentences up to ten times to obtain a possible answer.

The study also prompts a number of suggestions. First, the data show that students attend to error-specific feedback and correct their output accordingly, despite the opportunity to access the correct answer at any time. Thus, CALL programs can provide a meaningful practice environment — one in which students appreciate being informed about their errors and involved in a meaningful learner-computer interaction. Second, the data confirm previous studies which suggest that learner control is important. The study indicates that the quick route to the correct answer was not over-used and, in fact, was shunned by three students. Most of the time, students opted to work through the iterative correction process. Obtaining a correct answer on demand, however, serves to moderate student frustration. It is one option to facilitate learner control of the system.

The studies described in this section highlight the advantages and importance of error-specific feedback. Due to its apparent benefits, there have been a number of attempts to approximate the error-specific feedback generated by an ICALL system by manually encoding it into a non-parser-based system. However, anticipating and inserting each and every possible student response with its corresponding feedback message by hand is an impossibly onerous task. Hence, this can only be accomplished for a very limited number of grammatical constructions. At the same time, creating a parser-based system is also a very labor-intensive and costly task, but such a system is certainly more scalable. For instance, once the parser grammar has been written, no additional work is required to implement an extra set of tasks and/or exercises. A parser-based system also increases flexibility and exhibits more learner control, which we discuss in the following section.

4.6.3 Learner control and error correction

Holland et al. (1993), when discussing the role of parsers in language learning, draw our attention to a possible limitation of parser-based CALL and thus error-specific feedback:

> Moreover, the nature of the phenomenon modeled in this case, natural language, is so complicated that not all its patterns have been captured in a program of rules. The limitation leads to a second disadvantage

> of ICALL: Because parsers give the illusion of certainty, their feedback may at best confuse the students, who feel sure they are right when the system tells them they are wrong and it may at worst mislead students into mislearning. By contrast, in traditional CALL the very rigidity of the response requirements guarantees certainty. A system with a small set of well-defined response sets (such as multiple choice) will not tell the students they made a mistake when they did not, unless there is an authoring error or programming bug, which is usually obvious and easy to repair. In discourse analytic terms (Grice, 1975), the nature of the contract between student and CALL tutor is straightforward, respecting the traditional assumption that the teacher is right, whereas the ICALL contract is less well defined. (pp. 33–34)

However, the rigidity of traditional CALL in which the program controls the linguistic input by the learner to a very large extent, has often given rise to a criticism which accuses CALL developers and practitioners of relying on behaviorist programmed instruction. In these early CALL programs, based on behaviorist principles, students worked within a strict framework: navigation was generally hard-wired into the program (students were often trapped in an exercise unless they provided the correct answer) and help options were limited or non-existent. In contrast, modern CALL programs emphasize student control or, following Higgins (1983), the Pedagogue[12] Role of the computer (see also Späth, 1994). ICALL systems provide even more learner control than traditional drill and practice programs due to their sophisticated answer processing mechanisms, the NLP component. They are thus more likely to overcome the rigidity of the response requirements. In practical terms, users navigate more freely through the program, can terminate at any point, provide a wider range of language output and have a number of options while working on different tasks. Despite this extra user control, learners do not, of course, always use each and every option available. For example, Cobb and Stevens (1996) discovered that students did not make use of help options although they knew that such use could improve their learning outcome (see also Steinberg, 1989; Bland, Noblitt, Armington, & Gay, 1990; Chapelle, Jamieson, & Park, 1996).

Chapelle and Mizuno (1989) found in a study on learner-controlled CALL grammar lessons that there is a need for teachers and researchers alike to observe student use of CALL. Ideally, programs should be developed, tested and then revised to reflect student preferences and instructors' guidance towards appropriate use (Hubbard, 1992). While the past decade has contributed to a better understanding of learner control in CALL, a number of issues are, nevertheless, outstanding and more research in this area is needed.

In terms of error correction, van der Linden (1993) found, when comparing learner strategies in programs with different levels of feedback, that feedback about the type of error encouraged students to correct themselves. Does this apply in a learner-controlled grammar practice environment in which the student can access correct answers or even skip exercises? A study by Cobb and Stevens (1996) showed that students "who rely excessively on program-supplied help are not learning as much as those who try to solve problems through their own self-generated trial-and-error feedback" (p. 132). For this reason, while CALL programs should provide a degree of learner control (Steinberg, 1989), it is important that students do not over-use the quick route to the correct answer.

Heift (2002) investigated the impact of learner control on the error correction process within an online parser-based CALL program. Specifically, the study aimed to determine whether students correct themselves in a learner-controlled practice environment of an ICALL system. The study also examined whether proficiency level influences students' error correction behavior.

The data show that 85% of the 33 participants revised their sentences far more often than they peeked at the correct answer(s). The remaining students corrected themselves on occasion, but relied more often on system help. The data indicate that students skipped exercises in only 1% of the total server requests.

The study further identified four interaction types among the participants: *Browsers*, *Frequent Peekers*, *Sporadic Peekers*, and *Adamants*. The data indicate that the majority of students are *Sporadic Peekers*, preferring to work through the error correction process and to peek at the correct answer only occasionally. Language proficiency seems to be a determiner: In short, lower performers make more use of system help (peeks and skips) than higher performers, with the exception of very high performers, who may be skipping trivial material.

Heift's study confirms previous studies and indicates that students tended overwhelmingly to correct themselves and thus made appropriate and effective use of the system capabilities of an ICALL system. Students also showed distinct interaction patterns depending on their proficiency level, thus suggesting that a CALL program should allow for individualization of the learning process.

Klenner et al. (Klenner & Visser, 2003; Klenner, 2004) discuss DiBEx, a dialogue-based explanation facility, which engages in a tutorial dialogue if the student made a linguistic error. DiBEx attempts to guide the student to identify the location and nature of an error. It starts off by providing sparse feedback and adds new pieces of information if necessary (Klenner, 2004). In spite of the fact that DiBEx is only a research prototype, it shows that it is possible to adjust the level and verbosity of feedback in a student-computer interaction.

4.6.4 Feedback and linguistic output

Chapelle (1998) lists seven hypotheses "relevant for developing multimedia CALL" (p. 23). The two hypotheses most relevant to the discussion at hand are discussed below:

Learners need to notice errors in their own output

The hypothesis relates to the importance of noticing linguistic features of the target language. It states that the syntactic mode of processing helps learners to internalize new forms (Pica et al., 1989) and to improve the accuracy of their existing grammatical knowledge (Nobuyoshi & Ellis, 1993). The process of noticing can occur through the learner's own reflection and monitoring or through triggers provided by others. Swain and Lapkin (1995) describe the hypothesis as follows:

> In producing L2, a learner will on occasion become aware of (i.e., notice) a linguistic problem (brought to his/her attention either by external feedback (e.g., clarification requests) or internal feedback). Noticing a problem 'pushes' the learner to modify his/her output. In doing so, the learner may sometimes be forced into a more syntactic processing mode than might occur in comprehension. (p. 373)

Learners need to correct their linguistic output

> When errors are recognized in comprehensible output, the process of the learner's self-correction is also believed to be beneficial, particularly because the linguistic items for which self-correction occurs may be those for which the learner's knowledge is fragile. Error correction affords the opportunity to "focus on form" (Long, 1988). Focus on form is expected to be beneficial when it occurs during the process of attempting to construct meanings. In other words, it is important that the language containing the noticed error be used in communication rather than merely displaying examples of the target language. Corrections can come from learners' own hypothesis testing, from their requests for assistance from others, or from explicit correction. (Chapelle, 1998, p. 24)

Based on these hypotheses, Chapelle (1998, pp. 30–31) recommends the following output-related evaluation questions:

1. Is there evidence that learners notice their errors in their output?
2. Do learners correct their linguistic output?

These questions have been addressed in a number of studies which will be discussed in the following section.

4.6.5 Feedback and learner uptake

Issues regarding the role and contribution of corrective feedback for language learning have been central to second language acquisition (SLA) theory and pedagogy. Corrective feedback has received much attention in the oral classroom lately, in particular, studies that investigate the effectiveness of *recasts*. Following Lyster and Ranta (1997), recasts involve a teacher's reformulation of a student's utterance, minus the error, sometimes also referred to as "paraphrase" (Spada & Fröhlich, 1995).

Nicholas, Lightbown, and Spada (2001), for example, found that recasts appear to be most effective in contexts where it is clear to the learner that the recast is a reaction to the accuracy of the form, not the content, of the original utterance (Long, Inagaki, & Ortega, 1998; Mackey & Philp, 1998; Ellis, Basturkmen, & Loewen, 2001; Lyster, 2001). More generally, studies further indicate that the efficacy of corrective feedback in the oral classroom is determined by a number of factors. For instance, Havranek and Cesnik (2001) found that the success of corrective feedback is affected by its format, the type of error and certain learner characteristics. Of the learner characteristics taken into consideration, verbal intelligence, relative proficiency (within levels at school or university) and the learner's attitude towards correction proved to be most influential. Despite a vast interest in studying the role of corrective feedback in the oral classroom, very little research has been conducted for the CALL environment.[13] Due to a difference in modes of instruction, however, the studies and their outcomes will most likely vary for the two respective learning environments and thus independent research in both areas is needed.

The limited research that does exist for grammar instruction in CALL can be classified into two categories: performance-based and interaction-based studies. The goal of the former is to examine the effects of different types of feedback on the learning outcome. For example, Nagata (1993, 1996, 1997) found that meta-linguistic feedback — feedback that explains the type of an error — is more effective than feedback in the form of just a correct answer, location of error based on a string-to-string comparison, or based on anticipated incorrect answers (see Garrett, 1987; Nagata, 1993). A study group that received meta-linguistic feedback performed significantly better on a post-test than a control group which received no error explanation (see also van der Linden, 1993; Yang & Akahori, 1999). In contrast, interaction-based studies (Robinson et al., 1985; Bationo, 1992; Heift, 2001, 2002, 2003, 2004; Pujolà, 2001) are primarily concerned with the ways in which students use CALL applications. They research how students react to various types of feedback. Tracking technology, in particular if implemented in Web-based applications, allows researchers to collect large data sets for subsequent analyses. User responses and navigation patterns can be recorded in a data log. The findings can make suggestions for software design and thus optimal software usage, all of which will eventually contribute to a more effective language learning environment.

A study by Heift (2004), for instance, investigated learner feedback in CALL with respect to learner uptake, which she defined as student responses to corrective feedback. In other words, she studied whether and how learners attempt to correct their mistake(s) after receiving feedback from a CALL system. The study considered three distinct types of feedback that differ in the amount and specificity of information provided to the learner, as well as the presentation format. However, all three feedback types provide an interactive environment in which students receive corrective feedback that encourages them to attend to linguistic form and to revise their input. A study by Robinson et al. (1985), for instance, showed that greater learning gains were achieved with feedback that identified the existence of an error but still required the learner to locate the error and correct it. A question which arises is whether students are more inclined to revise their input and show more learner uptake for certain types of feedback than for others.

The interactionist Second Language Acquisition (SLA) theory (Pica, 1994; Long, 1996; Gass, 1997) and the Noticing Hypothesis (Schmidt, 1990) suggest that negotiated interaction can facilitate SLA and that one reason for this could be that, during interaction, learners may receive feedback on their utterances. According to Schmidt (1995), the Noticing Hypothesis states that "what learners notice in input becomes intake for learning" (p. 20). However, the following conditions apply (Hegelheimer & Chapelle, 2000; see also Cross, 2002):

Linguistic input needs to be both syntactically and semantically comprehended in order to be acquired by the learner (commonly referred to as intake).
Input is more likely to become intake if it is noticed.
Learners are most likely to notice linguistic form during interaction (negotiation of form).

Most useful are interactions that help learners comprehend the input and improve the comprehensibility of their linguistic output.

Given these assumptions, the quality of interaction between the computer and the learner is also determined by the type of feedback the system provides. Considering SLA theory, there are a number of studies that investigated corrective feedback and learner uptake in the oral classroom. For example, Lyster and Ranta (1997)[14] in their study of immersion classes at the primary level found the following types of feedback used by language instructors:

1. Explicit Correction
2. Recast
3. Clarification
4. Meta-linguistic Feedback
5. Elicitation
6. Repetition

The study further showed that feedback types 1–3 were most commonly used, 4 and 5 were most effective at eliciting uptake, and 6 often co-occurred with feedback types 1–5. Due to the medium, feedback in a CALL environment cannot be identical to feedback in the oral classroom, however, Table 4.6 illustrates the types of feedback found in classroom studies and their proposed CALL counterparts.

Explicit Correction and Recast are very similar with respect to learner uptake. Both feedback types provide the correct answer. Unlike Recast, however, Explicit Correction provides the correct form overtly to the learner (You mean ...). However, neither Explicit Correction nor Recast can lead to learner uptake in a CALL environment. Once the correct answer has been supplied by the system, learner uptake and thus a negotiation of form between the learner and the CALL program is not an option (Lyster, 2001).

Clarification with its *Try again!* counterpart in CALL provides no guidance to learners to correct their mistakes. In the absence of a language instructor, however, it is desirable to achieve a more enhanced interaction between the CALL program and the learner, one in which learners receive more detailed feedback on their work and progress. Nevertheless, there are successful implementations of this feedback type when augmented with guidance to additional learner resources. Levy (1999b), for example, in his CALL program for advanced ESL learners discusses the positive effects of learner guidance through the implementation of flashing lights. The exact wording of Clarification in a CALL environment certainly deserves more attention. Even the variation between *Try again!* and *I cannot understand.* might possibly reveal a difference in student behavior. This is especially

Table 4.6 Feedback types in the oral classroom and the CALL environment

Feedback type	*Oral classroom*	*CALL*
Explicit Correction	You mean ...	Correct answer
Recast	Teacher Reformulation	Correct answer
Clarification	What do you mean?	Try again!
Meta-linguistic Feedback	Explanation of error type	Explanation of error type
Elicitation	Ellipsis	Highlighting
Repetition	Intonation	Highlighting

important if one considers the control implications of the two requests: with *try again* the program assumes control, whereas with *I cannot understand/the program cannot analyze your answer* control remains with the student.

Both Elicitation and Repetition are rendered as highlighting in a study by Heift (2004). It is possible to highlight the error, which would be similar to repetition, or highlight the correct part of the utterance, which would be closer to elicitation, particularly if one compares this to the rendering in the oral classroom as ellipsis.

Heift (2004) conducted a study in which she investigated *Meta-linguistic* feedback, *Elicitation,* and *Repetition.* The goal of Heift's study was to examine the effects of corrective feedback on learner uptake. In particular, the following research questions were addressed:

What is the distribution of corrective feedback types in relation to learner uptake? Of interest to her study were the following feedback types: *Meta-linguistic*, *Meta-linguistic* + *Highlighting,* and *Repetition/Elicitation* + *Highlighting*?

What is the distribution of learner uptake in relation to learner variables?

How do students rate different types of feedback?

Figure 4.9, Figure 4.10, and Figure 4.11 in the following section illustrate the distinctions between the three feedback types.

The three feedback types

For the *Meta-linguistic* feedback, students receive a detailed error explanation. For example, for the input given in Figure 4.9, the feedback states that the sentence contains an error and that the past participle instead of the infinitive is needed (*Klaus has *bake* the cake). In case of a grammatical

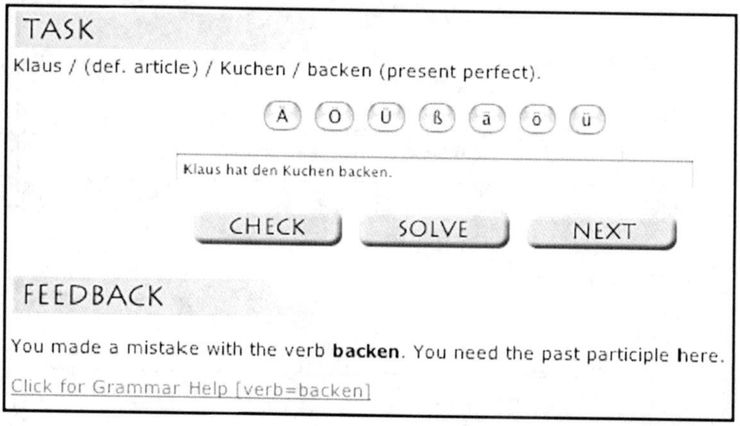

Figure 4.9 Meta-linguistic feedback in the *E-Tutor*

error, the *E-Tutor,* the ILTS used in the study, also displays a context-sensitive help link that provides an inflectional paradigm. In this example, the inflectional paradigm is that of the verb *backen* (to bake).

In the event of an error, students have a number of options. The student can either correct the error and resubmit the sentence by clicking the "CHECK" button, or peek at the correct answer(s) with the "SOLVE" button and/or skip to the next exercise with the "NEXT" button. If the student chooses to correct the sentence, it will be checked for further errors. The iterative correction process continues until the sentence is correct.

The current study investigated whether, given the various options and the three feedback types, students are more inclined to revise their input by attending to system feedback, or, whether they ignore system feedback by clicking the SOLVE and/or NEXT button, in which case there is no learner uptake.

For the feedback type *Meta-linguistic + Highlighting*, the system response is identical to that in Figure 4.9, except here the student input is also displayed in the feedback section and the error is highlighted, as given in Figure 4.10. In case of an error, students have the same options as described for the *Meta-linguistic* feedback type.

For the final feedback type, *Repetition + Highlighting*, the student input is repeated and the error is highlighted as with *Meta-linguistic + Highlighting* above, but here the student does not receive a detailed error explanation (Figure 4.11). Instead, the system only provides a hint as to which main error category has been violated, for example, a grammar versus a spelling mistake.[15] In case of an error, students have the same options as described for the two feedback types above.

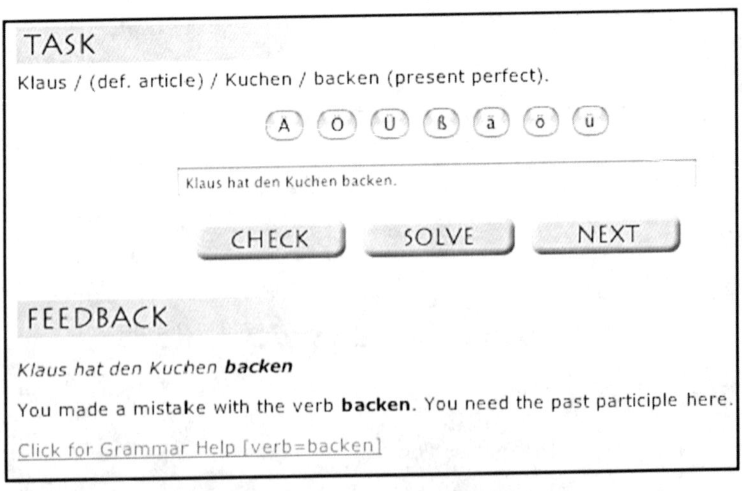

Figure 4.10 Meta-linguistic + highlighting in the *E-Tutor*

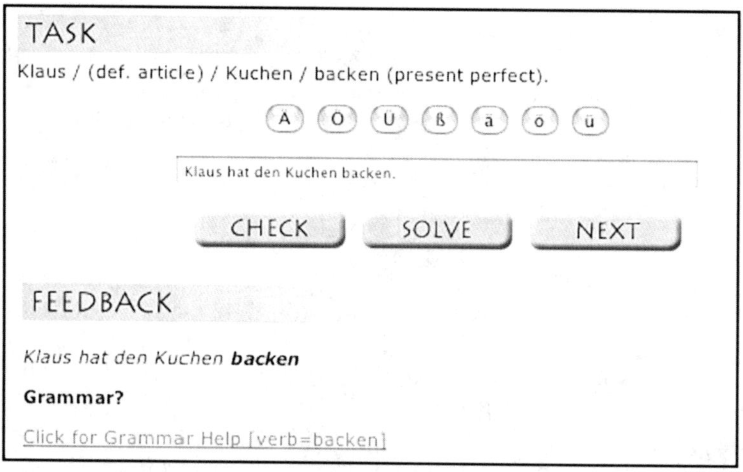

Figure 4.11 Repetition + highlighting in the *E-Tutor*

Comparison of the three feedback types

For a comparison of the three feedback types, Heift calculated the number of correct responses, the submissions that contained an error and the number of total submissions for each feedback type. The number of correct responses at first and subsequent tries was also counted. Finally, the log allowed to determine submissions where 1) the students looked up the answer (peeks), and 2) skipped the exercise altogether and moved on to another exercise (skips). In both instances, no learner uptake of the feedback could be observed. The results are given in Table 4.7.[16]

Table 4.7 indicates that the total number of submissions for the three feedback types is fairly balanced with slightly more submissions received for *Repetition + Highlighting* (17381). The data further show that most correct responses were achieved by *Meta-linguistic* (42.1%) and *Meta-linguistic + Highlighting* (43.4%). However, Heift was also interested at which point in the correction process a correct answer was achieved. While it is not surprising that students were more successful at obtaining a correct answer after several tries as opposed to at their first try, the difference between the two possibilities turned out to be minimal. This might be due to the fact that students had practiced the vocabulary and grammar constructions of each chapter in the oral classroom prior to completing the online exercises. As a result, students were probably quite successful at achieving a correct answer on their first try.

However, with respect to learner uptake it is of more interest how students responded to an error given their options:

Table 4.7 Submissions for each feedback type (Heift, 2004)

Submission types	*Feedback type*			*Totals*
	Meta-linguistic	*Meta-linguistic + highlighting*	*Repetition + highlighting*	
Correct	7,128 (42.1%)	7,508 (43.4%)	6,509 (37.4%)	21,145 (41%)
Correct on 1st try	3,364 (19.9%)	3,506 (20.3%)	3,104 (17.8%)	9,974 (19.3%)
Correct on 1+n tries	3,764 (22.3%)	4,002 (23.1%)	3,405 (19.6%)	11,171 (21.7%)
Errors	8,569 (50.7%)	8,610 (49.8%)	8,940 (51.5%)	26,119 (50.6%)
Peeks and skips	1,208 (7.2%)	1,176 (6.8%)	1,932 (11.1%)	4,316 (8.4%)
Total submissions	16,905 (100%)	17,294 (100%)	17,381 (100%)	51,580 (100%)

1. Students can attempt to correct the error and then resubmit the sentence for further analysis (learner uptake), or
2. students can choose to ignore the error and instead either look up the answer (peek) or skip the exercise altogether by moving on to the next exercise (skip). In both instances, however, there is no learner uptake, that is, no attempt at revising the input is made.

To investigate learner uptake, the uptake for each study participant was divided by the number of total submissions of the participant under each feedback condition. A three-way mixed ANOVA design with gender and language proficiency as between-subject factors completed the analysis.

Figure 4.12 shows the means of learner uptake for each feedback type. The data show that with *Meta-linguistic + Highlighting* our study participants are most likely to correct their mistakes (87.4%) while the least learner uptake occurs with *Repetition + Highlighting* (81.7%). The difference between *Meta-linguistic* feedback (86.9%) and *Meta-linguistic + Highlighting* (87.4%) is minor although it appears that highlighting has some effect on students attempting to correct their errors.

The test of within-subject effects with respect to the three feedback types indicates a statistically significant difference ($F = 11.251$; $p = 0.000$). To determine inter-group variation, a pair-wise comparison with significance level .05 revealed a significant difference between *Meta-linguistic* and *Repetition + Highlighting* (.000) and between *Meta-linguistic + Highlighting* and *Repetition + Highlighting* (.000).

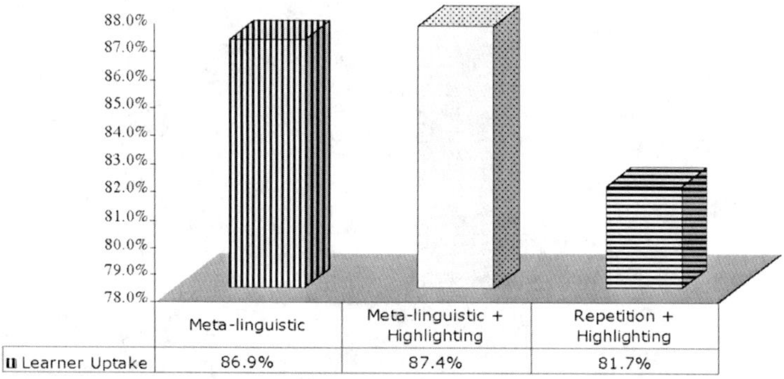

Figure 4.12 Learner uptake by feedback type (Heift, 2004)

Learner variables

Of further interest are learner characteristics that might affect learner uptake for the three feedback types. In her study, Heift considered two learner variables: language proficiency and gender. The study participants each belonged to one of three language skill levels: beginners, advanced beginners, and intermediates. There were 49 beginners, 105 advanced beginners, and 23 intermediates in the study. There were 112 females and 65 males.

The three-way mixed ANOVA design applied to feedback types with language proficiency and gender as between-subject factors revealed that the results are not statistically significant (see also Brandl, 1995). Although the results are not statistically significant, a comparison of the means for both language proficiency and gender is, nonetheless, interesting. The results are displayed in Figure 4.13 and Figure 4.14, respectively.

Figure 4.13 indicates that there is a decrease in learner uptake for all language skill levels if errors are merely repeated (*Repetition + Highlighting*) as opposed to explained (*Meta-linguistic* and *Meta-linguistic + Highlighting*). With respect to highlighting errors, students at the intermediate level seem to be least affected by the absence of such a feature, given that they achieved the same means for *Meta-linguistic* versus *Meta-linguistic + Highlighting*. It is quite possible that students at the intermediate level are familiar enough with grammar explanations that such a feature makes less of a difference to them than to learners at the beginner and advanced beginner levels.

Figure 4.14 illustrates that both female and male students show the most learner uptake with *Meta-linguistic + Highlighting* while the biggest difference occurs between *Meta-linguistic + Highlighting* and *Repetition + Highlighting*. In general, the female study participants attempted to correct their errors less often than the male students although the difference is not statistically significant.

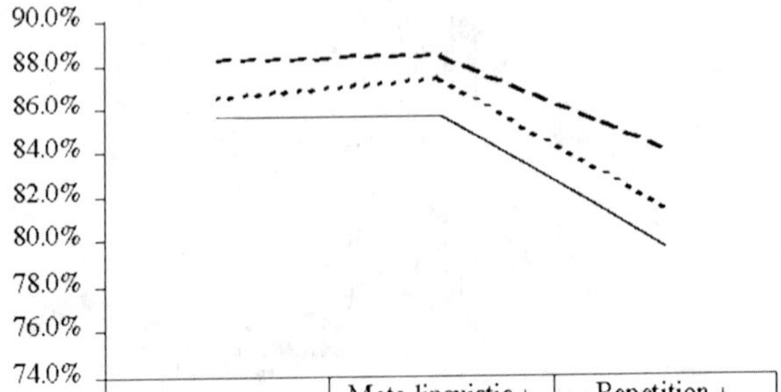

	Meta-linguistic	Meta-linguistic + Highlighting	Repetition + Highlighting
Beginners	88.3%	88.4%	84.1%
Advanced Beginners	86.5%	87.4%	81.2%
Intermediates	85.6%	85.6%	79.6%

Figure 4.13 Learner uptake by feedback type and language proficiency (Heift, 2004)

The distribution of females and males with respect to language proficiency was fairly even. Thus language proficiency was not a determining factor in the differences found in men's and women's responses to corrective feedback.

In addition to the quantitative data collection Heift (2004) considered two further questions that were part of a follow-up questionnaire:

1. Did you notice that the feedback differed in each chapter?
2. Would you prefer the most explicit feedback at all times?

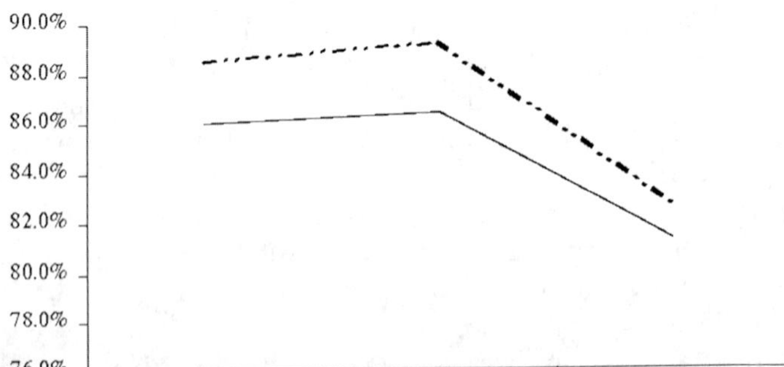

	Meta-linguistic	Meta-linguistic + Highlighting	Repetition + Highlighting
Women	86.0%	86.4%	81.3%
Men	88.5%	89.2%	82.6%

Figure 4.14 Learner uptake by feedback type and gender (Heift, 2004)

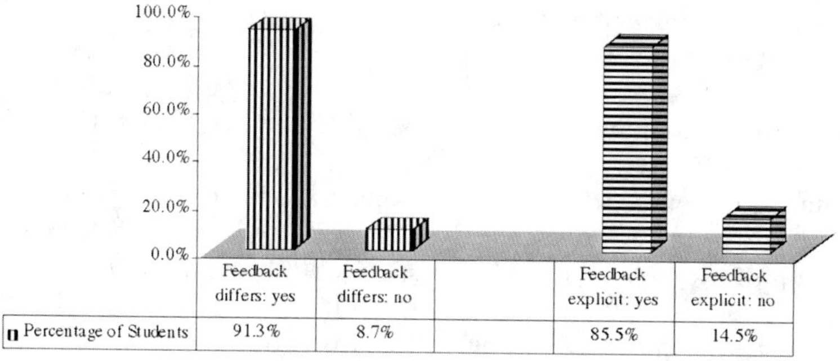

Figure 4.15 Student responses from the questionnaire (Heift, 2004)

The results, given in Figure 4.15, indicate that the vast majority of study participants (91.3%) noticed that the feedback differed during system use and that most of the students (85.5%) would prefer the most explicit feedback at all times.

It is surprising, however, that 8.7% of the students did not notice the change in feedback although the log confirmed that the students, all of whom were advanced beginners, had received each of the three feedback types. It is possible that students indeed did not notice the change, or maybe misunderstood the question on the questionnaire, or likely, that student self-report in this context is not very reliable.

A more detailed data analysis revealed that the majority of the students who stated that they do not prefer the most explicit feedback at all times were at the intermediate level. It is possible that more advanced students, in particular in the case of a trivial error, prefer to solve the task by themselves without explicit feedback. Considering these results, a further investigation of the effects of scaled feedback seems necessary (see Nassaji & Swain, 2000, for a discussion on feedback suited to learner expertise).

Overall, Heift's (2004) study suggests that feedback type has an effect on learner uptake: the more explicit and prominent the feedback the more likely students will revise their errors in written grammar and vocabulary exercises, independent of language proficiency and gender. However, it remains to be investigated to what extent the results are applicable and relevant to CALL with all its different facets and applications, for example, to the training of listening and reading skills (see also Chapelle, 2001).

In addition, there are a number of questions that call for further investigation:

What is the effect of other variables on learner uptake? For example, do certain error types elicit more learner uptake than others? What is the role of motivation, learning styles and learner strategies? Studies in the oral classroom, for instance, indicate that learners' attitudes have an effect on the success of corrective feedback (Havranek & Cesnik, 2001). Similar results might be found for a CALL environment.

What is the effect of additional learner resources on student responses to corrective feedback? For example, if a CALL program provides feedback that is coupled with context-sensitive help in form of a dictionary and/or grammar paradigms, are students less likely to be affected by different feedback types?

A final question addresses the language and format of the feedback that might have an impact on student responses to corrective feedback. For example, Mackey, Gass, and McDonough (2000) found that the nature as well as the content of feedback might affect learners' perceptions of corrective feedback in the oral classroom (see also Havranek & Cesnik, 2001). Does the same apply to a CALL environment? These questions are among the many that still need to be answered for a better understanding of feedback in CALL. The quality of feedback, however, is very closely linked to the quality of delivery and hence the design of the software.

4.7 SYSTEM DESIGN ISSUES

Over the past years, we have seen a significant increase in empirical research that investigates best practices in both CALL and parser-based CALL. Online systems, in particular, have enabled us to collect data that not only differ in size but also in kind. For instance, data sets are no longer limited to particular user groups, that is, most commonly, a single language learning class in a particular location. Instead, empirical studies often include study participants from all over the world. Moreover, there is a notable shift in focus from the traditional performance-based studies to empirical research that evaluates student use of CALL systems and, more generally, software design. Such studies are an excellent indication for the importance of software design in NLP in CALL.

Software design is a cyclical process and, ultimately, it is the user studies that inform us how learners are employing specific features in a CALL system (Hubbard, 1992; Levy, 1997, 1999a; Hémard, 2000; Chapelle, 2003; Colpaert, 2004). For that reason, we first need to investigate learner usage and then design and revise our systems accordingly. This will eventually lead to software that students use most effectively and therefore promote best results. It is often, however, surprising to discover that students use software quite differently from what designers had intended or even assumed. For instance, Heift (2006), examined design issues with groups of learners of German, in particular, she investigated their use of task guidance in the *E-Tutor*, the online parser-based system discussed in the previous sections. Task guidance is designed to help the user in solving and/or completing a task as opposed to operational guidance that is intended to assist the user with the functions of a computer program.

Task guidance is especially important in self-study programs where students are generally more reliant and dependent on auxiliary tools to achieve the learning objectives. Task guidance can be provided by means of online dictionaries, concordancers with learner corpora, transcripts, translations, recordings, cultural notes and inflectional paradigms, etc. Most commonly, learners can access these help options at their own convenience. Some of the help features may appear static although the information provided to the user may, nonetheless, be context-specific and thus dynamic. This applies, for instance, to a dictionary look-up that is linked to words in context. Additional modes of help options include user-adaptive versus more generic guidance. For example, we may specify help options for certain errors and not others. Moreover, help options may be individualized, that is, they address the needs of different learners. They also may come in different presentation modes such as oral versus written. For example, for all grammar and vocabulary exercises in the *E-Tutor*, the system provides error-specific feedback and additional help options in form of a dictionary and context-sensitive grammar help. For instance, in the example given in Figure 4.16, the student provided the incorrect definite article following the German dative preposition *nach*. To guide the learner towards a correct answer, the system provides the error explanation "There is a mistake with the article *das*. You need the dative case." along with links to additional error-specific help on the preposition *nach* and the definite articles.

The content for the context-sensitive help links is illustrated in Figure 4.17 and Figure 4.18, respectively. Figure 4.17 displays the grammar explanations on the usage of German prepositions: *nach* requires the dative case. Learners who require assistance with German articles can access the declensions of the definite article given in Figure 4.18.

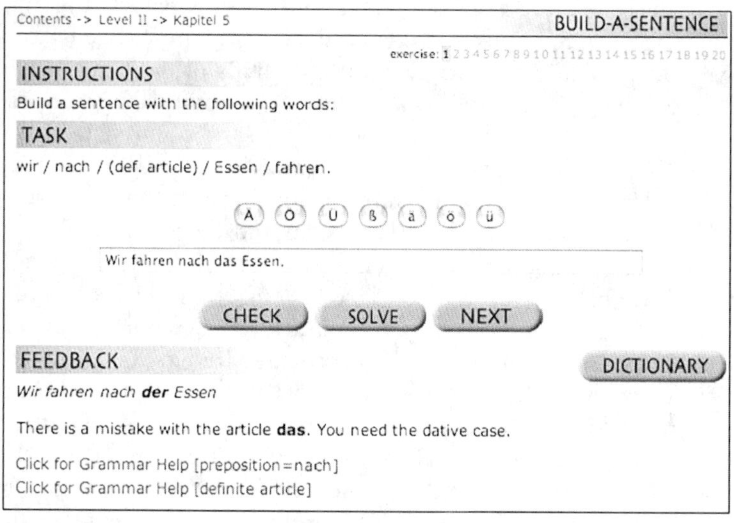

Figure 4.16 Context-sensitive help in the *E-Tutor*

Prepositions

Accusative Prepositions are prepositions that always take the **accusative** case.

durch	für	gegen
ohne	um	

Example: Das Geschenk ist *für ihn.*

Dative Prepositions are prepositions that always take the **dative** case.

aus	außer	bei	mit
nach	seit	von	zu

Example: Ich bin *mit dem Zug* gefahren.

Genitive Prepositions are prepositions that always take the **genitive** case.

wegen	trotz	statt	während

Example: Lisa ist *trotz des Schneesturms* gekommen.

Two-way Prepositions are prepositions that take *either* the **accusative** (toward a destination - *wohin*?) or **dative** case (in a fixed location - *wo*?).

an	auf	hinter	in	neben
über	unter	vor	zwischen	

Wohin=accusative: Ich hänge das Bild *an die Wand.*

Wo=dative: Das Bild hängt *an der Wand.*

QuickRef generated on 05-11-07-12:27:07

Figure 4.17 Context-sensitive help for the preposition *nach*

The information presented in Figure 4.17 and Figure 4.18 is context-specific, that is, it is specific to the error given in Figure 4.16. From an implementation point of view, this functionality requires a computer system that first identifies the error and then reacts to the user's request by providing relevant error explanations and/or linguistic paradigms. Given a comprehensive CALL system that may contain hundreds of individual exercises, which in turn may trigger all kinds of errors, it is not feasible to encode this knowledge manually. Instead this process needs to be automated.

In the *E-Tutor*, most of the help pages are dynamically generated, that is, each inflectional paradigm is created during run-time by extracting words from the main lexicon of the system and then inserting them into a template. This has several advantages with respect to system design and maintenance. For instance, if a new lexeme is added to the lexicon the context-specific help for this lexeme is automatically generated. In the *E-Tutor*, this is achieved by determining the inflectional paradigm of a lexeme by its word class, for example, verb. Each word class in turn has a template that contains place holders for the different inflections. During run-time, the system extracts each inflectional form from the lexicon and then inserts it into the appropriate place holder in the template. This also means that a change to a lexeme or its inflectional paradigm needs to be made in only one location, that is, the lexicon. This is certainly an important design consideration with a fairly large lexicon containing thousands of words.

Articles

Definite Article

	Singular			Plural
	Masculine	Feminine	Neuter	All Genders
Nominative	cer	die	das	die
Accusative	cen	die	das	die
Dative	cem	der	dem	den
Genitive	ces	der	des	der

Figure 4.18 Context-sensitive help for definite articles

In addition to dynamically generated help pages, the *E-Tutor*, however, also contains a few static help pages. For instance, these include notes on word order, or, more generally, pages that provide rule-specific content to the learner. An example of a static page is that of German prepositions, given in Figure 4.17.

Colpaert (2004) makes a useful classification of CALL software that considers the following functionality types[17]: Tool, Monitor, Mentor, Tutor and Lector (see also Levy, 1997). Most relevant to the discussion of user guidance presented here is the *Monitor* type. Colpaert (2004) states that

> the "Monitor" type gives advice on demand (like the F7-key in Word). For example, it can check spelling and grammar and provide translation, pronunciation, various hints, feedback, scores and reports. A typical example is context-sensitive help. Opening a help file is a tool functionality; opening a help file on the correct page needs more lines of code; the system reacts to user requests with an analysis of the situation and a relevant response, but it never initiates an action or intervenes without a request. The system's reaction is content related and relevant to the user's situation. It is supposed to help the learner from a linguistic-didactic point of view. Menu-driven content selection mechanisms may also be classified as monitoring functions, because they give content on demand. (p. 85)

However, when designing different kinds of task guidance as described by Colpaert, a number of issues related to conception and implementation need to be considered and addressed. For instance, what kind of help options do we provide to the user and what are the design criteria for the user interface? What are the effects of certain task and learner variables? How do multiple help features interact with each other, that is, when do multiple representations of information assist and when do they hinder learning? Do learners use help features and if so, how?

A number of researchers, for instance, have investigated dictionary use, in particular, they investigated the types of words that students look up and the influence of task and learner variables (see Laufer & Kimmel, 1997;

Atkins, 1998; Atkins & Varantola, 1998a; Bogaards, 1998; Hulstijn & Atkins, 1998; Nesi, 1998). These studies generally agree that learners do not look up all the words that cause problems. Instead they look up some types of words but not others. Moreover, studies indicate that there is some benefit to including illustrations in dictionary entries for some words, for example, concrete nouns. In addition to dictionary usage, Pujolà (2001, 2002) considered further help options in a reading and listening activity, for example, cultural notes, transcript, subtitles and play controls, feedback. He found that many variables affect the amount and quality of the use of help ranging from the learners' individual differences to the CALL environment itself (see also Plass, 1998; Hoven, 2003; Plass, Chun, Mayer, & Leutner, 2003). These kinds of findings assist us in designing system features that learners will use effectively and, ultimately, will address their learning needs.

The study by Heift (2006) builds on existing research and she investigated the relationship between task guidance, corrective feedback, task type, and learner variables. More specifically, the following research questions are addressed in her study:

1. Do language learners access context-sensitive help? If so, what is the relationship between different types of corrective feedback and learners' usage of context-sensitive help?
2. Are certain learner variables a predictor of learners' usage of context-sensitive help?
3. Does help access differ with respect to distinct exercise types?

Heift's study results indicate that help access differs significantly with respect to distinct modes of feedback, different exercise types and language proficiency. In general, learners rely more heavily on additional help options when system feedback is sparse, that is, the system merely repeats the error instead of providing an error explanation. This applies especially to beginner learners. Furthermore, help pages that are context-sensitive and dynamic have shown to be most useful to learners because students access help most often for morphological errors.

While it is not surprising that system feedback is a significant factor in student use of a CALL program, it is, to some extent, perplexing that a design feature such as task guidance is still not part of the general design of CALL programs. For instance, in 1999, Arneil and Holmes already recognized problems associated with the general design of Web applications and according to their experience, "the vast majority tend to be of the "one-click right/wrong" variety. They are typically multiple choice exercises and rarely provide useful feedback in the event of a wrong answer, or any additional information in response to a correct answer" (p. 13; see also Felix, 1999).

Two years later, Felix (2001) states that "CALL on the Web has limitations in terms of quality, speed and variety of interaction it offers" (p. 190). Similarly, Davies (2002) points out that

> there is an unfortunate trend for designers of Web-based CALL to adopt a point-and-click-let's-move-on-quick approach, concentrating on flashy presentations and neglecting features such as discrete error analysis, feedback and branching, all of which are well established in CALL research and development. (Module 2.3, Section 3.1)

In 2007, while the user interface has become much fancier, the pedagogy has still not caught up and, in fact, the average Web-based CALL application still lacks behind some of the earlier desktop-based CALL applications. This is surprising given that studies also indicate that users in general prefer the simple design that often came with better pedagogy. For instance, Hémard and Cushion (2000) state that in their studies "overwhelmingly, students opted for greater usability and learnability rather than complex, technology-driven functionality" (p. 109). This suggests that it is the designers rather than the users that need to be educated that pedagogy and learning content are far more important than whizz-bang features. However, software designers are generally not experts in second language acquisition which, at least to some extent, explains this lack of focus on pedagogy.

Undoubtedly, a fair amount of resources are required to design a system capable of providing context-sensitive task guidance. However, Heift's (2006) study prompts system suggestions that can certainly be implemented even in a non-parser-based application. For instance, the feedback in non-parser-based systems is generally fairly limited but, according to Heift's study, it is with these applications that students benefit most from additional resources in form of links to inflectional paradigms, additional grammar notes, etc. From a design point of view, these help features are just as onerous to create in a more generic application than in parser-based applications (see Laufer & Kimmel, 1997; Atkins, 1998; Atkins & Varantola, 1998b; Bogaards, 1998; Hulstijn & Atkins, 1998; Nesi, 1998 for various implementations of dictionary look-ups). The main difference lies in the fact that it is far more difficult and laborious to provide context-sensitive information in non-parser-based systems because a parser can identify the source of the error. Accordingly, the error can then be easily linked to additional information. Nonetheless, it is possible for a non-parser-based system to provide a search engine that allows the student to look for an inflectional paradigm most relevant to the task at hand. Alternatively, an additional link for each content word of the task can be included, in particular, for sentence-based tasks.

Heift's (2006) study provided a quantitative analysis of learner access of additional help options by also noting that access of dynamically generated help pages is much more frequent than that of static pages.[18] These results suggest that the overall content and quality of certain help features may also affect user rates. Further studies are necessary to support this claim, in particular, the long-term effect on student usage of task guidance needs to be examined closely. Moreover, there are many more possibilities of additional help options than presented in this article and different parameters need to be further tested with language learners. For instance, a subsequent study may determine the impact of further learner variables, static versus dynamically generated help and/or different display modes. Ultimately, user studies of this kind will assist us in designing CALL programs that learners will use effectively and that will address learners' needs.

While task guidance is only one example of possible design criteria that need to be considered and evaluated when designing CALL software Heift's study quite clearly indicates that students may use software quite differently from the way it was conceptualized and implemented. Here, adaptive systems have a distinct advantage. Such systems change their behavior according to the information they gathered about the learner. Usually, this collection of information about individual learners and the algorithms to interpret these data are termed student model. Student modeling is discussed in part 5.

5. Student modeling

5.1 INTRODUCTION

> A student model is any information which a teaching program has which is specific to the particular student being taught. The reason for maintaining such information is to help the program to decide on appropriate teaching actions. The information itself could range from a simple count of how many incorrect answers have been given, to some complicated data structure which purports to represent a relevant part of the student's knowledge of the subject. (O'Shea & Self, 1983, p. 143)

Individualized language instruction has long been recognized as a significant advantage of CALL over workbook tasks. A one size fits all approach is not appropriate for a learning environment. Students learn at their own pace and often work for their own purposes. Learners also vary with respect to prior language experience, aptitude, cognitive needs, beliefs, attitudes and/or learning styles and strategies. The Individual Differences Theory as described by Oxford (1995) suggests that learners learn in different ways and that no single methodology is effective for all. The theory further suggests "because each person is somewhat different, instruction must take these contrasts into account and provide a learning environment that optimizes the educational benefit of the contrasts" (p. 365). Accordingly, if learners learn differently, then they likely benefit from individualized instruction.

Despite the need for an individualized learning environment, student modeling has not been a strong focus of CALL. One likely reason is that in order for a computer program to adapt itself to different learner needs, the system needs a dynamic model of the strengths and weaknesses of the learner and this presents a difficult problem in itself (McCalla & Greer, 1992). However, a computer program that can analyze student errors can also keep a detailed record of student performance. The information can then be used to make system decisions based on the current student proficiency level and it assists in individualizing the language learning process with respect to learner feedback, assessment, and remediation (Heift & Nicholson, 2001). A student model enables the tutoring system to not only observe, record, and analyze surface phenomena of the learning activity such as text entered by language learners, but also to reason about the underlying causes of correct as well as incorrect responses.

This part discusses the theoretical issues surrounding student modeling and provides examples of parser-based CALL systems that have implemented various student modeling techniques. Student modeling has been at the center of attention in Computer-Aided Learning (CAL) and Intelligent Tutoring Systems (ITS) research. Self (1974) reviews student models of the time and comes to the conclusion that student modeling will provide better insights if it is "expressed in terms of a set of procedures in a high-level [programming] language" (p. 275).

Student models can be used in a number of ways (Elsom-Cook, 1993): corrective (providing tailored feedback), elaborative (extending the knowledge of the student), strategic (guiding decisions on teaching interventions), diagnostic (determining the knowledge state of the student), predictive (anticipating future student behavior), and evaluative (assessing the level of student achievement).[1] We start the discussion with an overview and review of some general aspects of user models and continue with a description of student models in ITS, as a subgroup of user models. The two terms *student model* and *learner model* are used synonymously and for stylistic reasons only. We conclude with a detailed discussion of learner models that are part of language learning systems, both parser-based and those built on pattern-matching and scoring algorithms.

5.2 AN OVERVIEW OF STUDENT MODELS

Artificial Intelligence (AI) has been interested in the development of user-adaptive systems for about thirty years. The goal of making software more responsive to its users and consequently more user-friendly, more efficient and more ergonomic is shared by all developers of user models. Up until the mid-1990s, a time when the World Wide Web became more and more widely used, user modeling concentrated on learner models and played an important role in instructional development. Student models are still important for the development of Intelligent Tutoring Systems (ITSs) and are still considered an essential part of user modeling. However, user modeling has also developed a strong record of achievement in many other areas, in particular, in personalizing the vast information the Web provides to its users. For example, user modeling is also concerned with areas such as:

- plan recognition — the user's goal and future steps in the plan are inferred from observed actions by the user (Brusilovsky, 2001). Plan recognition is also used to improve natural language understanding and generation (Chin, 2001).

- adaptive hypermedia — the content of webpages changes according to the information in the user model (Brusilovsky, 2001).
- universal access — user models are used to develop systems which adapt to a wide range of human abilities, skills, requirements, and preferences (Stephanidis, 2001).

Plan recognition is of limited use in language learning systems because text production can rarely be carried out by following a pre-defined and finite selection of plans or algorithms. Text production can be described as a problem solving activity. It is a process which has to overcome ill-defined problems. The solution state of these problems is not well-defined at the start of the problem solving activity and, for this reason, it is difficult to determine or follow a particular plan of action.

Adaptive hypermedia can play an important part in improving large language learning Web sites and online course management systems (Nakabayashi et al., 1997), but this aspect of user modeling will not be discussed here.[2] The applicability to *parser-based* CALL systems is more limited. In CALL, adaptive hypermedia are best applied to entire online courses.

Concepts from user modeling for universal access overlap with general attempts in learner modeling. Access is particularly relevant with regard to the student's ability and skill levels.

User models, in general, have a strong ethical dimension because they store and rely on personal information on human subjects. Here, issues of storing data about users securely and preventing misuse by third parties are highly relevant. A detailed discussion of the importance of privacy and security with regards to user modeling can be found in Schreck (2003). It suffices to say here that safe and transparent storage of student data should be a primary concern of any designer of a student model. It is best to familiarize oneself with the relevant legislation and guidelines in the country or countries where the software will be used.

Student models are more complex than other user models because misconceptions and inconsistencies in the student's knowledge have to be considered. Certain aspects of observable student behavior can only be described as stochastic. The following are possible reasons for students' inconsistent beliefs:

- In language learning, students are often testing hypotheses (see a discussion of the Output Hypothesis, Swain, 1985) and they expect feedback on these attempts. There are instances when students deliberately employ a wide variety of surface structures to try to convey the same meaning but to learn which of these will be accepted.

- Students are often unable to consider all relevant issues simultaneously when solving a problem because nobody has full access to one's full body of knowledge at all times.
- Students react adversely to external pressures.

For these reasons, learner models will always be approximations because of the noise present when inferring and maintaining the model (Mitrovic, Djordjevic-Kajan, & Stoimenov, 1996). Mitrovic et al. (1996) identify four different sources of this noise: inconsistent student behavior, dynamic and nonmonotonic nature of human learning, ambiguity of possible explanations for the observed behavior, and indeterminacy of student answers. Huang (1992), however, argues that students are capable of recognizing their inconsistent beliefs if they notice them. This leads him to assume that tutors can help students to remove such inconsistencies and misconceptions by drawing their attention to them.

Student models are challenging in a number of ways. Self (1979), in opposition to a number of other authors who list the advantages of student models, discusses the difficulties: how to capture what kind of information and how to maintain and implement it. Such difficulties have since been the subject of debate and, accordingly, we will provide glimpses of these discussions and report steps towards solving these problems.

Self (1989) demonstrates the difficulty of establishing the underlying cause of an error for a mathematical problem (integral of a given equation). He assumes that for the problem he presents there are 30 possible transformations (m). Each of them has approximately 5 mistransformations (n) and 10 steps (p) that need to be carried out. This results in $m(n+1)^p = 10^{24}$ paths that need to be explored. Self (1989) describes this as the intractable problem of student modeling and makes the following suggestions to bypass the problem:

- To design student-computer interactions for which the information to build the student model (especially about the student's goals?) is provided by the student while using the ITS and not inferred by the ITS from inadequate data.
- To explicitly link the proposed contents of student models with specific tutorial actions, ideally supported by educational evidence to determine the kind of information that is needed in the student model.
- To avoid viewing student models solely as devices to support remediation.
- To use student models "constructively" by regarding the contents as representations of student beliefs with no value judgment imposed by the ITS.

- To make the contents of the student model open to the student for them to reflect upon its contents and to remove all pretense that the ITS has a perfect understanding of them.
- To develop ITSs which adopt a more collaborative role, rather than a directive one, for then the style corresponds to a more adequate philosophy of knowledge acquired.

These suggestions have been implemented in a number of systems that are more focused and have more attainable goals. For example, cooperative, or also so-called, collaborative student models have been proposed with direct reference to Self's suggestions (e.g., Beck, Stern, & Woolf, 1997, p. 128). A collaborative learner model asks the student for information that it cannot infer from the input. For instance, it may ask students to assess their ability level for a particular skill. Self himself argues in 1994 that, even within the move toward Interactive Learning Environments (ILE), student models play a role by supporting autonomy and allowing alternative conceptions (Self, 1994, p. 4).

5.2.1 Different types of student models

Intelligent Tutoring Systems are traditionally described as consisting of three parts[3] (e.g., Beck, Stern, & Haugsjaa, 1996; Chin, 2001):

1. an expert model which contains the knowledge of the domain,
2. a teacher model which determines the system's teaching,
3. a student model which stores information about the learner[4]

According to Matthews (1992c), the main role of a student model (SM) is to enable "the Tutorial Module (TM) to adapt its behavior to the individual" (p. 16). He suggests a number of actions that can be carried out by a student model (and they frequently occur in conjunction with the tutorial module). For example, within error correction the SM can react in various ways:

- let the student try again;
- let the student examine an example of a similar type that she previously solved correctly;
- provide the correct version and let the student determine the mistake herself;
- provide overt correction with an explanation, and so on. (p. 16)

Kay (2001) argues that "the last decade has seen a considerable shift from this architecture" (p. 112) because learner control is now at the center of attention in ITS research and development. The learner interacts with a variety of tools and agents which simulate the domain, the teacher and peers. All of these interact with the learner model (Chin, 2001) and, to facilitate learner control, at least aspects of the model should be open to the learner. According to Chin (2001), "we need tools to support the learner in examining, exploring, correcting and scrutinizing the learner model" (p. 118).

A student model generally consists of four components (Néhémie, 1992):

1. a knowledge base about the student,
2. a query module that handles requests from other parts of the system and that produces responses based on the information it has about the student,
3. a module that updates the knowledge base depending on the student's interaction with the system,
4. a synthesis module that deduces a synthetic model of the student based on observed data.

The information recorded and maintained in the knowledge base broadly falls into two categories: a simpler model that only maintains some historical data of the user (scores, task completion, utterances produced, etc.)[5] and a more complex model, for which the system needs to deduce a more elaborate knowledge state of student beliefs. This can be problematic because the logs may contain contradictory data that first have to be analyzed and interpreted.

A further distinction is made between a surface level student model which "represents the scheduled problem solving plans and applied procedural knowledge" (Villano, 1992, p. 469) and a deeper level student model which "must infer and model the student's belief by interpreting the surface level student model" (Villano, 1992, p. 469).

In determining the quality of a learner model, the following questions play an essential role:

- How should the system deal with performance-related errors, that is, mistakes or lapses, as opposed to genuine competence-dependent errors?
- At which point should the system discard previous activity records that contain errors? For example, in determining the knowledge state of a particular student, should an error made three weeks ago be weighted equally as an error that was committed three hours ago?
- Is there a one-to-one mapping or, at least, a correlation between the surface error and the cause of the error for each student?

In general, student behavior is nonmonotonic, that is, learners exhibit contradictions in their behavior and in their beliefs. For this reason, a system needs to deal with inconsistent student answers and beliefs to obtain a more reliable student model, in particular, when using induction to build the student model.

Ideally, a student model is dynamic in that it reflects the student's learning progress over time. When the system attempts to predict the current knowledge state of the student, errors made when learning a new concept have to be assigned less weight than errors committed during or after the practicing phase. One way of achieving this is by data aging. Consider the following example from a study by Webb and Kuzmycz (1998):

> Data aging was implemented by reducing the accumulated score for each of $\#(C \rightarrow a)$ and $\#(C \rightarrow \neg a)$ [roughly speaking the number of correct and incorrect responses] for every a and C by the set aging rate after the prediction phase of each test round. Hence with an aging rate of 30%, if for some a and C $\#(C \rightarrow a)$ was 1 on every test, for prediction on round 5 [the last round] the cumulative value of $\#(C \rightarrow a)$ would be 2.533. The round 4 item would contribute 1.0, as it would not yet be aged. The round 3 item would contribute 0.7, as it would have aged once. The round 2 and 1 items would contribute 0.49 and 0.343 as they would be aged twice and three times respectively. (p. 388)

The authors report that data aging plays a positive role in predicting future test results. At the same time, they state "that such benefits are far from guaranteed" (p. 392). Webb and Kuzmycz (1998) experimented with different aging rates (between 5% and 50%) but they used arbitrarily fixed aging rates which is problematic. Aging rate is a dependent variable, that is, it is dependent on the student's learning progress. At the same time, student behavior and student beliefs are inconsistent which presents an additional challenge, in particular, in the domain of language learning.

Shute (1995), for example, proposes a student model paradigm called SMART which employs domain-specific (emerging knowledge and skills) and domain-independent information (initial aptitude). The paradigm was implemented and tested in Stat Lady, a program that teaches introductory statistics. The initial aptitude was computed on the basis of information on working memory capacity, inductive reasoning, processing speed and associative learning skill (Shute, 1995, p. 22). Domain-specific knowledge states were inferred from student results on various topics of the curriculum. These were then arranged in three difficulty-dependent hierarchies (symbolic knowledge [any symbol or formula], procedural skill [application of a formula], conceptual knowledge [relations among statistical concepts]).

However, not only aptitude plays a role in the domain-independent information about a learner; certain emotions as well as motivations and filters that depend on them are important variables in the quality of the learning process as well. Affective user modeling is concerned with the system's ability to model the user's affective states (Martinho, Machado, & Paiva, 2000). Emotions are ascribed by interpreting the user's behavior.

Martinho et al. discuss an affective user model for *Teatrix*, an ITS that teaches children narrative structures. They propose to appraise events relating to user goals to reason about possible emotions and to maintain information about the user's assumed attitudes and standards. It is their aim to "simulate the user's appraisal process" (Martinho et al., 2000, p. 72) by applying a two-stage affective cycle. In the first stage and, based on an assumed affective state, the system compares observed behavior to expected behavior and updates the model accordingly. In the second stage, the appraisal is simulated by inferring "what affective changes the observed events will activate and what actions are expected to occur" (p. 73).

Generally, it is difficult to elicit student-dependent information and, for this reason, it is often described in rather complex categories, for example, by using Gardner's multiple intelligences[6] or Bloom's learning goals.[7] Kelly and Tangney (2002) attempt to use both for their student model which aims at supporting the selection of appropriate instructional strategies. However, their conclusion suggests that both theoretical approaches lack granularity for precise modeling.

> It may indeed be possible to explicitly model how different categories of student [sic] preferred different models of presentation [of learning content]. However, this is time consuming and makes the assumption we know what the correct learning theory is. It also makes the assumption, that we can articulate the rules for updating the student model and for making pedagogical decisions. (p. 737)

Most learner models capture the knowledge state(s) of the student relative to the domain of learning. Far fewer models incorporate individual characteristics of the learner (Milne, Shiu, & Cook, 1996). However, the few examples above indicate that some work has been done in this area. Later in this part, we examine examples of student models in language learning systems that are primarily interested in personal traits such as beliefs about learning strategies. First, however, we present different modeling techniques that have been applied to ITSs.

5.2.2 Modeling techniques

A student model can be defined as a data structure that contains information about the student. Accordingly, the simplest way of maintaining this structure is by recording performance data in the form of scores. These scores, however, do not contain any information about the kind of knowledge that has been acquired, they only reflect how much knowledge has been gained (Gisolfi, Dattolo, & Balzano, 1992, p. 329).

Some learner models are merely a representation of the student's knowledge in a small number of key areas. Other learner models can be much more complex and may contain a representation of the student's learning styles and strategies as well as learner variables. Modeling additional student attributes will provide the system with more information and, in turn, the user with a more individualized experience. However, there is an increased difficulty in obtaining and using the information (Mabbott & Bull, 2004).

Over the last decade, great emphasis has been placed on inspectable or open learner models. These models can be inspected or even modified by the learner. Recent studies confirm that learning can be facilitated by allowing the learner to view their learner model as this promotes self-assessment, one of the meta-cognitive skills necessary for effective learning (Mitrovic & Martin, 2002). Hansen and McCalla (2003) further suggest that when students share their learner model with others, they may gain a greater understanding of their problems and their progress by directly comparing it to that of their peers.

A number of researchers have investigated the benefits of open learner models. Zapata-Rivera and Greer (2002), for example, suggest several ways to interact with models in order to support reflection, negotiated assessment and knowledge awareness. For instance, they believe that reflecting upon the learner model facilitates a new learning process. In their system ConceptLab, students can create and inspect their model. Morales, Pain, and Conlon (1999) also show that it is vital to construct learner models that can be studied and understood by the learner.

Open learner model systems can largely be divided into two categories: systems with inspectable learner models provide some view of the system's model to the students while a system with a negotiable learner model additionally allows some scope for the students to change their learner model. Open learner models need to meet the following criteria (Dimitrova, Brna, & Self, 2002):

- Understandability — here the authors argue for a representation using conceptual graphs. These are semantic networks with constraints attached to their nodes and links.
- Effective inspection — this means that the inspection of a learner model should provoke inferential processes and meta-cognition.
- Reduction of cognitive load — this is important because the load during inspections is generally very high. This supports the need for a graphical representation of the information contained in the student model. For instance, a study by Dimitrova et al. (2002) showed that, even after little initial training with conceptual graphs students appreciated the graphical knowledge representation.
- Expressiveness — this means that both the system and the learner need to be able to express their views of the model in a dialogue.

- Effective communication — this criterion builds on expressiveness and stipulates a scenario in which both the system and the learner need to be able to understand expressions constructed by the other party.
- Symmetry — this states that learner and system maintain the student model jointly.

Ohlsson (1992) discusses a number of different approaches to creating and maintaining a student model: the bug library technique, the machine learning approach, the model tracing technique, constraint-based student modeling, and Bayesian belief networks. These are discussed[8] in the following sections.

5.2.2.1 The bug library technique

Student modeling is a complex and computationally expensive undertaking. A number of ways have been suggested to reduce the complexity of the problem. For example, the bug library technique comprises error descriptions of student errors and their explanations. The error descriptions are very expensive to create because they are built on empirical analyses of errors previously encountered. The error libraries are also restricted in that they are not transferable from one student population to another. There are, however, ways to make such a system more reasonable. For example, one technique to greatly reduce the search space for alternative solutions of the next step and thus ease the prediction for possible correct and incorrect solutions, is to accept the concept of mastery learning, that is, for each step towards a solution only one correct answer is accepted.

Errors often occur because the student applied a similar rule, schema, or pattern to a new problem, or because the learner employed an existing correct rule which is not appropriate for the problem or the context of the problem at hand (Burton & Brown, 1982). Programs with a built-in expert system have been based all too often on the assumption that the student's knowledge is simply a subset of the knowledge of the expert system (e.g., Cerri, Cheli, & McIntyre, 1992). Accordingly, the main function of the system is to impart the complementary subset of facts and rules onto the student.

> This is, of course, a simplification of the teaching process. It has allowed research to focus on the critical task of representing expertise. But the subset viewpoint fails to represent the fashion in which the new knowledge evolves from old by such processes as analogy, generalization, debugging and refinement. (Burton & Brown, 1982, p. 51)

However, there is a close relationship between the student model, with its knowledge base of facts and rules about the student's belief system, and the expert system. Knowledge that the student possesses and that is stored in the student model is often encoded in a very similar way as the knowledge that is taught by the system and stored in the expert model. Naturally, this is rarely apparent to the system user. In this respect, however, glass-box and black-box expert systems are often distinguished (e.g., Burton & Brown, 1982, p. 81). The former contains knowledge that would be used in exactly the same way by human problem solvers and, as a result, can be articulated to the learner. Black boxes contain knowledge in the form of facts and rules that would not be employed in exactly this way by the learner.

The formal grammars in a parser-based CALL system are examples of black boxes, that is, its rules and facts would not be used by a learner in exactly this way. As a result, they also should not be communicated to the learner in such a manner.

> Since the implementation of a black-box Expert is not constrained by human-like algorithms, it potentially can be considerably more efficient and, therefore, more useful for evaluation [sic] of a student's move. However, the skills it uses to generate an optimal move are not analogous to the student's, so it can not be directly used for the skill determination task. This raises the possibility of combining an efficient and robust black-box Expert for evaluation with a less efficient glass-box Expert for skill determination. (Burton & Brown, 1982, p. 82)

Murray (1999) distinguishes two different ways of recording student bugs: runnable models and overlay models.

> Runnable models ... represent student knowledge as a subset of the expert system rules, along with buggy rules and can compare these rules to the student's behavior in precise ways. Overlay models assign competency (and sometimes certainty) values to curriculum topics according to inferences made during the tutorial. (p. 99)

A version of the bug catalogue is the so-called perturbation approach. Reyes (1998) suggests this approach to student modeling for the domain of Pascal programming. This technique does not rely on a set of buggy rules, that is, anticipated student errors. Instead, it uses transformations of rules that the expert system possesses. These transformations result in valid sections of programming code, which are semantically identical to the anticipated correct answer. In addition, she applies *perturbation*, that is, a set of meta-rules which modify operators, delete sub-expressions, exchange operands and alter variables (Mitrovic, 1998, p. 330). This approach is similar to the use of meta-rules in the parsing of erroneous input (see section 2.4.4).

5.2.2.2 The machine learning approach

The machine learning approach relies on a search of the space of possible models to identify the path that led to the incorrect solution. This approach assumes that students employ certain strategies when solving problems. However, it has since been proven that an "individual student has several strategies at each moment in time and he or she switches between them on a problem-by-problem basis" (Ohlsson, 1992, p. 432).

The application of machine learning techniques to learner models is dependent on a number of factors and challenges (Brusilovsky, 2001). First, large data sets are needed to achieve a high level of accuracy of the probabilities predicted. Second, for these data to be useful they need to be labeled. However, it is often impossible to infer from the user's behavior whether or not a text was helpful, understood and/or challenging. One solution is to require the user to provide additional information. This especially applies to instances where, for example, the system can only observe whether the user clicked on a page and displayed it for some time. Third, the fact that user models are dynamic, that is, they have to be modified and adapted over time, poses a challenge for machine learning approaches. From a machine learning perspective, this phenomenon is commonly labeled *concept drift* (Brusilovsky, 2001, p. 23). A possible solution to the problem is to place less weight on older observations without, however, neglecting the long-term collection of facts about the user. Finally, user modeling activities often have to be carried out in real time and for multiple users simultaneously, if run on a server. Here, computationally less expensive algorithms are needed when maintaining or improving the accuracy of the predictions in a reasonable timeframe.

In estimating the (future) usefulness of teaching interventions, researchers have claimed that a machine learning element on top of a student model is effective and has "advantages over hand coding teaching strategies" (Beck, 1997). The machine learning element acquires the long-term benefit of a teaching interaction while observing the student's performance in reinforcement tasks (here in mathematics). Reinforcement tasks are, however, of limited use in language learning. They contribute much to the knowledge about the language but little to the development of communicative L2 competence.

5.2.2.3 The model tracing technique

The model tracing technique monitors the student's steps in the problem solving process instead of attempting to infer from final answers. "The student is modeled as the set of rules which matched his or her steps in the traced performance" (Ohlsson, 1992, p. 433). The technique thus depends on a set of *correct* and *incorrect* rules and has to rely on anticipating the rules that might get violated.

Tasso, Fum, and Giangrandi (1992) developed a version of this technique, namely backward model tracing. It was implemented for a later version of *ET* (English Tutor), which concentrates on verb conjugation in English. Backward model tracing utilizes all techniques of model tracing, but does not rely "on an a priori established catalogue of correct and incorrect productions but is able to dynamically generate mal-rules necessary to explain the student performance" (p. 154). The student input is compared to a version of the same utterance. This utterance, however, is generated by not just relying on the expert system, but also on the information already contained in the student model. Accordingly, the actual student performance is compared to the expected student behavior as predicted by the learner model. Tasso et al. state:

> If the two answers are equal, the Modeler assumes that the student has applied the same knowledge utilized in the simulation process and this constitutes a useful piece of information for discriminating among possible hypotheses still active from preceding cycles. On the other hand, if the two answers are different, the Modeler executes the two analyses of commission [application of an inappropriate rule] and omission rules [ignoring of a necessary rule], which will eventually produce new hypotheses about the student knowledge. (p 158)

5.2.2.4 Constraint-based student modeling

Constraint-based modeling (CBM) originally was proposed by Ohlsson (see e.g., Mitrovic, 1998, p. 415). This approach concentrates on learner errors and attempts to correct them. It presupposes that diagnostic information is not attained from the (intractable) problem solving process the student undergoes. Instead it is obtained from the problem state at which the student arrives or the final results.

The constraint-based approach has similarities with the bug library technique described above. Both start with a knowledge base in the expert system. The bug library technique generates possible deviant solutions with meta-rules that transform rules and facts from the expert system. The constraint-based approach relaxes these constraints during the analysis in order to determine the rule(s) that might have been violated.

Each constraint consists of a relevance condition that, in turn, determines when to apply the satisfaction condition (Ohlsson, 1992, p. 437). For example, if the parser finds what could be a direct object, the phrase in question needs to be marked for accusative case. This approach is very similar to an approach employed in robust parsing of error-prone data (Menzel, 1988, 1992a, 1992b; Heift, 1998b; Heinecke, Kunza, Menzel, & Schröder, 1998; Menzel & Schröder, 1998a; Schulze, 1998, 1999; Heift & Nicholson, 2001; Schulze, 2001; Vandeventer, 2001; Schröder, 2002).

The constraint-based modeling approach is very efficient because it does not rely on the anticipation of student errors, as an intractable problem. However, it poses a set of different problems because it has to work with an immensely large search space. For example, parse forests, that is, all syntactic trees representing one and the same sentence or text fragment, get increasingly larger depending on the number and kind of constraints that can be violated. This potentially prolongs the analysis of student input. But, more importantly, it requires a selection of the most appropriate analysis of this input for feedback generation and for the maintenance of the student model. This, in itself, is a highly complex and time-consuming task.

Martin and Mitrovic (2000) have implemented constraint-based modeling in their *SQL Tutor.*[9] They employ a pattern-based approach to constraints by pattern-matching an error to generate a correct solution. They can successfully rely on patterns because of the rather limited domain of a querying language such as SQL (Standard Query Language). However, for a natural language this is a much more exhaustive and difficult task.

5.2.2.5 Computing probabilistic student models

For its student model, the *SQL Tutor* employs a Bayesian belief network. For single constraints, that is, rules that play a role in the syntax of SQL for databases, Martin and Mitrovic (2000) compute prior probabilities by analyzing data from previous studies and determining the ratio of correct versus incorrect student responses (Mitrovic, Martin, & Mayo, 2002). This approach is similar to computing the item difficulty in classical test theory. For each student the probability of mastering a single constraint is updated according to the following heuristics:

- If constraint c is satisfied, then $P(Mastered_c = YES)$ increases by 10% of $(1- P(Mastered_c = YES))$.
- If constraint c is violated and no feedback about c is given, then $P(Mastered_c = YES)$ decreases by 20%.
- If constraint c is violated but feedback is given about c, then $P(Mastered_c = YES)$ increases by 20% of $(1- P(Mastered_c = YES))$. (Mitrovic et al., 2002, p. 264)

Mitrovic et al. (2002) defend their use of dependent values for increasing and decreasing probabilities by stating that this approach results in smaller increases in the region of the boundary values of 0 and 1. "For example, if $P(Mastered_c = YES) = 0.4$, then satisfying c would result in a much more significant change to the student model than if $P(Mastered_c = YES)$ had been, for example, 0.95" (p. 264). The approach certainly reflects the system designers' faith in their feedback: they increase the probability of the student mastering the constraint in a subsequent try, even though it has just been violated.

Bayesian statistics are commonly used to calculate the probability of a future event given some prior probabilities. Bayesian belief networks are usefully employed in high-risk estimations (e.g., investment decisions) because the calculations required are generally statistically complex and computationally expensive. In addition to this complexity, prior probabilities of certain knowledge states and knowledge acquisition as well as conditional independence assumptions about these knowledge states would be useful (Murray, 1998, p. 425). We are not aware of any language learning software with a student model that relies on a Bayesian belief network. This is understandable since most CALL software certainly handles low-risk problems. For example, students will not suffer badly if a model underestimates their ability to case-mark German noun phrases. Belief networks are also difficult because it is not always possible to arrange linguistic problems in a linear fashion.

For these reasons, many developers found it more practical to employ simpler techniques than the ones discussed by Mitrovic et al. (2002) and outlined above. Zukerman and Albrecht (2001) discuss the predictive statistical models which are less computationally complex than Bayesian belief networks:

- Linear models which "take weighted sums of known values to produce a value for an unknown quantity" (p. 8).
- TFIDF-based models (term frequency inverse document frequency) which are used in information retrieval and which are based on terms contained in a document and weighted by frequency.
- Markov models which start with the assumption that "the occurrence of the next event depends only on a fixed number of previous events" (p. 9).
- Neural networks which are capable of representing non-linear decision networks.
- Classification and rule induction group sets of objects which are close to one another according to either attribute values or rules. New objects can then be treated in a similar way to known objects of the same class.
- Bayesian networks which have the highest level of computational complexity. They are briefly discussed below.

Everson (1995) lists Bayesian networks as one of three psychometric approaches to student modeling. The other two are: latent trait models and statistical pattern recognition models. Latent trait models mainly rely on item response theory (IRT) which computes the relationship "between performance on an item ... and achievement as a mathematical function" (p. 439). In contrast, "with statistical pattern recognition methods students are assigned to groups based on the analysis of task results in a specified domain" (p. 441). All three approaches have in common that they attempt to infer future task behavior, that is, they rely on data from past task behavior in order to optimize instruction and tutoring processes of the software. Item-response theoretical methods model only one underlying trait while Bayesian belief networks consider a variety of abilities (or traits) at the same time.[10] Bayesian belief networks are most often employed to update student models, that is, to incorporate new information on recently completed tasks.

Such Bayesian belief networks can be described as directed acyclic graphs. In these graphs each node represents a variable which can stand, for instance, for a concept, rule, problem, ability, or skill. The relationships between these variables could be prerequisite-of, part-of, etc. The conditional probabilities of these connections have to be defined (a priori probabilities) and then updated depending on student behavior (dynamic model).

Reye (1998) proposes the use of a Bayesian belief network to update the student model for an ITS which teaches programming languages. He argues for a two-phase model. In phase I the model incorporates the "state of knowledge as it was prior to the interaction" (p. 275) and in phase II the model records "the expected changes (if any) in the student's state of knowledge as a result of the interaction" (p. 275). A Bayesian belief network with rather complex computations is used to combine the results of the two phases. If one is willing to trade off some complexity, the number of a priori probabilities can be reduced greatly. Murray (1998) places his exercises in difficulty classes according to skill level and only needs prior probabilities for the skill levels, the likelihood of the student slipping (getting an answer wrong in spite of knowing the correct answer) and the likelihood of a lucky guess — the latter two tend to be close to zero.

McCalla, Vassileva, Greer and Bull (2000), however, argue that the way to improved efficiency of student modeling lies in a radically different approach in the future:

> Learner modelling will be a fragmented activity, performed on demand as a function of the people being modelled, purpose of the modelling and resources available. Learner modelling will occur for many reasons, extended from the traditionally narrower focus on diagnosis and assessment. ... This should be easier than in the past given the vast amount of information that will be available about learner interaction in the emerging information technology intensive world. (p. 61)

This conceptualization of a student model views modeling as a computation, that is, a continuous, fragmented process rather than a data structure. This reduces the immense development costs of learner models which others have tried to achieve with generic student models. Fung (1993), for example, states quite rightly that we know too little about learning and teaching processes to be able to develop domain and task independent models. She suggests the use of toolkits for various aspects of an ITS, including the student model. Others propose the use of a general (first-order) framework, that is, a set of object level theories and a meta-theory (Carlucci, Cialdea, & Nardi, 1993). According to the authors, this makes the design of student models more efficient.[11] To our knowledge, none of these approaches have had any significant impact on the design, development and implementation of learner models in ILTSs or other CALL systems. However, given the anticipated value of such approaches, their employment in CALL software would be desirable.

5.2.3 Initializing and maintaining a student model

The different approaches to learner modeling all need to begin with an initialization of the learner model. Initialization can be achieved in four different ways.[12]

In the first approach, the system assumes that the student has no prior knowledge of the domain. Alternatively, the student is placed in the middle of the ability range, in particular, for the purposes of diagnostic adaptive testing. Both assumptions, however, are arbitrary. In the second approach, the system administers a pre-test that is used to determine the student's current knowledge state. Third, it is also possible to take a pattern from models of similar students as a stereotype. In the final approach, the system uses *artificial* students, that is, vague models of students, to produce behavioral patterns that form the data for the learner model.

These approaches often result in the selection of a stereotype because the initial impression of the student is based on default assumptions that are refined and modified once the student starts using the system. The final result is a more detailed model. Kay (2000) defines a stereotype *M* as follows:

- a set of triggers (tM_i) which activate a stereotype;
- a set of retraction conditions (rM_i) for the different stereotypes, some retraction conditions correspond to the negation of essential triggers, others can be set by the learner to facilitate user control;
- a set of stereotypic inferences for each trigger (sM_i);
- the minimum probability (p_M) of each stereotype that it holds for a certain user population. (p. 28)

Kay (2000) argues that students have to be able to scrutinize the stereotypical knowledge of the model because this will eventually improve its accuracy. "Where the student models are based on stereotypic inference, there are even stronger arguments for scrutability since the inferences are only valid in a statistical sense" (p. 29) and not for each individual.

The lack of system knowledge of the new user is often compounded by the fact that beginning users produce less elaborate input and more errors.

For example, in the ICICLE system (Interactive Computer Identification and Correction of Language Errors) developed by Michaud and McCoy (2000), the first interactions will most likely contain a high number of errors and will be difficult to parse adequately. Accordingly, they adopt a two-pass approach where "a first pass through the piece evaluates such crude measures of writing competence as mean number of words per utterance or complexity of clause structure" (not paginated).

This measure is used to gain a general idea of the user's initial competence level. Michaud and McCoy (1999) use the concept of interlanguage to model second language acquisition for their system. The language produced by beginner learners is thought to be close to the mother tongue. It then moves along a continuum towards the target language when students continue to work with the second language and revise their internal representations of the language constantly. Michaud and McCoy (1999) explain the second basis of their model as follows:

> Research in second language acquisition and education indicates that as a learner masters a subject, there is always some subset of that material that is currently within his or her grasp to acquire. ... This subset has been termed the Zone of Proximal Development (ZPD) (Vygotsky 1986). ... In our model, ZPD corresponds to the portion of the interlanguage currently "in flux" and in the process of making a transition to the target grammar. (p. 49)

The problem of updating the system's knowledge of the learner's language learning and acquisition processes has also been discussed in more general terms. Ragnemalm (1996), for example, identifies three sub-processes in updating the student model: data acquisition, transformation and evaluation:

For data acquisition, Ragnemalm discusses issues of granularity, that is, how much and what kind of detail is needed for the student model. Transformation refers to processes of data structure conversion, in which the student's knowledge is brought closer to the knowledge representation of the expert system. It is questionable, however, whether this conversion can be captured as a sub-process of student modeling. In parser-based CALL, for example, it is the parser that performs the conversion of student input to a formal representation. Finally, for evaluation Ragnemalm proposes to infer underlying student beliefs.

5.2.4 Evaluation of student models

The previous discussion illustrates that the task of building student models is time-consuming and laborious. A number of issues are also very difficult or even impossible to capture in a formal, computational manner (intractability of student modeling) (see Mitrovic et al., 1996 for a brief overview of this discussion). It is therefore of utmost importance that the efficacy and efficiency of such efforts are evaluated adequately.

Little attention, however, has been paid to issues of empirical evaluation of user models in general, and learner models in particular. Chin (2001), for instance, makes a number of recommendations for the appropriate evaluation of learner models. First, he emphasizes the importance of general rules for experiments with human subjects such as randomness of group allocation, exclusion of distracting variables and ethics approval. He proposes the use of available measurement tests in order to obtain data on (personal) covariant variables such as aptitude and learning styles:[13]

- Ball Aptitude Battery (http://www.careervision.org/About/BallAptitudeBattery.htm)
- Kit for Factor-Referenced Cognitive Tests (http://www.ets.org/research/ekstrom.html)
- Human Information Processing Survey (http://walden.mvp.net/~stlsts/gift.shtml)
- Group Embedded Figures Test (http://www.acer.edu.au/scripts/product.php3?family_code=SH) (pp. 186-187)

Chin continues by proposing that researchers should report the following measures:

- the number, source and relevant background of the participants,
- the independent, dependent and covariant variables,
- the analysis method,
- the post-hoc probabilities,
- the raw data (if not too voluminous),
- the effect size (treatment magnitude) and the power (inverse sensitivity, which should be at least 0.8) (p. 189).

In addition to these quantitative measures, Chin (2001) lists ethnographic field studies, content analysis, case studies, self-reports and interviews as possible qualitative approaches (p. 191).

Very few empirical studies of learner models in parser-based CALL systems have been conducted. Heift (2005), however, analyzed students' use of an inspectable learner model, the *Report Manager,* which is part of her online *E-Tutor* system. The *Report Manager* is an interface to a persistent learner report that students can inspect and manipulate. The learner report collects and retains information on the learner's progress and performance that is saved between system visits. It also provides access to a journaling system that records prior inputs along with detailed error analyses and a bookmarking system that tracks exercise completion, that is, the student's current position in an exercise set. Finally, results can be printed or emailed to an instructor.

Heift (2005) conducted a study with 87 learners of German to determine their use of the *Report Manager.* More specifically, she investigated to what extent students' study habits are affected by an inspectable learner report. The following research questions were posed for the study:

- How frequently do students access the *Report Manager*?
- For which exercise types and at which point do students access the *Report Manager*?
- What are possible factors that influence students repeating entire exercise sets?

Online language learning holds much promise, however, expanded use of the internet has generally meant less, rather than more, emphasis on individualized instruction. For instance, learner progress and performance assessment is sparse in many online systems, or, when present, does not persist across sessions (visits). Learners commonly return to a site puzzled as to which exercises they have previously completed and what mistakes were made.

It is interesting, however, that over the past few years tracking technology has become sufficiently sophisticated to potentially address these pitfalls of online applications. But the vast amounts of data that are being collected with modern tracking tools are generally not shared with learners. Instead, the information is most commonly used for research and program design purposes. There exists a body of research, however, which suggests that this kind of information, frequently contained in a learner model, has a motivating effect on learners if shared with them (see Mitrovic & Martin, 2002). As part of the *E-Tutor,* Heift (2005) created an inspectable learner report with the aim to share the tracked data with the user.

Figure 5.1 shows the typical content of a chapter in the *E-Tutor.*[14] Besides different exercise types for both grammar and vocabulary practice, the *E-Tutor* provides additional chapter-related resources. For example, students can study the online grammar content for each chapter, access related Web links and pictures and listen to the chapter vocabulary. The *Report Manager* provides the interface to our inspectable learner report. The content page for each chapter provides a link to the journaling part of the *Report Manager* ("manage your reports"), followed by a brief explanation of the symbols used in Heift's system.

The *Report Manager* provides access to a bookmarking system that tracks exercise completion for each user and exercise set. The pencil icon, shown in front of the link "listen to a story about Gabi", for instance, indicates that the listening exercise is in progress but the student has not yet completed it. For each exercise type, the system saves the information for each student and session between visits to the site. This allows students to always continue their work from their last visit. The report card icon displayed in front of "fill in the blank" and "multiple choice" under "prac-

Figure 5.1 Content page for a chapter in the *E-Tutor*

tice your vocabulary", indicates that the exercise set has been completed. The dotted square icon that, for instance, appears in front of "translation" under "practice your grammar," indicates that the student has not yet accessed this particular exercise type.

In addition to the learner's progress, the *Report Manager* also saves information on the student's performance. The journaling system of the *Report Manager* records prior inputs along with detailed error reports. Figure 5.2 shows the summary page for the exercises that are either completed or in progress. Exercise types that the student has not yet worked on do not appear in the report.

The *Report Manager* displays the name of the exercise, the completion date and a final performance summary for each exercise. For example, on the build-a-sentence task in Figure 5.2 the student scored 80%. For exercises that are in progress students can resume the exercise ("resume"). If a student chooses to repeat an entire exercise set the associated report has to be deleted first by clicking the "delete" button. This will delete the previously saved summary of the student's performance of this exercise type.[15] Finally, students can also obtain a more detailed summary of their performance on a completed exercise type by clicking on "view report". Figure 5.3 shows a comprehensive report for the build-a-sentence exercise type. In addition to the completion date, students receive a summary of the total number of correct, incorrect, peeked and skipped exercises followed by a detailed break down of their errors.

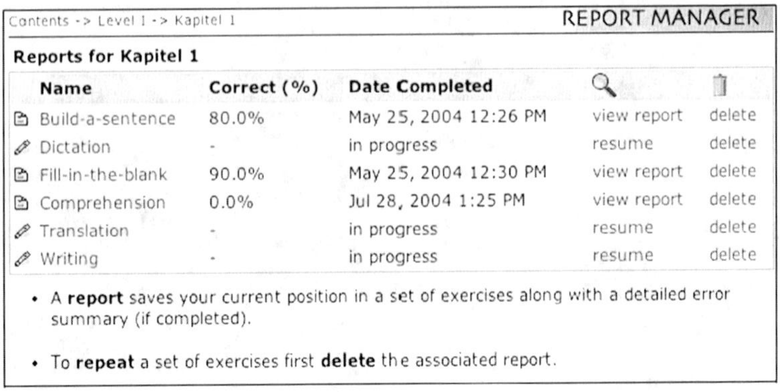

Figure 5.2 Progress report and performance summary

Figure 5.3 indicates that the student did not skip any exercises but for four of them, s/he looked up the answer (peeked) at some point in the error correction process. In the event of an error, students have a number of options in the *E-Tutor*. The student can either correct the error and resubmit the sentence, or peek at the correct answer(s) and/or skip to the next exercise. If the student chooses to correct the sentence, it will be checked for further errors. The iterative correction process continues until the sentence is correct.

The summary in Figure 5.3 further shows that for twelve out of the twenty exercises, the student obtained the correct answer on first try. For the remaining four exercises, the student required several tries, committing the errors given in the error break down in the lower half of Figure 5.3: the student made mistakes with the articles, spelling, verbs, and word order. The results for each exercise type can also be printed or emailed to an instructor. In addition to individual student assessment, the instructor can compile the information into a class error history by combining the errors that were made by all students in the class.

Heift's (2005) study indicates that students utilize the information contained in an inspectable learner report. Over the course of the semester, each student on average accessed the *Report Manager* approximately 33 times. 70% of learners repeated whole exercise sets after viewing their results suggesting that learners are influenced by the information contained in an inspectable learner report. Only 16% of the students never viewed a detailed error break down of their performance. The data further suggest that there are significant differences in the distribution of student access of the *Report Manager* with respect to different exercise types suggesting that the results are context-dependent. For all exercise types, students delete the exercises more often after having completed the entire exercise set. The differences noted in deletion of exercises that are in progress as opposed to completed are more prominent with *fill-in-the-blank* and *translation*

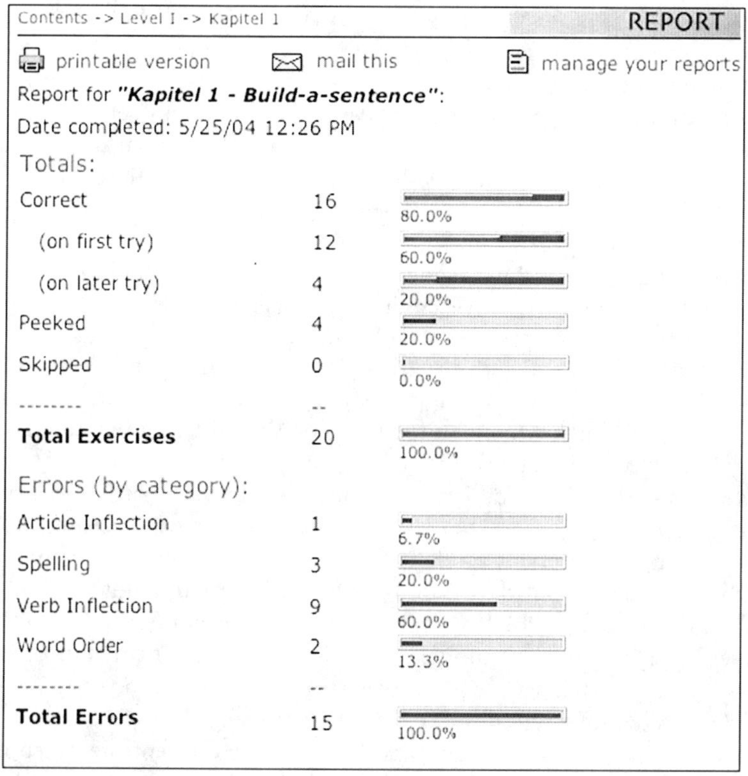

Figure 5.3 Viewing an error report

than with *build-a-sentence* and *dictation*. The time required to redo an entire exercise set may be a determining factor for students because the number of exercises for each exercise type differs. Finally, while Heift did not find any learner variables that significantly influenced student access of the *Report Manager*, the study suggests a significant positive correlation between number of mistakes and number of deletes. While students were not graded on the exercises, they were asked to send their results for each exercise and chapter to their instructor. It is possible that the mere fact that their results had to be submitted motivated students to repeat those exercises that, according to their judgment, contained too many mistakes.

The following sections concentrate on the intersection of NLP-based systems and learner modeling.

5.3 STUDENT MODELS IN PARSER-BASED CALL SYSTEMS

Student modeling has not been a strong focus of parser-based CALL systems, likely because the challenging task of representing the domain knowledge is still largely incomplete (Levin & Evans, 1995). Individualization of the learning process, however, is one of the features of a student-teacher interaction that distinguishes it from gross mainstreaming of students characteristic of workbooks. An ILTS can adapt itself to different learner needs. The requirement, however, is that the system incorporates and updates knowledge about the learner. Student modeling provides the key to individualized knowledge-based instruction (McCalla & Greer, 1992).

The development and implementation of student models is a time-consuming and labor-intensive engineering task (see Cerri et al., 1992). Research in both parser-based CALL and user modeling as part of the development of ITSs started in the late 1970s. According to Holland and Kaplan (1995) there are two trends in student modeling in language learning systems: the North American focus lies on the NLP module, that is, the domain knowledge. Due to the complexity of the NLP component, the student models in these systems generally focus on surface errors only, that is, subject matter performance. In contrast, European systems concentrate on more sophisticated student models by hypothesizing causes of errors (see Chanier et al., 1992) but they "opt for narrow NLP bandwidth" (Holland & Kaplan, 1995, p. 364). If the grammar is not accurate and complete, however, a precise student model cannot compensate. For instance, Holland (1994) states that a system which does not flag ambiguous and contingent errors accurately will obscure a student model.

ILTSs which do have a student model primarily concentrate on subject matter performance. Modeling students' errors, without speculating on possible reasons for the errors, assists in individualizing the language learning process and "is sufficient to model the student to the level of detail necessary for the teaching decisions we are able to make" (Elsom-Cook, 1993, p. 238). The technique aids in teaching the required skills and remediating the student's misconceptions.

The modeling techniques employed in language learning are distinct from those applied to procedural tasks as, for instance, found in mathematics. In procedural tasks, the modeling techniques presume that the student can learn the skill in terms of a number of formal steps. In contrast, languages are rule-governed systems and, while, we can represent linguistic ability in terms of formal step-by-step rules, we do not produce language by consciously following them (Bailin, 1990). As a result, the modeling techniques in language learning primarily diagnose the sources of errors rather than model strategies which students use in solving a particular problem. Bailin (1990), therefore, proposes for his program VERBCON[16] to first look for the most salient error and then to establish the most common error context. The most common error context is the morpho-syntactic feature that, most frequently, occurs with the error. In a last step, he envisages the determination of the most common correction context, for example, deciding on the expected tense when the student incorrectly used the present tense.

This approach is geared towards grammar learning in dedicated exercises with deterministic contexts. At the same time, it also exemplifies features in the student's text that can provide additional information on student beliefs about the phenomenon under investigation.

McCalla (1992) makes a distinction between implicit and explicit student modeling which is particularly useful in classifying the student models in ICALL systems. In addition, there is a body of research that focuses on collaborative student models.

An implicit student model is static, in the sense that the student model is reflected in the design decisions inherent to the system and derived from a designer's point of view. For instance, in an ILTS the native language of the learner can be encoded as a bug model and ultimately used to diagnose errors.

In contrast, an explicit student model is dynamic in that it is used to drive instructional decisions. For ICALL systems, for instance, the student model can assist in guiding the student through remedial exercises or it can adjust instructional feedback suited to the learner's proficiency level. In either case, the decisions are based on the previous performance history of the learner.

A collaborative student model is constructed in collaboration with the learner. Students can also inspect their model. This approach results in a more accurate student model although the students report about their own knowledge subjectively. However, it also involves the student in decisions about future instructional actions and thus emphasizes a more student-centered approach.

The following sections provide examples of ILTSs that have implemented implicit, explicit and collaborative student models. We also discuss their respective strengths and weaknesses.

5.3.1 Implicit student models

Implicit student modeling has been applied to ILTSs to diagnose errors. For example, in Catt and Hirst's (1990) system *Scripsi* the native language of the student represents the learner model. It is used to model the learner's interlanguage. With regard to student modeling, the pitfall of such an implementation is that it is a static conception. The system's view of the learner cannot change across interactions with the system. It has no impact on instructional decisions and provides only a gross individualization of the learning process when ideally, a student model is dynamic (Holt, Dubs, Jones, & Greer, 1994).

In a more individualized example, Bull (1994a) developed a system that teaches clitic pronoun placement in European Portuguese. The student model is based on the system's and the student's belief measures, language learning strategies, and language awareness. The system's belief measure is comprised of the proportion of incorrect/correct uses of a given rule; students provide the data for the student's belief measure by stating their confidence level in their answer when entering sentences. Learners also identify their preferred learning strategies when using the program. According to Bull (1994a), language awareness is achieved by allowing the student access to all information held in the system. None of the information, however, is used to drive the instructional process.

In addition, a number of studies have shown that students tend not to take advantage of the option to access additional information. For example, Cobb and Stevens (1996) found that in their reading program learners' use of self-accessible help was virtually non-existent, in spite of their previously having tried it in a practice session and also having doubled the success rate as compared to either a no help or dictionary help option in the practice session. Aleven and Koedinger (2000) argue that many students do not possess adequate meta-cognitive skills and therefore do not always know how to best make use of static as well as adaptive help facilities in an ITS. For this reason, "the tutor should help students to learn to develop effective meta-cognitive help-seeking strategies" (p. 301). According to Martin and Mitrovic (2000), students also have problems judging the difficulty of steps and monitoring their own competence.

In Kempen's (1992) system for the teaching of Dutch spelling to Dutch-speaking children, the student is modeled with the help of mal-rules for orthographical mistakes and the unification aspects of subject-verb agreement. The system teaches morphotactics (the different realization of morphemes according to their neighboring morphs), verb conjugation and subject-verb agreement.[17] The mal-rules generate possible student answers. If the system generates a solution that is identical to the one the student provided, the system assumes that the two must have taken the same path, a path that can provide an explanation of the error.

This approach might succeed in the limited domain of orthographical and agreement problems. However, it is less likely to be applicable to other, larger linguistic domains. Accordingly, Kempen (1992) notes quite rightly that

> rather than spending inordinate amounts of time and money on student modeling in ITSs for isolated and small-scaled L1 or L2 skills (as is current practice), one can more profitably develop simple diagnostic modules which, through the implementation of special malrules, are attuned to typical errors of well-defined L1 or L2 learner groups. (p. 198)

Kempen provides a valid alternative, however, it has the disadvantage of creating a rather static, often stereotypical picture of the learner. For a language learning environment to adapt to an individual learner, it is necessary to consider the design and implementation of an explicit student model.

5.3.2 Explicit student models

Developing an explicit student model typically entails making some initial assumptions about the learner based on pretests or stereotypical postulations, as discussed in section 5.2.3. Tsiriga and Virvou (2004), for example, use stereotypes for their learner model of the *Passive Voice Tutor*. They compute the difference between students in the same stereotype group in order to establish the closest neighbor of the student in question. This enables them to estimate how prone to errors a particular student is. The distance between two students is calculated as follows:

For any given value, the distance is 1 if this concept is unknown to at least one student. Nominal values, such as mother tongue, are assigned a distance of 0 if they are identical and 1 if they are not. For *real* values such as, for example, the percentage of correct answers on a particular concept, the distance is calculated using the following formula:

$$d_a(x,y)=\sqrt{(x-y)^2}$$

The actual distance between two students, taking into consideration the distance for all values, is the sum of all differences for these values. The authors claim that their framework, *Initializing Student Models*, has been successful in initializing learner models.

The *Passive Voice Tutor* focuses on a limited domain for which it attempts to perform a deeper error analysis (Virvou, Maras, & Tsiriga, 2000). It also constrains the number of values which have to be considered when calculating the distance between students of one and the same stereotype group. In addition, this precision is facilitated by the teaching approach employed in the *Passive Voice Tutor* because students only perform multiple choice and transformation exercises (active → passive; passive → active). Therefore, the linguistic analysis of student answers is relatively robust and, as a result, the technique provides a good basis for the maintenance of the student model.

Maintenance means that the student model adjusts to the student's behavior during the instructional process. This technique is used in explicit student models, for example, to make instructional decisions. Explicit student modeling has been used in a number of ICALL systems, often in the form of *tracking*. Tracking can be as simple as calculating percentages of correct answers or it can entail more sophisticated procedures that identify particular errors in the student's input. The information is then used to alter the instructional process, either in the form of further language tasks or feedback.

Bailin (1988, 1990) in his system *Verbcon/Diagnosis* employs the tracking method. *Diagnosis* provides practice in using English verb forms in written texts. All verbs are presented in their infinitival form challenging the student to provide the appropriate inflected verb form. The system tracks the most frequent error occurrence and the context in which the error occurred. The information is used to provide informative feedback based on contrasting correct and ungrammatical uses of tenses. In addition, *Diagnosis* suggests exercises for remediation.

Learner modeling is frequently based on students' final responses. A cognitive diagnosis, however, is required to determine and understand how the student arrived at a deviant answer. To provide error-specific feedback, a student model needs to reason about the path the student has taken and the underlying cause of an error. This is the goal of the *E-Tutor*. The student model in the *E-Tutor* (Heift, 1998b; Heift & McFetridge, 1999; Heift & Nicholson, 2000a, 2000b, 2001; Heift & Schulze, 2003b) is based on students' prior performance and it ultimately has two main functions: first, to select instructional feedback suited to learner expertise and second, to use the student's performance for assessment and remediation. To select instructional feedback suited to the level of the learner, the student model keeps track of 79 grammar constraints. These grammar constraints correspond to the grammatical concepts to be monitored for beginner and intermediate learners of German. The grammar constraints are split among the three clause types, main, subordinate and coordinate, each containing 25 nodes. In addition, there are two grammar constraints monitoring noun phrases practiced in isolation, one for verb-initial position in main-clauses and one for the entire sentence.

The student model assumes three types of learners: the novice, the intermediate and the expert. Each student level is represented by a range of values (novice: $20 \leq X \leq 30$; intermediate: $10 \leq X < 20$; expert: $0 \leq X < 10$). The ranges chosen for each student level roughly correspond to the average size of a grammar exercise unit. Since the default decrement for the error count is 1, successful completion of 10–15 exercises will record a change in student level. Initially, the learner is assessed with the value 15 for each grammar constraint, representing the mean score of the intermediate learner. The values are used by the student model to decide on the specificity of the instructional feedback being displayed. The intermediate learner has been chosen as a reasonable default. While the messages might be initially too overspecified for the expert and too underspecified for the novice, they will quickly adjust to the actual learner level. Pre-testing could be used to individualize the model from the outset.

For each learner level, the student model receives four pieces of information, that is, atoms from the analysis module which is responsible for parsing the student input and identifying correct and incorrect linguistic structures: the name of a grammar constraint, an increment/decrement, a Boolean value and in case of the latter being true, a feedback message. The counter of the grammar constraint determines which of the three learner responses is selected. If the number is 20 or greater, the system displays the message suited for the beginner. If it is less than 10, the system treats the learner as expert and any number in between points to an intermediate. The counter is bounded at 0 and 30.

Once the student model has selected the feedback message to be displayed to the learner, the counter is incremented by the incoming weighted constant. For the expert, the increment is generally 3, for the intermediate 2, and for the novice 1. The consequence of this sequence is that in case of errors, the student will switch quickly from expert to intermediate and somewhat less quickly from intermediate to novice. As a result, if a student is not an expert with a given grammatical construction after all, the feedback will quickly become more informative from the expert to the intermediate level. The transition from the intermediate to the beginner level is slower since the feedback for the former already points at a specific error type. Ultimately, it might be desirable to incorporate knowledge of the student's past performance. For example, at the end of each practice session the current error count for a particular grammar constraint could be averaged with a historical count representing the last N sessions. By considering a historical error count in determining student level, momentary lapses in performance would be balanced by previous performance.

In the case of a correct response, as indicated by the Boolean value *false* received from the analysis module, the constant of the grammar constraint is subtracted from the counter. The decrement for all grammar constraints is 1. Thus, the transition from novice to intermediate to expert is gradual. The result of assigning a small decrement at all learner levels is that any student has to apply a correct construction many times before the feedback becomes sparse.

The student model of the *E-Tutor* has a number of advantages. It takes into account students' previous performance and by adjusting the value to be incremented or decremented, it is adaptable to a particular grammatical constraint in an exercise or the pedagogy of a particular instructor. For example, a language instructor might rate some errors more salient than others in a given exercise. In such an instance, the increment/decrement of some grammar constraints can be tuned to change their sensitivity. Its main strength, however, lies in the fact that a single erroneous sentence will not drastically change the overall assessment of the student. The phrase descriptors describe a grammatical constraint and collect errors that indicate precisely the grammatical context of the mistake (see section 4.6.1.2 in part 4). This enables the analysis module to create grammar constraints which reflect very specific grammatical concepts that are maintained in the student model. The consequence is that a student can be at a different level for any given grammar constraint reflecting the performance of each particular grammar skill. This is desirable in a language teaching environment because as a student progresses through a language course a single measure is not sufficient to capture the knowledge of the learner and to distinguish among learners. The student model provides error-contingent and individualized remediation and can also be used for assessment. A branching program can be implemented where students' tasks are determined by their prior performance. The grammar constraints can also be weighted for a particular set of exercises, so as to be especially sensitive to salient errors. In an authoring program, these settings could be adjusted by the language instructor. Finally, the data obtained can be used for further research in improving the overall performance of the system and might prove useful in providing objective measures of student performance.

A different approach is used by Brown, Keim, Brammer, and Flagel (2004). They employ an incomplete grammar and argue "that an incomplete grammar and lexicon can be inferred from the parsing of ungrammatical input" (p. 346). Their system employs constituent and lexical production rules for both correct and incorrect input. A production rule consists of a rewriting rule and a confidence factor. The grammar of the target domain (English) remains incomplete, while the generated rules are used to infer and maintain the learner models.

An incomplete grammar is problematic for generating a complete student model. Learners that are observed over a lengthy period of time produce a large number of utterances that contain a limited number of grammatical structures. In the ICICLE system, for instance, this problem is addressed by augmenting the information from such direct observations (Michaud & McCoy, 2004). Michaud and McCoy assume that deaf students[18] learning (written) English employ correct rules when they have acquired a certain grammatical construct. For constructs that are being acquired but have not been mastered yet, they employ both correct and incorrect rules. Finally, for structures that are outside of their language competence, they use incorrect rules. These predictions may occur with high probability, but not with certainty. For instance, students slip and use an incorrect rule even though they have already mastered a construction. Along the same lines, they also use a correct rule by chance without knowing the correct rule for a particular linguistic construction.

Michaud and McCoy (2004) carried out a textual analysis of student texts. The texts were tagged for errors and students were profiled according to competence level. Following this analysis, Michaud and McCoy propose an empirically derived acquisition order for deaf learners of English where learner levels are correlated with probability of error frequencies. The authors note that future work not only needs to consider absolute error frequencies but also evaluate them in the context of how often a grammatical construction was attempted (relative error frequency).

Parsers produce a variety of parse trees for a single sentence, in particular, for one that contains errors. As a result, it is still problematic to update the student model with the most appropriate parsing result. This, in turn, makes it difficult for the student model to provide information to guide the selection of a suitable parse tree. At the same time, empirical evidence for an acquisition order for deaf learners has proven useful.

> By establishing which grammatical constructions are mastered to which degree at which levels of proficiency, we will have identified the order in which structures are typically acquired and those structures which are acquired concurrently by learners at the same level. With this information, we will be able to build links in the inference network that will enable SLALOM [Steps of Language Acquisition in a Layered Organization Model] to provide data on structures previously unseen in user's language production. (Michaud & McCoy, 2004, p. 346)

Murphy and McTear (1997) propose a student model for their RECALL project, which they describe as a simple model. It relies on three different groups of information: a student profile with personal information about the student (e.g., course, age, gender), the core model which they term student model and which estimates the learner's grammatical competence, and the cognitive model which contains the relatively stable learner characteristics such as learning preferences and knowledge of other languages. "Based on a simple test the learner is assigned to one of the four stereotype groups defined within CASTLE[19] (novice, beginner, intermediate, advanced)" (p. 307). The model is updated for each grammatical topic. Variables such as error proneness are calculated (number of errors divided by number of questions). Finally, the model recommends remedial exercises by considering final student scores.

Price, McCalla, and Bunt (1999) describe their model for the *L2tutor* as "an unusual type of learner for an intelligent learning environment" (p. 14). The *L2tutor* is a proof-of-theory prototype that engages learners of English in a mixed-initiative dialogue in a restaurant scenario. In the written exchange, the student plays a guest while the system takes on the role of a waiter. In a post-dialogue analysis, the text produced by the learner is analyzed for errors that result in a post-hoc learner model. This approach allowed the authors to experiment with a small parser which, at a later stage, can be replaced by a much more sophisticated one.

Systems such as FGA (Yazdani, 1990, 1992), XTRA-TE (Chen & Kurtz, 1989a, 1989b), the ILTS for German (Schwind, 1988, 1990a, 1995) and work by Menzel (1988) have been criticized for the fact that "the learner is never considered as an agent who creates knowledge and the acquisition of a second language is never understood as an elaborative process" (Chanier et al., 1992, pp. 136–137). Chanier et al. (1992) cite VP^2 (Schuster, 1986) and ALICE (Cerri, 1989) as examples of improved modeling of the student's knowledge. At the same time, they note that Schuster's use of Spanish rules to parse English text considers only a subset of error causes, namely those of transfer from the native language. The approach used in ALICE and later in Nobile, exhibits problems with scalability. The complex network generated for the domain of English conjugation is not necessarily directly transferable to other grammatical or even linguistic domains.

Chanier et al. (1992) further present aspects of the student model of their BELLOC system, a prototype for learners of French to practice questions in the domain of family relations. They introduce the notion of *applicable rule*, which can be either attributed to the knowledge of the learner (often containing a misconception) or the teacher (a rule of the French standard language) or both. Three types of applicable rules are distinguished:

1. Mal-rules on specific linguistic difficulties that can be predicted by expert teachers;
2. Formal linguistic rules which are based on descriptions of grammar in language learning textbooks, that is, a computational implementation of a relevant fragment of a learner grammar;
3. Meta-rules that describe learner strategies, that is, a set of rules that appear to be very close to perturbation rules.

In addition to implicit and explicit student models, a number of research projects have focused on collaborative student models. They are discussed in the following section.

5.3.3 Collaborative student models

Collaborative student models are generally constructed with the learner and they incorporate a wide set of variables. These data are elicited from the student and would be hard to establish otherwise. On the other hand, the fact that at least parts of the data are based on student judgment provided in a teaching context entails some caveats. These issues form part of the discussion in this section.

Bull, Pain, and Brna (1993, 1995) describe the design of an ICALL system that focuses on a collaborative student model. The model records the learner's past and current learning stages and attempts to anticipate future learning. Rules of different languages involved (L1, L2) are captured in the general part of the model. Actual learner beliefs about these languages are recorded in the individual part. Each rule is tagged by a numeric value (1-4) to indicate the level of rule mastering by a particular student and by an alphanumeric value (A-D) to indicate "the learner's own assessment of his ability" (p. 49). Error rules are tagged in the same way. If the recorded mastery values (numeric) and belief values (alphanumeric) are incompatible, the system initiates discussion. Information on the learner is elicited from the student. Bull et al. (1993) state:

> In order to determine the nature of an error, the system uses the student model in the following manner: The user's input is first parsed by the expert model to discover whether it is syntactically correct. Correct input allows the learner to enter a new sentence and the parsing process restarts at the above level with the second sentence. However,

> if the initial input is incorrect, the parse using the expert model will fail, leading to a parsing attempt of the first sentence by the current student model. A positive result here will lead to the misconception stage (see below). Failure will result in an attempt at parsing by the most recent version(s) of the learner's history; success in this is indicative of a simple forgetting of rules on the part of the learner. The material concerned would be reintroduced for revision. Failure to match to a previous history model will result in a parsing effort by the closest intermediate model. ... if a parse by an intermediate model succeeds ... this is an indication that the learner has in fact progressed, despite having produced a sentence containing an error. ... If all parses up to this point have failed, or if there has been a successful parse by the current model, the student model will become 'more traditional' in the sense that it will try to infer any underlying misconceptions the learner has. ... If all models fail, the final stage involves parsing by the grammars of other languages known by the student. ... By this stage, it is assumed that one of the above parses will have succeeded. However, if the sentence is so scrambled that it has failed all attempts, it is probably too anomalous to be usefully analyzed. (pp. 53–54)

We fully agree with the last point made by Bull et al. (1993), given that not even highly trained and experienced language teachers are able to make sense of each and every sentence produced by the learner. However, many learners and teachers expect a computational grammar checker to be able to analyze and correct all errors, which is clearly not the case and never will be. A good grammar checker should function similarly to a good spell checker. Potential errors should be flagged and suggestions for correction should be made but the decision to accept the feedback and thus correct the error certainly remains with the writer.

The approach pursued by Bull et al. (1993) is to parse the input a number of times using different rule sets. This clearly assists the system in assessing learner proficiency levels more accurately. However, this strategy is less efficient due to redundancy: the same input is being parsed repeatedly although parts of it are correct and thus will always parse in the same way.

Bull (1994b) outlines two components of a learner model to address the role of CALL software in the learning process: an *inspectable* student model and a *collaborator*. An *inspectable* model can be scrutinized or even modified by the learner. The *collaborator* is intended to help plan strategies and promote reflection. It performs the supporting tasks of a traditional teacher who

- shares his/her knowledge,
- is a co-learner who is always willing to discuss learning issues and thus encourages reflection and
- is a student.

Bull (1993) supports Vygotsky's claim that "the potential for an individual's development is located in the zone of proximal development (ZPD)" (p. 3) which refers to the difference between the current and the potential level of development. The latter corresponds to the level of the more competent learning partner.

> A good teacher creates his own model of a learner's beliefs and understandings of the domain. Likewise, computer assisted learning software should maintain a student model in order to effectively diagnose and respond to learner difficulties. However, the simple existence of a student model is not adequate to ensure useful system responses in many domains; the model must be sufficiently detailed in issues relevant to learning in the particular domain (and not only in student mastery/non-mastery of subsets of the domain). (Bull, 1994b, p. 34)

Bull's learner model aims to take into account the learner's performance, beliefs, native and other foreign languages, learning strategies,[20] typical acquisition order and awareness of language. Her proposed model is constructed in collaboration with the learner and it can also be inspected. The advantage is that the model incorporates a wide set of variables that can potentially influence second language learning. At the same time, at least parts of the data have to be elicited from the learner which has two major disadvantages:

First, it may prove difficult to base decisions of a language learning system on student judgments because, depending on their language learning experience and competence, they often may not be reliable enough. There are three possibilities with respect to information obtained from the user:

1. The information can be easily elicited and without doubt of correctness (e.g., age)
2. The information remains vague and ambiguous (e.g., time spent learning the foreign language) because the quality of the answer may be influenced by other factors (e.g., how effectively was the time spent due to effort, motivation, teaching input, etc.).
3. The information is based on subjective judgments by the learner (e.g., level of language competence).

The second disadvantage for relying on information elicited from the user relates to the fact that the information is extracted in a *teaching and learning* context. Learners are likely to treat these queries in a similar way to questions they receive in the normal course of their learning, that is, students may attempt to anticipate responses the teacher is expecting and answer accordingly. This, of course, invalidates at least some of the information and, as a result, it is impossible to determine which answers were given on the basis of this anticipation and which were not.

The list of extra-linguistic features that have a potential bearing on language learning goes even beyond the extensive list proposed by Bull (1994b). Ellis (1994), for example, discusses age, sex, social class, and ethnic identity as the social factors that influence L2 learning.

> With regard to age, it has been found that younger learners are generally more successful than older learners, possibly because their identity is less threatened by target-language norms. In the case of sex, mixed results have been obtained, but female learners generally outperform male language learners in classroom settings and also display more positive attitudes. Male learners do better in listening and vocabulary, however. The effects of social class may depend crucially on the setting; in language classrooms that emphasize formal language learning, working-class children are often less successful than middle-class children, whereas there is some evidence to suggest that in immersion settings they do as well. The central factor and the one that has attracted the most attention, is ethnic identity. A normative view emphasizes the effect of 'cultural distance' on L2 learning; learners who are close to the target-language culture are likely to outperform those who are more distant. (p. 210)

In a later study, Bull et al. (1996) pursue the idea of collaboration and extend the teacher-student collaboration to assessment. The dyads, one playing the role of a student and the other playing the role of a teacher, are asked to compare their assessments of rule knowledge on Portuguese pronouns. The assessment takes the form of confidence ratings about rule knowledge. In the conclusion, the authors argue that there is room for negotiation in assessment. Results of their pilot study indicate that students will often justifiably defend their own beliefs, a factor that will have to be considered when designing intelligent learning environments.

Bull (1997b) discusses how her student model, *Mr. Collins,* is used to teach students language learning strategies. She believes that the system needs to take into account student preferences and current approaches. The system should also introduce new strategies to the student. The learning strategy component of the system is only activated upon student request, or, if the system judges the student's performance inadequate and believes that the student will profit from the application of another strategy. Bull relies on the strategy catalogue by O'Malley and Chamot (1990) and lists the following strategies for *Mr. Collins*:

- Meta-cognitive — strategy planning, self-monitoring, self-evaluation;
- cognitive — use of resources, note taking, summarization, grouping, deduction, inferencing.

She describes two approaches that are used by students: substitution (in her case of Portuguese object pronouns) and translation. Bull (1997b) labels these *learning* strategies although they may be described, more suitably, as *interlanguage* strategies.

Bull (2000a) also designed a *diyM* (do it yourself model) using the same pronoun placement rules employed in earlier projects. In this version, however, students are asked to formulate rules by selecting the position of a pronoun, that is, pre-verbal, post-verbal, or as an infix. Furthermore, learners are requested to state their level of confidence. Students also need to provide grammaticality judgments on different positions of the same pronoun. In a third method, learners are given the order in simplified linear precedence rules and, again, they need to identify the one they believe to be correct. If students use more than one method to build their learner model and a conflict exists, then students are asked to identify the method they consider to be more reliable.

A small-scale study established the importance of providing users with different methods of constructing the student model because "a large majority of users would use more than one method" (Bull, 2000a, p. 181). Bull highlights that the *diyM* system can be used in different learning domains. It can also be employed as a component of systems that explicitly invite the learner to provide information for the student model.

In 2000, Bull introduced the LS-LS (learning style — learning strategies) system which is not tied to a particular language or a particular learning domain within a language. The system relies on a shorter, adapted version of the Myers-Briggs Type Indicator to establish an inventory of learning styles. The inventory is based on Oxford's Strategy Inventory for Language Learning. The results from these two inventories are used to construct a student model that suggests suitable strategies during the learning process.

Bull claims that the learning strategies suggested by the system should be in accordance with the learning styles of the students. Unfortunately, Oxford's questionnaire only elicits students' perceptions of language learning strategies as opposed to information on their usage of them. Students, however, can benefit from a broadened repertoire of learning strategies and thus the system needs to suggest underutilized strategies for students to test them. The model can then be updated with information about students' actual use of strategies and their developing learning style.

There is a widely held belief that computers and, more specifically, CALL software has the advantage to record learner data fairly easily. But what do we do with the data? What pieces of information can the computer record that cannot be captured otherwise? How can we structure the information to understand the interrelation of different items?

Levy (1997) reports on developments in ICALL that exploit the computer in order to develop a learning theory. He mentions the example of Harrington (1994) who uses his program *CompLex* as a research tool to study lexico-semantic development in L2. "Thus by tracking the learner as the program is used, the researcher can make adjustments and modifications and fine-tune the program as it is developed" (Levy, 1997, p. 219).

Yet another, quite different application of student models in parser-based systems is one that uses the learner model to disambiguate student input, which we describe in the next section.

5.3.4 Student models to disambiguate learner input

The initial goal of parsing a student's sentence is to choose the appropriate parse and, from it, select the error (if there is one) that the system will focus on for instruction.

A sentence which is unambiguous in many other NLP applications can nonetheless result in multiple sentence readings in a system designed to parse ill-formed input. For example, let us consider a system which relaxes the constraint on grammatical case. Without case marking, the parser has no way of knowing if a constituent is a subject or a verb complement. As a result, more than one sentence analysis will be produced and the errors flagged in each sentence reading can vary. For instance, for the German sentence *Sie liebt er* the parser can assign at least two legitimate syntactic structures. The two sentence readings are given in the following example:

Example 5.1
a* *Sie liebt er.*
Sie liebt ihn.
She loves him
b *Sie liebt er.*
It is her that he loves.

For the sentence *Sie liebt er*, *er* could be taken to be either the direct object or the subject of the sentence. Assuming that the choice between the two parses were arbitrary, sentence structure 5.1a, where *er* is the object of the sentence, contains an error and would yield the feedback *This is not the correct case for the direct object.* In contrast, the alternative sentence reading in Example 5.1b, where *er* is the subject of the sentence and the direct object *sie* is topicalized, contains no errors.

The example illustrates two important points. First, an algorithm that selects the appropriate parse by counting the numbers of errors flagged in each parse and selecting the one with the least number of errors (as in Weischedel, Voge, and James, 1978, and Covington & Weinrich, 1991) is inadequate. If the student is at an introductory level, the appropriate analysis is the sentence reading given in Example 5.1a, the parse that has more errors.[21] The algorithm implemented in the *E-Tutor* (Heift, 1998b; Heift & McFetridge, 1999; Heift & Nicholson, 2000a, 2000b, 2001; Heift & Schulze, 2003b) uses instead a set of licensing conditions to mark sentences for the rules that were used to parse them and select the appropriate sentence reading on the basis of the likelihood of a grammatical construction. This can be achieved with licensing conditions that distinguish multiple sentence readings conditioned by word order. The licensing conditions can license a sentence by ranking parses by the likelihood of the rule combinations that the parser applied.

Second, it is not sufficient to exclude all other alternatives whenever they appear. An advanced student may be practicing object topicalization and in that case the system should preferably choose the alternative parse given in Example 5.1b.

This consideration illustrates the importance of the student model in finding the intended interpretation with multiple parses. To provide input to the licensing conditions, Heift (1998b) generates a figure representing the student's overall mastery of the grammar by averaging expertise levels on each grammar constraint in the student model. A threshold of expertise is set, below which the analysis in Example 5.1a is preferred and above which that in Example 5.1b is chosen.

After licensing, a single parse is selected and a learner model update on each of the grammatical constraints present in the student's input is extracted. From a language teaching perspective, this technique reflects a pedagogically informed, student-centered approach. System decisions are based on a dynamic student model rather than static computational factors. As a consequence, the learning process is individualized throughout the analysis of student input.

The following section provides an overview of student models in non-parser-based CALL systems. It starts with a brief discussion of tracking.

5.4 STUDENT MODELS IN OTHER CALL SYSTEMS

Computer programs for tracking student-computer interaction have become a popular research tool in second language acquisition theories. By now, many learning management systems (LMSs) and CALL programs come with readily equipped logging capabilities (e.g., WebCT, Blackboard, Système-D, J-Edit, Trace-It, Sequitur, Jumbler) and researchers have also designed their own tracking devices, mainly to overcome the apparent limitations associated with off-the-shelf software (Heift & Nicholson, 2001). While off-the-shelf software is time-saving, researchers are, at the same time, restricted in the kinds of data they can track.

Tracking has been used extensively to monitor student writing and to record student navigation patterns (e.g., Glendinning & Howard, 2003; Roed, 2003). The studies generally suggest that learner strategies, learner variables, and system design features play a vital role in how students use a CALL program. For instance, with respect to navigational patterns, Beasley and Waugh (1997) showed that learners tend to use a systematic top-down, left-to-right navigation strategy and suggested that this preference was not only due to the constraints in the design of the environment but also to a strong cultural bias (see also Desmarais, Laurier, & Renie, 1998). Concerning student writing, New (1999) found that both good and poor writers revise their output but, more commonly, students make surface-level changes and do not revise the content.

Romano Hvid and Krabbe (2003) list the following reasons to employ tracking in the CALL classroom (see also Hwu, 2003):

- allows for automatic collection of research data
- enables research in CALL and SLA
- tests teaching methodology
- provides automatic feedback on the quality of the courseware
- facilitates real time tailoring of the courseware to the user

Heift (2005) suggests an additional and quite distinct benefit to tracking learner data. She proposes an inspectable user report whereby learners have access to the initially tracked data for self-inspection. Her parser-based *E-Tutor* system displays the grammatical and orthographical error categories to the student in addition to providing updates on completed exercises and other tracked information (see section 5.2.4).

This brief discussion of tracking has already indicated that although student modeling is an artificial intelligence technique, it does not have to rely on natural language processing technology. A number of CALL systems have implemented student models that rely on pattern-matching and similar techniques to evaluate student input. Thus the student model depends on a different kind of observation of student activity. However, if designed adequately, it can deduce considerable information about individual students. Many CALL programs incorporate a static, implicit student model. Examples of explicit and collaborative models are much more infrequent.

A system which comprises an explicit student model, but which does not make use of natural language processing, is *The Fawlty Article Tutor* (Néhémie, 1992). *The Fawlty Article Tutor* teaches correct article use in English. The system presents learning scenarios and students are asked to choose the appropriate article to fill a blank and select the rule (one out of eleven) for the context given. The tutor keeps an error count and a record of student beliefs of appropriate article rules. The system is individualized by altering the instructional process, that is, it selects language learning scenarios according to student performance. The underlying concept is a combination of explicit rule knowledge and selection of the actual answer. This results in a system that is very efficient in determining underlying student beliefs and in addressing misconceptions and knowledge gaps.

Another CALL program with a limited expert domain and a student model is COMPOUND (Danna & Sebillot, 1997). This project concentrates on the teaching of selected English noun compounds. Danna and

Sebillot discuss a number of possibilities in probabilistic reasoning. They conclude, however, that further studies are necessary to establish the pedagogic usefulness of the model. The combination of a very limited learning domain, a very labor and research intensive student model and a language fragment (compounding in English) leads to a model which can only predict whether or not a student mastered one of a limited set of compounding concepts.

Student models have also been implemented in computer-supported collaborative learning environments (CSCL). Ayala and Yano (1996), for example, describe GRACILE, a system that supports collaborative learning of grammatical patterns in Japanese. The system maintains a record of its beliefs about the student's ability, commitment and goals. It communicates with the models of other students to compute the "learner's group-based knowledge frontier". The knowledge frontier consists of the knowledge elements the learner is believed to have but has not yet acquired and the knowledge sets the other students have internalized. Accordingly, the system can generate a task that is suitable for collaboration.

Students are able to inspect the rules that they are believed to have internalized. In addition, learners can access the patterns for the task they are working on. Finally, the student can use solutions from other students or ask them for assistance because each learner model is accessible to every student. This type of student model is an interesting extension of inspectable learner models as discussed previously: learner models are not only inspectable by the student whose knowledge states are represented, but also by fellow students who are working in the same group (see Bull, 1993, 1994b; Bull et al., 1993).

Bull also worked on the *See Yourself Write* system which does not have a natural language processing component (Bull, 1997a). In this system, the learner produces a foreign language text. The teacher provides feedback by inserting information in a template. The system uses the feedback as input to construct the student model. Teachers select labels such as *superficial, good, okay, weak,* and so forth to describe the student's performance in areas such as content, structure, grammar, spelling, punctuation and style.

This "quantitative information" (see Bull, 1997a, p. 319) can be supplemented by textual (qualitative) annotations provided by the teacher. The student model is inspectable to give the learners the opportunity to reflect on their feedback and their general performance and progress.

Logging student information and maintaining a student model do not always go hand in hand. In a number of projects, the goal of student activity logs is for research purposes only. For example, researchers analyze the data logs to gain further insights into behavioral patterns in the learning process. Scott and New (1994), for instance, describe *Systéme-D*, a tool which allows the evaluation of the writing process of French texts.

In addition to an evaluation of the composition itself which is done by human tutors, the students' writing processes are analyzed and evaluated. The primary source of information is the *Systéme-D* log which includes the following information:

- the time when the student began the writing session;
- dictionary inquiries in both French and English;
- searches for examples of words and expressions used in context;
- inquiries of grammar, vocabulary and phrase indexes;
- the time of each inquiry;
- the time when the student ended the writing session. (Scott & New, 1994, p. 9)

The authors, however, do not specify whether the tracked data is shared with the learner and/or used to determine the nature of future instructional interventions.

Finally, there are instances in which the modeling of student knowledge has been based on an outdated understanding of second language acquisition processes. For example, Ogata, Liu, Ochi, and Yano (2000) used contrastive and behaviorist approaches[22] in determining differences in the use of Japanese and Chinese lexemes, that is, different mappings of meanings onto forms in the respective languages. They state that if, for instance, Chinese students of Japanese use the Japanese word for *translator*, then the system will notify them that there is another Japanese word for *interpreter* because the Chinese word can mean either. A possible correct understanding or a misunderstanding of such words is recorded in the student model.

The previous discussion illustrates that student modeling does not require a parser-based system. CALL applications without a parser can, nonetheless, provide a fairly sophisticated assessment of underlying student behavior, beliefs and, to some extent, an understanding of the domain. However, any design of language learning software needs to consider current research in SLA and CALL to determine in what ways language learning software that relies on student modeling techniques can best contribute to successful learning. Moreover, empirical studies that investigate authentic student behavior and their use of CALL programs will certainly assist in improving our understanding of issues pertinent to an individualization of the learning process.

6. The past and the future

Predictions are difficult, especially when they are about the future.
(attributed to the Danish physicist Niels Bohr)

6.1 PLOTTING THE PAST

In our discussion of artificial intelligence, in particular of NLP and CALL, we have looked at a period of about 25 years. During this quarter of a century, teachers, developers and researchers in CALL have witnessed a vast number of technological changes that had an impact on their perception of computer-assisted learning and their use of computers in general. To give just a few examples:

- Who would have thought that a machine which initially only processed capital letters for American English and a few punctuation signs, can now display, process and print character sets for a wide variety of languages? Via ASCII and ANSI standards for the encoding of different characters, we have come to Unicode and are able to use different character sets in one and the same text, write right-to-left languages as well as languages with extensive character sets such as traditional Chinese.
- Who would have thought that a machine which initially beeped at the user in high-pitched tones, whenever a wrong key within a prescribed sequence was pressed can now generate speech from written text? The computer's oral 'ability' has achieved such a high quality that blind people can *read* written texts on screen. Language learners can listen to audio examples of vocabulary items retrieved from an electronic dictionary and to computer-generated, spoken versions of second-language texts.
- Who would have thought that a machine which only stored short text with very limited formatting can now provide an entire encyclopedia with a multitude of audio and video samples? This encyclopedia, for

instance, is easily and quickly searched, cross-referenced and provides links to articles.

- Who would have thought that a machine which restricted its users to a small selection of cryptic keystroke sequences or commands when editing and formatting a document now responds to the spoken word and types out the text including formatting and other commands?
- And finally, who would have thought that a machine the size of a gigantic wardrobe with limited storage capacity and accessible from 'dumb' terminals could be replaced by wireless machines connected to billions of computers with billions and billions of documents and other files? These files are linked and searchable and thus retrievable within seconds. And it is not only computers which can be accessed over great distances, but the people at these computers can communicate effortlessly over the same great distances.

Such rapid developments of new technologies have also had a significant impact on developments in parser-based CALL. A large number of projects, which we discussed in section 2.5 and elsewhere in this book, were carried out on computers that have long become obsolete. Storage space for a grammar or a dictionary is no longer an obstacle. Storage devices have become much bigger and cheaper over the last quarter of a century. The same is true for computer memory: Stack sizes which were troublesome for developers of parsing software that used charts and temporarily stored partial parsing results no longer present a problem. Dictionaries are widely available online due to larger hard disks. This increase in capacity coincides with an overall increase in processing speed. For instance, early parsers measured the total processing time for sentence analysis. Papers proudly reported that a particular parser had reduced its processing time by seconds, or in some extreme cases, it was reduced from minutes to seconds. Today, even if the parser does not use the most efficient algorithms, the hardware components are so efficient that processing speed has resulted in almost instantaneous parsing results. These developments have meant that grammars, dictionaries, user profiles and models are no longer limited by storage capacity or processing speed.

However, not only the hardware has changed over the past two or three decades. New programming languages (e.g., Prolog, Java) have become available, while others have almost vanished or changed beyond recognition (e.g., BASIC). The possibility of writing declarative programs[1] provided developers with an opportunity to write grammatical rules and have the parser decide on which rules to use. Declarative programming languages have also been augmented by development shells for grammars. These are specialized tools for writing grammatical and other linguistic rules and they reduce the effort required for developing large grammars. Newer programming languages appear to converge: object-oriented programming languages, which are in a way similar to declarative languages, enable developers to write rules as well as procedures. Most new programming languages have an intuitive interface for visualizing information on the screen. For instance, program menus, buttons and text boxes can be drawn on the screen instead of writing pages of computer code. Most programming languages and operating systems have also improved drastically in the way characters and, more generally, strings are processed. Most modern development tools can handle Unicode and thus work with a huge variety of languages, character sets and writing conventions.

The software has not just changed for programmers. Teachers and instructional designers have also been working with tools that allow them to concentrate on the creation of teaching materials without having to learn a programming or scripting language. Much improved and extended linguistic resources have become available for developers. Annotated, lexically tagged and/or syntactically parsed corpora are available. The same is true for shells to experiment with different grammatical formalisms. Also, word lists and spelling algorithms no longer have to be written from scratch. These tools are all freely available for non-commercial purposes.

The development and subsequent availability of such linguistic resources is interdependent with developments in linguistics in general and developments in formal and computational linguistics in particular. The past 25 years have seen new powerful linguistic formalisms that had a great influence on advances in natural language processing, for example, Head-Driven Phrase Structure Grammar and Lexical Functional Grammar. Complex linguistic phenomena such as word order rules of languages with a relatively free word order, or morphological structures of languages with an elaborate inflectional morphology have been described using grammatical formalisms. This provided the basis for successful computer implementations.

However, it was not just the processing of naturally occurring languages that has seen advances in the last quarter century. Student models, for example, are about as old as the application of NLP in CALL. Yet, the conceptualization of these models has become far more complex, as illustrated in our discussion in part 5 on student modeling. We have also seen implementations of student models with complex statistical algorithms, such as Bayesian belief networks that predict future performance in addition to relatively simple student profiles that maintain scores and results from user interactions and react to established thresholds. More recently, however, a number of AI researchers have moved away from complex, often monolithic user models and, instead, are working with intelligent agents (e.g., Ayala & Yano, 1998). These smaller programs are highly specialized in their capacities and behavior. They interact with the 'host' program and each other in order to predict user behavior. They also support user individualization in a more "intelligent" way.

However, it is not just the technology that has changed in the time period considered in this book. Our understanding of language learning methodology has also changed considerably. When the first programs with NLP components were written for CALL in the late seventies, the communicative approach in language teaching was in its infancy. Language learning methodology was informed by behaviorist learning psychology and Contrastive Analysis as well as Error Analysis. Many language learning programs, not just the ones which incorporated NLP technology, placed great and, sometimes, exclusive emphasis on the enforcement and reinforcement of grammatical patterns. Such programs for grammar learning still exist and are being produced today but they are usually regarded as only one of the many components of the language learning process. This process strongly emphasizes the learner's ability to communicate in the target language in a meaningful way. The focus on communication has also resulted in a greater use of multimedia capabilities of modern computers. This certainly meant that other endeavors such as, for example, the analysis of written input for meaningful, contextualized and individualized feedback, have been neglected.

In the last 10 to 15 years, language learning methodology has increasingly focused on task-based approaches to teaching, that is, embedding foreign language communication with its negotiation of meaning and its focus on form in often complex learning tasks. Researchers in SLA have become more interested in learning processes and products, learning communities and individual differences. Learning styles, learning strategies, multiple intelligences, etc., are seen as important variables that have an effect on language learning behavior and hence on success or failure in the learning of a foreign language. This leads to the question of whether or not it is possible to extrapolate from such trends and identify qualitative progress and challenges that lie ahead. Will it be possible to determine a research and development agenda?

6.2 PREDICTING THE FUTURE

> Attempting to predict future trends is risky at best. Where technology is involved, the success rate has been embarrassingly poor. (Underwood, 1989)

How can our understanding of past developments in technology, artificial intelligence, natural language processing and computer-assisted language learning facilitate our prediction of future developments? How can it assist us in making plans for the future that are more likely to be met with success? Why is it important to anticipate future developments in any of these areas?

A frequent complaint about CALL has always been that the field is often driven by advances in technology. Yet, arguing for the primary role of pedagogy, in our case language teaching methodology, forces us to anticipate emerging technologies: the prediction of future advances is a necessary prerequisite for maintaining the primary role of pedagogy because, only when a particular technology is emerging or is in its infancy, can we shape technology according to pedagogic goals and suited to our needs. This interdependency of advances in technology and pedagogy and the necessary primacy of pedagogy have led to some aspects of CALL lagging behind technological developments. In other words, if new technological developments, original research in computer science, artificial intelligence and media technologies are ignored by CALL research they will, nonetheless, be adopted by learners and teachers. However, they may possibly not be implemented, at least initially, in the most effective way or fully integrated into the learning process. Accordingly, it is of utmost importance for CALL researchers to closely follow technological innovation and to, at least, attempt to predict the future path of certain technologies. This is necessary for two reasons: First, it is necessary to be able to shape "young," emerging technologies so that they become better suited to learning and communicating. Second, in order to maintain the primacy of pedagogy, the new technologies have to be understood and utilized to the best of our abilities. Yet, how can technological and, consequently, societal change be predicted?

One area that "lives off" predictions by imagining the future is, of course, science fiction. Already in 1976, Stanislaw Lem, a well-known Polish science fiction author, contemplated the idea[2] that huge amounts of information which have reached a critical density — namely 10^{12} bits per liter — are converted to mass, or more precisely, protons. Martin Warnke (2005) who quotes from the story by Lem identifies a number of information resources which contain at least 10^{12} bits: 1) the number of neurons in the brain, 2) the very large database by Sears, Roebuck and Co., and 3) the backup of the Internet done by the Californian company Alexa in 1997.

We appear to have reached a level of technological development at which a new, very different quality is a possibility due to the large quantity of new information, new inventions and new technologies. This perception of technological change as a sudden leap is often explained by describing technological change as exponential growth over time. Curves of exponential functions are rather flat at the beginning and become increasingly steeper as they progress.[3] Gordon Moore, the inventor of the integrated circuit and one of the founders of Intel was the first to observe this exponential growth in the world of computing. He noticed that the surface of transistors that are used for integrated circuits is reduced by half every year. In 1975, he revised the rhythm of change to two years: An observation and subsequently a prediction that concurs with the actual development of processors (Kurzweil, 1999, pp. 20–21).

Ray Kurzweil[4] uses this assumption of exponential growth not just for predictions in the world of computing. He also plots historical events in the development of our planet and in evolution in order to estimate the curve that represents this exponential growth. His diagrams resemble an s-shape.

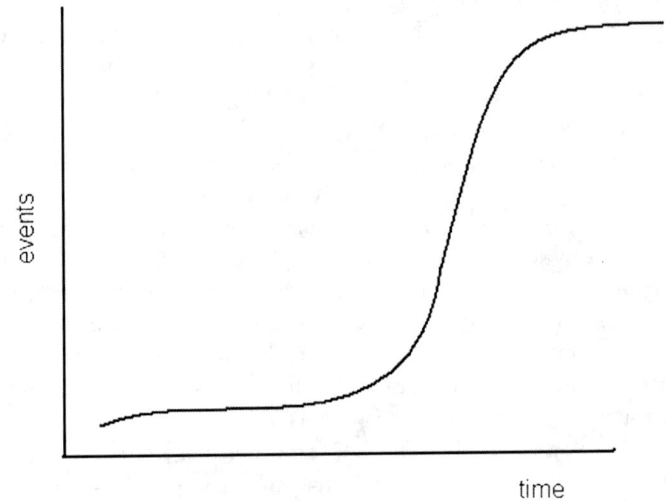

Figure 6.1 Exponential s-curve (sketch)

The exponential s-curve starts out rather flat, becomes very steep and flattens again in the upper part, as illustrated in Figure 6.1.

He further calculates changes that are likely to occur in the (often unforeseeable) future. Kurzweil (1999) formulated the Law of Accelerating Returns which states that "the time interval between salient events grows shorter as time passes" (p. 30). According to him,

> an analysis of the history of technology shows that technological change is exponential, contrary to the common-sense "intuitive linear" view. So we won't experience 100 years of progress in the 21st century — it will be more like 20,000 years of progress (at today's rate). (Kurzweil, 2001, not paginated)

Already in 1990, Kurzweil argued that computer technology needs to reach a critical mass before any transformation of learning can take place. He lists eight developments:

- Every child has a computer. Computers are as ubiquitous as pencils and books.
- They are portable laptop devices about the size of a large book.
- They include very high resolution screens that are as easy to read as books.
- They include a variety of devices for entering information, including a keyboard and a track ball (or possibly a mouse).
- They support high quality two-way voice communication, including natural-language understanding.

- They are extremely easy and intuitive to use.
- A great variety of high-quality interactive intelligent and entertaining courseware is available.
- Computers are integrated into wireless networks. (pp. 430–431)

At this point, we are leaving it up to the reader to judge the validity of such predictions. However, in 1999, Kurzweil (1999) asserts that intelligent courseware will have "emerged as the common means of learning" (p. 197) by 2009, and, by 2019, intelligent courseware will work with handheld displays and "intelligent software-based simulated teachers" (p. 204). Finally, by 2029 it will be possible to enhance the brain through neural implants. "The implants improve memory and perception, but it is not yet possible to download knowledge directly" (p. 227).

> As computer-assisted instruction (CAI) becomes more intelligent the ability to individualize the learning experience for each student will greatly improve. New generations of educational software are capable of modeling the strengths and weaknesses of each student and develop strategies to focus on the problem area of each learner. (Kurzweil, 2005, pp. 336–337)

Kurzweil (2001), in his book *The Singularity is Near. When Humans Transcend Biology*, explains that the human body will be augmented with nanotechnology and artificial intelligence research will reach a level at which it will surpass human abilities. Such singularity technology would change our lives beyond recognition. In futurism, a technological singularity is a predicted point in the development of a civilization at which technological progress accelerates beyond the ability of present-day humans to fully comprehend or predict. This prognosis is based on statistical data showing the acceleration of various trends in the human civilization. As a reason for the likelihood of such developments, Kurzweil argues that accumulated knowledge can be transferred from one machine to another in a very short period of time. This occurs without any loss of information, whereas the transmission of information from one human to another can only be done via communication. This process is rather slow, fraught with errors and prone to information loss.

Of course, there are also voices of caution and criticism,[5] for example, Wolf Singer, director of the Max-Planck-Institute for Brain Research, states:

> Ich glaube, daß Kurzweil einem riesigen Mißverständnis aufsitzt, wenn er glaubt, daß Vermehrung der Rechengeschwindigkeit allein zu einem qualitativen Umschlag führt. Die Analogie zwischen Computer und Gehirn ist bestenfalls eine oberflächliche. Beide Systeme können zwar logische Operationen ausführen, aber die Systemarchitekturen sind radikal verschieden. (quoted in Dittmann, 2005, p. 139)[6]

The impact and results of technological innovation, whether or not we will have tiny nanobots working in our bodies and supporting our brain functions, or robots which behave in a way which matches or even surpasses human capacities, remain open to debate and can only be answered in a definite way in hindsight. However, it is a fact that we are witnessing radical technological change and its speed increases at an incredible rate. This needs to be considered when thinking about future directions of CALL and NLP in CALL.

Technological change is often considered and discussed by CALL researchers. For instance, in the chapter which concludes the selection of articles on research in technology and second language learning (Zhao, 2005b), Zhao (2005a) identifies five current trends which are relevant for the future of CALL:

- "Increasing accessibility to technologies" (p. 446), indicated by more wide-spread computer and Internet use,
- "increasing capacity for content manipulation and fast multimedia communication" (p. 448), facilitated by advances in speech technology, computer-mediated communication, Web and multimedia technologies,
- "increasing availability of readily usable content and tools" (p. 450), for example, DVDs, Web sites that can be readily used in language learning,
- "increasing pressure of more uses of technology" (p. 451), referring to the need to make more frequent and efficient use of the existing technologies, and
- "increasing need for system-level uses" (p. 452), explaining that increasingly more learning materials are not designed as supplementary materials but, instead, constitute the entire course material.

After identifying these trends, Zhao argues for future research to be more responsive to education policy needs. This is a move away from development-oriented research toward an evaluation of technology use, learner and teacher-centered research as well as research that supports the integration of diverse existing technologies.

Zhao (2005a) correctly identifies the contributions language technology can make to future development in CALL but fails to acknowledge the actual and potential contributions of parser-based technologies to speech technology and CALL. His view that research should focus on the evaluation of existing technologies (pp. 453–454) ignores the fact that technologies are best shaped during their development. Moreover, he overlooks that the (language) teaching profession with its research and development probably knows best what technologies are needed and how these technologies should function in the (language) learning process. Levy (1999a) concludes his discussion of design processes in CALL by stating unequivocally that

CALL researchers need to provide detailed information on all variables of the learning process so "that designers might be able to construct specific design features with confidence" (p. 100).

6.3 THE FUTURE OF AI IN CALL

We are certainly not the first in the field of NLP in CALL to speculate on future developments in an attempt to adjust a research and development agenda. Often such plans are made as part of a project proposal. A recent one illustrates this point.

Antoniadis, Lebarbé, Loiseau, and Ponton (2004) propose *Mirto*, an NLP-based platform for teachers with four different levels: function, script, activity and scenario. The function level contains the NLP tools and carries out technical processes such as tokenization and language identification. It is completely hidden from teachers and students alike. The next higher level is that of scripts. On this level, NLP specialists and language (teaching) specialists work together. This is essentially envisaged as an NLP-CALL interface. The example given for this level is an automated gap-filling exercise. The activity level is maintained by language teachers and provides links to possible aids (which again could be NLP tools), the exercise description and an evaluation system. At the scenario level, the teacher defines a sequence of activities. Antoniadis et al. (2004) have set themselves ambitious goals and anticipate that they will need three years for a working platform.

This project is symptomatic for many recent projects. Existing NLP technologies are re-used and integrated in a new system and hence a significant reduction of development time and effort is achieved. The focus shifts to designing an "effortless" interface for instructors and students. The NLP tools work in the background and support text manipulation and/or error correction. Gamper and Knapp (2002), after having reviewed 40 CALL projects[7] that employ NLP tools (including speech technology), come to the conclusion that

> Artificial Intelligence offers many possibilities to improve computer-assisted language learning systems. However, the application of most of these technologies is not mature yet and still requires more research. Many interesting and promising systems remained in a prototypical stage. ... Most of the CALL systems using NLP techniques concentrate on syntax, few of them include semantic components, even less [sic] try to address the problem of pragmatics. (pp. 338–339)

This critical assessment of the state of affairs provides a good starting point for a glimpse into the future of technology in ICALL. The assessment of the relative immaturity of products in ICALL is probably as frequent as the complaint about the lack of language technology in CALL. The fact that NLP tools are under-utilized in CALL has often been lamented (e.g., Handke, 1989b, p. 30; Kohn, 1994, p. 32). Handke, for instance, argued in 1989 that the introduction of NLP technology in CALL is just a question of time because the necessary technical prerequisites, that is, hardware as well as software, are becoming more and more widely available. He concludes that the use of computers in language learning will remain in its infancy if the procedures, research and development in CALL and NLP are not integrated in a meaningful way. Such an integration would necessitate an interest by computational linguists in CALL and by CALL researchers in computational linguistics.

With respect to computational linguists, ten Hacken argues that a revolution took place in the field of machine translation in the 1990s. He detects a major shift between the holistic approach based on linguistic theory in pre-revolutionary machine translation and a more recent approach whose focus is on "a special problem of practical communication" (ten Hacken, 2003, not paginated). Ten Hacken considers machine translation as the main applied focus of computational linguistics in the past. As a result, he argues, which is evident from the title of his paper *Computer-Assisted Language Learning and the Revolution in Computational Linguistics*, that a change in computational linguistics has taken place and it is bound to have an effect on CALL. He concludes that "CALL is likely to be among the typical fields of application of CL in the future" (ten Hacken, 2003, not paginated).

Similar predictions have been made from within CALL. Underwood (1989) predicted that three types of intelligent CALL systems would be developed further in the 1990s: intelligent tutoring systems, intelligent microworld systems and dialogue systems (pp. 73–77). In spite of a number of intelligent tutoring systems that were developed, we did not witness a large-scale introduction of such systems. New hypermedia and multimedia technologies, the Internet and the World Wide Web have absorbed the bulk of research and development efforts in CALL.

However, it is not only the concentration on the use of hypermedia and multimedia in language learning which has prevented ICALL systems to become part of the mainstream in CALL. One of the reasons that ITSs have not been widely accepted is "the problem of technology transfer" (Schoelles & Hamburger, 1996, p. 1). This general claim also seems to hold for intelligent tutoring systems for language learning. "A good approach is to think of technology transfer as a 'political' process where you are trying to get your technology 'elected'. Successful technology transfer requires satisfying all of your 'special interest groups' [upper management, instructors, students, developers] in order to get their 'vote'" (Schoelles & Hamburger, 1996, p. 8).

We are optimistic and certainly hope that the challenges of closer collaboration on projects with a practical focus by both CALL and CL researchers as well as the challenge of successful technology transfer will be met in the near future for the following reasons:

First, all the ingredients such as powerful hardware, large corpora and their tools, elaborate grammars (or at least interesting fragments thereof) are available. Second, interest in possible contexts for NLP tools such as multimedia environments, virtual reality, and computer-mediated communication tools provide a good opportunity and motivation for the integration of NLP tools. Of course, progress will mostly depend on research and development efforts that are concentrated in certain areas. They also focus on relevant problems for which NLP tools and techniques can provide or facilitate a solution.

Nerbonne (2003) lists the following NLP technologies that may contribute to CALL: concordancing, lemmatization, text alignment, speech recognition and synthesis, morphological processing, syntactic processing and machine translation. He considers concordancing (the retrieval and display of text material with an identical lexical token from large corpora) and lemmatization (the generation of word forms with one and the same stem or root) as particularly useful for corpora used in language learning. He also adds text alignment (the parallel display of two texts written in different languages but of the same content) as a technique that has largely been overlooked by CALL. However, he believes that it could be very useful for bilingual corpora for language learning. Granger (2002, p. 28) sees three avenues for future research in corpus analysis: research on linguistically annotated corpora, longitudinal learner studies as well as a combination of quantitative product-oriented and qualitative process-oriented studies. All three areas would benefit from the employment of NLP. Furthermore, NLP-based CALL will benefit greatly from results of empirical studies in corpus analysis. Nerbonne (2003) concurs with Zock, who argued in his introduction to a special issue on French CALL that

> there seems to be a paradigm shift: at last NLP technology and techniques of artificial intelligence are being used in CALL systems. What seems still to be lacking though are teams of researchers with all the expertise needed for building high-level systems: linguists, computer scientists and pedagogues, to name but a few! (Zock, 1998, p. 472)

If that spirit of collaboration were to prevail in the coming years, the contribution of computational linguistics and artificial intelligence to CALL could be immense.

Naturally, there are not only changes and improvements in natural language processing which will influence the progress of ICALL. Language learning in general, and the role of computers in language learning in particular, have changed significantly over the last decades. The saying that computers will not replace teachers but that teachers who use computers will replace those who do not, has almost become a cliché given the ubiquity of computers (see e.g., Zhao, 2005a). Students have become used to working with computers and other electronic tools so that many of them would be surprised if computers were not utilized in their learning and in foreign-language communication. This process of normalization, that is, a piece of technology has been so widely adopted that people have ceased to look at it as technology, appears to be at its beginning in CALL (Bax, 2003, p. 23). Bax sees normalization as the goal for future developments in CALL — an "invisible," fully integrated technology.

> This will almost certainly require changes in technology, in the size, shape and position of the classroom computer. [And more importantly, it] will require change in attitudes, in approach and practice amongst teachers and learners; it will require fuller integration into administrative procedures and syllabuses. (Bax, 2003, p. 27)

Attitudes among learners are certainly changing. Linguistic and, in particular, writing skills are not just taught using computers as tools but learners acquire these skills in order to work with computers. Warschauer (2004, p. 19) makes this case convincingly for learners of English and a similar case can be made for language learning, in general. However, this does not mean that for language learners to be successful they need to be comfortable with hardware and software. To the contrary, learners need to be trained to successfully employ technology when learning a language (Hubbard, 2004). It is a misguided belief to assume that, just because a wealth of information is at the learners' finger tips, (language) learning will take place. Nobody would expect a learner to acquire a language just by sitting in a large library. Along the same lines, providing learners with a computer with lots of CALL software and access to the Internet does not guarantee success either.

However, the availability of technology might not be a sufficient prerequisite for successful language learning but it may become a necessary one. Students learn to operate new technologies such as gameboys, cellphones, iPods and computers before they even embark on language learning. In this sense, computer literacy becomes a prerequisite for foreign-language literacy. On the other hand, learners and teachers need to be informed about the possible advantages and limitations of a particular (language) technology. For example, a spell checker or a grammar checker, although still limited, can be put to good use in the language classroom as long as learners and teachers are aware of its precise functionality and its limitations. Students must also have the opportunity to reflect on the task results and discuss them with their instructors.

However, it is not just the learning of languages that undergoes change. Languages themselves, that is, their status and spread are changing too. One of these shifting processes is often referred to as globalization. The following portmanteau describes the dialectic developments of globalization and localization.

> Social theorists now use this term, however, to refer not only to the fact that globalism can strengthen localism, as we have just observed, but also to the rather paradoxical fact that localism is now a global phenomenon. (Trudgill, 2004)

English has been established as the global language while, at the same time, other languages are used more and more frequently on the Internet. The use of the Russian language, for example, grew between 2000 and 2005 by 664.5%.[8] Out of the more than 6,000 languages spoken worldwide, many less commonly taught languages gain wider acceptance and increased importance in certain regions. In recognizing the importance and the value of Europe's multilingualism, the European Union tries to protect the cultural and linguistic identity of its people and supports the goal that all Europeans learn two foreign languages (see Commission of the European Communities, 2005). Languages, and consequently language learning, remain important in a variety of global contexts. Technology will play an increasingly important role in providing an international forum for "local" languages as well as a medium for just-in-time and group-oriented language learning. What do these changes in language learning as well as in language and computer technologies mean for the future of research and development in parser-based CALL?

6.4 FUTURE RESEARCH IN NLP IN CALL

CALL, as a relatively young academic discipline, has had its fair share of discussions on research agendas, foci and methodologies. In a recent book dedicated to research in CALL, Egbert and Petrie (2005) list the following research perspectives as prevalent in CALL:

- Research from sociocultural perspectives, which is, among others, based on activity theoretical approaches (Vygotsky, 1978; Leontiev, 1981), contributes to our understanding of the computer and other newer technologies as tools and considers CALL in its various contexts (e.g., distance education, classroom instruction, learning at home) (see Warschauer, 2005).
- Interactionist SLA theory (Pica, 1994; Long, 1996) with its analysis of discourses facilitates a better understanding of language learning processes. CALL research benefits distinctly from the strong theoretical grounding of SLA theory (see Chapelle, 2005).
- A similar focus on discourses by learners is advocated by proponents of systemic functional linguistics (e.g., Halliday, 1994). However, this

approach relies on an analysis that bears in mind a view of grammar that is functional, meaning-centered, text-oriented and flexible (Mohan & Luo, 2005).
- Others do not emphasize the influence of any theory or school of thought entirely, but instead, argue for a particular theoretical focus in CALL research (e.g., meta-cognitive knowledge (Hauck, 2005), visuality (Petrie, 2005), authenticity (Lotherington, 2005), culture (Gade Brander, 2005)).

Empirical work for the above-mentioned research perspectives can clearly benefit from an in-depth textual analysis supported by NLP tools such as taggers, lemmatizers and parsers. Moreover, learner texts with information that has been obtained from a structural analysis can assist researchers in better understanding learner products and at the same time shed light on second language learning processes. However, insights from research in SLA-based CALL and SLA research, in general can inform design as well as evaluation processes in ICALL.

Hirschman and Thompson (1996) identify three kinds of evaluation that are relevant to NLP:

- adequacy evaluation tests the fitness for a particular purpose of the system,
- diagnostic evaluation produces a system profile by running a widely used test suite such as a corpus that has been compiled for evaluation purposes,
- performance evaluation looks at selected aspects of the system and measures variables such as speed, precision and error rate.

Hirschman and Thompson (1996), after first presenting some of the successes of evaluation in NLP research, such as the availability ot test corpora, discuss the limitations of evaluation methods and practice. For instance, evaluation frequently ignores the interaction of the system with the end-user. Moreover, testing is often application-dependent. Thus, for a fair comparison, the same testing tools would have to be used. Finally, evaluation deals with issues of portability. "There is no evaluation methodology for assessing how portable systems are to new application domains. The current high costs of porting language-based systems to new applications hinders transition of this technology to the commercial marketplace" (Hirschman & Thompson, 1996, not paginated).

All of these problems are even more prominent in ICALL. For instance, very few systems have undergone a thorough and transparent evaluation and, if so, most of these evaluations were performance-based. Accordingly, very few systems have been tested with respect to system-user interaction and/or task suitability. Yet, research findings from SLA can provide useful parameters for test design in NLP in CALL. Task-based language teaching (Willis, 1996; Börner, 1999; Bygate, Skehan, & Swain, 2001; Ellis, 2003, 2005), for instance, can inform task design for different NLP systems and, by implication, for the language learning domain. This, in turn, provides a solid theoretical background for system adequacy and diagnostic evaluation.

There are also areas in which NLP can contribute directly to research in CALL and, more generally to a better understanding of second language acquisition and language learning. For instance, much of the data for studies in error analysis, interlanguage and closely related fields can be directly derived from an analysis of student input by a parser. The system can identify the errors made by different learners in different learning environments. At the same time, off-the-shelf database software has made it much easier to analyze vast amounts of data (see also Nerbonne, 2003 who calls for more quantitative research in these areas).

Harrington (1996), in discussing the relationship of parser-based CALL and second language research, correctly states that

> an ICALL system is a controlled environment in which second language processes can be systematically examined, and research in the area can contribute to the development of theory and practice in several fields. ICALL can inform theories of learning by forcing researchers to operationalize terms that are currently quite vague. Likewise, the need to develop increasingly robust parsers will force existing linguistic theories to handle a wider range of language use and errors. Finally, ICALL is particularly well-suited to tracking learner development and provides a means to systematically study the development of interlanguage, a process that is extremely complex and inherently variable. (not paginated)

To conclude, we may predict that the contributions that NLP will make to development and research in CALL will be significant by building on nearly 30 years of research and development in ICALL. These contributions will have an impact on the effectiveness of language learning processes in a very practical sense. By the same token, ICALL will facilitate new empirical and theoretical insights into second language learning.

Notes

PART 1

1. Translated from the German original: “Ich will einen Test anbieten auf die Ernsthaftigkeit der Behauptung, daß ein Computer Bewußtsein hat. Das glaube ich nur dem jenigen, der bereit ist, *einem Computer etwas zu schenken*. Wenn er antwortet: Das geht doch gar nicht, würde ich entgegnen: Eben. Der Computer hat keine Welt, sondern bloß Informationen, die er nach Programm verarbeitet, und dies kann er besser als wir. Wir aber können außerdem über uns erschrecken, wenn wir bemerken, daß wir bloß noch automatisch, ohne Sinn und Verstand und ohne Rücksicht auf die Welt, in der wir leben, ein Programm abarbeiten.”
2. The acronym CALL will be used throughout this book. A number of synonymous acronyms have been used in the literature (see Levy, 1997, pp. 77–79 for an overview).
3. In addition, the system also contains an interaction module.
4. Parsers and parsing will be discussed in some detail in part 2.

PART 2

1. The game Noughts and Crosses has become known, as Tic Tac Toe in North America.
2. Taylor, Heimy F., & Bate, Bryce W. *TUCO II Version 2.3*. New York: Gessler Educational Software, Inc.
3. Pattern matching can be based on a bit-by-bit comparison where all letters have to appear in identical positions. Fuzzier matches are also possible, for example, all blanks, or even punctuation signs can be ignored in the match. A number of systems have made clever use of bracketing structures to push pattern matching to its limit. With a number of different operators (e.g., brackets to separate parts of the string, Boolean operators such as *and* and *or*, as well as *wildcards*), formulae can be created that represent different answers. J. R. Allen, (1995) discusses algorithms for detecting errors in French texts which are based on the smart manipulation of surface strings rather than a structural analysis. The algorithms are also combined with a bracketing system to encode a variety of possible answers. However, no matter how clever and successful the algorithms may be, they all have two limitations: first, the developer has to anticipate all correct and incorrect responses and, second, each of the responses has to be painstakingly encoded.

4. For further details, see the following Web sites: http://www.questionmark.com, http://www.halfbakedsoftware.com/index.php, http://cali.arizona.edu/docs/wmaxa/ (accessed on January 15, 2007).
5. For further details, see the following Web sites: http://www.webct.com, http://www.blackboard.com, http://www.cllinc.com, http://moodle.com (accessed on January 15, 2007).
6. Parsing is usually discussed in the context of natural language understanding and due to the scope of this book, some aspects of this large area of research can only be touched upon. A very readable and widely used introduction can be found in J. Allen (1995). Individual areas of computational linguistics are introduced in Mitkov (2003). Felshin (1995) offers a good discussion of a parser in the context of her discussion of the Athena project. NLP tools can be found at the following addresses (accessed on January 15, 2007): http://www-nlp.stanford.edu/links/statnlp.html (Christopher Manning), http://www.redbrick.dcu.ie/~ace/translate.html (Aoife Cahill), http://www.ldc.upenn.edu/ (Linguistic Data Consortium).
7. Error detection and correction using NLP will be discussed in detail in part 3 of this book.
8. ELIZA is one of the best-known conversational programs. It was developed by Joseph Weizenbaum in 1966 at MIT. Weizenbaum, a well-known computer scientist, showed how powerful, yet limited computer programs of the time were. Eliza could carry on a plausible conversation with a human typing at a terminal. The topic of conversation would depend on the nature of Eliza's script. The most famous, however, was a psychologist that responded to the user's complaints. The program was based on a sophisticated pattern-matching algorithm. The software has often been imitated and several Web-based versions have been written. For an example, check http://www-ai.ijs.si/eliza/eliza.html (accessed on January 15, 2007). It is interesting to note that Weizenbaum developed ELIZA to demonstrate the limitations of such programs and he was astonished to learn that there were psychiatrists who thought this program could replace them (Weizenbaum, 1976).
9. During a dictionary look-up, the parser retrieves a lexical item from the computerized dictionary, often with its grammatical and semantic features.
10. Nagata uses CALI as the acronym for Computer Assisted Language Instruction but, for reasons of consistency, the acronym CALL will be used whenever possible.
11. Flynn, S. (1986). "Production vs. comprehension: Differences in underlying competences." Studies in Second Language Acquisition 8, 135–164.
12. A lexeme is the fundamental unit of the lexicon of a language. For example, *eat*, *eats*, *ate* and *eating* are forms of the English lexeme *eat*.
13. Definite Clause Grammars (DCGs) are a special notation provided in most Prolog systems which provide a convenient way of defining grammar rules, that is, the DCG preprocessor takes the DCG rule and translates it into pure Prolog (see Gazdar & Mellish, 1989 for a detailed discussion of DCGs).
14. Matthews uses Kurtz's first name, Barry, to reference this article.
15. Note that some scholars would argue that PPT is not nearly formal enough for computational use.
16. The Kleene star * is used in mathematical logic and in computer science to describe the operation of closure. Closure of a set creates a new set which contains all combinations of its members (with the possibility to repeatedly use any member in all different orders, e.g., the closure of the set {x, y} would be {ε, x, y, xy, yx, xx, yy, xxy, yyx, xxx, yyy,...}).
17. The parser for *Textana* was written by A. Ramsay. The German grammar was implemented by M. Schulze.

18. Razi (1985) (apparently working with Weischedel and Sondheimer) discusses the problem of the heurism used by Weischedel and Sondheimer. They used the longest-spanning arc in their ATN to which they then applied the meta-rule. Razi shows that this is not always possible because partial parsers might block the necessary meta-rule. His proposal is to use a different heurism: "A promising alternative to the above heuristics is to parse the utterance from right to left (RL) after the blockage of the left to right (LR) parse" (p. 70).
19. Bottom-up parsers start by combining terminal symbols, that is, words to larger units until the entire input sentence is reconstructed. Top-down parsers, on the other hand, start with a high-level production rule such as S -> NP, VP and attempt to *fill* it until all terminal symbols have been used.
20. In addition to these four approaches, we also find statistical and finite-state approaches to processing ill-formed input. For a detailed discussion of statistical and finite state approaches, see Hashemi (2003).
21. This approach is used by Weischedel and Sondheimer (1983) and has been criticized by Mellish (1989).
22. With *b-rule* the authors refer to re-write rules while with *p-rule* they refer to preference rules in the context of tree-building.
23. Precision and recall are the basic measures used in evaluating search strategies. *Precision* is the ratio of the number of relevant records retrieved to the total number of records retrieved. It is usually expressed as a percentage. *Recall* is the ratio of the number of relevant records retrieved to the total number of relevant records in the database. It is usually expressed as a percentage.
24. See *Speech and Language Processing* by Jurafsky and Martin (2000) for a more detailed introduction to the topic.
25. Weischedel et al. (1978) reference earlier work in CALL, for example, an article by Nelson, Ward, Desch and Kaplow (1976) in which the authors argue: "What is needed if CALI [Computer Aided Language Instruction, the term for CALL dominant in North America at the time] is to provide the student with a meaningful analysis of his input is a means of including information about the structure of the language in general, and about each individual sentence in the program, so that the program does not have to refer to a long list of anticipated responses for the sentence" (p. 32).
26. Loritz et al. (Loritz et al., 1990; Loritz, 1992) discuss the implementation of ATNs in parser-based CALL systems.
27. Meta- and buggy rules will be explained in some detail in sections 2.4.3 and 2.4.4.
28. According to Richards (1971) such strategies appear to be universally employed when a learner is exposed to second language data. This is confirmed by the observation that many errors in second language communication occur regardless of the native language of the speaker. Error Analysis (Corder, 1974) states that equal weight can be given to interlingual and overgeneralization errors.
29. Colmerauer's (1978) Metamorphosis Grammar is a logic grammar. Definite Clause Grammars (DCGs) (Pereira & Warren, 1980), which were developed later, have their origins in Metamorphosis Grammar.
30. These three features are specific to nouns in German and do not cover the declension of adjectives. The declension of adjectives in German also depends on whether or not they are preceded by a definite or indefinite article.
31. See also Weischedel and Sondheimer (1983). The authors present a very similar analysis of semantic networks. However, it is not as complete as the one by Schwind (1983).

32. More recently, the research for the U.S. military in this area appears to concentrate on speech recognition for languages such as Korean and Arabic.
33. Note that this particular pedagogical focus of NLP-based projects has been highly criticized for contributing little to the development of a language learner's communicative competence. These types of exercises generally focus on acquiring knowledge about the language with its rules and principles instead of grammar learning.
34. Note that these analyses are run in quasi batch mode.
35. Post-parsing activities (parsing of parse output to find missing structures) are proposed by Hamel (Schulze & Hamel, 1998) in an earlier project.
36. The XTAG lexicon is available at http://www.cis.upenn.edu/~xtag/ (accessed on January 15, 2007).
37. This example also has an incorrect sentence boundary. The CALIFORNIA is a heading.
38. The *German Tutor* (Heift, 1998b) was rewritten and enhanced in 2002 and subsequently renamed *E-Tutor.*
39. In the dissertation, they are referred to as *time words.*
40. Regular expressions are string patterns with alternatives and wildcards, that is, a string which matches a set of strings that follow its rules. Regular expressions can be quite powerful as in the case of Perl (http://www.perl.org; accessed on January 15, 2007), a programming language with extensive text manipulation capabilities.
41. Johnston borrowed the idea from the UNIX system in which regular expressions play a role.
42. Sicstus Prolog was used by Schulze (2001) (http://www.sics.se/sicstus/; accessed on January, 2007).
43. Electronic Learner Dictionary German-Italian.
44. See http://pages.unibas.ch/LIlab/projects/wordmanager/wordmanager.html (accessed January 15, 2007).

PART 3

1. For a more detailed discussion on spell checkers and second language learning, see Rimrott and Heift (2005).
2. With respect to language influence, Rimrott and Heift (2005) make a distinction between interlingually- and intralingually-motivated errors. Interlingual errors are due to a transfer of patterns from the native language to the target language. According to Richards (1974b), intralingual errors reflect the "general characteristics of rule learning, such as faulty generalization, incomplete application of rules and failure to learn conditions under which rules apply." (p. 174). In addition, many of the misspellings can be attributed to interlingual sources.
3. Rimrott and Heift (2005) define lexical errors as spelling mistakes at the word-level where the actual spelling differs from the target spelling because of a deviant representation of the target word in the writer's mental lexicon. When writing *<Zeitelesung> instead of <Zeitung> *newspaper*, for example, the writer's mental representation wrongly consists of a blend of the two distinct items <Zeitung> *newspaper* and <lesen> read.

   Unlike lexical errors which affect the entire word, morphological misspellings concern morphemes and can be attributed to incorrect applications of inflectional paradigms. For example, there are German verbs that require a stem vowel change in the 2nd and 3rd person singular of the present tense and/or in the past participle. These irregularities in general pose difficulties to second language learners and may result in a spelling error.

Phonological errors are instances where the (assumed or actual) phonology of a word has an influence on its orthography. In *<Meite> for <Miete> *rent*, for example, the phoneme /i/ is represented with the grapheme <ei> instead of the correct <ie>. Here, the writer has chosen an English phoneme-grapheme correspondence rule whereby /i/ can be represented as <ei> instead of the German rule that converts the phoneme /i/ into the grapheme <ie>.

The final category consists of orthographic misspellings. They tend to resemble the target word most closely as the errors are comprised of single substitutions (i.e., capitalization errors) or the addition or omission of a single space (i.e., word boundary errors).

4. In this context it is important to note that a study by Lawler concluded that LINGER was not usable in a language learning classroom even with a larger dictionary (Lawler, 1990, p. 49).
5. Commercially available grammar checkers for French, for example, include programs such as *Antidote* and *Le Correcteur. Antidote Prisme* was designed as a tool for native French speakers and the grammar checker now has a setting for non-native French speakers. *Le Correcteur Bilingue* is a grammer checker for Anglophones writing in French or Francophones writing in English.
6. Lennon, who also relies on Corder (1974), lists five stages: (1) selection of a corpus of language; (2) identification of errors in the corpus; (3) classification of the errors identified; (4) explanation of the psycholinguistic causes of the errors; (5) evaluation or error gravity/ranking of the errors (Lennon, 1991, p. 181).
7. For example, grammaticality judgments are often, to a degree, subjective. They also depend on the designer's linguistic background (e.g., regional dialect, social class, education).
8. A distinction between *error* and *mistake* is made by Corder and described here. Note, however, that, for the remainder of the book, the terms are used interchangeably.
9. To mention just one exception, Menzel et al. embedded their parsing activities in a graphically represented market place scenario. This allows them to also parse violations of semantic and pragmatic constraints (Menzel & Schröder, 1999). See also the discussion on microworlds in ICALL in the section 'Virtual Contexts' in part 2.
10. The notion of trust and credibility has received increased attention in recent research about human-computer interaction (for a detailed discussion, see Fogg & Tseng, 1999).
11. A learner model can be a representation of the student's knowledge in a small number of key areas or it can be much more complex and may contain a representation of the student's learning styles and strategies as well as learner variables. See part 5 of this book for an overview of student models.
12. Part of speech classifications are, in some cases, not straight-forward and, for this reason, they have been subject to debate for many languages (e.g., uninflected adjectives vs. adverbs, particles vs. adverbs).
13. Note that in a computational context, words are defined as strings of symbols that are separated from other strings by spaces or punctuation signs.
14. Adjectives can also occur as obligatory subject or object complements. However, if these complements are omitted it cannot be determined whether an adjectival phrase or a noun phrase was missing. In this case, we will just record the fact that a complement was missing.

15. Nouns subsume the pronouns that do not act as determiners or relativizers.
16. Juozulynas (1994) analyzed errors in an approximately 400-page corpus of German essays by American college students in second-year language courses. His study shows that "syntax is the most problematic area, followed by morphology. These two categories make up 53% of errors ... The study, a contribution to the error analysis element of a syntactic parser of German, indicates that most student errors (80%) are not of semantic origin and therefore, are potentially recognizable by a syntactic parser" (p. 5).
17. For a practical introduction to using corpora and conducting simple analyses of a corpus, in particular the creation and use of concordances, see Sinclair (2003).
18. The best-known corpus with part of speech as well as syntactic annotations is the PENN TREEBANK compiled at the University of Pennsylvania (Marcus, Santorini, & Marcinkiewicz, 2004 [1993]).
19. For an example of such an analysis, see Mindt (2004 [1996]). On the basis of selected frequency data from corpora he concludes that the order in which most L2 learners of English use modals, future-time orientation and conditional clauses is not appropriate.
20. In parallel corpora the text is displayed in two languages side by side.

PART 4

1. Note that this is our translation from the German original.
2. Cybernetics, as the study of information-processing systems, was defined by Norbert Wiener (see Wiener, 1948).
3. These criticisms have also shaped what is known today as second language acquisition (SLA) theory.
4. Taylor, Heimy F. and Bate, Bryce W. (Ohio State University) *TUCO II Version 2.3*. Gessler Educational Software, Inc., New York.
5. *Übungsgrammatik Deutsch* is the drill-and-practice program that accompanies *Lehr- und Übungsbuch der deutschen Grammatik* (Dreyer & Schmitt, 1994).
6. This understanding of a formal grammar was briefly introduced in section 2.3.3 when discussing the parsing of ill-formed input.
7. See sections 2.3.3, 2.3.4, and 2.4 for a detailed discussion on computational solutions for ill-formed input.
8. The error types for determiners are more fine-grained indicating the incorrect article that has been used. For example, *den*error indicates that the student incorrectly used the determiner *den* for the indirect object (for a detailed discussion see Heift, 1998b).
9. For a detailed analysis of errors in linear precedence, see Heift (1998b). For alternative approaches to error detection, see Reuer (2003), L'Haire and Vandeventer (2003), the work by Menzel et al. (Heinecke et al., 1998; Menzel & Schröder, 1998a, 1998b, 1998d, 1999; Schröder, 2002) and McCoy et al. (McCoy et al., 1996b; Schneider & McCoy, 1998; Michaud & McCoy, 1999, 2000, 2004).
10. The whole concept of student modeling will be discussed in part 5. Here we only mention it in relation to feedback.
11. In addition to the grammar and parser, our system includes a spell checker which ensures that the words contained in the student input are correctly spelled before the sentence is sent to the parser (see Heift & Nicholson, 2001).

12. This word and the metaphor refer to *paidagogos*, the slave who accompanied the Greek boy to school or the gymnasium, would help and protect him, was often very educated and could give advice, but as a slave was not allowed to control the child.
13. This was confirmed in conference presentations by both U. Felix and P. Bangs at Eurocall 2002 (Bangs, 2002; Felix, 2002).
14. A related study was conducted by Ferreira and Bañados (2005).
15. Prior to this study, Heift (2003) learnt that, in a CALL environment, the main error category needs to be included with this feedback type because there are examples where the error cannot be repeated or highlighted in the student input. This applies to instances where the student leaves out an entire word.
16. The distribution of correct versus wrong submissions is fairly consistent with an earlier study (Heift, 2002).
17. Note that the types are provided in order of increasing system initiative and decreasing learner initiative.
18. Sinyor (1997) analyzed errors by 100 students who used the beta version of an Italian CALL software. She describes in detail that learners made very little use of the static information provided in the program such as *vocabulary screens* and *grammar recap*. Sinyor laments the lack of involvement on the part of students which, however, might have been due to the static, non-individualized nature of the help features given.

PART 5

1. See the discussion in Woolf and Murray (1994) which identifies similar areas of use, but describes them in more practical terms (also quoted in Metrovic, Djordjevic-Kajan, & Stoimenov, 1996, p. 279).
2. See Brusilovsky, Ritter, and Schwarz (1997) for an example of adaptive hypermedia applied to intelligent tutoring in the realm of Mathematics.
3. This is usually based on Wenger (1987).
4. In addition, the system also contains an interaction module, that is, a user interface.
5. In this case the model is frequently described as a *student profile* or *student (activity) log*.
6. Gardner (1999) lists eight intelligences a human possesses, for example, linguistic, logical-mathematical, musical and interpersonal.
7. Kelly and Tangney (2002) took the second axis of their analysis from a 50-year old book on pedagogy: Bloom, B., Engelhart, M., Hill, W., Furst, E, & Krathwohl, D. (1956): *Taxonomy of Educational Objectives. The Classification of Educational Goals. Handbook I: Cognitive Domain*. Longman Green. The learning goals are defined at three levels: the memorization of facts, the understanding of concepts and the ability to solve problems.
8. In section 5.2.2.5, we discuss different probabilistic approaches to student modeling but focus mainly on Bayesian belief networks.
9. The constraint-based approach was also used in the *SQL Tutor* to generate exercises by using the information contained in the domain model (Martin & Mitrovic, 2002).
10. Millán and Pérez-de-la-Cruz (2002) discuss a student model which relies on both the ideas of adaptive testing/item response theory and Bayesian belief networks. They tested their integrated model successfully with simulated students.

11. In this case, the student model is based on the expert model.
12. Note that Tsiriga and Virvou (2004) review three of them.
13. The URLs below are provided by Chin. They were accessed January 15, 2007 and updated appropriately.
14. After a pre-test students used the E-Tutor for a period of 15 weeks. Each student completed a total of five chapters, each containing about 50 individual exercises. A final post-test and questionnaire completed the data set. The entire study was conducted online (see http://www.e-tutor.org).
15. For computational and pedagogical reasons, the system only stores the current report for each exercise type.
16. VERBCON is a "program which gives students practice in using English verb forms in written contexts" (Bailin, 1990, p. 12).
17. See also Pijls, Daelemans and Kempen (1987).
18. The students use American Sign Language (ASL) in face-to-face communication and are learning English writing.
19. CASTLE is the name of the English language learning software the authors were working on in the RECALL project.
20. In a small-scale study, Bull (1994a) was able to show that students appreciated the opportunity to discuss language background and learning strategies.
21. Object topicalization is not a grammatical construction explicitly taught at the introductory level where the focus is on the grammar of more commonly used rules of German. Object topicalization is a rare construction, even at a more advanced level.
22. The project titles, nonetheless, suggest a communicative approach (Communicative Gap Model; Network-Based Communicative Kanji Learning Environment).

PART 6

1. See section 2.3.4 for a detailed discussion of declarative programming languages.
2. This story is entitled *Profesor A. Donda* and appeared in the story collection *Maska* (The Mask). This professor predicted the melt-down of the digital information in all libraries, archives and universities; this melt-down actually happens in this story and results in the creation of one gram of mass.
3. This phenomenon is best explained by the well-known anecdote about the inventor of the chess game. He was asked by the emperor what kind of reward he would like to receive for inventing this challenging game. The chess inventor responded: a corn of rice for the first field of the chess board, two for the second, four for the third, and so forth. The emperor laughed about the ostensibly modest inventor until he realized that the chess inventor was asking for almost the entire rice production of the time. For the first couple of fields he would have received only a few corns of rice. However, the exponential growth in numbers means that, for instance, for field number 21 he would already receive $2^{19} = 1{,}048{,}576$ corns. For field 31 he would be given more than 1 billion corns of rice. For field 64, the last of the chess board, the inventor would have been rewarded with almost 10^{19} corns of rice. Compared to the figures at the end, the increase at the beginning is almost unnoticeable.
4. Ray Kurzweil was the principal developer of the first omni-font optical character recognition, the first print-to-speech reading machine for blind people, the first CCD flat-bed scanner, the first text-to-speech synthesizer, the first music synthesizer capable of recreating the grand piano and other orchestral

instruments and the first commercially marketed large-vocabulary speech recognition. He founded nine businesses in OCR, music synthesis, speech recognition, reading technology, virtual reality, financial investment, cybernetic art, and other areas of artificial intelligence. All of these technologies continue today as market leaders. His Web site, http://www.kurzweilai.net/, is a leading resource on artificial intelligence (see also http://www.kurzweiltech.com/aboutray.html) (accessed January 15, 2007).

5. In chapter 9, Kurzweil (2005) addresses criticisms raised against his theory of accelerating returns and his prediction of singularity events at the intersection of nano-bio-technology and artificial intelligence.
6. Undoubtedly, an increase in processing power alone will not lead to a qualitative change. The analogy of computer and brain is at best superficial. Both systems can carry out logical operations but the system architectures are radically different.
7. This review was part of Knapp's PhD project (Knapp, 2004).
8. For these data and other statistics see http://www.internetworldstats.com/stats7.htm (accessed January 15, 2007).

Bibliography

Abeillé, Anne. (1992). The Lexicalised Tree Adjoining Grammar for French and Its Relevance to Language Teaching. In M. L. Swartz & M. Yazdani (Eds.), *Intelligent Tutoring Systems for Foreign Language Learning. The Bridge to International Communication* (pp. 65–88). Berlin: Springer Verlag.

Aijmer, Karin, & Altenberg, Bengt. (Eds.). (2004). *Advances in Corpus Linguistics. Papers from the 23rd International Conference on English Language Research on Computerized Corpora (ICAME 23) Göteborg 22–26 May 2002* (Vol. 49). Amsterdam: Rodopi.

Aldabe, Itziar, & Maritxalar, Montse. (2005). *IRAKAZI: A Web-Based System to Assess the Learning Process of Basque Language Learners.* Paper presented at the Eurocall 2005, Krakow, Poland.

Aleven, Vincent, & Koedinger, Kenneth R. (2000). Limitations of Student Control: Do Students Know When They Need Help? In G. Gauthier, C. Frasson & K. VanLehn (Eds.), *Intelligent Tutoring Systems. 5th International Conference, ITS 2000, Montréal, Canada, June 2000, Proceedings* (pp. 292–303). Berlin: Springer Verlag.

Aljaafreh, Ali, & Lantolf, James P. (1994). Negative Feedback as Regulation and Second Language Learning in the Zone of Proximal Development. *The Modern Language Journal, 78*(iv), 465–483.

Allen, James. (1995). *Natural Language Understanding.* New York: Benjamins/Cummings.

Allen, John Robin. (1995). The Ghost in the Machine: Generating Error Messages in Computer Assisted Language Learning Programs. *CALICO Journal, 13*(2), 87–103.

Allerton, David J., Tschichold, Cornelia, & Wieser, Judith (Eds.). (2005). *Linguistics, Language Learning and Language Teaching.* Basel: Schwabe.

Anderson, Don D. (1995). Machine Translation as a Tool in Second Language Learning. *CALICO Journal, 13*(1), 68–97.

Annett, John. (1969). *Feedback and Human Behaviour. The Effects of Knowledge of Results, Incentives and Reinforcement on Learning and Performance.* Middlesex: Penguin Books.

Antoniadis, Georges, Echinard, Sandra, Kraif, Oliver, Lebarbé, Thomas, Loiseau, Mathieu, & Ponton, Claude (2004). *NLP-Based Scripting for CALL Activities.* Paper presented at the eLearning for Computational Linguistics and Computational Linguistics for eLearning. Workshop at COLING — The 20th International Conference on Computational Linguistics, Geneva.

Antos, Gerd. (1982). *Grundlagen einer Theorie des Formulierens. Textherstellung in geschriebener und gesprochener Sprache.* Tübingen: Niemeyer.

Arneil, Stewart, & Holmes, Martin. (1999). Juggling Hot Potatoes: Decisions and Compromises in Creating Authoring Tools For the Web. *ReCALL, 11*(2), 12–19.

Atkins, B.T. Sue (Ed.). (1998). *Using Dictionaries: Studies of Dictionary Use by Language Learners and Translators*. Tübingen: Max Niemeyer.

Atkins, B. T. Sue, & Varantola, Krista. (1998a). Language Learners Using Dictionaries: The Final Report on the EURALEX / AILA Research Project on Dictionary Use. In B. T. S. Atkins (Ed.), *Using Dictionaries: Studies of Dictionary Use by Language Learners and Translators* (pp. 21–82). Tübingen: Niemeyer.

Atkins, B. T. Sue, & Varantola, Krista. (1998b). Monitoring Dictionary Use. In B. T. Sue Atkins (Ed.), *Using Dictionaries: Studies of Dictionary Use by Language Learners and Translators* (pp. 83–122). Tübingen: Niemeyer.

Ayala, Gerardo, & Yano, Yoneo. (1996). Learner Models for Supporting Awareness and Collaboration in a CSCL Environment. In C. Frasson, G. Gauthier, & A. Lesgold (Eds.), *Intelligent Tutoring Systems. Third International Conference, ITS'96, Montréal, Canada, June 1996, Proceedings* (pp. 158–168). Berlin: Springer Verlag.

Ayala, Gerardo, & Yano, Yoneo. (1998). A Collaborative Learning Environment Based on Intelligent Agents. *Expert Systems with Applications, 14*(1–2), 129–137.

Bailin, Alan. (1988). Artificial Intelligence and Computer-Assisted Language Instruction. *CALICO Journal, 5*(3), 25–45.

Bailin, Alan, & Thomson, Philip. (1988). The Use of Natural Language Processing in Computer-Assisted Language Instruction. *Computers and the Humanities, 22*, 99–110.

Bailin, Alan, & Levin, Lori S. (1989). *Intelligent Computer-Assisted Language Instruction. Computers and the Humanities (Special Issue)* (Vol. 23).

Bailin, Alan. (1990). Skills in Context and Student Modeling. *CALICO Journal, 8*(1), 7–22.

Bailin, Alan (Ed.). (1991). *Special Issue of the CALICO Journal on ICALL* (Vol. 9 (1)).

Bailin, Alan. (1995). Intelligent Computer-Assisted Language Learning: A Bibliography. *Computers and the Humanities, 29*(5), 375–387.

Baker, Mona, Francis, Gill, Sinclair, John McHardy, & Tognini-Bonelli, Elena. (1993). *Text and technology: In Honour of John Sinclair*. Amsterdam/Philadelphia: Benjamins.

Bangs, Paul. (2002). *Why is Feedback Dying of Starvation? — Let's Try to Revive It....* Retrieved November 6, 2002, from http://members.aol.com/bangspaul/EuroCall2002.htm

Bangs, Paul. (2003). Engaging the Learner - How to Author for Best Feedback. In U. Felix (Ed.), *Language Learning Online: Towards Best Practices*. Lisse: Swets & Zeitlinger.

Barchan, Jonathan. (1986). New Approaches in Computer Aided Language Learning. In K. Cameron, W. S. Dodd, & S. P. Q. Rathz (Eds.), *Computers and Modern Language Studies* (pp. 93–99). Chichester: Ellis Horwood.

Barchan, Jonathan, Woodmansee, B., & Yazdani, Masoud. (1986). A Prolog-Based Tool for French Grammar Analysis. *Instructional Science, 15*, 21–48.

Barker, Philip, G., & Yeates, Harry. (1985). *Introducing Computer Assisted Learning*. Englewood Cliffs; London: Prentice-Hall.

Barrutia, Richard. (1985). Communicative CALL with Artificial Intelligence: Some Desiderata. *CALICO Journal, 3*(1), 37–42.

Bationo, Bernadin D. (1992). The Effects of Three Feedback Forms on Learning Through a Computer-Based Tutorial. *CALICO Journal, 10*(1), 45–52.

Bax, Stephen. (2003). CALL — Past, Present and Future. *System, 31*, 13–28.

Beasley, Robert E., & Waugh, Michael L. (1997). Predominant Initial and Review Patterns of Navigation in a Fully Constrained Hypermedia Hierarchy: An Empirical Study. *Journal of Educational Multimedia and Hypermedia, 6*(2), 155–172.

Beck, Joseph, Stern, Mia, & Haugsjaa, Erik. (1996). *Applications of AI in Education.* Retrieved April 27, 2005, from http://www.acm.org/crossroads/xrds3-1/aied.html

Beck, Joseph. (1997). *Modelling the Student With Reinforcement Learning.* Paper presented at the 6th Annual Conference on User Modelling, Sardinia, Italy.

Beck, Joseph, Stern, Mia, & Woolf, Beverly Park. (1997). Cooperative Student Models. In B. H. du Boulay & R. Mizoguchi (Eds.), *Artificial Intelligence in Education: Knowledge and Media in Learning Systems. Proceedings of AI-ED'97, 8th World Conference on Artificial Intelligence in Education, Kobe, Japan, 18–22 August 1997* (pp. 127–134). Amsterdam: IOS Press.

Belz, Julie A. (2004). Learner Corpus Analysis and the Development of Foreign Language Proficiency. *System, 32*(4), 577–591.

Bender, Emily M., Flickinger, Dan, Oepen, Stephan, Walsh, Annemarie, & Baldwin, Timothy. (2004). *Arboretum: Using a Precision Grammar for Grammar Checking for CALL.* Paper presented at InSTIL/ICALI 2004, Venice.

Bennett, Paul. (1995). *A Course in Generalized Phrase Structure Grammar.* London: UCL.

Berghel, Hal L. (1987). A Logical Framework for the Correction of Spelling Errors in Electronic Documents. *Information Processing & Management: an International Journal, 23*(5), 477–494.

Biber, Douglas, Conrad, Susan, & Reppen, Randi. (1998). *Corpus Linguistics: Investigating Language Structure and Use.* Cambridge: Cambridge University Press.

Black, Allan W. (1986). *Formal Properties of Feature Grammars.* Retrieved March 28, 2006, from http://www.cs.cmu.edu/~awb/papers/gram86.ps

Bland, Susan K., Noblitt, James S., Armington, Susan, & Gay, Geri. (1990). The Naive Lexical Hypothesis: Evidence from Computer-Assisted Language Learning. *Modern Language Journal, 74*(4), 440–450.

Bogaards, Paul. (1998). What Type of Words Do Language Learners Look Up? In B. T. S. Atkins (Ed.), *Using Dictionaries: Studies of Dictionary Use by Language Learners and Translators* (pp. 151–157). Tübingen: Max Niemeyer.

Bolt, Philip. (1992). An Evaluation of Grammar-Checking Programs as Self-Help Learning Aids for Learners of English as a Foreign Language. *Computer Assisted Language Learning, 5*(1-2), 49–91.

Bolt, Philip, & Yazdani, Masoud. (1998). The Evolution of a Grammar-Checking Program: LINGER to ISCA. *Computer Assisted Language Learning, 11*(1), 55–112.

Borchardt, Frank L. (1995). Language and Computing at Duke University: or, Virtue Triumphant, for the Time Being. *CALICO Journal, 12*(4), 57–83.

Borin, Lars, & Dahllöf, Mats. (1999). A Corpus-Based Grammar Tutor for Education in Language and Speech Technology. In *EACL'99. Computer and Internet Supported Education in Language and Speech Technology. Proceedings of a Workshop Sponsored by ELSNET and the Association for Computational Linguistics* (pp. 36–43). Bergen: Association for Computational Linguistics.

Borin, Lars, Lindberg, Inger, Kokkinakis, Sofie Johansson, Kokkinakis, Dimitrios, Gronostaj, Maria Toporowska, Olsson, Fredrik, et al. (2003). *Network of Excellence: Supporting Second Language Acquisition with Human Language Technology.* Unpublished manuscript, Göteborg.

Borissova, Elena. (1988). Two-Component Teaching System That Understands and Corrects Mistakes. In D. Vargha (Ed.), *Coling Budapest. Proceedings of the 12th Conference on Computational Linguistics* (pp. 68–70). Budapest: John von Neumann Society for Computing Sciences.
Börner, Wolfgang. (1999). Fremdsprachliche Lernaufgaben. *Zeitschrift für Fremdsprachenforschung, 10*(2), 209–230.
Bos, Edwin, & van de Plassche, Joke. (1994). A Knowledge-Based, English Verb-Form Tutor. *Journal of Artificial Intelligence in Education, 5*(1), 107–129.
Bouwer, Anders. (1998). An ITS for Dutch Punctuation. In B. P. Goettl, H. M. Halff, C. Redfield Luckhardt, & V. J. Shute (Eds.), *Intelligent Tutoring Systems. 4th International Conference, ITS '98, San Antonio, Texas, August 16–19, 1998. Proceedings* (pp. 224–233). Berlin: Springer-Verlag.
Bowerman, Christopher. (1991). *The Importance of Knowledge: A Look at an ITS for German Writing from a Different Angle. Paper Presented at PEG91 in Italy*. Retrieved Nov. 3, 2004, from http://osiris.sunderland.ac.uk/cbowww/html/papers.html
Bowerman, Christopher. (1993). *Intelligent Computer-Aided Language Learning. LICE: A System to Support Undergraduates Writing in German*. Unpublished PhD Thesis, UMIST, Manchester.
Brand, James. (1987). A Program That Acquires Language Using Positive and Negative Feedback. *CALICO Journal, 5*(1), 15–31.
Brandl, Klaus K. (1995). Strong and Weak Students' Preferences for Error Feedback Options and Responses. *The Modern Language Journal, 79*(ii), 194–211.
Braun, Sabine. (2005). From Pedagogically Relevant Corpora to Authentic Language Learning Contents. *ReCALL, 17*(1), 47–64.
Brehony, Tom, & Ryan, Kevin. (1994). Francophone Stylistic Grammar Checking (FSGC) Using Link Grammars. *Computer Assisted Language Learning, 7*(3), 257–269.
Bresnan, Joan. (1982). *The Mental Representation of Grammatical Relations*. Cambridge, Mass: MIT Press.
Briscoe, Edward John, & Carroll, J. A. (2004 [1995]). Developing and Evaluating a Probabilistic LR Parser of Part-of-Speech and Punctuation Labels. In G. R. Sampson & D. McCarthy (Eds.), *Corpus Linguistics. Readings in a Widening Discipline* (pp. 267–275). London: Continuum.
Brocklebank, Christopher Paul. (1998). *An Experiment in Developing a Prototype Intelligent Teaching System from a Parser Written in Prolog*. Unpublished MPhil Thesis, UMIST, Manchester.
Brookshear, J. Glen. (1997). *Computer Science. An Overview*. Reading, Mass.: Addison-Wesley.
Brown, Charles Grant. (2002). Inferring and Maintaining the Learner Model. *Computer Assisted Language Learning, 15*(4), 343–355.
Brown, Charles Grant, Keim, Nathan, Brammer, Kevin, & Flagel, Lorne. (2004). *The Incomplete Grammar Approach to the Development of a Strong AI-Based ICALL System*. Paper presented at the InSTIL/ICALI 2004, Venice.
Brusilovsky, Peter, Ritter, Steven, & Schwarz, Elmar. (1997). *Distributed Intelligent Tutoring on the Web*. Retrieved November 16, 1999, from http://www.contrib.andrew.cmu.edu/~plb/AIED97_workshop/Brusilovsky/Brusilovsky.html.
Brusilovsky, Peter. (2001). Adaptive Hypermedia. *User Modeling and User-Adapted Interaction, 11*, 87–110.
Buchmann, Beat. (1987). Early History of Machine Translation. In M. King (Ed.), *Machine Translation Today: The State of the Art* (pp. 3–21). Edinburgh: University Press.

Bull, Susan. (1993). Towards User/System Collaboration in Developing a Student Model for Intelligent Computer-Assisted Language Learning. *Computer Assisted Language Learning, 8*, 3–8.

Bull, Susan, Pain, Helen, & Brna, Paul. (1993). Collaboration and Reflection in the Construction of a Student Model for Intelligent Computer Assisted Language Learning. In *Proceedings of PEG93. AI Tools and the Classroom: Theory into Practice. Vol. I* (pp. 48–56).

Bull, Susan. (1994a). Student Modeling for Second Language Acquisition. *Computers and Education, 23*(1–2), 13-20.

Bull, Susan. (1994b). Learning Languages: Implications for Student Modelling in ICALL. *ReCALL, 6*(1), 34–39.

Bull, Susan, Brna, Paul, & Pain, Helen. (1995). Extending the Scope of the Student Model. *User Modeling and User-Adapted Interaction, 5*, 45–65.

Bull, Susan. (1997a). See Yourself Write: A Simple Student Model to Make Students Think. In A. Jameson, C. Paris, & C. Tasso (Eds.), *User Modeling: Proceedings of the Sixth International Conference, UM97* (pp. 315–326). Berlin: Springer Verlag.

Bull, Susan. (1997b). Promoting Effective Learning Strategy Use in CALL. *Computer Assisted Language Learning, 10*(1), 3–39.

Bull, Susan. (2000a). 'Do It Yourself' Student Models for Collaborative Student Modelling and Peer Interaction. In B. P. Goettl, H. M. Halff, C. Redfield Luckhardt, & V. J. Shute (Eds.), *Intelligent Tutoring Systems. 4th International Conference, ITS '98, San Antonio, Texas, USA, August 16–19, 1998 Proceedings* (pp. 176–185). Berlin: Springer Verlag.

Bull, Susan. (2000b). Individualized Recommendations for Learning Strategy Use. In G. Gauthier, C. Frasson, & K. VanLehn (Eds.), *Intelligent Tutoring Systems. 5th International Conference, ITS 2000, Montréal, Canada, June 2000, Proceedings* (pp. 594–603). Berlin: Springer Verlag.

Burstein, Jill, Kaplan, Randy, Wolff, Susanne, & Lu, Chi. (1996). Using Lexical Semantic Techniques to Classify Free-Responses. In *Proceedings of SIGLEX 1996 Workshop, 34th Annual Meeting of the Association for Computational Linguistics, University of California, Santa Cruz, June 28* (pp. 20–27). Morristown, NJ: Association for Computational Linguistics.

Burstein, Jill, & Chodorow, Martin. (1999). Automatic Essay Scoring for Nonnative English Speakers. In M. B. Olsen (Ed.), *Computer Mediated Language Assessment and Evaluation in Natural Language Processing. Proceedings of a Symposium Sponsored by the Association for Computational Linguistics and the International Association of Language Learning Technologies* (pp. 68–75). College Park, Maryland: Association for Computational Linguistics.

Burston, Jack. (1998). Antidote 98. *CALICO Journal, 16*(2), 197–212.

Burton, Richard R., & Brown, John Seely. (1982). An Investigation of Computer Coaching for Informal Learning Activities. In D. Sleeman & J. S. Brown (Eds.), *Intelligent Tutoring Systems* (pp. 79–88). London: Academic Press.

Bygate, Martin, Skehan, Peter, & Swain, Merrill. (2001). *Researching Pedagogic Tasks: Second Language Learning, Teaching, and Testing.* Harlow, England; New York: Longman.

Calico, Eurocall, & IALLT. (1999). *Scholarly Activities in Computer-Assisted Language Learning: Development, Pedagogical Innovations, and Research.* Retrieved 13 October 13, 2004, from http://www.calico.org/CALL_document.html.

Cameron, Keith (Ed.). (1999). *Computer-Assisted Language Learning. Media, Design and Applications.* Lisse: Swets & Zeitlinger.

Carlucci, Luigia Aiello, Cialdea, Marta, & Nardi, Daniele. (1993). Reasoning About Student Knowledge and Reasoning. *Journal of Artificial Intelligence in Education, 4*(4), 397–413.

Carroll, Susanne, & Swain, Merrill. (1993). Explicit and Implicit Negative Feedback: An Empirical Study of the Learning of Linguistic Generalizations. *Studies in Second Language Acquisition, 15*, 357–386.

Cathcart, Ruth L., & Olsen, Judy E.W.B. (1976). Teachers' and Students' Preferences for Correction of Classroom Conversation Errors. In J. F. Fanselow & R. H. Crymes (Eds.), *On TESOL '76: Selections Based on Teaching Done at the Tenth Annual TESOL Convention, New York, New York, March 2–7, 1976* (pp. 41–53). Washington, DC: Teachers of English to Speakers of Other Languages.

Catt, Mark Edward. (1988). *Intelligent Diagnosis of Ungrammaticality in Computer-Assisted Language Instruction.* Unpublished Master's Thesis, University of Toronto, Toronto.

Catt, Mark Edward, & Hirst, Graeme. (1990). An Intelligent CALI System for Grammatical Error Diagnosis. *Computer Assisted Language Learning, 3*, 3–27.

Cerri, Stefano A., & Merger, Marie-France. (1983). Learning Translation Skills with a Knowledge-Based Tutor: French-Italian Conjunctions in Context. In *Proceedings of the First Conference of the European Chapter of the Association of Computational Linguistics* (pp. 133–138). Pisa, Italy: Association for Computational Linguistics.

Cerri, Stefano A. (1989). ALICE: Acquisition of Linguistic Items in the Context of Examples. *Instructional Science, 18*, 63–92.

Cerri, Stefano A., Cheli, Elena, & McIntyre, Angus. (1992). Nobile: Object-Based User Model Acquisition for Second Language Learning. In M. L. Swartz & M. Yazdani (Eds.), *Intelligent Tutoring Systems for Foreign Language Learning. The Bridge to International Communication* (pp. 171–190). Berlin: Springer Verlag.

Chanier, Thierry, Pengelly, Michael, Twidale, Michael, & Self, John A. (1992). Conceptual Modeling in Error Analysis in Computer-Assisted Language Learning Systems. In M. L. Swartz & M. Yazdani (Eds.), *Intelligent Tutoring Systems for Foreign Language Learning: The Bridge to International Communication* (pp. 125–150). New York: Springer Verlag.

Chanier, Thierry. (1994). Special Issue on Language Learning. *Journal of Artificial Intelligence in Education, 5*.

Chapelle, Carol A., & Mizuno, Suesue. (1989). Student's Strategies with Learner-Controlled CALL. *CALICO Journal, 7*(2), 25–47.

Chapelle, Carol A., Jamieson, Joan, & Park, Yuhsoon (1996). Second Language Classroom Traditions: How Does CALL Fit?. In M. C. Pennington (Ed.), *The Power of CALL*. Houston: Athelstan Publications.

Chapelle, Carol A. (1997). Call in the Year 2000: Still In Search of Research Paradigms? *Language Learning & Technology, 1*(1), 19–43.

Chapelle, Carol A. (1998). Mulitmedia CALL: Lessons to be Learned from Research on Instructed SLA. *Language Learning & Technology, 2*(1), 22–34.

Chapelle, Carol A. (2001). Innovative Language Learning: Achieving the Vision. *ReCALL, 13*(1), 3–14.

Chapelle, Carol A. (2003). *Linking SLA Task Theory to Technology Based Tasks.* Paper presented at the Conference on Technology for SLL, Memorial Union, Iowa State University.

Chapelle, Carol A. (2005). Interactionist SLA Theory in CALL Research. In J. Egbert & G. M. Petrie (Eds.), *CALL Research Perspectives* (pp. 53–64). Mahwah, N.J.: Erlbaum Associates.

Chen, Li, & Kurtz, Barry L. (1989a). XTRA-TE: Using Natural Language Processing Software to Develop an ITS for Language Learning. In D. Bierman, J. Breuker & J. Sandberg (Eds.), *Artificial Intelligence and Education. Proceedings of the 4th International Conference on AI and Education* (pp. 54–63). Amsterdam: IOS.

Chen, Li, & Kurtz, Barry L. (1989b). XTRA-TE: Using Natural Language Processing Software to Develop an ITS for Language Learning. *Journal of Artificial Intelligence in Education, 80*, 54–63.

Chen, Liang, & Tokuda, Naoyuki. (2003). A New Template-Template-Enhanced ICALL System for a Second Language Composition Course. *CALICO Journal, 20*(3), 561–578.

Chen, Si-Qing, & Xu, Luomai. (1990). Grammar-Debugger: A Parser for Chinese EFL Learners. *CALICO Journal, 8*(2), 63–75.

Chenoweth, N. Ann, Day, Richard R., Chun, Ann E., & Luppescu, Stuart. (1983). Attitudes and Preferences of ESL Students to Error Correction. *Studies in Second Language Acquisition, 6*(1), 79–87.

Chin, David N. (2001). Empirical Evaluation of User Models and User-Adapted Systems. *User Modeling and User-Adapted Interaction, 11*, 181–194.

Chomsky, Noam. (1981). *Lectures on Government and Binding*. Dordrecht, Holland Foris, 1981.

Chomsky, Noam. (1986). *Knowledge of Language: Its Nature, Origin, and Use*. New York: Praeger.

Church, Kenneth. (1988). *A Stochastic Parts Program and Noun Phrase Parser for Unrestricted Text*. In Second Conference on Applied Natural Language Processing. Proceedings of the COnference (pp. 136–143). Austin, Texas.

Claydon, Peter, Hietala, Pentti, & Nissilä, Kimmo. (1992). A Knowledge-Based Learner Companion for Aspects of Academic Writing: Problems or Potential. In J. Thompson & C. Zähner (Eds.), *Proceedings of the ICALL Workshop, UMIST, September 1991* (pp. 12–21). Hull: University of Hull, CTI Centre for Modern Languages.

Cobb, Thomas, & Stevens, Vance (1996). A Principled Consideration of Computers and Reading in a Second Language. In M. C. Pennington (Ed.), *The Power of CALL* (pp. 115–137). Houston: Athelstan.

Cole, Ronald. (1996). *Foreword. Survey of the State of the Art in Human Language Technology*. Retrieved October 13, 2004, from http://cslu.cse.ogi.edu/HLTsurvey/foreword_cole.html.

Colmerauer, Alain. (1978). Metamorphosis Grammars. In L. Bolc (Ed.), *Natural Language Communication with Computers* (pp. 133–189). Berlin: Springer Verlag.

Colpaert, Jozef. (2004). *Design of Online Interactive Language Courseware: Conceptualization, Specification and Prototyping. Research into the Impact of Linguistic-Didactic Functionality on Software Architecture*. University of Antwerp, Antwerp.

Commission of the European Communities. (2005). *A New Framework Strategy for Multilingualism (COM(2005) 596 final)*. Retrieved April 12, 2006, from http://europa.eu.int/languages/servlets/Doc?id=913.

Conrad, K. Bernd (1996). CALL-Non-English L2 Instruction. *Annual Review of Applied Linguistics, 16*, 158–181.

Cook, Vivian, & Fass, Dan. (1986). Natural Language Processing by Computer and Language Teaching. *System, 14*(2), 163–170.

Cook, Vivian. (1988). Designing a BASIC Parser for CALL. *CALICO Journal, 6*(1), 50–67.

Cook, Vivian, & Newson, Mark. (1996). *Chomsky's Universal Grammar. An Introduction (second edition)*. Oxford: Blackwell.

Corder, Steven Pit. (1974). Error Analysis. In J. P. B. Allen & P. Corder (Eds.), *The Edinburgh Course in Applied Linguistics. Volume 3 - Techniques in Applied Linguistics* (pp. 122–131). London: Oxford University Press.

Corder, Steven Pit. (1981). *Error Analysis and Interlanguage.* Oxford: Oxford University Press.

Courtin, Jaques, Dujardin, Danièle, Kowarski, Irène, Genthial, Damien, & De Lima, Véra Lucia. (1991). Towards a Complete Detection / Correction System. In M. Nagao (Ed.), *Proceedings of the International Conference on Current Issues in Computational Linguistics* (pp. 158–173). Penang, Malaysia.

Covington, Michael A., & Weinrich, Kevin B. (1991). Unification-Based Diagnosis of Language Learners' Syntax Errors. *Literary and Linguistic Computing, 6*(3), 149–154.

Covington, Michael A. (1994). *Natural Language Processing for Prolog Programmers.* Englewood Cliffs, N. J.: Prentice Hall Inc.

Cowan, Ron, Choi, Hyun Eun, & Kim, Doe Hyung. (2003). Four Questions for Error Diagnosis and Correction in CALL. *CALICO Journal, 20*(3), 451–463.

Cross, Jeremy. (2002). 'Noticing' in SLA: Is it a Valid Concept? *TESL-EJ, 6*(3), A-2.

Culley, Gerald, Mulford, George W., & Milbury-Steen, John. (1986). A Foreign-Language Adventure Game: Progress Report on an Application of AI to Language Instruction. *CALICO Journal, 4*(2), 69–87.

Cunningham, Pat A., Iberall, Thea, & Woolf, Beverly W. (1987). CALEB: An Intelligent Silent Second Language Tutor. In *Proceedings of IEEE International Conference on Systems, Man, and Cybernetics* (pp. 1210–1215). Los Alamitos, CA: Computer Society IEEE.

Dagneaux, Estelle, Denness, Sharon, & Granger, Sylviane. (1998). Computer-Aided Error Analysis. *System, 26*(2), 163–174.

Dalgish, Gerard M. (1991). Computer-Assisted Error Analysis and Courseware Design: Applications for ESL in the Swedish Context. *CALICO Journal, 9*(2), 39–56.

Damerau, Fred J. (1964). A Technique for Computer Detection and Correction of Spelling Errors. *Communications of the ACM, 7*(3), 171–176.

Danna, Frederic, & Sebillot, Pascale. (1997). A Formalization of Student Modeling. *Computer Assisted Language Learning, 10*(2), 121–147.

Dansuwan, Suyada, Nishina, Kikuko, Akahori, Kanji, & Shimizu, Yasutaka. (2001). Development and Evaluation of a Thai Learning System on the Web Using Natural Language Processing. *CALICO Journal, 19*(1), 67–88.

Davies, Graham. (2002). *ICT4LT: Module 2.3, Section 3.1.* Retrieved March 24, 2006, from http://www.ict4lt.org.

Davies, Graham. (1988). CALL Software Development. In U. O. H. Jung (Ed.), *Computers in Applied Linguistics and Language Learning. A CALL Handbook* (pp. 29–47). Frankfurt: Peter Lang.

Davies, Graham. (1996). *Total-text Reconstruction Programs: A Brief History.* Maidenhead: Camsoft Monograph (unpublished manuscript).

de Haan, Ab, & Oppenhuizen, Tinus. (1994). SPELLER: A Reflexive ITS to Support the Learning of Second Language Spelling. *Computers in Human Behavior, 10*(1), 21–31.

Delmonte, Rodolfo. (2002). Feedback Generation and Linguistic Knowledge in 'SLIM' Automatic Tutor. *ReCALL, 14*(2), 209–234.

Delmonte, Rodolfo. (2003). Linguistic Knowledge and Reasoning for Error Diagnosis and Feedback Generation. *CALICO Journal, 20*(3), 513–532.

Delmonte, Rodolfo. (2004). *Evaluating Students' Summaries with GETARUNS.* Paper presented at InSTIL/ICALI 2004, Venice.

Desmarais, Lisa, Laurier, Michel, & Renie, Delphine. (1998). The Analysis of Navigation Patterns in CALL. *Computer Assisted Language Learning, 11*(3), 309–315.

DeSmedt, William H. (1995). Herr Kommissar: An ICALL Conversation Simulator for Intermediate German. In V. M. Holland, J. D. Kaplan & M. R. Sams (Eds.), *Intelligent Language Tutors: Theory Shaping Technology* (pp. 153–174). Mahwah, NJ: Erlbaum Associates.

Diaz de Ilarranza, Arantza, Maritxalar, Montse, & Oronoz, Maite. (1998). Reusability of Language Technology in Support of Corpus Studies in an ICALL Environment. In S. Jager, J. A. Nerbonne & A. van Essen (Eds.), *Language Teaching and Language Technology* (pp. 149–166). Lisse: Swets & Zeitlinger.

Diaz de Ilarranza, Arantza, Maritxalar, Aitor, Maritxalar, Montse, & Oronoz, Maite. (1999). IDAZKIDE: An Intelligent Computer-Assisted Language Learning Environment for Second Language Acquisition. In M. Schulze, M.-J. Hamel & J. Thompson (Eds.), *Language Processing in CALL. ReCALL Special Publication (Proceedings of a One-Day Conference "Natural Language Processing in Computer-Assisted Language Learning" Held at UMIST, 9 May 1998, Organised by the Centre of Computational Linguistics, UMIST, in Association with Eurocall)* (pp. 12–19). Hull: CTICML.

Dimitrova, Vania, Brna, Paul, & Self, John A. (2002). The Design and Implementation of a Graphical Communication Medium for Interactive Open Learner Modelling. In S. A. Cerri, G. Gouardáeres, & F. Paraguaçu (Eds.), *Intelligent Tutoring Systems. 6th International Conference, ITS 2002, Biarritz, France and San Sebastian, Spain, June 2–7, 2002, Proceedings* (pp. 432–441). Berlin: Springer-Verlag.

Dini, Luca, & Malnati, Giovanni. (1993). Weak Constraints and Preference Rules. In P. Bennett & P. Paggio (Eds.), *Preference in Eurotra* (pp. 75–90). Luxembourg: Commission of the European Communities.

Dittmann, Frank. (2005). Maschinenintelligenz zwischen Wunsch und Wirklichkeit. In C. Pias (Ed.), *Zukünfte des Computers* (pp. 133–155). Zürich: Diaphanes.

Dodigovic, Marina. (2005). *Artificial Intelligence in Second Language Learning.* Clevedon: Multilingual Matters.

Dokter, Duco, & Nerbonne, John. (1998). A Session with Glosser-RuG. In S. Jager, J. A. Nerbonne & A. van Essen (Eds.), *Language Teaching and Language Technology* (pp. 89–95). Lisse: Swets & Zeitlinger.

Dokter, Duco, Nerbonne, John, Schürcks-Grozeva, Lily, & Smit, Petra. (1998). Glosser-RuG: A User Study. In S. Jager, J. A. Nerbonne, & A. van Essen (Eds.), *Language Teaching and Language Technology* (pp. 169–178). Lisse: Swets & Zeitlinger.

Douglas, Sarah A. (1995). LingWorlds: An Intelligent Object-Oriented Environment for Second Language Tutoring. In V. M. Holland, J. D. Kaplan & M. R. Sams (Eds.), *Intelligent Language Tutors: Theory Shaping Technology* (pp. 201–220). Mahwah, NJ: Erlbaum Associates.

Dreyer, Hilke, & Schmitt, Richard. (1994). *A Practice Grammar of German.* München: Verlag für Deutsch.

Dulay, Heidi C., & Burt, Marina K. (1974). You Can't Learn without Goofing. In J. C. Richards (Ed.), *Error Analysis: Perspectives on Second Language Acquisition* (pp. 95–123). London: Longman.

Dulay, Heidi C., Burt, Marina K., & Krashen, Stephen D. (1982). *Language Two.* New York: Oxford University Press.

Durrell, Martin, & Hammer, Alfred E. (2002). *Hammer's German Grammar and Usage* (4th ed.). Chicago, Ill.; Toronto, Ont.: McGraw-Hill.

Egbert, Joy, & Petrie, Gina Mikel (Eds.). (2005). *CALL Research Perspectives.* Mahwah, N.J.: Erlbaum Associates.
Egedi, Dania, & Martin, Patrick. (1994). *A Freely Available Syntactic Lexicon for English.* Paper presented at the International Workshop of Sharable Natural Language Resources, Nara, Japan.
Ellis, Rod. (1994). *The Study of Second Language Acquisition.* Oxford: Oxford University Press.
Ellis, Rod, Basturkmen, Helen, & Loewen, Shawn. (2001). Learner Uptake in Communicative ESL Lessons. *Language Learning, 51*(2), 281–318.
Ellis, Rod. (2003). *Task-Based Language Learning and Teaching.* Oxford, U.K.: Oxford University Press.
Ellis, Rod (Ed.). (2005). *Planning and Task Performance in a Second Language.* Amsterdam: John Benjamins.
Elsom-Cook, Mark. (1993). Student Modeling in Intelligent Tutoring Systems. *Artificial Intelligence Review, 7*(3-4), 227–240.
Emanuelli, Annie J. (1986). Artificial Intelligence and Computer Assisted Language Learning. *UEA Papers in Linguistics, 25–26*, 43–56.
Emirkanian, Louisetta, & Bouchard, Lorne H. (1988a). Knowledge Integration in a Robust and Efficient Morpho-Syntactic Analyzer for French. In D. Vargha (Ed.), *Coling Budapest. Proceedings of the 12th International Conference on Computational Linguistics* (Vol. 1, pp. 166–171). Budapest: John von Neumann Society for Computer Sciences.
Emirkanian, Louisetta, & Bouchard, Lorne H. (1988b). Towards a Knowledge-Based Tool for Correcting French Text. In F. Lovis & E. D. Tagg (Eds.), *Computers in Education* (pp. 583–588). Amsterdam: Elsevier Science.
Eurocall, Calico, & IALLT. (1999). *Eurocall Research Policy Statement.* Retrieved October 13, 2004, from http://www.eurocall-languages.org/research/research_policy.html.
European Commission. (1996). *Language and Technology. From the Tower of Babel to the Global Village.* Brussels: Office for Official Publications of the European Communities.
Evans, Roger (Ed.). (1992). *An Introduction to the Sussex Prolog DATR System.* Brighton: University of Sussex.
Everson, Howard T. (1995). Modeling the Student in Intelligent Tutoring Systems: The Promise of a New Psychometrics. *Instructional Science, 23*, 433–452.
Fallman, Daniel. (2002). *The Penguin: Using the Web as a Database for Descriptive and Dynamic Grammar and Spell Checking.* Paper presented at CHI 2002, Conference on Human Factors in Computing Systems, Minneapolis, MN.
Farghaly, Ali. (1989). A Model for Intelligent Computer Assisted Language Instruction (MICALI). *Computers and the Humanities, 23*(3), 235–250.
Fass, Dan, & Wilks, Yorick. (1983). Preference Semantics, Ill-formedness, and Metaphor. *American Journal of Computational Linguistics, 9*(3–4), 178–187.
Felix, Uschi. (1998). *Virtual Language Learning. Finding the Gems amongst the Pebbles.* Melbourne: Language Australia.
Felix, Uschi. (1999). Web-based Language Learning: A Window to the Authentic World. In R. Debski & M. Levy (Eds.), *WorldCALL: Global Perspectives on Computer-Assisted Language Learning* (pp. 85–98). Lisse, The Netherlands: Swets & Zeitlinger.
Felix, Uschi (Ed.). (2001). *Beyond Babel: Language Learning Online.* Melbourne: Language Australia.
Felix, Uschi. (2002). Teaching Language Online — Deconstructing Myths. Paper presented at *EUROCALL.* Jyväskylä, Finland.
Felix, Uschi (Ed.). (2003). *Language Learning Online: Towards Best Practice.* Lisse: Swets & Zeitlinger.

Felshin, Sue. (1995). The Athena Language Learning Project NLP System: A Multilingual System for Conversation-Based Learning. In V. M. Holland, J. D. Kaplan & M. R. Sams (Eds.), *Intelligent Language Tutors: Theory Shaping Technology* (pp. 257–272). Mahwah, NJ: Erlbaum Associates.

Ferreira, Anita, & Bañados, Emerita. (2005). Effective Corrective-Feedback Strategies in Second Language Teaching with Implications for Intelligent Tutorial Systems (ITS) for Foreign Languages (FL), *CALICO*. Michigan State University, East Lansing.

Ferris, Dana R. (2004). The "Grammar Correction" Debate in L2 Writing: Where Are We, and Where Do We Go from Here? (and What Do We Do in the Meantime ...?). *Journal of Second Language Writing, 13*, 49–62.

Feuerman, Ken, Marshall, Catherine, Newman, David, & Rypa, Marikka. (1987). The CALLE Project. *CALICO Journal, 4*(2), 25–34.

Finlay, Janet, & Dix, Alan. (1996). London: UCL Press.

Flämig, Walter. (1991). *Grammatik des Deutschen : Einführung in Struktur- und Wirkungszusammenhänge. Erarbeitet auf der theoretischen Grundlage der "Grundzüge einer deutschen Grammatik"*. Berlin: Akademie Verlag.

Fogg, B.J., & Tseng, Hsiang. (1999). *The Elements of Computer Credibility*. Paper presented at the Human Factors in Computing Systems (CHI-99), Pittsburg, PA.

Fortmann, Christian, & Forst, Martin. (2004). *An LFG Grammar Checker for CALL*. Paper presented at InSTIL/ICALI 2004, Venice.

Foth, Kilian, Menzel, Wolfgang, & Schröder, Ingo. (2005). Robust Parsing with Weighted Constraints. *Natural Language Engineering, 11*(1), 1–25.

Fotos, Sandra, & Browne, Charles. (2004). The Development of CALL and Current Options. In S. Fotos & C. Browne (Eds.), *New Perspectives on CALL for Second Language Classrooms*. Mahwah, N.J.: Erlbaum Associates.

Fujiwara, Miho, & Yamura-Takei, Mitsuko. (2002). Zero-Checker: A CALL Program for Reading and Writing Japanese. In *Proceedings of the Third International Conference of Computer Assisted Systems for Teaching and Learning Japanese* (pp. 205–208).

Fum, Danilo, Giangrandi, Paolo, & Tasso, Carlo. (1988). The ET Project: Artificial Intelligence in Second Language Teaching. In F. Lovis & E. D. Tagg (Eds.), *Computers in Education* (pp. 511–516). Amsterdam: Elsevier Science.

Fum, Danilo, Giangrandi, Paolo, & Tasso, Carlo. (1989). Tense Generation in an Intelligent Tutor for Foreign Language teaching: Some Issues in the Design of the Verb Expert. In *Proceedings of the Fourth Conference of the European Chapter of the Association for Computational Linguistics* (pp. 124–129). Manchester: Association for Computational Linguistics.

Fum, Danilo, Pani, Bruno, & Tasso, Carlo. (1991). *Teaching the English Tense: Integrating Naive and Formal Grammars in an Intelligent Tutor for Foreign Language Teaching. Paper Presented at the Fifth Conference of the European Chapter of the Association for Computational Linguistics*. Retrieved Nov. 3, 2004, from http://www.dimi.uniud.it/~tasso/EUROACL1991.html.

Fum, Danilo, Pani, Bruno, & Tasso, Carlo. (1992). Naive vs. Formal Grammars: A Case for Integration in the Design of a Foreign Language Tutor. In M. L. Swartz & M. Yazdani (Eds.), *Intelligent Tutoring Systems for Foreign Language Learning. The Bridge to International Communication* (pp. 51–64). Berlin: Springer Verlag.

Fung, Patricia. (1993). Do-It-Yourself Student Modeling. *Computers and Education, 20*(1), 81–87.

Gade Brander, Brigitte. (2005). Considering Culture in CALL Research. In J. Egbert & G. M. Petrie (Eds.), *CALL Research Perspectives* (pp. 141–153). Mahwah, N.J.: Erlbaum Associates.

Gamper, Johann, & Knapp, Judith. (2002). A Review of Intelligent CALL Systems. *Computer Assisted Language Learning, 15*(4), 329–342.

Garrett, Nina. (1987). A Psycholinguistic Perspective on Grammar and CALL. In W. F. Smith (Ed.), *Modern Media in Foreign Language Education: Theory and Implementation* (pp. 169–196). Lincolnwood, IL: National Textbook.

Gaskell, Delian, & Cobb, Thomas. (2004). Can Learners Use Concordance Feedback for Writing Errors? *System, 32*(4), 301–319.

Gass, Susan M. (1997). *Input, Interaction, and the Second Language Learner.* Mahwah, NJ: Erlbaum Associates.

Gass, Susan M., & Selinker, Larry. (2001). *Second Language Acquisition. An Introductory Course.* Mahwah, NJ: Erlbaum Associates.

Gazdar, Gerald, Klein, Ewan, Pullum, Geoffrey K., & Sag, Ivan A. (1985). *Generalized Phrase Structure Grammar.* Cambridge, MA: Harvard University Press.

Gazdar, Gerald, & Mellish, Chris. (1989). *Natural Language Processing in PROLOG: An Introduction to Computational Linguistics* (Vol. xv). Wokingham: Addison-Wesley.

Gillard, Patrick, & Gadsby, Adam. (1998). Using a Learners' Corpus in Compiling ELT Dictionaries. In S. Granger (Ed.), *Learner English on Computer* (pp. 159–171). London: Longman.

Gisolfi, Antonio, Dattolo, Antonina, & Balzano, Walter. (1992). A Fuzzy Approach to Student Modeling. *Computers and Education, 19*(4), 329–334.

Glendinning, Eric, & Howard, Ron. (2003). Lotus ScreenCam as an Aid to Investigating Student Writing. *Computer Assisted Language Learning, 16*(1), 31–46.

Granger, Sylviane, & Meunier, Fanny. (1994). Towards a Grammar Checker for Learners of English. In U. Fries, G. Tottie, & P. Schneider (Eds.), *Creating and Using English Language Corpora: Papers from the Fourteenth International Conference on English Language Research on Computerized Corpora, Zürich 1993* (pp. 79–91). Amsterdam/Atlanta: Rodopi.

Granger, Sylviane, & Tribble, Christopher. (1998). Learner Corpus Data in the Foreign Language Classroom: Form-Focused Instruction and Data-Driven Learning. In S. Granger (Ed.), *Learner English on Computer* (pp. 199–209). London: Longman.

Granger, Sylviane. (2002). A Bird's-Eye View of Learner Corpus Research. In S. Granger, J. Hung, & S. Petch-Tyson (Eds.), *Computer Learner Corpora, Second Language Acquisition and Foreign Language Teaching* (pp. 3–33). Amsterdam/Philadelphia: John Benjamins.

Granger, Sylviane. (2003). Error-tagged Learner Corpora and CALL: A Promising Synergy. *CALICO Journal, 20*(3), 465–480.

Greer, Jim E., & McCalla, Gordon I. (1989). A Computational Framework for Granularity and Its Application to Educational Diagnosis. In *Proceedings of the 11th International Joint Conference on Artificial Intelligence, Detroit* (pp. 477–482): Morgan Kaufman.

Grice, P. (1975). Logic and Conversation. In D. Cole & J. Morgan (Eds.), *Syntax and Semantics: Speech Acts* (pp. 41–58). New York: Academic Press.

Güvenir, H. Altay. (1992). Drill and Practice for Turkish Grammar. In M. L. Swartz & M. Yazdani (Eds.), *Intelligent Tutoring Systems for Foreign Language Learning. The Bridge to International Communication* (pp. 275–291). Berlin: Springer Verlag.

Hackenberg, Robert G. (1984). Generate: A Natural Language Sentence Generator. *CALICO Journal, 2*(2), 5–8.

Hagen, Kirk L. (1995). Unification-Based Parsing Applications for Intelligent Foreign Language Tutoring Systems. *CALICO Journal, 12*(2&3), 5–31.

Halliday, Michael A. K. (1994). *An Introduction to Functional Grammar*. London: Edward Arnold.

Hamburger, Henry, & Hashim, Raza. (1992). Foreign Language Tutoring and Learning Environment. In M. L. Swartz & M. Yazdani (Eds.), *Intelligent Tutoring Systems for Foreign Language Learning. The Bridge to International Communication* (pp. 201–218). Berlin: Springer Verlag.

Hamburger, Henry, Tufis, Dan, & Hashim, Raza. (1993). Structuring Two - Medium Dialog for Learning Language and Other Things. In O. Rambow (Ed.), *Intentionality and Structure in Discourse Relations. Proceedings of a Workshop Sponsored by the Special Interest Group on Generation of the Association of Computational Linguistics* (pp. 27–30). Columbus, Ohio.

Hamburger, Henry. (1994). Foreign Language Immersion: Science, Practice, and a System. *Journal of Artificial Intelligence in Education, 5*(4), 429–453.

Hamburger, Henry. (1995). Tutorial Tools for Language Learning by Two-Medium Dialogue. In V. M. Holland, J. D. Kaplan & M. R. Sams (Eds.), *Intelligent Language Tutors: Theory Shaping Technology* (pp. 183–199). Mahwah, NJ: Erlbaum Associates.

Hamburger, Henry, Schoelles, Michael, & Reeder, Florence. (1999). More Intelligent CALL. In K. Cameron (Ed.), *Computer-Assisted Language Learning* (pp. 183–202). Lisse: Swets & Zeitlinger.

Hamel, Marie-Josée. (1996). NLP Tools in CALL for Error Diagnosis. *Revue de l'ACLA/Journal of the CAAL, 18*(2), 125–141.

Handke, Jürgen. (1989a). INTELTEXT - CALL Software mit natürlichsprachlichem Wissen. In K. Dette (Ed.), *Mikrocomputer-Pools in der Lehre* (pp. 54–64). Berlin: Springer Verlag.

Handke, Jürgen. (1989b). Computer Assisted Language Learning und Künstliche Intelligenz. *Die Neueren Sprachen, 88*(1), 21–32.

Handke, Jürgen. (1990). Intelligente Tutorielle Systeme - Theorie und Realisierung auf dem PC. *Innsbrucker Beiträge zur Kulturwissenschaft, 3*, 274–290.

Handke, Jürgen. (1992). WIZDOM: A Multiple-Purpose Language Tutoring System Based on AI Techniques. In M. L. Swartz & M. Yazdani (Eds.), *Intelligent Tutoring Systems for Foreign Language Learning. The Bridge to International Communication* (pp. 293–306). Berlin: Springer Verlag.

Hansen, C., & McCalla, Gordon I. (2003). Assisting Students by Analysing their Interaction and Learning. In V. Aleven, H. U. Hoppe, J. Kay, R. Mizoguchi, H. Pain, F. Verdejo & K. Yacef (Eds.), *Supplementary Proceedings of Artificial Intelligence in Education Conference (AIED2003), Sydney, Australia* (pp. 258–268). Sydney: university of Sydney.

Harrington, Michael. (1994). *CompLex*: A Tool for the Development of L2 Vocabulary Knowledge. *Journal of Artificial Intelligence in Education, 5/4*, 481–500.

Harrington, Michael. (1996). Intelligent Computer-Assisted Language Learning, *ON-CALL* (Vol. 10).

Harroff, Susan. (1986). Die Sprachmaschine: A Microworld for Language Experimentation. *CALICO Journal, 3*(4), 32–34, 48.

Hart, Robert S. (1995). The Illinois PLATO Foreign Languages Project. *CALICO Journal, 12*(4), 15–37.

Hashemi, Sylvana S. (2003). *Automatic Detection of Grammar Errors in Primary School Children's Texts: A Finite State Approach.*, Göteborg, Göteborg University, Sweden.

Hauck, Mirjam. (2005). Metacognitive Knowledge, Metacognitive Strategies, and CALL. In J. Egbert & G. M. Petrie (Eds.), *CALL Research Perspectives* (pp. 65–86). Mahwah, N.J.: Erlbaum Associates.

Havranek, Gertraud, & Cesnik, Hermann. (2001). Factors Affecting the Success of Corrective Feedback. In S. H. Foster-Cohen & A. Nizegorodcew (Eds.), *EUROSLA Yearbook* (Vol. 1, pp. 99–122). Amsterdam: John Benjamins.

Hegelheimer, Volker, & Chapelle, Carol A. (2000). Methodological Issues in Research on Learner-Computer Interactions in CALL. *Language Learning & Technology, 4*(1), 41–59.

Heidorn, George E., Jensen, Karen, Miller, Lance A., Byrd, Roy J., & Chodorow, Martin. (1982). The EPISTLE Text-Critiquing System. *IBM Systems Journal, 21*(3), 305–326.

Heift, Trude. (1998a). An Interactive Intelligent Tutor over the Internet. In T. Otman & I. Tomak (Eds.), *Proceedings of ED-MEDIA 98, World Conference on Educational Multimedia, Hypermedia and Telecommunications* (pp. 556–560). Charlottesville, VA: AACE.

Heift, Trude. (1998b). *Designed Intelligence: A Language Teacher Model.* Unpublished PhD Thesis, Simon Fraser University, Burnaby.

Heift, Trude, & McFetridge, Paul. (1999). Exploiting the Student Model to Emphasize Language Teaching Pedagogy in Natural Language Processing. In M. B. Olsen (Ed.), *Computer Mediated Language Assessment and Evaluation in Natural Language Processing. A joint ACL-IALL Symposium Tuesday, June 22, 1999* (pp. 55–62). Retreived Jan. 8, 2000 from University of Maryland: http://umiacs.umd.edu/~molsen/acl-iall/Accepted/heift-mcfetridge.rtf.

Heift, Trude, & Nicholson, Devlan. (2000a). Theoretical and Practical Considerations for Web-based intelligent Language Tutoring Systems. In G. Gauthier, C. Frasson, & K. VanLehn (Eds.), *Intelligent Tutoring Systems. 5th International Conference, IITS 2000, Montréal, Canada, June 19–23, 2000. Proceedings* (pp. 354–362). Montreal: Springer Verlag.

Heift, Trude, & Nicholson, Devlan. (2000b). Enhanced Server Logs for Intelligent, Adaptive Web-Based Systems. In *Intelligent Tutoring Systems. Proceedings of the Fifth International Conference, ITS 2000* (pp. 354–362).

Heift, Trude. (2001). Error-Specific and Individualized Feedback in a Web-Based Language Tutoring System: Do They Read It? *ReCALL, 13*(2), 129–142.

Heift, Trude, & Nicholson, Devlan. (2001). Web Delivery of Adaptive and Interactive Language Tutoring. *International Journal of Artificial Intelligence in Education, 12*(4), 310–325.

Heift, Trude. (2002). Learner Control and Error Correction in ICALL: Browsers, Peekers and Adamants. *CALICO Journal, 19*(3), 295–313.

Heift, Trude. (2003). Multiple Learner Errors and Feedback: A Challenge for ICALL Systems. *CALICO Journal, 20*(3), 549–560.

Heift, Trude, & Schulze, Mathias (Eds.). (2003a). *Error Analysis and Error Correction. Special Issue of the CALICO Journal,* 20 (3).

Heift, Trude, & Schulze, Mathias. (2003b). Student Modeling and ab initio Language Learning. *System, 31*(4), 519–535.

Heift, Trude. (2004). Corrective Feedback and Learner Uptake in CALL. *ReCALL, 16*(2), 416–431.

Heift, Trude. (2005). Inspectable Learner Reports for Web-Based Language Learning. *ReCALL, 17*(1), 32–46.

Heift, Trude. (2006). Context-sensitive Help in CALL. *Computer Assisted Language Learning,* 19(2+3), 243–259.

Heinecke, Johannes, Kunze, Jürgen, Menzel, Wolfgang, & Schröder, Ingo. (1998). Eliminative Parsing with Graded Constraints. In *Proceedings of Coling-ACL'98* (pp. 526–530).

Hellwig, Harold. (1987). Problems and Solutions in Parsing. *CALICO Journal, 5*(1), 49–64.

Hémard, D., & Cushion, S. (2000). From Access to Acceptability: Exploiting the Web to Design a New CALL Environment. *Computer Assisted Language Learning, 13*(2), 103–118.

Hendrickson, James M. (1979). Evaluating Spontaneous Communication Through Systematic Error Analysis. *Foreign Language Annals, 12*(5), 357–364.

Hergenhahn, Baldwin R., & Olson, Matthew. (1997). *An Introduction to Theories of Learning*. London: Prentice-Hall International.

Higgins, John. (1983). Can Computers Teach? *CALICO Journal, 1*(2), 4–6.

Higgins, John. (1987). Artificial Unintelligence: Computer Uses in Language Learning. *TESOL Quarterly, 21*(1), 159–165.

Hirschman, Lynette, & Thompson, Henry S. (1996). 13.1 Overview of Evaluation in Speech and Natural Language Processing. In R. A. Cole, J. Mariani, H. Uszkoreit, A. Zaenen, V. Zue, G. B. Varile, & A. Zampolli (Eds.), *Survey of the State of the Art in Human Language Technology*. http://cslu.cse.ogi.edu/HLTsurvey/HLTsurvey.html.

Holland, V. Melissa, Maisano, Richard, Alderks, Cathie, & Martin, Jeffery. (1993). Parsers in Tutors: What Are They Good For? *CALICO Journal, 11*(1), 28–46.

Holland, V. Melissa. (1994). Lessons Learned in Designing Intelligent CALL: Managing Communication Across Disciplines. *Computer Assisted Language Learning, 7*(3), 227–256.

Holland, V. Melissa, Kaplan, Jonathan D, & Sams, Michelle R (Eds.). (1995). *Intelligent Language Tutors: Theory Shaping Technology*. Mahwah, NJ: Erlbaum Associates.

Holland, V. Melissa, & Kaplan, Jonathan D. (1995). Natural Language Processing Techniques in Computer Assisted Language Learning: Status and Instructional Issues. *Instructional Science, 23*, 351–380.

Holmes, Glyn, & de Moras, Nadine. (1997). A French Language Grammar Analyzer: What Use for Anglophone Students? In P. Liddell, M. Ledgerwood & A. Iwasaki (Eds.), *FLEAT III: Foreign Language Education and Technology - Proceedings of the Third Conference* (pp. 91–106). Victoria: University of Victoria.

Holt, Peter, Dubs, S., Jones, M., & Greer, Jim E. (1994). The State of Student Modelling. In J. E. Greer & G. I. McCalla (Eds.), *Student Modelling: The Key to Individualized Knowledge-Based Instruction* (pp. 3–39). Berlin: Springer Verlag.

Hoven, Debra. (2003). What Learners Use and How They React. *Australian Review of Applied Linguistics, Supplement 17*, 125–148.

Huang, Xueming. (1992). Inconsistent Beliefs, Attention, and Student Modeling. *Journal of Artificial Intelligence in Education, 3*(4), 417–428.

Hubbard, Philip. (1990). Obermeier, Klaus K. Natural Language Processing Technologies in Artificial Intelligence: The Science and Industry Perspective. and Last, Rex W. Artificial Intelligence Techniques in Language Learning. (Book Review). *Modern Language Journal, 74*, 512–513.

Hubbard, Philip. (1992). A Methodological Framework for CALL Courseware Development. In M. C. Pennington & V. Stevens (Eds.), *Computers in Applied Linguistics: An International Perspective* (pp. 39–65). Clevedon, Avon: Multilingual Matters.

Hubbard, Philip. (2004). Learner Training for Effective Use of CALL. In S. Fotos & C. Browne (Eds.), *New Perspectives on CALL for Second Language Classrooms* (pp. 45–67). Mahwah, N.J.: Erlbaum Associates.

Hull, C. L. (1943). *Principles of Behaviour*. New York: Appleton-Century-Crofts.

Hulstijn, Jan H., & Atkins, B.T. Sue. (1998). Empirical Research on Dictionary Use in Foreign-Language Learning: Survey and Discussion. In B. T. S. Atkins (Ed.), *Using Dictionaries: Studies of Dictionary Use by Language Learners and Translators* (pp. 7–19). Tübingen: Max Niemeyer.

Hutchins, John. (1986). *Machine Translation - Past, Present and Future.* New York: Ellis Horwood.

Hwu, Fenfang. (2003). Learners' Behaviors in Computer-Based Input Activities Elicited Through Tracking Technologies. *Computer Assisted Language Learning, 16*(1), 5–29.

Imlah, W J, & du Boulay, B. H. (1985). Robust Natural Language Parsing in Computer-Assisted Language Instruction. *System, 13*(2), 137–147.

Jager, Sake, Nerbonne, John A., & van Essen, Arthur (Eds.). (1998). *Language Teaching and Language Technology.* Lisse: Swets & Zeitlinger.

Jehle, Fred. (1987). A Free-Form Dialog Program in Spanish. *CALICO Journal, 5*(2), 11–22.

Jensen, K., Heidorn, G.E, Miller, L.A, & Ravin, Y. (1984). Parse Fitting and Prose Fixing: Getting a Hold on Ill-Formedness. *American Journal of Computational Linguistics, 9*(3–4), 147–160.

Johns, Tim. (1991a). From Printout to Handout: Grammar and Vocabulary Teaching in the Context of Data-Driven Learning. *ELR Journal, 4*, 27–45.

Johns, Tim. (1991b). Should You Be Persuaded - Two Samples of Data-Driven Learning Materials. *ELR Journal, 4*, 1–16.

Johns, Tim, King, Philip, & University of Birmingham. Centre for English Language Studies. (1991). *Classroom concordancing.* Birmingham: Centre for English Language Studies University of Birmingham.

Johns, Tim. (1994). From Printout to Handout: Grammar and Vocabulary Teaching in the Context of Data-Driven Learning. In T. Odlin (Ed.), *Perspectives on Pedagogical Grammar* (pp. 293–313). Cambridge: Cambridge University Press.

Johns, Tim. (1997). Contexts: the Background, Development and Trialling of a Concordance-based CALL Program. In A. Wichmann, S. Fligelstone, T. McEnery & G. Knowles (Eds.), *Teaching and Language Corpora* (pp. 100–115). London: Longman.

Johnson, Rod. (1983). Parsing with Transition Networks. In M. King (Ed.), *Parsing Natural Language* (pp. 59–73). London: Academic Press.

Johnston, Ian. (1988). *Gibber.* Unpublished PhD Thesis, University of Dundee, Dundee.

Jung, Udo O. H. (2002). An International Bibliography of Computer Assisted Language Learning: Fifth Installment. *System, 30*, 349–398.

Juozulynas, Vilius. (1994). Errors in the Composition of Second-Year German Students: An Empirical Study of Parser-Based ICALI. *CALICO Journal, 12*(1), 5–17.

Jurafsky, Dan, & Martin, James H. (2000). *Speech and Language Processing: An Introduction to Natural Language Processing, Computational Linguistics, and Speech Recognition.* Upper Saddle River, NJ: Prentice Hall.

Kagegawa, Junichi, Kanda, Hisayuki, Fujioka, Eitaro, Itami, Makoto, & Itoh, Kohji. (2000). Diagnostic Processing of Japanese for Computer-Assisted Second Language Learning. In *Proceedings of the 38th Annual Meeting of the Association for Computational Linguistics* (not paginated).

Kang, Yun-Sun, & Maciejewski, Anthony A. (2000). A Student Model of Technical Japanese Reading Proficiency for an Intelligent Tutoring System. *CALICO Journal, 18*(1), 9–40.

Kaplan, Jonathan D, Sabol, Mark A, Wisher, Robert A, & Seidel, Robert J. (1998). The Military Language Tutor (MILT) Program: An Advanced Authoring System. *Computer Assisted Language Learning, 11*(3), 265–287.

Kaplan, Jonathan D., & Holland, V. Melissa. (1995). Application of Learning Principles to the Design of a Second Language Tutor. In V. M. Holland, J. D. Kaplan, & M. R. Sams (Eds.), *Intelligent Language Tutors: Theory Shaping Technology* (pp. 273–287). Mahwah, NJ: Erlbaum Associates.

Karttunen, Lauri. (1984). Features and Values. In *10th International Conference on Computational Linguistics and 22nd Annual Meeting of the Association of Computational Linguistics. Proceedings of the Coling84* (pp. 28–33). Stanford: Association for Computational Linguistics.

Kaszubski, Przemyslaw. (1998). Enhancing a Writing Textbook: A National Perspective. In S. Granger (Ed.), *Learner English on Computer* (pp. 172–185). London: Longman.

Kay, Judy. (2000). Stereotypes, Student Models and Scrutability. In G. Gauthier, C. Frasson & K. VanLehn (Eds.), *Intelligent Tutoring Systems. 5th International Conference, ITS 2000, Montréal, Canada, June 19–23, 2000. Proceedings* (pp. 19–30). Berlin: Springer-Verlag.

Kay, Judy. (2001). Learner Control. *User Modeling and User-Adapted Interaction, 11*, 111–127.

Kelly, Declan, & Tangney, Brendan. (2002). Incorporating Learning Characteristics into an Intelligent Tutor. In S. A. Cerri, G. Gouardáeres, & F. Paraguaçu (Eds.), *Intelligent Tutoring Systems. 6th International Conference, ITS 2002, Biarritz, France and San Sebastian, Spain, June 2–7, 2002, Proceedings* (pp. 729–737). Berlin: Springer-Verlag.

Kempen, Gerard. (1992). Language Technology and Language Instruction: Computational Diagnosis of Word Level Errors. In M. L. Swartz & M. Yazdani (Eds.), *Intelligent Tutoring Systems for Foreign Language Learning. The Bridge to International Communication* (pp. 191–198). Berlin: Springer Verlag.

Kenning, Marie-Madeleine, & Kenning, M. J. (1990). *Computers and Language Learning.* New York: Ellis Horwood.

Kiss, Tibor, Fox, Deirdre, Geurts, Bart, Gediga, Günther, Hamilton, Simon, Krüger, Anja, et al. (1997). *RECALL: Repairing Errors in Computer-Assisted Language Learning (Final Report)* (No. LE1/1615).

Klein, Wolfgang, & Dittmar, Norbert. (1979). *Developing Grammars. The Acquisition of German Syntax by Foreign Workers.* Berlin: Springer Verlag.

Klenner, Manfred, & Visser, Henriëtte. (2003). What Exactly Is Wrong and Why? Tutorial Dialogue for Intelligent CALL Systems. *Linguistik online, 17*(5), 81–98.

Klenner, Manfred. (2004). *Tutorial Dialogue in DiBEx.* Paper presented at InSTIL/ICALI 2004, Venice.

Knapp, Judith. (2004). *A New Approach to CALL Content Authoring.* Unpublished Doctoral Dissertation, Universität Hannover, Hannover.

Knight, Kevin. (1989). Unification: A Multidisciplinary Survey. *ACM computing surveys, 21*(1), 93–124.

Kohn, Kurt. (1994). Distributive Language Learning in a Computer-Based Multilingual Communication Environment. In H. Jung & R. Vanderplank (Eds.), *Barriers and Bridges: Media Technology in Language Learning. Proceedings of the 1993 CETaLL Symposium on the Occasion of the 10th AILA World Congress in Amsterdam* (pp. 31–43). Frankfurt am Main: Peter Lang.

Kramsch, Claire, Morgenstern, Douglas, & Murray, Janet H. (1985). An Overview of the MIT Athena Language Learning Project. *CALICO Journal, 2*(4), 31–34.

Krashen, Stephen D. (1982). *Principles and Practice in Second Language Acquisition*. Oxford: Pergamon.

Krüger, Anja, & Hamilton, Simon. (1997). RECALL: Individual Language Tutoring through Intelligent Error Diagnosis. *ReCALL, 9*(2), 51–58.

Krüger-Thielmann, Karin. (1992). *Wissensbasierte Sprachlernsysteme. Neue Möglichkeiten für den computergestützten Sprachunterricht*. Tübingen: Gunter Narr.

Kukich, Karen. (1992). Techniques for Automatically Correcting Words in Text. *ACM Computing Surveys, 24*(4), 377–439.

Kulhavy, Raymond W. (1977). Feedback in Written Instruction. *Review of Educational Research, 47*(1), 211–232.

Kulik, James A., & Kulik, Chen-Lin C. (1988). Timing of Feedback and Verbal Learning. *Review of Educational Research, 58*(1), 79–97.

Kunichika, Hidenobu, Takeuchi, Akira, & Otsuki, Setsuko. (1998). Automatic Generation of Questions for a Comprehension Test in English Learning. In T. Ottmann & I. Tomek (Eds.), *Proceedings of ED-MEDIA/ED-TELECOM 98, World Conference on Education Multimedia and Educational Telecommunications* (Vol. 1, pp. 767–772). Charlottesville, VA: AACE.

Künzel, Sebastian. (1995). Processor Processing: Learning Theory and CALL. *CALICO Journal, 12*(4), 106–113.

Kurtz, Barry L., Chen, Li, & Huang, Xiuming. (1990). An English-Chinese Language Learning System Using Adaptive Correction and Multipass Error Diagnosis. *Journal of Artificial Intelligence in Education, 1*(4), 51–64.

Kurzweil, Raymond. (1990). *The Age of Intelligent Machines*. Cambridge, Mass.: MIT Press.

Kurzweil, Raymond. (1999). *The Age of Spiritual Machines*. London: Viking Press.

Kurzweil, Raymond. (2000). *Homo s@piens. Leben im 21. Jahrhundert. Was bleibt vom Menschen? (Aus dem Englischen von Helmut Dierlamm, Enrico Heinemann, Ute Mihr, Thomas Pfeiffer, Reiner Pfleiderer)*. München: Econ Taschenbuch Verlag.

Kurzweil, Raymond. (2001). *The Law of Accelerating Returns*. Retrieved March 20, 2006, from http://www.kurzweilai.net/meme/frame.html?main=/articles/art0134.html.

Kurzweil, Raymond. (2005). *The Singularity is Near: When Humans Transcend Biology*. New York: Viking.

L'Haire, Sébastien, & Vandeventer Faltin, Anne. (2003). Error Diagnosis in the FreeText Project. *CALICO Journal, 20*(3), 481–496.

Labrie, Gilles, & Singh, Lal P. S. (1991). Parsing, Error Diagnostics and Instruction in a French Tutor. *CALICO Journal, 9*, 9–25.

Lado, Robert. (1957). *Linguistics Across Cultures: Applied Linguistics for Language Teachers*. Ann Arbor: The University of Michigan Press.

Langenscheidt Redaktion (Ed.). (1985). *Computergestützter Fremdsprachenunterricht*. Berlin: Langenscheidt.

Last, Rex. (1986). The Potential of Artificial Intelligence-Related CALL at the Sentence Level. *Literary and Linguistic Computing, 1*(4), 197–201.

Last, Rex. (1989). *Artificial Intelligence Techniques in Language Learning*. Chichester: Ellis Horwood.

Last, Rex. (1992). Computers and Language Learning: Past, Present - and Future? In C. S. Butler (Ed.), *Computers and Written Texts* (pp. 227–246). Oxford: Blackwell.

Laufer, Baria, & Kimmel, Michal. (1997). Bilingualised Dictionaries: How Learners Really Use Them. *System, 25*(3), 361–369.

Lawler, Robert W. (1990). Dual Purpose Learning Environments. *Computer Assisted Language Learning, 4*, 46–52.

Lawler, Robert W. (1993). Dual Purpose Learning Environments. In M. Yazdani (Ed.), *Multilingual Multimedia. Bridging the Language Barrier with Intelligent Systems* (pp. 73–84). Oxford: Intellect.

Leather, C. H. (1932). *Common Errors in German with Rapid Corrective Exercises.* London, Toronto, Vancouver, Melbourne, Wellington: J. M. Dent and Sons Ltd.

Lee, Mi Ja. (2003). *Error Analysis of Written Texts by Learners of German as a Foreign Language.* Unpublished Master's Thesis, University of Waterloo, Waterloo, Ontario.

Leech, Geoffrey. (1997). Teaching and Language Corpora: A Convergence. In A. Wichmann, S. Fligelstone, T. McEnery & G. Knowles (Eds.), *Teaching and Language Corpora* (pp. 1–23). London: Longman.

Lehman, Jill Fain. (1999a). *Adaptive Parsing: Self-Extending Natural Language Interfaces.* Norwell, MA: Kluwer Academic Publishers.

Lehman, Jill Fain. (1999b). Toward the Use of Speech and Natural Language Technology in Intervention for a Language-Disordered Population. *Behaviour & Information Technology, 18*(1), 45–55.

Lelouche, Ruddy. (1994). Dealing with Pragmatic and Implicit Information in an ICALL System. *Journal of Artificial Intelligence in Education, 5*(4), 501–532.

Lennon, Paul. (1991). Error: Some Problems of Definition, Identification, and Distinction. *Applied Linguistics, 12*(2), 180–196.

Leontiev, Alexei Alexeyevich. (1981). *Psychology and the Language Learning Process.* Oxford: Pergamon.

Lessard, Greg, Maher, Daniel, Tomel, Ivan V., & Levison, Michael. (1994). Modeling Second Language Learner Creativity. *Journal of Artificial Intelligence in Education, 5*(4), 455–480.

Levin, Lori S., Evans, David A., & Gates, Donna M. (1991). The ALICE System: A Workbench for Learning and Using Language. *CALICO Journal, 9*(1), 27–54.

Levin, Lori S., & Evans, David A. (1995). ALICE-chan: A Case Study in ICALL Theory and Practice. In V. M. Holland, J. D. Kaplan, & M. R. Sams (Eds.), *Intelligent Language Tutors: Theory Shaping Technology* (pp. 77–99). Mahwah, NJ: Erlbaum Associates.

Levy, Mike. (1997). *Computer-Assisted Language Learning. Context and Conceptualisation.* Oxford: Clarendon.

Levy, Mike. (1998). Two Conceptions of Learning and their Implications in CALL at the Tertiary Level. *ReCALL, 10*(1), 86–94.

Levy, Mike. (1999a). Design Processes in CALL: Integrating Theory, Research and Evaluation. In K. Cameron (Ed.), *Computer-Assisted Language Learning* (pp. 83–108). Lisse: Swets & Zeitlinger.

Levy, Mike. (1999b). Theory and Design in a Multimedia CALL Project in Cross-Cultural Pragmatics. *Computer Assisted Language Learning, 12*(1), 29–57.

Lian, Andrew. (1992). Intelligence in Computer-Aided Learning. In M. C. Pennington & V. Stevens (Eds.), *Computers in Applied Linguistics: An International Perspective* (pp. 66–76). Clevedon, Avon, England: Multilingual Matters.

Lieberman, David. (1990). *Learning. Behavior and Cognition.* Belmont, California: Wadsworth.

Lightbown, Patsy M., & Spada, Nina. (1990). Focus-on-Form and Corrective Feedback in Communicative Language Teaching: Effects on Second Language Learning. *Studies in Second Language Acquisition, 12*, 429–448.

Liou, Hsien-Chin. (1991). Development of an English Grammar Checker. A Progress Report. *CALICO Journal, 9*, 27–56.
Long, Michael H. (1988). Inside the "Black Box": Methodological Issues in Classroom Research on Language Learning. *Language Learning, 30*, 1–42.
Long, Michael H. (1991). Focus on Form: A Design Feature in Language Teaching Methodology. In K. de Bot, D. Coste, R. Ginsberg, & C. Kramsch (Eds.), *Foreign Language Research in Cross-Cultural Perspectives* (pp. 39–52). Amsterdam: John Benjamins.
Long, Michael H. (1996). The Role of the Linguistic Environment in Second Language Acquisition. In W. C. Ritchie & T. K. Bhatia (Eds.), *Handbook of Second Language Acquisition* (pp. 413–468). San Diego: Academic Press.
Long, Michael H., Inagaki, Shunji, & Ortega, Lourdes. (1998). The Role of Implicit Negative Feedback in SLA: Models and Recasts in Japanese and Spanish. *The Modern Language Journal, 82*(iii), 357–371.
Loritz, Donald. (1987). An Introductory Lisp Parser. *CALICO Journal, 4*(4), 51–70.
Loritz, Donald, Parhizgar, A., & Zambrano, R. (1990). Diagnostic Parsing in CALL. *Computer Assisted English Language Learning, 1*(4), 9–13.
Loritz, Donald. (1992). Generalized Transition Network Parsing for Language Study: The GPARS System for English, Russian, Japanese and Chinese. *CALICO Journal, 10*(1), 5–22.
Loritz, Donald. (1995). GPARS: A Suite of Grammar Assessment Systems. In V. M. Holland, J. D. Kaplan & M. R. Sams (Eds.), *Intelligent Language Tutors: Theory Shaping Technology* (pp. 77-99). Mahwah, NJ: Erlbaum Associates.
Lotherington, Heather. (2005). Authentic Language in Digital Environments. In J. Egbert & G. M. Petrie (Eds.), *CALL Research Perspectives* (pp. 97–107). Mahwah, N.J.: Erlbaum Associates.
Lusuardi, Carlo. (2005). *The Use of Natural Language Processing in CALL for the Purpose of Error Diagnosis*. Paper presented at the Eurocall 2005, Krakow, Poland.
Lyster, Roy, & Ranta, Leila. (1997). Corrective Feedback and Learner Uptake: Negotiation of Form in Communicative Classrooms. *Studies in Second Language Acquisition, 19*, 37–66.
Lyster, Roy. (2001). Negotiation of Form, Recasts, and Explicit Correction in Relation to Error Types and Learner Repair in Immersion Classrooms. *Language Learning, 51*(Supplement 1), 265–301.
Mabbott, Andrew, & Bull, Susan. (2004). Alternative Views on Knowledge: Presentation of Open Learner Models. In J. C. Lester, R. M. Vicari, & F. Paraguacu (Eds.), *Intelligent Tutoring Systems: 7th International Conference* (pp. 689–698). Berlin: Springer-Verlag.
Mackey, Alison, & Philp, Jenefer. (1998). Conversational Interaction and Second Language Development: Recasts, Responses, and Red Herrings? *The Modern Language Journal, 82*(iii), 338–356.
Mackey, Alison, Gass, Susan M., & McDonough, K. (2000). How do Learners Perceive Interactional Feedback? *Studies in Second Language Acquisition, 22*(471–497).
Mansilla, Juan Rafael Zamarano. (2004). *Text Generators, Error Analysis and Feedback*. Paper presented at InSTIL/ICALI 2004, Venice.
Marcus, Mitchell P., Santorini, Beatrice, & Marcinkiewicz, Mary Ann. (2004 [1993]). Building a Large Annotated Corpus of English: The Penn Treebank. In G. R. Sampson & D. McCarthy (Eds.), *Corpus Linguistics. Readings in a Widening Discipline* (pp. 242–257). London: continuum.
Marshall, D.V. (1988). *CAL/CBT - The Great Debate*. Bromley: Chartwell-Bratt.

Martin, Brent, & Mitrovic, Antonija. (2000). Tailoring Feedback by Correcting Student Answers. In G. Gauthier, C. Frasson & K. VanLehn (Eds.), *Intelligent Tutoring Systems. 5th International Conference, ITS 2000, Montréal, Canada, June 2000, Proceedings* (pp. 383–392). Berlin: Springer Verlag.

Martin, Brent, & Mitrovic, Antonija. (2002). Automatic Problem Generation in Constraint-Based Tutors. In S. A. Cerri, G. Gouardáeres & F. Paraguaçu (Eds.), *Intelligent Tutoring Systems. 6th International Conference, ITS 2002, Biarritz, France and San Sebastian, Spain, June 2–7, 2002, Proceedings* (pp. 388–397). Berlin: Springer-Verlag.

Martinho, Carlos, Machado, Isabel, & Paiva, Ana M. (2000). A Cognitive Approach to Affective User Modeling. In A. M. Paiva (Ed.), *Affective Interactions* (pp. 64–75). Berlin: Springer-Verlag.

Matthews, Clive. (1992a). *Intelligent CALL (ICALL) Bibliography*. Hull: CTI Centre for Modern Languages.

Matthews, Clive. (1992b). Fundamental Questions in ICALL. In J. Thompson & C. Zähner (Eds.), *Proceedings of the ICALL Workshop, UMIST, September 1991* (pp. 77–89). Hull: University of Hull, CTI Centre for Modern Languages.

Matthews, Clive. (1992c). Going AI. Foundations of ICALL. *Computer Assisted Language Learning, 5*(1–2), 13–31.

Matthews, Clive. (1993). Grammar Frameworks in Intelligent CALL. *CALICO Journal, 11*(1), 5–27.

Matthews, Clive. (1994). Intelligent Computer Assisted Language Learning as Cognitive Science: The Choice of Syntactic Frameworks for Language Tutoring. *Journal of Artificial Intelligence in Education, 5*(4), 533–556.

McCalla, Gordon I. (1992). The Centrality of Student Modelling to Intelligent Tutoring Systems. In E. Costa (Ed.), *New Directions for Intelligent Tutoring Systems* (pp. 107–131). Berlin: Springer Verlag.

McCalla, Gordon I., & Greer, Jim E. (1992). Special Issue on Student Modelling: Editors' Introduction. *Journal of Artificial Intelligence in Education, 3*(4), 377–380.

McCalla, Gordon I., & Greer, Jim E. (1994). Granularity-Based Reasoning and Belief Revision in Student Models. In J. E. Greer & G. I. McCalla (Eds.), *Student Modelling: The Key to Individualized Knowledge-Based Instruction* (pp. 39–62). Berlin: Springer Verlag.

McCalla, Gordon I., Vassileva, Julita, Greer, Jim E., & Bull, Susan. (2000). Active Learner Modelling. In G. Gauthier, C. Frasson, & K. VanLehn (Eds.), *Intelligent Tutoring Systems. 5th International Conference, ITS 2000, Montréal, Canada, June 2000, Proceedings* (pp. 53–62). Berlin: Springer Verlag.

McCoy, Kathleen F., Pennington, Christopher A., & Suri, Linda Z. (1996a). *Considering the Effects of Second Language Learning on Generation. Paper Presented at the Eighth International Natural Language Generation Workshop (INLG'96)*. Retrieved Nov. 3, 2004, from http://acl.ldc.upenn.edu/W/W96/W96-0408.pdf.

McCoy, Kathleen F., Pennington, Christopher A., & Suri, Linda Z. (1996b). *English Error Correction: A Syntactic User Model Based on Principled "Mal-Rule" Scoring. Paper Presented at the Fifth International Conference on User Modeling*. Retrieved Nov 3, 2004, from http://www.cis.udel.edu/~mccoy/publications/1996/McCoPenn96a.ps.

McFetridge, Paul, & Heift, Trude. (1995). Grammar and Analysis for Implementing Granularity in Computer-Assisted Language Instruction. In *Educational Multimedia and Hypermedia* (pp. 460–465). Graz, Austria: Association for the Advancement in Computing in Education.

Mellish, Chris S. (1989). Some Chart-Based Techniques for Parsing Ill-Formed Input. In *Proceedings of the 27th Annual meeting of the Association for Computational Linguistics* (pp. 102–109): Association for Computational Linguistics.

Menzel, Wolfgang. (1988). Error Diagnosing and Selection in a Training System for Second Language Learning. In *Proceedings of the Twelfth International Conference on Computational Linguistics* (pp. 414–419).

Menzel, Wolfgang. (1990). Anticipation-Free Diagnosis of Structural Faults. In *Proceedings of COLING* (pp. 422–424). Helsinki.

Menzel, Wolfgang. (1992a). *Modellbasierte Fehlerdiagnose in Sprachlernsystemen*. Tübingen: Niemeyer.

Menzel, Wolfgang. (1992b). Constraint-Based Diagnosis of Grammatical Faults. In J. Thompson & C. Zähner (Eds.), *Proceedings of the ICALL Workshop, UMIST, September 1991* (pp. 89–101). Hull: University of Hull, CTI Centre for Modern Languages.

Menzel, Wolfgang, & Schröder, Ingo. (1998a). Constraint-Based Diagnosis for Intelligent Language Tutoring Systems. In *Proceedings of the IT&KNOWS Conference at IFIP'98 Congress* (pp. 484–497). Wien/Budapest.

Menzel, Wolfgang, & Schröder, Ingo. (1998b). Error Diagnosis for Language Learning Systems. In *Proceedings of NLP+IA'98* (pp. 526–530).

Menzel, Wolfgang, & Schröder, Ingo. (1998c). Decision Procedures for Dependency Parsing Using Graded Constraints. In S. Kahane & A. Polguère (Eds.), *Proceedings of the Joint Conference COLING/ACL Workshop: Processing of Dependency-Based Grammars* (pp. 78–87). Montreal.

Menzel, Wolfgang, & Schröder, Ingo. (1999). Error Diagnosis for Language Learning Systems. In M. Schulze, M.-J. Hamel, & J. Thompson (Eds.), *Language Processing in CALL. ReCALL Special Publication (Proceedings of a One-Day Conference "Natural Language Processing in Computer-Assisted Language Learning" Held at UMIST, May 9, 1998, Organised by the Centre of Computational Linguistics, UMIST, in Association with Eurocall)* (pp. 20–30). Hull: CTICML.

Menzel, Wolfgang. (2004). *Errors, Intentions, and Explanations: Feedback Generation for Language Tutoring Systems.* Paper presented at InSTIL/ICALI 2004, Venice.

Meyer, Charles F., Grabowski, Roger, Han, Hung-Yul, Mantzouranis, Konstantin, & Moses, Stephanie. (2003). The World Wide Web as Linguistic Corpus. In P. Leistyna & C. F. Meyer (Eds.), *Corpus Analysis: Language Structure and Language Use* (pp. 241–254). Amsterdam: Editions Rodopi B. V.

Michaud, Lisa N., & McCoy, Kathleen F. (1999). Modeling User Language Proficiency in a Writing Tutor for Deaf Learners of English. In M. B. Olsen (Ed.), *Computer Mediated Language Assessment and Evaluation in Natural Language Processing. Proceedings of a Symposium Sponsored by the Association of Computational Linguistics and International Association of Language Learning Technologies* (pp. 47–54). University of Maryland: Association for Computational Linguistics.

Michaud, Lisa N., & McCoy, Kathleen F. (2000). Supporting Intelligent Tutoring in CALL by Modeling the User's Grammar. In *Proceedings of the Thirteenth Annual International Florida Artificial Intelligence Research Symposium, May 22–24, 2000, Orlando, Florida* (pp. 50–54). Menlo Park, CA: AAAI Press.

Michaud, Lisa N., & McCoy, Kathleen F. (2004). Empirical Derivation of a Sequence of User Stereotypes for Language Learning. *User Modeling and User-Adapted Interaction, 14*, 317–350.

Michel, Johan, & Lehuen, Jérôme. (2002). Conception of a Language Learning Environment Based on the Communicative and Actional Approaches. In S. A. Cerri, G. Gouardáeres & F. Paraguaçu (Eds.), *Intelligent Tutoring Systems. 6th International Conference, ITS 2002, Biarritz, France and San Sebastian, Spain, June 2–7, 2002, Proceedings* (pp. 651–660). Berlin: Springer-Verlag.

Millán, Eva, & Pérez-de-la-Cruz, José Luis. (2002). A Bayesian Diagnostic Algorithm for Student Modeling and Its Evaluation. *User Modeling and User-Adapted Interaction, 12*, 281–330.

Milne, Sue, Shiu, Edward, & Cook, Jean. (1996). Development of a Model of User Attributes and Its Implementation within an Adaptive Tutoring System. *User Modeling and User-Adapted Interaction, 6*, 303–335.

Milton, John. (1998). Exploiting L1 and Interlanguage Corpora in the Design of an Electronic Language Learning and Production Environment. In S. Granger (Ed.), *Learner English on Computer* (pp. 186–198). London: Longman.

Mindt, Dieter. (2004 [1996]). English Corpus Linguistics and the Foreign-Language Teaching Syllabus. In G. R. Sampson & D. McCarthy (Eds.), *Corpus Linguistics. Readings in a Widening Discipline* (pp. 293–303). London: continuum.

Mislevy, Robert J., & Gitomer, Drew H. (1996). The Role of Probability-Based Inference in an Intelligent Tutoring System. *User Modeling and User-Adapted Interaction, 5*, 253–282.

Mitchell, Rosamond, & Myles, Florence (Eds.). (1998). *Second Language Learning Theories*. London: Arnold.

Mitkov, Ruslan (Ed.). (2003). *The Oxford Handbook of Computational Linguistics*: Oxford University Press.

Mitrovic, Antonija, Djordjevic-Kajan, Slobodanka, & Stoimenov, Leonid. (1996). INSTRUCT: Modeling Students by Asking Questions. *User Modeling and User-Adapted Interaction, 6*, 273–302.

Mitrovic, Antonija. (1998). Experiences in Implementing Constraint-Based Modeling in *SQL-Tutor*. In B. P. Goettl, H. M. Halff, C. L. Redfield, & V. J. Shute (Eds.), *Intelligent Tutoring Systems. 4th International Conference, ITS 1998, San Antonio, Texas, USA, August 1998, Proceedings* (pp. 414–423).

Mitrovic, Antonija, & Martin, Brent. (2002). Evaluating the Effects of Open Student Models on Learning. In *Adaptive Hypermedia and Adaptive Web-Based Systems. Second International Conference. AH 2002. Malaga, Spain, May 29–31, 2002. Proceedings* (pp. 296–305). Berlin: Springer-Verlag.

Mitrovic, Antonija, Martin, Brent, & Mayo, Michael. (2002). Using Evaluation to Shape ITS Design: Results and Experiences with SQL Tutor. *User Modeling and User-Adapted Interaction, 12*, 243–279.

Mitton, Roger. (1996). Spellchecking by Computer. *Journal of the Simplified Spelling Society, 1*(20), 4–11.

Mohan, Bernhard, & Luo, Lynn. (2005). A Systemic Functional Linguistics Perspective on CALL. In J. Egbert & G. M. Petrie (Eds.), *CALL Research Perspectives* (pp. 87–96). Mahwah, N.J.: Erlbaum Associates.

Molla, Steven R., Sanders, Alton F., & Sanders, Ruth H. (1988). Artificial Intelligence in a German Adventure Game: Spion in Prolog. *CALICO Journal, 6*(1), 9–23.

Morales, R., Pain, Helen, & Conlon, T. (1999). From Behavior to Understandable Presentation of Learner Models: A Case Study. In R. Morales, H. Pain, S. Bull, & J. Kay (Eds.), *Proceedings of the Workshop on Open, Interactive, and Other Overt Approaches to Learner Modelling* (pp. 15–24). Le Mans, France: AIED'99 Conference.

Morgenstern, Douglas. (1986). The Athena Language Learning Project. *Hispania, 69*(3), 740–745.

Mostow, Jack, Aist, Greg, Beck, Joseph, Chalasani, Raghuvee, Cuneo, Andrew, Peng, Jia, et al. (2002). A La Recherche du Temps Perdu, or As Time Goes By: Where Does the Time Go in a Reading Tutor That Listens? In S. A. Cerri, G. Gouardères, & F. Paraguaçu (Eds.), *Intelligent Tutoring Systems. 6th International Conference, ITS 2002, Biarritz, France and San Sebastian, Spain, June 2–7, 2002. Proceedings* (pp. 320–329). Berlin; New York: Springer.

Mulford, George W. (1989). Semantic Processing for Communicative Exercises in Foreign-Language Learning. *Computers and the Humanities, 23*, 31–44.

Murphy, Maureen, & McTear, Michael. (1997). Learner Modeling for Intelligent CALL. In A. Jameson, C. Paris & C. Tasso (Eds.), *User Modeling: Proceedings of the Sixth International Conference, UM97* (pp. 301–312). Vienna; New York: Springer Verlag.

Murphy-Judy, Kathryn. (2003). Review of Sans-Faute Writing Environment. *CALICO Journal, 21*(1), 209–220.

Murray, Janet H. (1991). Anatomy of a New Medium: Literary and Pedagogic Uses of Advanced Linguistic Computer Science. *Computers and the Humanities, 25*(1), 1–14.

Murray, Janet H. (1995). Lessons Learned from the Athena Language Learning Project: Using Natural Language Processing, Graphics, Speech Processing, and Interactive Video for Communication-Based Language Learning. In V. M. Holland, J. D. Kaplan & M. R. Sams (Eds.), *Intelligent Language Tutors: Theory Shaping Technology* (pp. 243–256). Mahwah, NJ: Erlbaum Associates.

Murray, Tom. (1999). Authoring Intelligent Tutoring Systems: An Analysis of the State of the Art. *International Journal of Artificial Intelligence in Education, 10*, 98–129.

Murray, William R. (1998). A Practical Approach to Bayesian Student Modeling. In B. P. Goettl, H. M. Halff, C. L. Redfield, & V. J. Shute (Eds.), *Intelligent Tutoring Systems. 4th International Conference, ITS 1998, San Antonio, Texas, USA, August 1998, Proceedings* (pp. 424–433).

Nagata, Noriko. (1992). *A Study of the Effectiveness of Intelligent CALI as an Application of Natural Language Processing.* Unpublished PhD Thesis, University of Pittsburgh, Pittsburgh.

Nagata, Noriko. (1993). Intelligent Computer Feedback for Second Language Instruction. *Modern Language Journal, 77*, 330–338.

Nagata, Noriko. (1995). An Effective Application for Natural Language Processing in Second Language Instruction. *CALICO Journal, 13*(1), 47–67.

Nagata, Noriko, & Swisher, M. Virginia. (1995). A Study of Consciousness-Raising by Computer: The Effect of Metalinguistic Feedback on Second Language Learning. *Foreign Language Annals, 28*(3), 337–347.

Nagata, Noriko. (1996). Computer vs. Workbook Instruction in Second Language Acquisition. *CALICO Journal, 14*(1), 53–75.

Nagata, Noriko. (1997). An Experimental Comparison of Deductive and Inductive Feedback Generated by a Simple Parser. *System, 25*(4), 515–534.

Nagata, Noriko. (1998a). Input vs. Output Practice in Educational Software for Second Language Acquisition. *Language Learning & Technology, 1*(2), 23–40.

Nagata, Noriko. (1998b). The Relative Effectiveness of Production Comprehension Practice in Second Language Acquisition. *Computer Assisted Language Learning, 11*(2), 153–177.

Nagata, Noriko. (2002). BANZAI: An Application of Natural Language Processing to Web-Based Language Learning. *CALICO, 19*(3), 583–599.

Nakabayashi, Kiyoshi, Mina, Maruyama, Koike, Yoshimasa, Kato, Yasuhisa, Touhei, Hirofumi, & Fukuhara, Yoshimi. (1997). *Architecture of an Intel-*

ligent Tutoring System on the WWW. Retrieved Nov. 16, 1999, from http://www.contrib.andrew.cmu.edu/~plb/AIED97_workshop/Nakabayashi/Nakabayashi.html.

Nassaji, H., & Swain, Merrill. (2000). A Vygotskian Perspective on Corrective Feedback in L2: The Effect of Random Versus Negotiated Help on the Learning of English Articles. *Language Awareness, 9*(1), 34–35.

Ndiaye, Mar, & Vandeventer Faltin, Anne. (2003). A Spell Checker Tailored to Language Learners. *Computer Assisted Language Learning, 16*(2-3), 213–232.

Néhémie, Patrick. (1992). A Systematic Approach for Student Modelling in a Multi-Agent Aided Learning Environment. In C. Frasson, G. Gauthier, & G. I. McCalla (Eds.), *Proceedings of the Second International Conference on Intelligent Tutoring Systems, June 1992* (pp. 475–482). Berlin; New York: Springer Verlag.

Nelson, G. E., Ward, Jean Renard, Desch, Samuel H, & Kaplow, Roy. (1976). Two New Strategies for Computer-Assisted Language Instruction (CALI). *Foreign Language Annals, 10*, 28–37.

Nerbonne, John A. (Ed.). (1998). *Linguistic Databases*. Stanford: CSLI.

Nerbonne, John A., Dokter, Duco, & Smit, Petra. (1998). Morphological Processing and Computer-Assisted Language Learning. *Computer Assisted Language Learning, 11*(5), 543–559.

Nerbonne, John A., Jager, Sake, & van Essen, Arthur. (1998). Introduction. In S. Jager, J. A. Nerbonne & A. van Essen (Eds.), *Language Teaching and Language Technology* (pp. 1–10). Lisse: Swets & Zeitlinger.

Nerbonne, John A., & Dokter, Duco. (1999). An Intelligent Word-Based Language Learning Assistant. *Traitement Automatique des Languages, 40*(1), 125–142.

Nerbonne, John A., Kleiweg, Peter, Smit, Petra, Kuipers, Edwin, & Dokter, Duco. (2001). A Web-Based Foreign Language Assistant. In M. Bax & J.-W. Zwarts (Eds.), *Essays in Language, Language Education, and the History of Linguistics in Honour of Arthur van Essen* (Vol. 2000, pp. 341–348). Amsterdam and Philadelphia: John Benjamins.

Nerbonne, John A. (2003). Computer-Assisted Language Learning and Natural Language Processing. In R. Mitkov (Ed.), *The Oxford Handbook of Computational Linguistics* (pp. 670–698). Oxford: Oxford University Press.

Nesi, Hilary. (1998). Defining a Shoehorn: The Success of Learners' Dictionary Entries for Concrete Nouns. In B. T. S. Atkins (Ed.), *Using Dictionaries: Studies of Dictionary Use by Language Learners and Translators* (pp. 159–178). Tübingen: Max Niemeyer.

New, Elizabeth. (1999). Computer-Aided Writing in French as Foreign Language: A Qualitative and Quantitative Look at the Process of Revision. *Modern Language Journal, 83*(i), 80–97.

Nicholas, Howard, Lightbown, Patsy M., & Spada, Nina. (2001). Recasts as Feedback to Language Learners. *Language Learning, 51*(4), 719–758.

Nobuyoshi, J., & Ellis, Rod. (1993). Focused Communication Tasks. *English Language Teaching Journal, 47*, 203–210.

Norman, D. (1988). *The Psychology of Everyday Things*: Basic Books.

O'Brien, Paul. (1993). eL: AI in CALL. In M. Yazdani (Ed.), *Multilingual Multimedia. Bridging the Language Barrier with Intelligent Systems* (pp. 85–139). Oxford: Intellect.

O'Malley, J. M., & Chamot, A. U. (1990). *Learning Strategies in Second Language Acquisition*. Cambridge: Cambridge University Press.

O'Shea, Tim, & Self, John A. (1983). *Learning and Teaching with Computers*. Brighton: Harvester.

Obermeier, Klaus K. (1985). Computers and Their Frame of Mind — The Linguistic Component. In S. Williams (Ed.), *Humans and Machines* (pp. 154–165). Norwood, NJ: Ablex.

Ogata, Hiroaki, Liu, Yuqin, Ochi, Youji, & Yano, Yoneo. (2000). Agent-Mediated Language Learning Environment Based on Communicative Gaps. In G. Gauthier, C. Frasson, & K. VanLehn (Eds.), *Intelligent Tutoring Systems. 5th International Conference, ITS 2000, Montréal, Canada, June 19–23, 2000. Proceedings* (pp. 454–463). Berlin: Springer-Verlag.

Ohlsson, Stellan. (1992). Constraint-Based Student Modeling. *Journal of Artificial Intelligence in Education, 3*(4), 429–447.

Olohan, Maeve. (2003). *Introducing Corpora in Translation Studies*. London: Routledge.

Olsen, Mari Broman (Ed.). (1999). *Computer Mediated Language Assessment and Evaluation in Natural Language Processing. Proceedings of a Symposium Sponsored by the Association of Computational Linguistics and International Association of Language Learning Technologies*. University of Maryland: Association for Computational Linguistics.

Oxford, Rebecca L. (1993). Intelligent Computers for Learning Languages: The View for Language Acquisition and Instructional Methodology. *Computer Assisted Language Learning, 6*(2), 173–188.

Oxford, Rebecca L. (1995). Linking Theories of Learning with Intelligent Computer-Assisted Language Learning (CALL). In V. M. Holland, J. D. Kaplan, & M. R. Sams (Eds.), *Intelligent Language Tutors: Theory Shaping Technology* (pp. 359–369). Mahwah, NJ: Erlbaum Associates.

Pain, Helen, Bull, Susan, & Brna, Paul. (1996). *A Student Model 'For its Own Sake'*. Retrieved February 17, 2005, from http://cblpc0142.leeds.ac.uk/~paul/papers/euroaiedpapers96/smpaper/smpaper.html.

Paramskas, Dana M. (1999). The Shape of Computer-Mediated Communication. In K. Cameron (Ed.), *CALL - Media, Design and Applications* (pp. 13–34). Lisse: Swets & Zeitlinger.

Patten, Terry. (1992). Computers and Natural Language Parsing. In C. S. Butler (Ed.), *Computers and Written Texts* (pp. 29–52). Oxford: Blackwell.

Payette, Julie, & Hirst, Graeme. (1992). An Intelligent Computer-Assistant for Stylistic Instruction. *Computers and the Humanities, 26*, 87–120.

Pedler, Jennifer. (2001). Computer Spellcheckers and Dyslexics - A Performance Survey. *British Journal of Educational Technology, 32*(1), 23–37.

Pereira, Fernando C. N., & Warren, David H. D. (1980). Definite Clause Grammars for Language Analysis - A Survey of the Formalism and a Comparison with Augmented Transition Networks. *Artificial Intelligence, 13*, 231–278.

Peterson, James L. (1980). Computer Programs for Detecting and Correcting Spelling Errors. *Communications of the ACM, 23*(12), 676–687.

Petrie, Gina Mikel. (2005). Visuality and CALL Research. In J. Egbert & G. M. Petrie (Eds.), *CALL Research Perspectives* (pp. 97–107). Mahwah, N.J.: Erlbaum Associates.

Pica, Teresa, Holliday, Lloyd, Lewis, Norah, & Morgenthaler, Lynelle. (1989). Comprehensible output as an outcome of linguistic demands on the learner. *Studies in Second Language Acquisition, 11*, 63–90.

Pica, T. (1994). Research on Negotiation: What Does It Reveal about Second-Language Learning Conditions, Processes, and Outcomes? *Language Learning, 44*(3), 493–527.

Pijls, Fieny, Daelemans, Walter, & Kempen, Gerard. (1987). Artificial Intelligence Tools for Grammar and Spelling Instruction. *Instructional Science, 16*, 319–336.

Plass, Jan L. (1998). Design and Evaluation of the User Interface of Foreign Language Multimedia Software: A Cognitive Approach. *Language Learning & Technology, 2*(1), 35–45.

Plass, Jan L., Chun, Dorothy M., Mayer, Richard E., & Leutner, Detlev. (2003). Cognitive Load in Reading a Foreign Language Text with Multimedia Aids and the Influence of Verbal and Spatial Abilities. *Computers in Human Behavior, 19*, 221–243.

Pollard, Carl J., & Sag, Ivan A. (1987). *Information-Based Syntax and Semantics.* Chicago: University Press.

Pollard, Carl J., & Sag, Ivan A. (1994). *Head-Driven Phrase Structure Grammar.* Chicago: University Chicago Press.

Pollock, Joseph J., & Zamora, Antonio. (1984). Automatic Spelling Correction in Scientific and Scholarly Text. *Communications of the ACM, 27*(4), 358–368.

Price, Charlotte, McCalla, Gordon I., & Bunt, Andrea. (1999). L2tutor: A Mixed Initiative Dialogue System for Improving Fluency. *Computer Assisted Language Learning, 12*(2).

Price, Robert V. (1991). *Computer-Aided Instruction: A Guide for Authors.* Pacific Grove, CA: Brooks/Cole.

Pujolà, Joan-Tomàs. (2001). Did CALL Feedback Feed Back? Researching Learners' Use of Feedback. *ReCALL, 13*(1), 79–98.

Pujolà, Joan-Tomàs. (2002). CALLing for Help: Researching Language Learning Strategies Using Help Facilities in a Web-Based Multimedia Program. *ReCALL, 14*(2), 235–262.

Pulman, S. G. (1984). Limited Domain Systems for Language Teaching. In *Proceedings of Coling84: Tenth International Conference on Computational Linguistics and 22nd Annual Meeting of the Association for Computational Linguistics* (pp. 84–87). Stanford: Stanford University.

Ragnemalm, Eva L. (1996). Student Diagnosis in Practice; Bridging a Gap. *User Modeling and User-Adapted Interaction, 5*, 93–116.

Razi, Amir. (1985). Two Strategies of Robustness in Natural Language Understanding Systems. In S. Williams (Ed.), *Humans and Machines* (pp. 67–72). Norwood, NJ: Ablex.

Reuer, Veit. (2003). Error Recognition and Feedback with Lexical Functional Grammar. *CALICO Journal, 20*(3), 497–512.

Reye, Jim. (1998). Two-Phase Updating of Student Models Based on Dynamic Belief Networks. In B. P. Goettl, H. M. Halff, C. L. Redfield, & V. J. Shute (Eds.), *Intelligent Tutoring Systems. 4th International Conference, ITS 1998, San Antonio, Texas, USA, August 1998, Proceedings* (pp. 274–283).

Reyes, Rhodora L. (1998). A Domain Theory Extension of a Student Modeling System for Pascal Programming. In B. P. Goettl, H. M. Halff, C. L. Redfield, & V. J. Shute (Eds.), *Intelligent Tutoring Systems. 4th International Conference, ITS 1998, San Antonio, Texas, USA, August 1998, Proceedings* (pp. 324–333).

Reynar, Jeffrey, & Ratnaparkhi, Adwait. (1997). *A Maximum Entropy Approach to Identifying Sentence Boundaries.* Paper presented at the Fifth Conference on Applied Natural Language Processing, Washington, DC.

Richards, Jack C. (1971). Error Analysis and Second Language Strategies. *Language Sciences, 17*, 12–2.

Richards, Jack C. (1974a). *Error Analysis: Perspectives on Second Language Acquisition.* London: Longman.

Richards, Jack C. (1974b). A Non-Contrastive Approach to Error Analysis. In J. C. Richards (Ed.), *Error Analysis: Perspectives on Second Language Acquisition* (pp. 172–188). London: Longman.

Richardson, Stephen D., & Braden-Harder, Lisa C. (1988). The Experience of Developing a Large-Scale Natural Language Text Processing System: Critique. In *Proceedings of the Second Conference on Applied Natural Language Processing. Association for Computational Linguistics* (pp. 195–202). Austin, TX.

Rimrott, Anne, & Heift, Trude. (2005). Language Learners and Generic Spell Checkers in CALL. *CALICO Journal, 23*(1), 17–48.

Robinson, G., Underwood, John H., Rivers, W., Hernandez, J., Rudisill, C., & Eseñat, C. . (1985). *Computer-Assisted Instruction in Foreign Language Education: A Comparison of the Effectiveness of Different Methodologies and Different Forms of Error Correction.* San Francisco: Center for Language and Crosscultural Skills. ERIC ED 262 626.

Roed, Jannie. (2003). Language Learner Behaviour in a Virtual Environment. *Computer Assisted Language Learning, 16*(2–3), 155–172.

Rogers, Margaret. (1982). Interlanguage Variability: Verb Placement Errors in German. In G. Nickel & D. Nehls (Eds.), *Error Analysis, Contrastive Linguistics and Second Language Learning* (pp. 43–83,). Heidelberg: Groos.

Romano Hvid, Carmit, & Krabbe, Jens. (2003). *Improving CALL Research: The Development of Methods and Tools for Tracking.* Paper presented at the WorldCALL, Banff.

Roosmaa, Tiit, & Prószéky, Gabor. (1998). GLOSSER - Using Language Technology Tools for Reading Texts in a Foreign Language. In S. Jager, J. A. Nerbonne, & A. van Essen (Eds.), *Language Teaching and Language Technology* (pp. 101–107). Lisse: Swets & Zeitlinger.

Rumelhart, David E., & Norman, Donald A. (1975). *Explorations in Cognition.* San Francisco: Freeman.

Rüschoff, Bernd. (1987). The "Intelligence" of Intelligently Programmed Adaptive CALL Materials for Self-Study. In L. Legenhausen & D. Wolff (Eds.), *Computer Assisted Language Learning and Innovative EFL Methodology* (pp. 74–82). Augsburg: Universität Augsburg.

Russell Valezy, Jane, & Spada, Nina. (2006). The Effectiveness of Corrective Feedback for Second Language Acquisition: A Meta-Analysis of the Research. In J. M. Norris, & L. Ortega (Eds.), *Synthesizing Research on Language Learning and Teaching* (pp. 133–164). Amsterdam: John Benjamins.

Rypa, Marikka, & Feuerman, Ken. (1995). CALLE: An Exploratory Environment for Foreign Language Learning. In V. M. Holland, J. D. Kaplan & M. R. Sams (Eds.), *Intelligent Language Tutors: Theory Shaping Technology* (pp. 55–76). Mahwah, NJ: Erlbaum Associates.

Sag, Ivan A., Wasow, Thomas, & Bender, Emily M. (2003). *Syntactic Theory: A Formal Introduction* (2nd ed.). Stanford, Calif.: Center for the Study of Language and Information.

Salaberry, M. Rafael. (2001). The Use of Technology for Second Language Learning and Teaching: A Retrospective. *The Modern Language Journal, 85*(1), 39–56.

Salaberry, Rafael. (1996). A Theoretical Foundation for the Development of Pedagogical Tasks in Computer-Mediated Communication. *CALICO Journal, 14*(1), 5–34.

Salaberry, Rafael. (2000). Review of 'Language Teaching and Language Technology'. *Language Learning & Technology, 4*(1), 22–25.

Sampson, Geoffrey Richard, & McCarthy, Diana (Eds.). (2004). *Corpus Linguistics. Readings in a Widening Discipline.* London: Continuum.

Sams, Michelle R. (1995). Advanced Technologies for Language Learning: The BRIDGE Project within the ARI Language Tutor Program. In V. M. Holland,

J. D. Kaplan, & M. R. Sams (Eds.), *Intelligent Language Tutors: Theory Shaping Technology* (pp. 7–21). Mahwah, NJ: Erlbaum Associates.

Sanders, Alton F., & Sanders, Ruth H. (1982). Spion: 'Intelligent' Computer Games for German Language Teaching. In *Proceedings of the Foreign Language Instructional Technology Conference* (pp. 141–146). Monterey, CA: Goethe Institute and Defense Language Institute.

Sanders, Alton F., & Sanders, Ruth H. (1987). Designing and Implementing a Syntactic Parser. *CALICO Journal, 5*(1), 77–86.

Sanders, Alton F., & Sanders, Ruth H. (1989). Syntactic Parsing: A Survey. *Computers and the Humanities, 23*, 13–30.

Sanders, Ruth H. (1984). Pilot-Spion: A Computer Game for German Students. *Unterrichtspraxis, 17*(1), 123–129.

Sanders, Ruth H. (1985). Pilot, Snobol, and Logo as Computing Tools for Foreign-Language Instruction. *CALICO Journal, 3*(2), 41–47.

Sanders, Ruth H. (1991). Error Analysis in Purely Syntactic Parsing of Free Input. The Example of German. *CALICO Journal, 9*, 72–89.

Sanders, Ruth H. (1995). Thirty Years of Computer Assisted Language Instruction: Introduction. *CALICO Journal, 12*(4), 5–14.

Sanders, Ruth H., & Sanders, Alton F. (1995). History of an AI Spy Game: Spion. In V. M. Holland, J. D. Kaplan, & M. R. Sams (Eds.), *Intelligent Language Tutors: Theory Shaping Technology* (pp. 141–151). Mahwah, NJ: Erlbaum Associates.

Sanders, Ruth H., & Sanders, Alton F. (1999). A German Parser and Error Checker. In R. Rapp (Ed.), *Sprachwissenschaft auf dem Weg in das dritte Jahrtausend: Akten des 34. Linguistischen Kolloquiums in Germersheim 1999* (pp. 795–802). Frankfurt: Peter Lang.

Schachter, Jacquelyn. (1974). An Error in Error Analysis. *Language Learning, 27*, 205–214.

Schachter, Jacquelyn. (1984). A Universal Input Condition. In W. E. Rutherford (Ed.), *Language Universals and Second Language Acquisition* (pp. 167–183). Amsterdam: Benjamins.

Schachter, Jacquelyn. (1986). The Epistemological Status of Second Language Acquisition. *Second Language Research, 2*, 120–159.

Schegloff, Emanuel A., Jefferson, Gail, & Sacks, Harvey. (1977). The Preference for Self-Correction in the Organization of Repair in Conversation. *Language, 53*(2), 361–382.

Schmidt, Richard. (1990). The Role of Consciousness in Second Language Learning. *Applied Linguistics, 11*(2), 129–158.

Schmidt, Richard. (1995). Consciousness and Foreign Language Learning: A Tutorial on the Role of Attention and Awareness. In R. Schmidt (Ed.), *Attention and Awareness in Foreign Language Teaching and Learning (Technical Report No. 9)* (pp. 1–64). Honolulu: University of Hawai'i at Manoa.

Schmitz, Ulrich. (1992). *Computerlinguistik*. Opladen: Westdeutscher Verlag.

Schneider, David, & McCoy, Kathleen F. (1998). Recognizing Syntactic Errors in the Writing of Second Language Learners. In *Proceedings of COLING-ACL '98 (36th Annual Meeting of the Association for Computational Linguistics and 17th International Conference on Computational Linguistics), Montreal, Quebec, Canada, August 10–14, 1998*. (Vol. 2, pp. 1198–1204).

Schoelles, Michael, & Hamburger, Henry. (1996). Teacher-Usable Exercise Design Tools. In C. Frasson, G. Gauthier & A. Lesgold (Eds.), *Intelligent Tutoring Systems. Second International Conference, ITS'96, Montréal, Canada, June 1996, Proceedings* (pp. 102–110). Berlin: Springer Verlag.

Schreck, Jörg. (2003). *Security and Privacy in User Modeling*. Dordrecht; Boston ; London: Kluwer Academic Publishers.

Schröder, Ingo. (2002). *Natural Language Parsing with Graded Constraints.* Unpublished PhD Thesis, University of Hamburg, Hamburg.

Schröder, Richard. (1998). Aliens lachen nicht. Das Bewußtsein wird sich nie im Labor nachweisen lassen. *Die Zeit, 2/7/1998,* 63.

Schulze, Mathias. (1998). Teaching Grammar — Learning Grammar: Aspects of Second Language Acquisition. *Computer Assisted Language Learning, 11*(2), 215–228.

Schulze, Mathias, & Hamel, Marie-Josée. (1998). Use and Re-Use of Syntactic Parsers in CALL. Towards Diagnosing Learner Errors. In *Proceedings of WorldCALL* (pp. 203–204). Melbourne: Melbourne University.

Schulze, Mathias. (1999). From the Developer to the Learner: Computing Grammar - Learning Grammar. *ReCALL, 11*(1), 117–124.

Schulze, Mathias, Hamel, Marie-Josée, & Thompson, June (Eds.). (1999). *Language Processing in CALL. ReCALL Special Publication (Proceedings of a One-Day Conference "Natural Language Processing in Computer-Assisted Language Learning" Held at UMIST, May 9, 1998, Organised by the Centre of Computational Linguistics, UMIST, in Association with Eurocall).* Hull: CTICML.

Schulze, Mathias. (2001). *Textana - Grammar and Grammar Checking in Parser-Based CALL.* Unpublished PhD Thesis, UMIST, Manchester.

Schulze, Mathias. (2003). Grammatical Errors and Feedback: Some Theoretical Insights. *CALICO Journal, 20*(3), 437–450.

Schuster, Ethel. (1986). The Role of Native Grammars in Correcting Errors in Second Language Learning. *Computational Intelligence, 2,* 93–98.

Schwind, Camilla B. (1988). Sensitive Parsing: Error Analysis and Explanation in an Intelligent Language Tutoring System. In *Proceedings of the Twelfth International Conference on Computational Linguistics* (pp. 608–613).

Schwind, Camilla B. (1990a). An Intelligent Language Tutoring System. *International Journal of Man-Machine Studies, 33*(5), 557–579.

Schwind, Camilla B. (1990b). Artificial Intelligence Techniques in Language Learning, by Last, Rex (1989) (Book Review). *Computational Linguistics, 16*(4), 242–244.

Schwind, Camilla B. (1990c). Feature Grammars for Semantic Analysis. *Computer Intelligence, 6,* 172–178.

Schwind, Camilla B. (1995). Error Analysis and Explanation in Knowledge Language Tutoring. *Computer Assisted Language Learning, 8*(4), 295–324.

Scott, Virginia M., & New, Elizabeth. (1994). Computer Aided Analysis of Foreign Language Writing Process. *CALICO Journal, 11*(3), 5–18.

Segond, Frédérique, & Parmentier, Thibault. (2004). *NLP Serving the Cause of Language Learning.* Paper presented at the eLearning for Computational Linguistics and Computational Linguistics for eLearning. Workshop at COLING — The 20th International Conference on Computational Linguistics, Geneva.

Self, John A. (1974). Student Models in Computer-Aided Instruction. *International Journal of Man-Machine Studies, 6,* 261–276.

Self, John A. (1979). Student Models and Artificial Intelligence. *Computers and Education, 3*(4), 309–312.

Self, John A. (1989). Bypassing the Intractable Problem of Student Modeling. In C. Frasson & G. Gauthier (Eds.), *Intelligent Tutoring Systems: At the Crossroad of Artificial Intelligence and Education* (pp. 107–123). Norwood, NJ: Ablex.

Self, John A. (1994). The Role of Student Models in Learning Environments. *IEICE Transactions on Information and Systems, 77*(1), 8.

Selinker, Larry. (1974). Interlanguage. In J. C. Richards (Ed.), *Error Analysis : Perspectives on Second Language Acquisition* (pp. 31–54). London: Longman.

Selinker, Larry. (1992). *Rediscovering Interlanguage*. London: Longman.

Sharples, Mike. (1989). *Computers and Thought: A Practical Introduction to Artificial Intelligence*. Cambridge, Mass.: MIT Press.

Shaughnessy, Mina P. (1979). *Errors and Expectations: A Guide for the Teacher of Basic Writing*. New York: Oxford University Press.

Shermis, Mark D., & Burstein, Jill. (2003). *Automated Essay Scoring: A Cross-disciplinary Perspective*. Mahwah, NJ; London: Erlbaum Associates.

Shneiderman, Ben. (1992). *Designing the User Interface. Strategies for Effective Human-Computer Interaction*. Reading, Mass.: Addison-Wesley.

Shute, Valerie J. (1995). SMART: Student Modeling Approach for Responsive Tutoring. *User Modeling and User-Adapted Interaction, 5*, 1–44.

Sinclair, John McHardy. (2003). *Reading Concordances*. Harlow: Longman.

Sinclair, John McHardy. (2004a). Intuition and Annotation — The Discussion Continues. In K. Aijmer & B. Altenberg (Eds.), *Advances in Corpus Linguistics. Papers from the 23rd International Conference on English Language Research on Computerized Corpora (ICAME 23) Göteborg 22–26 May 2002*. Amsterdam: Rodopi.

Sinclair, John McHardy (Ed.). (2004b). *How to Use Corpora in Language Teaching*. Philadelphia: J. Benjamins.

Sinyor, Roberta. (1990). Artificial Intelligence Techniques in Language Learning by Rex Last (Book Review). *Canadian Modern Language Review, 47*, 543–544.

Sinyor, Roberta. (1997). An Analysis of Student Behavior and Error Sources in an Italian CALL Context. *CALICO Journal, 14*(2--4), 51–64.

Smith, Wm. Flint (Ed.). (1987). *Modern Media in Foreign Language Education: Theory and Implementation*. Lincolnwood, IL: National Textbook.

Smrž, Pavel. (2004). *Integrating Natural Language Processing into E-Learning - A Case of Czech*. Paper presented at eLearning for Computational Linguistics and Computational Linguistics for eLearning. Workshop at COLING — The 20th International Conference on Computational Linguistics, Geneva.

Soria, J. (1997). Expert CALL: Data-Based versus Knowledge-Based Interaction and Feedback. *ReCALL, 9*(2), 43–50.

Spada, Nina, & Fröhlich, Maria. (1995). *COLT. Communicative Orientation of Language Teaching Observation Scheme: Coding Conventions and Applications*. Sydney, Australia: National Centre for English Teaching and Research.

Späth, Preben. (1994). "Hypertext" und Expertensysteme im Sprachunterricht. In J. Fechner (Ed.), *Neue Wege im computergestützten Fremdsprachenunterricht* (pp. 81–97). Berlin: Langenscheidt.

Steinberg, Esther R. (1989). Cognition and Learner Control: A Literature Review, 1977–1988. *Journal of Computer-Based Instruction, 16*(4), 117–121.

Stephanidis, Constantine. (2001). Adaptive Techniques for Universal Access. *User Modeling and User-Adapted Interaction, 11*, 159–179.

Stillings, Neil A., Weisler, Steven E., Chase, Christopher H., Feinstein, Mark H., Garfield, Jay L., & Rissland, Edwina, L. (1995). *Cognitive Science. An Introduction*. Cambridge: MIT Press.

Sutcliffe, Alistair. (1995). *Human-Computer Interface Design*. London: Macmillan.

Swain, Merill. (1985). Communicative Competence: Some Roles of Comprehensible Input and Comprehensible Output in Its Development. In S. M. Gass & C. G. Madden (Eds.), *Input in Second Language Acquisition* (pp. 235–253). Rowley: Newbury House.

Swain, Merill, & Lapkin, Sharon. (1995). Problems in Output and the Cognitive Processes they Generate: A step towards Second Language Learning. *Applied Linguistics, 16*, 371–391.

Swartz, Merryanna L., & Yazdani, Masoud. (1992). *Intelligent Tutoring Systems for Foreign Language Learning: The Bridge to International Communication* (Vol. 80). New York: Springer Verlag.

Tasso, Carlo, Fum, Danilo, & Giangrandi, Paolo. (1992). The Use of Explanation-Based Learning for Modelling Student Behavior in Foreign Language Tutoring. In M. L. Swartz & M. Yazdani (Eds.), *Intelligent Tutoring Systems for Foreign Language Learning. The Bridge to International Communication* (pp. 151–170). Berlin: Springer Verlag.

Taylor, Helen S. (1998). *Computer Assisted Text Production: Feedback on Grammatical Errors Made by Learners of English as a Foreign Language*. Unpublished Master's Thesis, University of Manchester, Manchester.

ten Hacken, Pius. (2003). Computer-Assisted Language Learning and the Revolution in Computational Linguistics. *Linguistik online, 17*(5), 23–39.

Teutsch, Philippe. (1996). Un modèle de situation d'évaluation pour le suivi de formation en langue étrangère. In C. Frasson, G. Gauthier, & A. Lesgold (Eds.), *Intelligent Tutoring Systems. Third International Conference, ITS'96 Montréal, Canada, June 12–14, 1996. Proceedings* (pp. 315–323). Berlin: Springer.

Thompson, June, & Zähner, Christoph (Eds.). (1992). *Proceedings of the ICALL Workshop, UMIST, September 1991*. Hull: University of Hull, CTI Centre for Modern Languages.

Thorndike, E. (1913). *Educational Psychology: The Psychology of Learning*. New York: Teachers College Press.

Thurmair, G. (1990). Parsing for Grammar and Style Checking. In *Proceedings of the Thirteenth International Conference on Computational Linguistics* (pp. 365–370).

Tokuda, Naoyuki, Heift, Trude, & Chen, Liang. (2002). *Special Issue on ICALL. Computer-Assisted Language Learning Vol. 15 No. 4*. Lisse: Swets & Zeitlinger.

Tolman, E. C. (1932). *Purpose Behavior in Animals and Men*. New York: Appleton-Century-Crofts.

Tomlin, Russell S. (1995). Modeling Individual Tutorial Interactions: Theoretical and Empirical Bases of ICALL. In V. M. Holland, J. D. Kaplan & M. R. Sams (Eds.), *Intelligent Language Tutors: Theory Shaping Technology* (pp. 221–241). Mahwah, NJ: Erlbaum Associates.

Toole, Janine, & Heift, Trude. (2002). *Task Generator:* A Portable System for Generating Learning Tasks for Intelligent Language Tutoring Systems. In P. Barger & S. Rebelsky (Eds.), *Proceedings of ED-MEDIA 02, World Conference on Education Multimedia, Hypermedia & Telecommunications* (pp. 1972–1978). Charlottesville, VA: AACE.

Trahey, Martha, & White, Lydia. (1993). Positive Evidence and Preemption in the Second Language Classroom. *Studies in Second Language Acquisition, 15*(2), 181–204.

Trahey, Martha. (1996). Positive Evidence in Second Language Acquisition: Some Long-Term Effects. *Second Language Research, 12*(2), 111–139.

Trudgill, Peter. (2004). Glocalisation and the Ausbau Sociolinguistics of Modern Europe. In A. Duszak & U. Okulska (Eds.), *Speaking from the Margin: Global English from a European Perspective*. Frankfurt: Peter Lang (also http://www.york.ac.uk/depts/lang/Jack_Chambers/globalisation.pdf).

Tschichold, Cornelia, Bodmer, Frank, Cornu, Etienne, Grosjean, François, Grosjean, Lysiane, Kübler, Natalie, et al. (1994). Detecting and Correcting Errors in Second Language Texts. *Computer Assisted Language Learning, 7*(2), 151–160.

Tschichold, Cornelia. (1999a). Intelligent Grammar Checking for CALL. In M. Schulze, M.-J. Hamel & J. Thompson (Eds.), *Language Processing in CALL. ReCALL Special Publication (Proceedings of a One-Day Conference "Natural Language Processing in Computer-Assisted Language Learning" Held at UMIST, May 9, 1998, Organised by the Centre of Computational Linguistics, UMIST, in Association with Eurocall)* (pp. 5–11). Hull: CTICML.

Tschichold, Cornelia. (1999b). Grammar Checking for CALL: Strategies for Improving Foreign Language Grammar Checkers. In K. Cameron (Ed.), *Computer-Assisted Language Learning* (pp. 203–222). Lisse: Swets & Zeitlinger.

Tsiriga, Victoria, & Virvou, Maria. (2004). A Framework for the Initialization of Student Models in Web-Based Intelligent Tutoring Systems. *User Modeling and User-Adapted Interaction, 14*, 289–316.

Underwood, John H. (1982). Simulated Conversation as CAI Strategy. *Foreign Language Annals, 15*, 209–212.

Underwood, John H. (1984). *Linguistics, Computers, and the Language Teacher*. Rowley, Massachusetts: Newbury House Publishers.

Underwood, John H. (1989). On the Edge: Intelligent CALL in the 1990s. *Computers and Humanities, 23*, 71–84.

Upshall, Michael. (1993). *The Hutchinson Concise Encyclopedia (Updated 1994 Edition)*. Oxford: Helicon.

van der Linden, E. (1993). Does Feedback Enhance Computer-Assisted Language Learning? *Computers and Education, 21*(1–2), 61–65.

Van Noord, G. (1997). An Efficient Implementation of the Head-Corner Parser. *Computational Linguistics, 23*(3), 425–456.

Vandeventer, Anne. (2000). Research on NLP-Based CALL at the University of Geneva. *TELL & CALL, 2/2000*, 10--13.

Vandeventer, Anne, & Hamel, Marie-Josée. (2000). Reusing a Syntactic Generator for CALL Purposes. *ReCALL, 12*(1), 79--91.

Vandeventer, Anne. (2001). Creating a Grammar Checker for CALL by Constraint Relaxation: A Feasibility Study. *ReCALL, 13*(1), 110–120.

Vandeventer Faltin, Anne. (2003). Natural Language Processing Tools for Computer Assisted Language Learning. *Linguistik online, 17*(5), 137–153.

Venezky, Richard L. , & Osin, Luis. (1991). *The Intelligent Design of Computer-Assisted Instruction*. New York: Longman Publishing Group.

Vigil, Neddy A., & Oller, John W. (1976). Rule Fossilization: A Tentative Model. *Language Learning, 26*(2), 281–295.

Villano, Michael. (1992). Probabilistic Student Models: Bayesian Belief Networks and Knowledge Space Theory. In C. Frasson, G. Gauthier, & G. I. McCalla (Eds.), *Intelligent Tutoring Systems. Second International Conference, ITS'96, Montréal, Canada, June 1992, Proceedings* (pp. 491–498). Berlin: Springer Verlag.

Virvou, Maria, & Maras, Dimitris. (1999). An Intelligent Multimedia Tutor for English as a Second Language. In B. Collis & R. Oliver (Eds.), *World Conference on Educational Multimedia, Hypermedia & Telecommunications* (Vol. 2, pp. 928–932). Charlottesville, VA: AACE.

Virvou, Maria, Maras, Dimitris, & Tsirigia, Victoria. (2000). Student Modelling in an Intelligent Tutoring System for the Passive Voice of English Language. *Educational Technology and Society, 3*(4), http://ifets.ieee.org/periodical/vol_4_2000/virvou.html.

Virvou, Maria, & Moundridou, Maria. (2001). Adding an Instructor Modeling Component to the Architecture of ITS Authoring Tools. *International Journal of Artificial Intelligence in Education, 12*, 185–211.

von Wittich, Barbara. (1967). Error Analysis: Implications for the Teaching of Foreign Languages. *Foreign Language Annals, 12*(4), 315–317.
Vosse, Théo. (1992). Detecting and Correcting Morpho-Syntactic Errors in Real Texts. In *Proceedings of the Third Conference on Applied Natural Language Processing, ACL* (pp. 111–118). Trento, Italy.
Vygotsky, Lev S. (1978). *Mind and Society: The Development of Higher Mental Processes.* Cambridge, MA: Harvard University Press.
Wang, Yang, & Garigliano, Roberto. (1992). An Intelligent Language Tutoring System for Handling Errors Caused by Transfer. In C. Frasson, G. Gauthier, & G. I. McCalla (Eds.), *Intelligent Tutoring Systems* (pp. 395–404). Berlin: Springer Verlag.
Wang, Yang, & Garigliano, Roberto. (1995). Empirical Studies and Intelligent Language Tutoring. *Instructional Science, 23*, 47–64.
Ward, Robert D. (1986). Natural Language Processing and the Language Impaired. *Programmed Learning & Educational Technology, 23*, 144–149.
Ward, Robert D., Foot, R., & Rostron, A. B. (1999). Language Processing in Computer-Assisted Language Learning: Language with a Purpose. In M. Schulze, M.-J. Hamel, & J. Thompson (Eds.), *Language Processing in CALL. ReCALL Special Publication (Proceedings of a One-Day Conference "Natural Language Processing in Computer-Assisted Language Learning" Held at UMIST, 9 May 1998, Organised by the Centre of Computational Linguistics, UMIST, in Association with Eurocall)* (pp. 40–49). Hull: CTICML.
Warnke, Martin. (2005). Size Does Matter. In C. Pias (Ed.), *Zukünfte des Computers* (pp. 17–27). Zürich: Diaphanes.
Warschauer, Mark. (1996). Computer-Assisted Language Learning: An Introduction. In S. Fotos (Ed.), *Multimedia Language Teaching* (pp. 3–20). Tokyo: Logos International.
Warschauer, Mark. (2004). Technological Change and the Future of CALL. In S. Fotos & C. Browne (Eds.), *New Perspectives on CALL for Second Language Classrooms* (pp. 15–26). Mahwah, N.J.: Erlbaum Associates.
Warschauer, Mark. (2005). Sociocultural Perspectives on CALL. In J. Egbert & G. M. Petrie (Eds.), *CALL Research Perspectives* (pp. 41–51). Mahwah, N.J.: Erlbaum Associates.
Webb, Geoffrey I., & Kuzmycz, Mark. (1998). Evaluation of Data Aging: A Technique for Discounting Old Data during Student Modeling. In B. P. Goettl, H. M. Halff, C. L. Redfield, & V. J. Shute (Eds.), *Intelligent Tutoring Systems. 4th International Conference, ITS 1998, San Antonio, Texas, USA, August 1998, Proceedings* (pp. 384–393).
Wei, Yu Hong, & Davies, Graham. (1997). Do Grammar Checkers Work? In J. Kohn, B. Rüschoff & D. Wolff (Eds.), *New Horizons in CALL: Proceedings of EUROCALL 96.* Szombathely, Hungary: Dániel Berzsenyi College.
Weinberg, Amy, Garman, Joe, Martin, Jeffery, & Merlo, Paola. (1995). A Principle-Based Parser for Foreign Language Tutoring in German and Arabic. In V. M. Holland, J. D. Kaplan, & M. R. Sams (Eds.), *Intelligent Language Tutors: Theory Shaping Technology* (pp. 23–44). Mahwah, NJ: Erlbaum Associates.
Weischedel, Ralph M., Voge, Wilfried M., & James, Mark. (1978). An Artificial Intelligence Approach to Language Instruction. *Artificial Intelligence, 10*, 225–240.
Weischedel, Ralph M., & Black, John E. (1980). Responding Intelligently to Unparsable Inputs. *American Journal of Computational Linguistics, 6*(2), 97–109.
Weischedel, Ralph M., & Sondheimer, Norman K. (1983). Meta-Rules as a Basis for Processing Ill-Formed Input. *American Journal of Computational Linguistics, 9*(3–4), 161–177.

Weizenbaum, Joseph. (1976). *Computer Power and Human Reason: From Judgment to Calculation*. San Francisco W.H. Freeman, 1976.

Wenger, Etienne. (1987). *Artificial Intelligence and Tutoring Systems - Computational and Cognitive Approaches to the Communication of Knowledge*. Los Altos: Morgan Kaufmann.

White, Lydia. (1991). Adverb Placement in Second Language Acquisition: Some Effects of Positive and Negative Evidence in the Classroom. *Second Language Research, 7*(2), 133–161.

Wiener, N. (1948). *Cybernetics, or Control and Communication in the Animal and the Machine*: Cambridge, Massachusetts: The Technology Press; New York: John Wiley & Sons, Inc.

Wiese, Richard. (1983). *Psycholinguistische Aspekte der Sprachproduktion: Sprechverhalten und Verbalisierungsprozesse*. Hamburg: Buske.

Wilks, Yorick, & Farwell, David. (1992). Building an Intelligent Second Language Tutoring System from Whatever Bits You Happen to Have Lying Around. In M. L. Swartz & M. Yazdani (Eds.), *Intelligent Tutoring Systems for Foreign Language Learning. The Bridge to International Communication* (pp. 263–274). Berlin: Springer Verlag.

Willis, Jane. (1996). *A Framework for Task-Based Learning*. Harlow, UK: Longman.

Wolff, Dieter. (1991). Artificial Intelligence Techniques in Language Learning by Rex Last (Book Review). *System, 19*, 332–335.

Wolff, Dieter. (1993). New Technologies for Foreign Language Teaching. In *Foreign Language Learning and the Use of New Technologies. Conference Proceedings. London 1993*. Brussels: Bureau Lingua.

Woolf, Beverly Park, & Murray, Tom. (1994). Using Machine Learning to Advise a Student Model. In J. E. Greer & G. I. McCalla (Eds.), *Student Modeling: The Key to Individualized Knowledge-Based Instruction*. Berlin: Springer-Verlag.

Yamura-Takei, Mitsuko, Fujiwara, Miho, Yoshie, Makoto, & Aizawa, Teruaki. (2002). Automatic Linguistic Analysis for Language Teachers: The Case of Zeros. In *Proceedings of Coling 2002: The Seventeenth International Conference on Computational Linguistics* (not paginated). Taipei: Association for Computational Linguistics.

Yang, Jie Chi, & Akahori, Kanji. (1995). Error Analysis in Japanese Writing and Its Implementation in a Computer Assisted Language Learning System on the World Wide Web. *CALICO Journal, 15*(1–3), 47–64.

Yang, Jie Chi, & Akahori, Kanji. (1997). Development of Computer Assisted Language Learning System for Japanese Writing Using Natural Language Processing Techniques: A Study on Passive Voice. In P. Brusilovsky, K. Nakabayashi, & S. Ritter (Eds.), *Proceedings of the Workshop "Intelligent Educational Systems on the World Wide Web" at AI-ED'97, 8th WorldConference on Artificial Intelligence in Education, Kobe, Japan, 18–22 August 1997* (pp. 99–103). Amsterdam: IOS Press.

Yang, Jie Chi, & Akahori, Kanji. (1999). An Evaluation of Japanese CALL Systems on the WWW Comparing a Freely Input Approach with Multiple Selection. *Computer Assisted Language Learning, 12*(1), 59–79.

Yannakoudakis, E.J., & Fawthrop, D. (1983). The Rules of Spelling Errors. *Information Processing & Management, 19*(2), 87–99.

Yasuda, Keiji, Sumita, Eiichiro, Kikui, Genichiro, Sugaya, Fumiaki, Takezawa, Toshiyuki, & Yamamoto, Seiichi. (2004). *Automatic Measuring of English Language Proficiency Using MT Evaluation Technology*. Paper presented at eLearning for Computational Linguistics and Computational Linguistics for eLearning. Workshop at COLING — The 20th International Conference on Computational Linguistics, Geneva.

Yazdani, Masoud (Ed.). (1984). *New Horizons in Educational Computing.* Chichester: Ellis Horwood.

Yazdani, Masoud, & Uren, J. (1988). Generalising Language-Tutoring Systems: A French/Spanish Case Study, Using LINGER. *Instructional Science, 17,* 179–188.

Yazdani, Masoud. (1990). An Artificial Intelligence Approach to Second Language Learning. *Journal of Artificial Intelligence in Education, 1*(3), 85–90.

Yazdani, Masoud. (1991). The Linger Project An Artificial Intelligence Approach To Second-Language Tutoring. *Computer Assisted Language Learning, 4*(2), 107–116.

Yazdani, Masoud. (1992). LINGERing On! Steps towards an 'Intelligent' Language Tutoring Environment. In J. Thompson & C. Zähner (Eds.), *Proceedings of the ICALL Workshop, UMIST, September 1991* (pp. 109–118). Hull: University of Hull, CTI Centre for Modern Languages.

Yazdani, Masoud (Ed.). (1993). *Multilingual Multimedia. Bridging the Language Barrier with Intelligent Systems.* Oxford: Intellect.

Zähner, Christoph. (1991). Word Grammars in CALL. In H. Savolainen & J. Telenius (Eds.), *Eurocall 1991. International Conference on Computer Assisted Language Learning. Proceedings* (pp. 291–295). Helsinki: Helsinki School of Economics and Business Administration.

Zapata-Rivera, Juan-Diego, & Greer, Jim E. (2002). Construction and Inspection of Learner Models. In *Proceedings of Computer Support For Collaborative Learning CSCL 2002* (pp. 495–497).

Zhao, Yong. (2005a). The Future of Research in Technology and Second Language Education: Challenges and Possibilities. In Y. Zhao (Ed.), *Research in Technology and Second Language Education: Developments and Directions* (pp. 445–457). Greenwich, Conn.: IAP-Information Age Pub.

Zhao, Yong (Ed.). (2005b). *Research in Technology and Second Language Education: Developments and Directions.* Greenwich, Conn.: IAP-Information Age Pub.

Zock, Michael, Sabah, Gérard, & Alviset, Christophe. (1986). From Structure to Process. Computer-Assisted Teaching of Various Strategies for Generating Pronoun Constructions in French. In *Proceedings of COLING* (pp. 566–569). Bonn.

Zock, Michael. (1988). Language Learning as Problem Solving. Modeling Logical Aspects of Inductive Learning to Generate Sentences in French by Man and Machine. In *Coling Budapest. Proceedings of the Twelfth International Conference on Computational Linguistics* (Vol. 2, pp. 806–811). Budapest: John von Neumann Society for Computing Sciences.

Zock, Michael. (1992). SWIM or Sink: The Problem of Communicating Thought. In M. L. Swartz & M. Yazdani (Eds.), *Intelligent Tutoring Systems for Foreign Language Learning. The Bridge to International Communication* (pp. 235–247). Berlin: Springer Verlag.

Zock, Michael. (1996). Computational Linguistics and its Use in Real World: The Case of Computer Assisted Language Learning. In *Proceedings of Coling'96: The Sixteenth International Conference on Computational Linguistics* (Vol. 1, pp. 1002–1004). Copenhagen: Center for Sprogteknologi.

Zock, Michael. (1998). Guest Editorial. (to the special issue: French Contributions to CALL). *Computer Assisted Language Learning, 11*(5), 467–473.

Zukerman, Ingrid, & Albrecht, David W. (2001). Predictive Statistical Models for User Modeling. *User Modeling and User-Adapted Interaction, 11,* 5–18.

Index